GOVERNABLE PLACES

To Timothy, Amelia, and Alissa

Advances in Criminology
Series Editor: David Nelken

Titles in the Series

Engendering Resistance: Agency and Power in Women's Prisons
Mary Bosworth

Integrating a Victim Perspective with Criminal Justice
International debates
Adam Crawford and Jo Goodey

Contrasts in Criminal Justice
David Nelken

Critique and Radical Discourses on Crime
George Pavlich

Blood in the Bank
Social and legal aspects of death at work
Gary Slapper

Governable Places
Readings on governmentality and crime control
Russell Smandych

Governable Places
Readings on Governmentality and Crime Control

Edited by
RUSSELL SMANDYCH

DARTMOUTH

Aldershot • Brookfield USA • Singapore • Sydney

Published by
Dartmouth Publishing Company Limited
Ashgate Publishing Limited
Gower House
Croft Road
Aldershot
Hants GU11 3HR
England

Ashgate Publishing Company
Old Post Road
Brookfield
Vermont 05036
USA

British Library Cataloguing in Publication Data
Governable places : readings on governmentality and crime
  control. – (Advances in criminology)
  1. Criminal justice, Administration of   2. Crime prevention
  I. Smandych, Russell C. (Russell Charles)
  353.4

Library of Congress Cataloging-in-Publication Data
Governable places : readings on governmentality and crime control /
  edited by Russell Smandych.
    p.   cm.
  Includes bibliographical references and index.
  ISBN 1-84014-726-1
  1. Criminal justice. Administration of.   2. Crime prevention.
  3. Political sociology.   4. Sociological jurisprudence.
  I. Smandych, Russell Charles.
  HV7405.G68   1998
  364–dc21   98–40530
                                                                  CIP

ISBN 1 84014 726 1

Typeset by Manton Typesetters, 5–7 Eastfield Road, Louth, Lincs, LN11 7AJ, UK.
Printed and bound in Great Britain by MPG Books Ltd, Bodmin, Cornwall

Contents

Notes on Contributors

Nick Blomley is Associate Professor in the Department of Geography, Simon Fraser University, Burnaby, BC, Canada. Dr Blomley is currently exploring opposing conceptions of land and property in Vancouver's Downtown Eastside, a low-income area confronting the threat of gentrification. He is more generally interested in the intersections of power, geography, and legal discourse and practice, and is the author of *Law, Space and the Geographies of Power* (New York: Guilford, 1994).

Richard Ericson is Principal of Green College, Professor of Law and Professor of Sociology at the University of British Columbia. During the 1998–9 academic year he is Canada Council Killam Research Fellow and Visiting Fellow of All Souls College, Oxford. His most recent book is *Policing the Risk Society* (Oxford Press and University of Toronto Press, 1997), co-authored with Kevin Haggerty. Dr Ericson is currently developing theories of governance and risk communication through research on the insurance industry.

David Garland is Professor in the School of Law and the Department of Sociology, New York University. He is the author of many works on the sociology of punishment, the history of criminology, and social theory. His recent works include *Punishment and Modern Society* (Chicago University Press 1990), *A Reader on Punishment* (with A. Duff, Oxford 1994) and 'Limits of the Sovereign State', *British Journal of Criminology* (1996). He is also the Editor-in-Chief of *Punishment and Society: The International Journal of Penology*.

Kevin Haggerty has recently completed his PhD at the University of British Columbia in the Department of Anthropology/Sociology. His dissertation, entitled *Making Crime Count*, is an analysis of the institutional production of criminal justice statistics considered in the context of the importance of aggregate knowledges to practices of governance. He is also a co-author with Richard Ericson of *Policing The Risk Society* (1997). From autumn 1998, Dr Haggerty will be undertaking post-doctoral research at the Centre of Criminology, University of Toronto, working on a project exploring the introduction of DNA testing into criminal justice.

Bryan Hogeveen has recently completed his MA degree in Sociology at the University of Manitoba, Winnipeg, Canada. From autumn 1998, he will be pursuing his PhD at the Centre of Criminology, University of Toronto. Bryan's current research interests include the governance of childhood in nineteenth-century Canada and the implications of Foucault's later work for socio-legal studies.

Maria Loś (PhD, 1971, University of Warsaw) is Professor of Criminology at the University of Ottawa. Her publications include: *Privatizing the Police-State* (London: Macmillan Press, forthcoming) (with A. Zybertowicz); *The Second Economy in Marxist States* (ed.) (London: Macmillan Press, 1990); *Communist Ideology, Law and Crime* (London: Macmillan Press, 1988); and *Multi-Dimensional Sociology* (London: Routledge & Kegan Paul, 1979) (with A. Podgorecki).

Sally Engle Merry is the Class of 1949 Professor in Ethics/Professor of Anthropology at Wellesley College, USA. She is the author of *Urban Danger: Life in a Neighborhood of Strangers* (Temple University, 1981), *Getting Justice and Getting Even: Legal Consciousness among Working Class Americans* (University of Chicago Press, 1990) and co-editor with Neal Milner of *The Possibility of Popular Justice* (University of Michigan Press, 1993). She is a former president of the Law and Society Association and current president of the Association for Political and Legal Anthropology and is currently finishing a book on law and the 'civilizing process' in nineteenth-century Hawaii which explores the nature of American colonialism in the Pacific.

Pat O'Malley is Professor of Law and Legal Studies at La Trobe University Melbourne and was formerly a member of the Premier's Drug Advisory Council (Victoria). His current research is focused on risk models of governance in the history of modern capitalism, and his most recent publications include two edited books: *Crime Prevention in Australia* (Federation Press, 1997) with Adam Sutton, and *Crime and the Risk Society* (Dartmouth, 1998).

George Pavlich is a Senior Lecturer in Sociology at the University of Auckland. He is the author of several articles in the fields of law and society, social theory and criminology. His most recent book was published by Routledge

(1996) and is entitled, *Justice Fragmented: Mediating Community Disputes Under Postmodern Conditions*. He is currently working on a book that reassesses the notion of critique in the context of radical criminology.

John Pratt is a Reader in Criminology, Victoria University of Wellington, New Zealand. He has taught, researched and published extensively on the history and sociology of punishment. His most significant publications are *Punishment in a Perfect Society* (1993) and *Governing the Dangerous* (1998). His current research is on penal culture and modern society.

James Sheptycki is a Research Fellow in the Centre for Law and Society, University of Edinburgh. Dr Sheptycki completed his PhD in criminology (London School of Economics, 1991) on the topic of policing domestic violence. A portion of this work was published as a book entitled, *Innovations in Policing Domestic Violence* (Avebury, 1993). In his current work, Dr Sheptycki is seeking to bring together concerns from the disciplines of international law, international relations and criminology in order to illuminate the emergent phenomenon of 'transnational policing'. He has published widely on these topics. He is also currently editor of *Policing and Society: An International Journal*. Recent publications include: 'Law Enforcement, Justice and Democracy in the Transnational Arena; Reflections on the War on Drugs', *International Journal of the Sociology of Law* (1996); 'Transnationalism, Crime Control and the European State System', *International Criminal Justice Review* (1997); and 'The Global Cops Cometh: Reflections on Transnationalisation, Knowledge Work and Policing Subculture', *British Journal of Sociology* (1998).

Russell Smandych is Associate Professor of Sociology at the University of Manitoba, Winnipeg, Canada. He has written mostly in the areas of the history and sociology of social control, Canadian legal history, law and colonialism, and comparative criminology. His recent publications include: 'Administering Justice without the State', *Canadian Journal of Law and Society* (1996) (with R. Linden); 'The Development of Criminal Law Courts in Pre-1870 Manitoba,' *Manitoba Law Journal* (1996) (with K. Sacca); 'Images of Aboriginal Childhood: Contested Governance in the Canadian West to 1850', in R. Halpern and M. Daunton (eds), *Empire and Others: British Encounters with Indigenous Peoples, 1600–1850*, (London: UCL Press, 1999) (with A. McGillivray); and 'The Exclusionary Effect of Colonial Law: Indigenous Peoples and English Law in the Canadian West to 1860', in L. Knafla and J. Swainger (eds), *Essays in the History of Canadian Law, Vol. 8: The Middle Kingdom: The Northwest Territories and Prairie Provinces, 1670–1945*, Toronto: The Osgoode Society, 1999.

Jeff Sommers is a community worker in Vancouver and a graduate student in the Department of Geography at Simon Fraser University. His dissertation research examines the representation and institutionalization of community in inner city Vancouver. His research interests also include constructions of urban poverty, the regulation of space and urban development.

Kevin Stenson is Professor of Social Policy at Buckinghamshire University College, UK. He has published studies of social and youth work, youth culture, policing, crime prevention strategies, social deprivation and anti-deprivation strategy. Publications include (with David Cowell), *The Politics of Crime Control* (Sage).

Acknowledgements

This book brings together some of the most important recent work in the emerging field of governmentality studies and crime control. Specifically, the collection includes the work of leading researchers in the field from the United States, Canada, Britain, Australia, and New Zealand. While I undertook the relatively easy task of bringing together the work of these authors, they, of course, deserve all the credit for the important empirical and theoretical contributions contained in the book. Without exception, my experience working with the contributing authors has been positive and rewarding, and I would like to thank each of them for giving me the opportunity to edit their scholarly work.

Several of the chapters contained in the book were originally presented as conference papers at the international conference on 'New Forms of Governance: Theory, Research, and Practice', held at the University of Toronto in October, 1996. I would like to thank the sponsors, including the Social Sciences and Humanities Research Council of Canada, the Ontario Law Foundation and the Legal Research Institute of the University of Manitoba, who made the conference possible. I would also like to extend a special thanks to Marianna Valverde, Willem De Lint and Clifford Shearing for helping organize the conference.

Finally, I would like to acknowledge the encouragement and administrative help provided by my Department Head, Rod Kueneman, and the support staff in the Department of Sociology, University of Manitoba, Sandy Froese, Diane Bulback, and Kathy Olafson.

This book is dedicated to my children, Timothy, Amelia, and Alissa, for helping me appreciate the everyday relevance of Foucault's thinking on the art of government.

Series Preface

The new series *Advances in Criminology* builds on the success of the *International Library of Criminology, Criminal Justice and Penology*. But rather than being dedicated to anthologising the best of existing work this venture seeks to publish original cutting-edge contributions to these fields. Volumes so far in press include discussions of Foucault and *governmentality*; critical criminology; victims and criminal justice; corporate crime; postmodern policing; and women's prisons.

The collection of papers on *Governable Places* by Russell Smandych is an excellent contribution to the series. It explores changing patterns of crime and crime control in the light of ideas about 'governmentality' in the later work of Michel Foucault. The book's particular strengths lie in the way contributors, drawn from a variety of intellectual disciplines, range widely across countries and periods so as to show the potential and limits of this way of looking at the regulation of criminal behaviour. Foucault's arguments are linked for example to current debates about risk and 'actuarial justice' and related to the changes being brought about by the globalization of the world economy. The value of such reflections for theoretical advance in criminology hardly needs to be underlined.

DAVID NELKEN
Series Editor

1 Introduction: The Place of Governance Studies in Law and Criminology

Russell Smandych

Recent years have witnessed an apparent erosion of state power accompanied by the rise of many different and new forms of governance which are beginning to take the place of state law and state justice institutions. Partly as a result of Michel Foucault's articulation of the need to decentre the state from social analysis (Foucault 1977, 1991), over the past 20 years researchers from numerous disciplines have directed attention to investigating the historical emergence and development of various forms of non-state or extra-state governance. Indeed, Foucault's (1991) effort at theorizing forms of governance – or *governable places* – which often exist outside the immediate view or interest of 'the state' has generated a huge amount of theoretical and empirical research across a wide range of social science and humanities disciplines (cf. Barry *et al.* 1996; Davidson 1997; O'Farrell 1997). In recent years, researchers in law and criminology have begun to use a variety of terms – including 'private justice', 'informalism', 'legal pluralism' and, most recently, 'governmentality' – to try to describe and develop a theoretical understanding of the complicated linkages connecting the various forms of state and non-state governance that appear to characterize modern societies. In addition, numerous studies have now been completed that provide data on the effect these new and changing forms of governance are having on individuals, communities and nation-states. The studies completed by socio-legal and criminology researchers have been pitched at several different levels of contemporary analysis, including: the study of community mediation as a political technology used in the formation of self-regulating citizens (Pavlich 1996a, 1996b); the discursive analysis of community crime prevention and community-based policing movements

(O'Malley 1992; Stenson 1993; Pavlich, Chapter 5 in this volume); analyses of the changing character of labour law and labour–capital relations in an era of declining state power (Arthurs 1996); and the study of shifting power relations and agencies of governance in recently emerging post-communist and post-apartheid states (Loś 1994, 1995; Nina 1995; Shearing and Brogden 1993). Foucault's influence is also evident in historical work now being undertaken by both socio-legal and post-colonial researchers on the nature of 'colonial governmentality' (Scott 1995; Pels 1997; Hogeveen, Chapter 12 in this volume) and the way in which law may be implicated as a tool of European colonialism (Smandych and Lee 1995; Smandych and Linden 1996). Studies of this type (see also Ericson and Haggerty 1997; Feeley and Simon 1994; Fitzpatrick 1988, 1992; Garland 1996; Hunt and Wickham 1994; Hunt 1996; O'Malley 1991; Merry 1990, 1992; Rose and Miller 1992) have been accompanied by related recent attempts at developing a more adequate theoretical understanding of the significance of such changing forms of governance for constituted postmodern/post-colonial societies (see especially Cohen 1994; Merry 1995; Santos 1992, 1995). Although theoretically diverse, a common feature of this large body of work is the manner in which different authors have recognized the need for research aimed at unravelling the complex character of the relationship linking state and non-state forms of governance. In addition, a number of authors have made explicit use of Foucault's (1991) concepts of 'government' and 'governmentality' as a starting point for carrying out this research.

One of the issues raised in recent discussions, including those taken up in subsequent chapters of this current collection, is the question of the meaning and usefulness of these concepts for guiding socio-legal and criminological research. However, for present purposes, we can start with Hunt and Wickham's (1994: 52) observation that, for Foucault, 'Modernity ... is marked by the emergence of "government" and "governmentality"'. Hunt and Wickham, among others, point out that Foucault 'uses the term "government" in a way that is very different from the conventional sense of state executives and legislatures', and in a way that is 'consistent with his downgrading of the importance of the state'. In essence, he argues that government is 'not a matter of imposing laws on men, but rather of disposing things, that is to say to employ tactics rather than laws, and if need be to use the laws themselves as tactics' (Foucault 1991: 95). Another of Foucault's central contributions that has caught the attention socio-legal scholars and criminologists is his use of 'the neologism "governmentality" to capture the dramatic changes in techniques of government developed in the western world from the eighteenth century onwards' (Hunt and Wickham 1994: 175). According to Foucault, these changes included the development of 'a range of multiform tactics' for the government of populations outside the state, as well as 'the governmentalisation of the state' itself (Foucault 1991: 95, 101). Consequently, for him, (1991: 87), the study of the 'art of government' involved addressing questions of 'How to govern oneself, how to be governed, how to govern others, by whom the people will accept to be governed, and how to become the best possible governor' (ibid.: 87).

Most of the authors whose work appears in the present volume have been greatly influenced by Foucault's writings of the late 1970s and early 1980s, in which he considered the topic of government in relation to a wide range of issues, from that of 'the correct government of one's self to the pedagogic question of the government of children and the question of the government of the state by the monarch' (McNay 1994: 113). The influence of Foucault's thinking is increasingly coming to be reflected in the work of critical socio-legal scholars and criminologists who – like most of those included in the present volume – have begun to recognize that the study of the 'art of government' involves the study of a sweeping range of questions concerning the nature and form of various techniques, strategies and rationalities of liberal government.

This volume highlights the work that has been completed to date by leading English-speaking researchers working in the field of governmentality and crime control. Despite the argument that much of the current work of 'governmentality researchers' can be subsumed within the discipline of sociology (Garland 1997 and Chapter 2 in this volume), the current collection of essays clearly reflects the multidisciplinary character of the field, with 13 authors representing the six ostensibly separate disciplines of law, sociology, anthropology, geography, social work and criminology. The volume also reflects the growing international importance of studies of governmentality and crime control, as measured both by the country of origin of the contributing authors and the substantive and geographical focus of their research. Contributing authors represent countries including Canada, the UK, New Zealand, Australia and the United States, while specific essays investigate either historical or contemporary developments surrounding governmentality and crime control in the UK (David Garland, Kevin Stenson), Australia (Pat O'Malley), New Zealand (George Pavlich), Eastern Europe (Maria Loś), Hawai'i (Sally Merry), Canada (Nicholas Blomley and Jeff Somers, Richard Ericson and Kevin Haggerty, Bryan Hogeveen), and cross-nationally (John Pratt, James Sheptycki). Collectively, the arguments and findings presented by these authors pose profound implications for future socio-legal and criminological research on a wide range of topics that can be seen to fall within the field of governmentality and crime control.

In his essay on '"Governmentality" and the Problem of Crime' David Garland (Chapter 2) offers a critique of the growing body of governmentality literature in law and criminology. He argues that while 'the governmentality literature offers a powerful framework for analysing how crime is problematized and controlled', it also has several limitations and problems. One of the problems with most governmentality research, according to Garland, is the tendency for researchers to look at 'government' as 'a problem-solving activity' mainly '*through* the perceptual grid of the programmes and rationalities that the authorities generate to deal with them'. This methodological weakness is one of basically taking the statements of authorities concerning crime control at face value without trying to glean knowledge about crime control programmes and rationalities from other possible sources. Combined with this problem, Garland argues, is the tendency of governmentality researchers to direct their analyses towards 'technical and knowledge-based' crime-control rationalities, while neglecting 'the expressive, emotionally driven and morally toned currents' that play a large part in shaping crime control policy. Added to this, Garland argues, is the somewhat false impression given by governmentality researchers that their approach is unique and different from other discipline-based approaches to the study of crime and crime control, particularly sociological. On the contrary, Garland claims that the work of governmentality researchers shares a close affinity to theorizing and research that has a long history in the discipline of sociology, and that future work could benefit from extending governmentality studies by drawing on more critical forms of sociological theory.

Kevin Stenson (Chapter 3) offers a critique of Garland's claim about the principally sociological nature of governmentality studies. According to Stenson, Garland's argument is based on only a partial understanding of Foucault's key concepts of sovereignty, discipline and governmentality. In his programmatic discussion of these concepts, Foucault attempted to provide, in abstract form, a diagrammatic account of the contours of power and the conditions of possibility for making the institution of government and also for governance operating within delimited institutional spheres both thinkable and operable. While this attempt has helped to generate productive work on shifting modes of government/governance, Stenson maintains that it has also generated ambiguities in our understanding of these issues and what may count as acceptable research agendas. Most problematically, researchers following Foucault's lead have focused on forms of governmental knowledge, particularly as they tend to be seen in textual or written forms in legal and other professional contexts. Stenson argues that it is possible to further develop Foucault's key concepts of sovereignty, discipline and governmentality as tools for describing and analysing the complex interrelations of governing practices. Here the emphasis shifts from knowledge, more narrowly conceived, towards governing practices in which oral and textual forms of knowledge interpenetrate and are embedded in practices. According to Stenson, this shift in research agenda requires different forms of evidence, including ethnographic and other field-derived sources. He provides several examples from his own ethnographic research, including his work on the government of ethnic-based youth gangs in inner-city London, to illustrate his methodological prescriptions.

While Garland and Stenson offer contending theoretical and methodological prescriptions for future work in the field of governmentality and crime control, the remaining chapters of the book provide a variety of examples of the type of research that is now being completed by socio-legal scholars and criminologists who have begun to enter the field. While some of the analyses of different, and often shifting, programmes and strategies of government offered in the following chapters make limited direct reference to Foucault, others draw quite openly and heavily on Foucault's key concepts and arguments. Nevertheless, the work of these authors provides many illustrations of the substantive topics and new theoretical approaches that are now being developed by socio-legal scholars and criminologists who are working in the wake of the critical postmodern tide that is now entering law and criminology, partly through the influence of Foucault.

In her essay on the changing governance of sexuality and gender violence in Hawai'i, Sally Engle Merry (Chapter 4) draws on Foucault to provide a starting point for her analyses of laws that criminalize specific gendered aspects of family life. Specifically, Merry notes that, in his analysis of the development of the art of government to the mid-eighteenth century, Foucault recognizes a shift in the significance of the family; as governmentality increasingly focuses on populations, the family disappears as a model of government and instead becomes an element within the population and a fundamental instrument in its governance. Merry extends Foucault's analysis, arguing that, since the mid-eighteenth century, there have been significant variations within this pattern in response to particular cultural configurations and processes such as capitalist transformation, colonialism and globalization. Moreover, Merry contends that recently in advanced capitalist societies, the family as a sovereign unit of governance seems to be becoming more effaced, and that individuals are coming more directly under state systems of governance, particularly within subordinate class groups. In her essay, she compares two instances in which the laws of Hawai'i have criminalized certain practices of family life. The first, in the 1840s and 1850s, redefined all sexual relations outside the marriage bond as crimes. The second, in the 1990s, redefined acts of violence against women within marriages as crimes. According to Merry, both of these changes reflect the legal construction and reconstruction of family relationships through criminal law. At the same time, these examples illuminate historical variations in the way the governance of the family is embedded in the governance of the state.

George Pavlich (Chapter 5) explores another pervasive development in criminal justice in the 1990s that can be more adequately understood by taking into account Foucault's insights on governmentality – namely, community crime prevention. According to Pavlich, in recent decades, and in a variety of contexts, rationales of 'social governance' have been affected by the rising popularity of an amorphous quest for 'community' regulation. Like other observers (cf. Cohen 1985), Pavlich notes that, consequently, in recent years, 'community-based' crime prevention schemes have been put into place alongside residual patterns of 'state' social control. In his essay, Pavlich analyses emerging neo-liberal governmental rationales around community crime prevention measures in Aotearoa/New Zealand, recognizing that there are important parallels with commensurate 'community' crime initiatives elsewhere. His overall thesis is that 'the rise of community crime prevention is not just a slight adjustment to political technique; rather, the very notions of who is governed, who governs and what governance entails are in the process of significant revision'. According to Pavlich, 'along with altering governmental rationalities come changes in the objects of governance (abnormal individuals in society versus prudent and "at-risk" groups or victims in the community), and who governs (individual social science experts as opposed to rational, responsible, managerially focused, enterprising, prudent selves). Finally, the very notion of what it is to govern is recast, and the emphasis on corrective disciplinary techniques is shifted with the rise of actuarial technologies and techniques of self that seek to "manage" risk in the "self-interests" of predefined communities.' Pavlich also offers an analysis of possible dangers associated with this ongoing shift from 'social-welfare' to 'neo-liberal' crime prevention measures and rationalities.

John Pratt (Chapter 6) studies the extent to which recent reforms made to laws governing 'dangerous offenders' have also been influenced by emergent 'neo-liberal' thinking about crime control. Pratt points out that the issue of how to govern the dangerous has been a prominent theme of criminological discourse over the last century in all English common-law-based countries. Moreover, he acknowledges that this has been the case, irrespective of whatever political party has been in power and irrespective of broader shifts in political rationalities; – for example, 'welfarism' for much of the twentieth century, and 'neo-liberalism' during its last two decades. Nevertheless, Pratt argues that, in recent years, a series of new tactics, strategies and forms of expertise which bear the influence of neo-liberal thinking have brought about important shifts in the way in which governing the dangerous is modulated. Surveying legislation from a number of countries, Pratt points out how the concept of dangerousness has been broadened, from including primarily dangerous repeat violent and sex offenders, to including a much wider range of so-called 'persistent' (property and less seriously violent) offenders. Examples of this include California's 'Three Strikes and Out' legislation which is now being mimicked in other US states, along with legislation proposed and debated in Australia, the UK, and New Zealand. Characteristic of such legislation is 'the creation of new risk groups and new strategies of risk management'. Pratt argues that these penal developments affecting the governance of dangerousness are, at least in part, the result of 'the shift in political rationalities – from welfarism to neo-liberalism' which has occurred to a greater or lesser extent in each of these countries over the last two decades.

Richard Ericson and Kevin Haggerty (Chapter 7) apply a similar line of reasoning in attempting to understand current developments related to 'governing the young'. Criminologists have typically taken a narrow perspective when studying youth, and this has led them to focus mainly on the causes of youth crime and the processing of juvenile offenders. In contrast, Ericson and Haggerty recognize the importance of studying the myriad ways in which adults attempt to govern the young, both within and outside of the criminal justice system. They argue that governance 'is organized by state institutions acting at a distance through collaboration with myriad institutions beyond the state'. In turn, these institutions 'use surveillance and risk management technologies that simultaneously identify dangers and help to do something about them'. According to Ericson and Haggerty, '[a] major component of risk management is sorting people into population categories that identify who poses risks and who is at risk'. Ericson and Haggerty apply this logic to demonstrating how adults deal with 'youth as a population that [both] poses risks and is at risk'. The authors do this through drawing on findings of their study of three police-initiated surveillance and risk management programmes for governing the young: specifically, school-based programmes for 'youths at risk'; interagency programmes aimed at identifying and tracking 'high risk youths'; and cooperative police–media–voluntary sector programmes for tracing missing children. Analysis of each of these programmes illustrates how the police operate at the fulcrum of risk communication systems for governing the young.

Pat O'Malley (Chapter 8) offers an analysis of the manner in which neo-liberal risk management thinking has begun to infuse programmes aimed at the 'government of drug-users' in Australia. In 1987 the Australian federal government launched a new drug use 'harm minimization programme'. This programme shifted attention from attacking supposed social problems linked to 'addicts', 'addiction', and 'drug abuse', to a newly recognized need to educate 'users' about the risks associated with 'drug use'. O'Malley explores the emerging discourse of governing drugs through harm minimization, examining this development in terms of the ways in which government plans and blueprints effect a reimagination of what it is to govern drug consumption. The chapter examines a series of questions in order to map out this emerging governmental framework, including: 'what kinds of drug-taking subjects are being thought into existence to displace the "addict" and the "drug abuser" in these discourses? How are the drugs and their effects being recast as problems for rule? ... What techniques are to be deployed in relation to such modes of governing? Why and how is it believed that these changes will govern drug consumption "better" than existing regimes?' O'Malley identifies neo-liberalism – with its inherent precepts of 'free will', 'individual choice' and 'risk' – as the key force underlying this contemporary shift in sensibilities about the government of drug-users. According to O'Malley, in neo-liberal discourses around drug use 'choice and risk' are commonly used complementary terms. 'The imagery of the choice-making drug-user is thus of a "normal" subject who seeks pleasure through the consumption of drugs, but whose choices are conditioned by an *environment* of risk rather than a restrictive polity. The drug-user is neither totally free nor compelled, but must make choices among risk-bearing options.' Complementing concerns raised by the authors of earlier chapters – that is, Pavlich (Chapter 5) and Ericson and Haggerty (Chapter 7) – O'Malley also looks at the 'dark side to the expansion of choice that harm minimization seems to deliver to a drug using society', noting that '[n]ow, it is not simply the addict who will be treated, nor the minority of users who are punished. *All* users are exposed to a regime of self-governance, constantly responsible for monitoring their behaviour, governing themselves without pause.'

James Sheptycki (Chapter 9) addresses the topic of transnational policing and the marketization of insecurity. Working from a critical postmodern perspective, Sheptycki begins with an historical overview of the use of the term 'police' in Western European countries. According to Sheptycki, '[t]he genealogy of police reveals it to be a form of governmentality based on the rule of law, with a mandate to use force in the maintenance of social order broadly conceived'. He argues that, just as the development of police was central to the imposition of the nation-state system of Europe in the eighteenth and nineteenth centuries, recent cross-national developments in policing are 'part of the larger global process of the restructuring of the nation-state system.' Sheptycki introduces and describes four postulates of 'postmodern police' as a way of illuminating broad changes to the transnational-state-system in which policing is now embedded. These postulates are conceptualized more precisely as two dual processes or dyads. The first duality is the marketization of insecurity and of state-provided social control. The second is the transnationalization of clandestine markets and of policing. The marketization of insecurity is visible in the worldwide expansion of private justice and private security, reflected in developments ranging from the work of police death squads in Brazil to fortified neighbourhoods in the suburban USA. At the same time, the marketization of public policing can be seen in such developments as the marketing of 'community policing' programmes and police–community crime prevention 'partnerships' (which is also discussed specifically in the New Zealand context by Pavlich in Chapter 5). Concerning the second duality, Sheptycki shows how the global move toward free market reform – which has included the creation and expansion of transnational regulatory regimes such as the European Union and NAFTA, along with the collapse of communist regimes in Eastern Europe – has been linked to both a dramatic increase in opportunities for transnational crime, and the increasing transnationalization of policing. According to Sheptycki, as free market reform continues to reshape the state system, the growing prevalence of 'market-based' transnational crime (ranging from international drug trafficking, to trafficking nuclear and radioactive substances and illegal immigrant smuggling) is pulling public policing further into the realm of transnational policing.

Maria Loś (Chapter 10) undertakes a parallel assessment of the effect of a move toward free market reform and the collapse of communism on the redefinition of property rights in East/Central Europe. While not employing concepts taken directly from Foucault, her study is essentially about governing through property. Loś notes that one of the universal features of the post-1989 East/Central European transformation was a conversion of the communist ruling class's political assets into economic ones (that is, capitalist property) and argues that, contrary to the outward appearance of the delegitimation and discrediting of the communist elite, the move toward free market reform and privatization simply gave the *nomenklatura* class the opportunity to formally legitimate its former 'informal property rights' through the acquisition and control of capitalist property. According to Loś, in the post-communist era the bulk of the *nomenklatura* class has succeeded in retaining its privileged position by exerting control over the spontaneous and formal privatization processes, capital formation and the creation of new economic and financial institutions. Moreover, having first traded its political capital for economic capital, it has tended to use the latter to regain political power. Apart from the transfer of economic property rights from the state to themselves, another factor of critical importance in this unprecedented process of privatization has been the *nomenklatura* members' ability to establish their property claims, first, through the domination of the discursive spaces with their own rhetoric – which has often involved reconstructing recent national and personal histories – and, second, through the privatization of the former police state apparatus, which has turned an enormous pool of former state-controlled information into strategic private property.

While Maria Łoś examines the process of governing through property at a national and transnational level, Nick Blomley and Jeff Sommers (Chapter 11) analyse the geographical reordering of cities that can occur when competing discourses emerge around the issue of property ownership and property use rights. Their study also provides a significant example of the impact made by Foucault's ideas on governmentality on researchers working in the field of law and geography. According to Blomley and Sommers, if power, as Foucault argues, is simultaneously spatial and decentred, it seems necessary to try to make sense of its local geographies. Using Vancouver's Downtown Eastside – one of the city's poorest neighbourhoods – as a site for their research, the authors examine the competing discourses behind intense struggles over gentrification, which pitted developers and planners against local residents. As part of their analysis, they consider the significance and functions of various forms of 'mapping' to both groups, arguing that the marking, naming and rendering of neighbourhood space is implicated in prevailing power relations and their contestation. Building on Foucault, Blomley and Sommers argue that the production of a 'governable' population presupposes the production of an abstract 'space', and that technologies of mapping play a pivotal role in the process.

The notion of producing a governable population through creating and controlling space is also central to Bryan Hogeveen's study of the governance of plains Aboriginal peoples in western Canada from 1870 to 1890 (Chapter 12). Empirically, Hogeveen focuses on how the overlapping duties of the Department of Indian Affairs and the North West Mounted Police in the late nineteenth-century prairie provinces of Canada combined to create a system of intrusive and knowledgeable government which sought to shape the lives of the indigenous peoples. This state control of indigenous peoples was backed by prevailing nineteenth-century modes of liberal rationality and was achieved through employing a range of invented governmental technologies and practices designed to remove indigenous peoples from the path of European settlers and undermine their traditional culture and forms of social organization. Theoretically, Hogeveen, like O'Malley (Chapter 5), draws on Foucault's argument that liberal governance rationalities presupposes the existence of 'free will' and 'choice'. Discourses reflected in the colonial archives left by Indian agents and police, who were given the task of 'governing at a distance', showed that indigenous peoples were frequently given a 'choice' about whether they wanted to continue with their traditional mode of life or take up the more sedentary reservation-based life being prescribed by the government in Ottawa. Ironically, Hogeveen points out that, while the nineteenth-century discourse of liberalism stressed freedom and non-intrusion into individuals' lives, this same rationality provided a way of intruding into the lives of indigenous peoples, reshaping them as a spatially isolated 'governable' population.

This collection of essays provides an indispensable starting point for the study of empirical and theoretical issues crossing a broad range of topics in critical criminology and law. Each of the topics covered in the book – the legal regulation of sexuality and gender-related violence, crime prevention and the quest for 'community' regulation, penal developments affecting the governance of dangerousness, the application of risk management thinking to governing youth and drug-users, developments in transnational policing and the marketization of insecurity, and governing through the control of different types of capitalist property and geographical space – is in itself important and worthy of more detailed study by critical criminologists and law and society researchers. Collectively, the data and arguments presented by the contributing authors pose a challenge to the approach taken by more conventional criminologists and legal scholars who remain unfamiliar with the essential ideas of Foucault. Hopefully, this book will be of interest to both students and researchers now involved in studying issues related to governmentality and crime control, as well as those who want to become familiar with the exciting work that is now emerging in this field.

References

Arthurs, Harry (1996), 'Labour Law Without the State', *University of Toronto Law Journal*, **46** (1): 1–45.

Barry, Andrew, Thomas Osborne and Nikolas Rose (eds) (1996), *Foucault and Political Reason: Liberalism, Neo-Liberalism and Rationalities of Government*, Chicago: University of Chicago Press.

Cohen, Stanley (1985), *Visions of Social Control: Crime Punishment and Classification*, Cambridge: Polity Press.

Cohen, Stanley (1994), 'Social Control and the Politics of Reconstruction' in David Nelken (ed.), *The Futures of Criminology*, London: Sage.

Davidson, Arnold (ed.) (1997), *Foucault and his Interlocutors*, Chicago: University of Chicago Press.

Ericson, Richard and Kevin Haggerty (1997), *Policing the Risk Society*, Toronto: University of Toronto Press.

Feeley, Malcolm and Jonathan Simon (1994), 'Actuarial Justice: The Emerging New Criminal Law', in David Nelken (ed.), *The Futures of Criminology*, London: Sage.

Fitzpatrick, Peter (1988), 'The Rise and Rise of Informalism', in Roger Matthews (ed.), *Informal Justice?*, London: Sage.

Fitzpatrick, Peter (1992), 'The Impossibility of Popular Justice', *Social and Legal Studies*, **1** (2), 199–216.

Foucault, M. (1977), *Discipline and Punish: The Birth of the Prison*, New York: Pantheon.

Foucault, M. (1991), 'Governmentality', in G. Burchell, C. Gordon and P. Miller (eds), *The Foucault Effect: Studies in Governmentality*, Chicago: University of Chicago Press.

Garland, David (1996), 'The Limits of the Sovereign State: Strategies of Crime Control in Contemporary Society', *British Journal of Criminology*, **36** (4), 445–71.

Garland, David (1997), '"Governmentality" and the Problem of Crime: Foucault, Criminology, Sociology', *Theoretical Criminology*, **1** (2), 173–214.

Hunt, Alan (1996), *Governance of the Consuming Passions: A History of Sumptuary Law*, New York: St Martin's Press.

Hunt, Alan and Gary Wickham (1994), *Foucault and Law: Towards a Sociology of Law and Governance*, London: Pluto Press.

Loś Maria (1994), 'Property Rights, Markets and Historical Justice: Legislative Discourses in Poland', *International Journal of the Sociology of Law*, **22** (1), 39–58.

Loś Maria (1995), 'Lustration and Truth-Claims: Unfinished Revolutions in Central Europe', *Law and Social Inquiry*, **20** (1), 117–62.

McNay, Lois (1994), *Foucault: A Critical Introduction*, New York: Continuum.

Merry, Sally (1990), *Getting Justice and Getting Even: Legal Consciousness among Working Class Americans*, Chicago: University of Chicago Press.

Merry, Sally (1992), 'Popular Justice and the Ideology of Social Transformation', *Social and Legal Studies*, **1** (2), 161–76.

Merry, Sally (1995), 'Resistance and the Cultural Power of Law', *Law and Society Review*, **29** (1), 11–26.

Nina, Daniel (1995), *Re-Thinking Popular Justice: Self-Regulation and Civil Society in South Africa*, Cape Town: Community Peace Foundation.

O'Farrell, Clare (ed.) (1997), *Foucault: The Legacy*, Brisbane: Queensland University of Technology.

O'Malley, Pat (1991), 'Legal Networks and Domestic Security', *Studies in Law, Politics, and Society*, **11**, 171–90.

O'Malley, Pat (1992), 'Risk, Power and Crime Prevention', *Economy and Society*, **21** (3), 252–75.

Pavlich, George (1996a), 'The Power of Community Mediation: Government and the Formation of Self-Identity', *Law and Society Review*, **30** (4), 707–33.

Pavlich, George (1996b), *Justice Fragmented: Mediating Community Disputes Under Postmodern Conditions*, New York: Routledge.

Pels, Peter (1997), 'The Anthropology of Colonialism: Culture, History, and the Emergence of Western Governmentality', *Annual Review of Anthropology*, **26**, 163–83.

Rose, Nikolas and P. Miller (1992), 'Political Power Beyond the State: Problematics of Government', *British Journal of Sociology*, **43** (2), 173–205.

Santos, Boaventura De Sousa (1992), 'State, Law and Community in the World System: An Introduction', *Social and Legal Studies*, **1** (2), 131–42.

Santos, Boaventura De Sousa (1995), *Toward a New Common Sense: Law, Science and Politics in the Paradigmatic Transition*, New York: Routledge.

Scott, David (1995), 'Colonial Governmentality', *Social Texts*, **5** (3), 191–220.

Shearing, Clifford and Mike Brogden (1993), *Policing for a New South Africa*, New York: Routledge.

Smandych, Russell and Gloria Lee (1995), 'Women, Colonialization, and Resistance: Elements of an Amerindian Autohistorical Approach to the Study of Law and Colonialism', *Native Studies Review*, **10** (1), 21–46.

Smandych, Russell and Rick Linden (1996), 'Administering Justice Without the State: A Study of the Private Justice System of the Hudson's Bay Company to 1800', *Canadian Journal of Law and Society*, **11** (1), 21–61.

Stenson, Kevin (1993), 'Community Policing as a Governmental Technology', *Economy and Society*, **22** (3), 373–89.

2 'Governmentality' and the Problem of Crime[1]

David Garland

Michel Foucault's *Discipline and Punish* (1977) made a huge impression on criminology, providing it with a theoretical language with which to analyse the practices of punishment, as well as with a heightened sense of criminology's own status as a power/knowledge apparatus linked into these very practices.

Now, a dozen years after his death, Foucault has begun to exert a theoretical influence of a quite different kind. From 1978 until his death in 1984, his work developed around a new theme, 'the government of others and the government of one's self', which focused particularly on the relations between two poles of governance – the forms of rule by which various authorities govern populations and the technologies of the self through which individuals work on themselves to shape their own subjectivity. These analyses of Foucault – broadly described as studies of 'governmentality' – have inaugurated a vigorous research programme and an impressive scholarly literature, anatomizing practices of government across a range of social and economic fields (see Burchell *et al.* 1991; Rose and Miller 1992; Barry *et al.* 1993, 1996; Dean 1994; Hunt and Wickham 1994). Analyses of this kind have recently begun to consider the field of crime control and criminal justice (Stenson 1993; O'Malley 1996), suggesting that a second, and rather different, 'Foucault effect' might be about to be felt within theoretical criminology.

At a time when criminologists are trying to come to terms with a reconfigured criminological field (see Feeley and Simon 1992; Garland 1996), the governmentality literature offers a powerful framework for analysing how crime is problematized and controlled. It is focused on the present – particularly on the shift from 'welfarist' to 'neo-liberal' politics – and avoids reductionist or totalizing analyses, encouraging instead an open-ended, positive account of practices of governance in specific fields. It aims

15

to anatomize contemporary practices, revealing the ways in which their modes of exercising power depend on specific ways of thinking (rationalities) and specific ways of acting (technologies), as well as on specific ways of 'subjectifying' individuals and governing populations. It also problematizes these practices by subjecting them to a 'genealogical' analysis – a tracing of their historical lineages that aims to undermine their 'naturalness' and open up a space for alternative possibilities.

In the first part of this chapter, I discuss the usefulness of this governmentality approach in opening up new ways of understanding the discourses, problems and practices of contemporary crime control. I then turn to consider some of the limitations and problems of this framework and argue, against some of its proponents, that an engagement with (certain forms of) sociological analysis would allow governmentality studies to overcome some of these limitations.

Governmentality and the Problem of Crime

The governmentality literature does not offer a general thesis that can be 'applied' to the field of crime control. Nor does it provide a unified account of the present – such as 'post-modernity' or 'risk society' – under which can be subsumed the facts of criminal policy or the developmental tendencies of the criminal justice system. It does, however, isolate a series of objects of analysis and suggest certain lines of enquiry that strike me as having great potential for researching and interpreting current developments in this field.

Pat O'Malley (1996) and Kevin Stenson (1993) have already suggested ways in which crime prevention and community policing can be illuminated by reference to this framework, and O'Malley's claim that neo-liberal social policy is increasingly promoting 'prudentialism' and the 'responsible individual' helps make sense both of the expansion of the demand for private security and the declining influence of 'social criminologies'. Similarly, Feeley and Simon's account of 'the new penology' points to the increasing influence of 'managerialism', 'risk-management' and 'actuarial justice' in US criminal justice (see Feeley and Simon 1992, 1994; Simon and Feeley 1995). In the following pages, I sketch some further ways in which an analytic of 'governmentality' might deepen our understanding of contemporary crime control and criminal justice.

Rationalities of Crime Control

The idea of a 'governmental rationality' is of crucial importance in pointing us towards a quite specific dimension of crime control that otherwise goes unnoticed. The dimension it identifies is not quite that of policy statements, nor the legitimatory rhetorics that are used by officials to gloss the practice of institutions. Nor is it precisely the same thing as the criminological theories or the reform programmes that influence these practices. The idea of 'governmental rationalities' refers instead to the ways of thinking and styles of reasoning that are embodied in a particular set of practices. It points to the form of rationality that organize these practices and supply them with their objectives and knowledge and forms of reflexivity.

Rationalities are thus *practical* rather than theoretical or discursive entities. They are forged in the business of problem solving and attempting to make things work. Consequently they manifest a logic of practice, rather than of analysis, and tend to bear the hallmarks of the institutional settings out of which they emerged.[2]

If we use this idea of 'rationalities' to think about crime control, it prompts the following questions. How have authorities understood their role in relation to the problem of crime? How has the problem of governing crime been problematized and rationalized? Through what technologies and assemblages, and using what forms of knowledge, have authorities exercised governance in this area?

It seems plausible to suggest that, in recent decades, the governance of crime has come to be problematized in new ways, partly in reaction to chronically high crime rates and the failure of criminal justice controls (Garland 1996), and partly under the influence of broader shifts away from welfarist styles of government towards neo-liberal ones. It also seems plausible to argue that, in response to this emergent field of problems and political forces, a new rationality for the governance of crime is coming into existence, together with a new rationality for the governance of criminal justice. Described in very broad terms, this is a governmental style that is organized around economic forms of reasoning, in contrast to the social and legal forms that have predominated for most of the twentieth-century.

By an 'economic' rationality, I don't mean simply that value-for-money considerations and fiscal restraint have nowadays become prominent and explicit aspects of crime control discourse and practice – although this is certainly a feature of the contemporary scene. I mean to point to:

1   the increasing reliance upon an *analytical language* of risks and rewards, rationality, choice, probability, targeting and the demand and supply of opportunities – a language that translates 'economic' forms of reasoning and calculation into the criminological field;
2   the increasing importance of *objectives* such as compensation, cost control, harm reduction, economy, efficiency and effectiveness; and

3   the increasing resort to *technologies* such as audit, fiscal control, market competition and devolved management to control penal decision-making.

For example, the now recurring image of the 'rational criminal' and the concern to govern this figure by manipulating incentives and risks, replicates the standard thought patterns of economic analysis. So, too, does the image of the victim as a supplier of criminal opportunities, and the idealized figure of *home prudens* (Adams 1995; O'Malley 1996) projected by crime prevention literature and insurance contracts. These new ways of thinking strip away the sociological and psychological layers in which twentieth-century criminology had clothed its conception of the criminal offender, and try to rethink the dynamics of crime and punishment in pseudo-economic terms.[3]

This kind of thinking developed first in the private sector – in the practices of insurance companies, private security firms and commercial enterprises, concerned to reduce those costs of crime that fall on them. Commercial and insurance-based thinking about crime control focuses upon reducing or displacing the costs of crime, upon prevention rather than punishment and upon minimizing risk rather than ensuring justice. Commercially situated attempts to control 'reactive risk', 'morale hazard' and 'risk compensation' (see Adams 1995; Heimer 1985; Litton 1990) or to weigh the costs of crime against the cost – to the enterprise – of its prevention or prosecution, led to the elaboration of this style of reasoning about crime and its control. Only later, in the 1980s, did it begin to influence state agencies and practices, most of which are in the control of professional groups allied to social and legal ways of conceiving the problem of crime.

This way of thinking also draws upon other sources. One such source is the work of Gary Becker (1968) and other economic analysts of crime, whose ideas have recently been imported into the language of criminal policy (Cook 1986; van Dijk 1994). Another is the cluster of criminological theories – rational choice theory, routine activity theory and the various approaches that view crime as a matter of opportunity – which I have described elsewhere as 'the new criminologies of everyday life' (Garland 1996). In contrast to older criminologies, which assumed that the individual offender could be differentiated and corrected, these theoretical frameworks view crime as a normal, mundane event, requiring no special disposition or abnormality on the part of the offender. Crime is viewed as a routine phenomenon – as something that happens in the course of events, rather than a disruption of normality that has to be specially explained. The everyday conduct of economic and social life supplies countless opportunities for illegitimate transactions. Viewed *en masse*, criminal events are regular, predictable and systematic, in the way that road traffic accidents are. It follows that action on crime should cease to be primarily action on deviant individuals and become, instead, action designed to govern social and economic routines.

Since their emergence, these theories have received considerable critical scrutiny, usually from the perspective of rival criminological traditions whose proponents complain that the new theories fail to identify the root causes of crime, or else that they take too superficial a view of human nature and of criminal conduct. In contrast to that kind of critique, the Foucauldian approach aims to address the substance of these discourses and the practical programmes that they support, paying careful attention to what they say, how they say it, and to the complex of preconditions that make these statements sayable, and which govern their emergence, functioning and transformation. It aims to describe how agents, knowledges, powers and techniques are assembled into specific apparatuses for the exercise of new ways of governing crime, thus transforming these ways of thinking into practical ways of acting. And, although this approach will tend to imply a critical stance – insofar as it is describing modes of exercising power and of projecting forms of subjectivity that are otherwise hidden – it seeks to maintain the neutral gaze of an analyst rather than the hostile glare of a rival with competing claims to truth. This strikes me as a valuable way of coming to terms with the currently emerging configuration of crime control, the very newness of which tends to undercut our conventional stock of 'critical' and 'progressive' positions, most of which derive from an earlier period in the history of the field.

The Criminogenic Situation

One of the effects of the new criminologies discussed above has been to bring into view – and therefore into existence for the purposes of knowledge and of government – an entity which might be termed *the criminogenic situation*. This constitutes a new site of intervention for governmental practices – a new practicable object, quite distinct from the individual delinquents and legal subjects that previously formed the targets for crime control. Moreover, the criminogenic situation is like 'the economy' or 'the population' in that it is a domain with its own internal dynamics and processes, populated by active human subjects whose interests and actions shape these processes, and with functional ends of its own that are easily disturbed by heavy-handed regulation.

Criminogenic situations are commonplace in modern society. They take a variety of forms and come in all shapes and sizes: unsupervised car parks, town squares late at night, deserted neighbourhoods, poorly lit streets, shopping malls, football games, bus stops, subway stations and so on. Their status as more or less 'criminogenic' – as hot spots of crime or low-rate, secure areas – are established by reference to local police statistics, victim surveys and crime pattern analysis. Their fundamental dynamics can be represented by a few simple parameters – the presence of valuable targets and criminally-inclined individuals, and the absence of effective guardians or situational controls – that emulate the commodity–buyer–price formulae of neo-classical economics. A new body of research on 'situational crime prevention' – offering phenomenological descriptions of situations that 'invite' crime, 'natural histories' of criminal events and 'environmental risk indexes' that calculate vulnerability – has begun to develop a working knowledge of this variable entity.

'The criminogenic situation' poses difficulties for government because it generally has a commercial or social value of its own which sets limits on crime control. Precisely because crime occurs in the course of routine social and economic transactions, any crime-reducing intervention must seek to preserve 'normal life' and 'business as usual'. The characteristic modes of intervention involve the implantation of non-intrusive controls in the situation itself, or else attempts to modify the interests and the incentives of the actors involved (see Shearing and Stenning 1985). The situation can be 'governed', but it cannot be completely or coercively controlled. Practices of situational governance must operate lightly and unobtrusively, working with and through the actors involved. The aim is to align the actors' objectives with those of the authorities; to make them active partners in the business of security and crime control. In this way the situation is allowed to retain its 'natural' character, but is made more secure against the occurrence of criminal events. The parallels with the problems of 'securing' economic processes through 'liberal' government suggest themselves forcefully.

This analysis also calls to mind Foucault's suggestion that the forms of modern power might be viewed as a 'triangle of sovereignty–discipline–government'. Thus we find, coexisting on the terrain of crime control, three practicable objects and three forms of exercising power in respect of them:

1   the *legal subject*, governed by sovereign command and obliged to obey or be punished;
2   the *criminal delinquent*, governed by discipline and required to conform or be corrected; and now
3   the *criminogenic situation*, governed by the manipulation of interests and the promotion of mechanisms of self-regulation.

Each of these stands for a particular way of acting on the problem of crime, supported by a complex of laws, institutional practices and forms of expertise, and each way of acting commands the support of particular groups (the judiciary, the social work establishment, the new crime prevention agencies and so on). The interweaving of these different modes of 'governing crime' produces an intricate web of policies and practices that cannot be reduced to a single formula. There is no phased historical progression from 'sovereign punishment' to 'discipline' to 'government at a distance', nor is there an easy or coherent relationship between these different conceptions and practices of crime control. In any concrete conjecture, the field of crime control will manifest an uneven (and often incoherent) combination of these modes of action, the specific 'mix' depending on the balance of power between the different groups involved, as well as the residues of past practices and institutional arrangements. The value of Foucault's analysis (which is both genealogical and typological) is that it allows us to analyse the crime control field as *a field of power relations and subjectifications* and draws attention to the impact of new knowledges and technologies on the power relations between governmental actors, as well as between the rulers and the ruled.

The attempt to govern criminogenic situations has led to a set of new objectives – the reduction of crime and the fear of crime, the promotion of a culture of security consciousness, the enhancement of public safety and so on – which are seen to be best achieved by acting through (rather than acting on) the actors involved. This gives rise to a 'responsibilization strategy' whereby state authorities (typically the police or the Home Office) seek to enlist other agencies and individuals to form a chain of coordinated action that reaches into criminogenic situations, prompting crime-control conduct on the part of 'responsibilized' actors (see Garland 1996). Central to this strategy is the attempt to ensure that all the agencies and individuals who are in a position to contribute to these crime-reducing ends come to see it as being in their interests to do so. 'Government' is thus extended and enhanced by the creation of 'governors' and 'guardians' in the space between the state and the offender.

Whereas older strategies sought to govern crime directly, through the specialist apparatus of criminal justice, this new approach entails a more indirect form of government-at-a-distance, involving 'interagency' cooperation and the responsibilization of private individuals and organizations. This practice of enlisting and enrolment, of seeking to build chains of action and to instil crime-conscious attitudes gives rise, in turn, to the development of new forms of knowledge and expertise – about the problems of coordinated action, about the costs of crime and ways to reduce them, and about technologies of situational prevention. Complex assemblages (comprising of specific combinations of agents, knowledges, techniques and practices) are thus pieced together in an attempt to translate the new rationalities and programmes into practical effects. There has been a real spurt of inventiveness at the level of security technologies (see, for example, the publications of the government's Crime Prevention Unit) partly due to government interest in the project and partly because of the formation of a market in security which speeds up the development and the (very unequal) distribution of such devices.

The Criminal Justice System as an Entity to be Governed

A striking feature of the present period is the degree to which official attention has become focused not just on the government of crime, but also on the problem of governing criminal justice. Rises in the flow of cases through the criminal justice system, resulting in crowded court calendars and overcrowded prisons, prompted government concern about new problems such as costs, efficiency and coordination in criminal justice. This, in turn, led to the development of techniques for representing and controlling these problems. Over time, there was a transformation in the way that 'criminal justice' was understood. What was previously viewed as a loosely coupled series of independent agencies – police, prosecution, courts, prison, probation, each with its own objectives and working ideologies and each with its own sphere of autonomous action – came to be seen instead as a 'system' which can be known and governed. It has become a practicable object of government, with the Home Office increasingly constituting itself as a centre of calculation and management, oriented to that governmental task.

The system's processes and internal dynamics have been theorized, using concepts and tools borrowed from 'systems management'. Models have been constructed to simulate the workings of the system. Monitoring devices, auditing requirements and decision-making guidelines have been implanted at key points so that the flow of cases can be predicted and controlled from a central point in a way that was previously quite impossible. Similarly, the day-to-day practice of practitioners working in the various agencies has been standardized and subjected to greater managerial control by the use of 'government-at-a-distance' techniques (budgetary limits, national standards, 'gatekeeping' guidelines) by which the central authorities exert broad control over decision-making while still leaving a space for the exercise of localized judgement on the part of the individual professionals.

As many commentators have pointed out – see Peters (1986), Heydebrand and Seron (1990), Tuck (1991), Feeley and Simon (1992), Walker (1993) – the rendering of criminal justice into a 'system' that can be known and centrally governed presupposes a new way of thinking about the processes involved. The focus of attention is shifted from individuals to aggregates, from specific cases to population flows and from individualized justice to the management of resources. The discretionary powers of professionals are curtailed and their jurisdictions are narrowed. The system is rendered more homogenous, more knowable and more governable. There is a centralization of powers and a shift from a patchwork of particular expertise to a more homogenized field of risk and resource management. Precisely because of these curtailments and centralized controls, this development has provoked resistance from some of the professional groups involved. The judiciary is especially forceful in its opposition to this attempt to 'systematize' and govern its conduct, and the need 'to treat the merits of the individual case' is used as a counter-claim by judges and social workers alike.

Active Subjects

Crime control practices embody a conception of the subjects they seek to govern. For most of the twentieth-century, the subjects of crime control have been the 'individual delinquent' and the 'legal subject'. The new economic rationality attempts to make up new kinds of individuals, or rather to create and impart new forms of subjectivity which individuals and organizations will adopt for themselves.

One new form of 'subjectification' is the responsibilized, security-conscious, crime-preventing subject – *homo prudens* – analysed by O'Malley (1992) and Adams (1995). A related, though opposed, figure is what has been called 'situational man' (see Clarke and Cornish 1986) who is criminology's version of the economic subject of interest. He (or, less often, she) is a moderately rational, self-interested individual, unfettered by any moral compass or super-ego controls – a consumer who is alert to criminal opportunities and responsive to situational inducements.

The questions to be asked of subjects of this kind are not 'how did their attitudes and personalities come to be abnormal? or 'how can they be corrected?' but rather 'how do such persons reason and act in criminogenic situations?', 'how do they choose?' and 'how can their actions be channelled away from crime by modifying situational controls?'.

Unlike *homo prudens*, situational man is not a preferred form of subjectivity that is promoted and projected by the authorities. It is an assumption about the real subjectivity of already formed individuals. But in assuming the reality of situational man, the authorities begin to give substance to it, projecting it on to real men and women and 'making people up' in this form. Thus research is conducted into the reasoning processes of burglars or robbers, offenders are officially identified as career criminals, sentencers shape their sentences on the basis of these perceptions, and convicted offenders are treated as entrepreneurial actors rather than as subjects of need or candidates for rehabilitative treatment.

Penal Technologies of the Self

In contemporary prison and probation regimes one sees a similar characterization of the criminal justice and a determined effort to assimilate individual offenders into its terms by means of new 'technologies of the self'. Techniques of correction stress the offender's responsibility for his or her criminal actions and insist that he or she must 'address' and 'take responsibility' for them. This is not merely a reversion to an older punitive mode which assumes that the offender has the attributes of a free-willed legal subject. On the contrary, instead of assuming that all adult individuals are 'naturally' capable of responsible, self-directed action and moral agency, contemporary penal regimes treat this as a problem to be remedied by procedures that actively seek to 'subjectify' and to 'responsibilize' individuals.'[4]

One vivid illustration of this is the Personal Development File, which the Scottish Prison Service offers to long-term prisoners as part of its programme of creating 'the responsible prisoner'. This programme is presented as a 'training for freedom' – a scheme that enlists the prisoner both as an agent in his own rehabilitation and an entrepreneur of his own personal development, rather than an objectified or infantalized client upon whom therapeutic solutions are imposed.

The Personal Development File consists of a series of exercises in decision-making and self-assessment, which individual prisoners are encouraged to work their way through. It is a secular, basic-literacy version of the techniques of self-examination, diary-keeping and spiritual exercise that have been used for centuries to help individuals 'subject' themselves. But whereas in the past, these ways of training one's self were in the service of spiritual or moral ends, the prison procedures are primarily concerned to teach prudent, self-interested decision-making.

The exercises are designed to help the prisoner examine different aspects of his or her life – drug use, drinking, relationships, attitudes to authority and criminal behaviour. Rather than 'preach' that such activities are wrong, or harmful to others, the message is that indulgence in bad practices is imprudent, self-defeating and leads ultimately to becoming a 'loser' who ends up in prison. Prisoners are taught to become 'responsible', prudent subjects – in prison and, more optimistically, after release – by techniques that assume an alignment between the self-interest of the prisoner and the governing interests of the authorities. (The prisoner who enjoys criminal behaviour, or who embraces the consequence of crime, or for whom a law-abiding life is not a viable option, will be deemed 'irresponsible', no matter how self-aware and autonomous his or her actions are.) Working on the file and, in the process, working on one's self, is part of a 'contract' that the prisoner enters into with the prison authorities.

Prisoners who succeed in rendering themselves 'responsible', and behaving accordingly, are rewarded by a Sentence Planning Scheme which allows them to take part in the government of their own confinement. They are permitted to choose their preferred options from within the available range of developmental activities or prison employment, and even to choose the prisons in which they will serve different parts of their sentence. By these means, 'responsible' choice is practised and rewarded, insofar as this is possible within the constraints of a resource-starved prison system. Prisoners are thus governed, and learn to govern themselves, in ways that emphasize individual agency and autonomy. One should take care, however, not to confuse 'agency' with 'freedom'.[5] As Scottish prisoners frequently complain – although not quite in these terms – they are by no means free to exercise 'autonomy' just as they choose. On the contrary, the form of agency sanctioned by the institution is that of the self-confining, prudent individual whose behaviour is aligned with the goals of the prison authorities (Gemmell 1993; Ferrant 1997).

The new emphasis on the offender's 'autonomy' and 'responsibility' can also be seen in recent policy on community penalties and the idea of 'punishment in the community'. Part of the appeal of probation and community service and monetary penalties is that they avoid the 'objectifying' tendencies of imprisonment and organize a process of penal control in which the offender is enlisted. Instead of removing the individual into the near-total control of a custodial confinement, these community measures seek to insert regulatory devices into the offender's natural habitat and daily routines, producing a light framework of supervision but leaving plenty of opportunity for the offender to practise self-control. Techniques such as intermittent supervision and reporting, electronic monitoring, tracking, drug-testing and attendance for work, are used, as are alliances with other sources of social control (such as the family, landladies, employers, bail hostel workers, and so on), to try to build an environment conducive to self-control and the practice of a responsibilized freedom.[6]

No doubt there are other lines of research which a governmentality analytic would help open up for criminologists. The 'neo-liberal' strategies involved in the 'privatization' or 'contracting out' of crime-control functions, the new linkages being formed between 'public' and 'private' forms of crime control, the impact of insurance on criminal behaviour and the conduct of victims, and the shift in police policy towards a more generic concern with the promotion of security and good order reminiscent of the older programme of 'police' are some that come to mind. And, of course, historical work on the development of crime control, criminal justice and a professionalized police has much to learn from the genealogical writings of Foucault and Foucauldian scholars such as Dean (1991), Burchell (1991) and Pasquino (1991). But I hope I have said enough to suggest that the field of crime control is certainly one in which 'governmental' analyses can be effectively and productively employed.

This chapter is written in the hope of encouraging such work and suggesting lines of enquiry. However, and in anticipation of such work being done, it might be useful to indicate some of the limitations of this analytical scheme, as well as some of the problems inherent in the governmentality literature.

The Limits of 'Governmentality' Analysis

If the governmentality literature is to become a resource for considering contemporary patterns of crime control, it will be necessary to elaborate and more precisely define some of its key concepts, and to build upon the genealogical analyses that Foucault developed.

Some of the governmentality concepts are neologisms ('bio-power', 'pastoral power', 'governmentality'); others are historical terms ('police', *'raison d'État'*) and others are conventional terms of analysis to which Foucault imparts a slightly unconventional meaning (for example, his use of the terms 'liberalism' and 'security'). This can lead to some confusion. It is not clear, for example, how 'pastoral power', 'bio-power' and 'security' relate to one another; are they distinct kinds of practices or different names for the same kind of thing? Nor is it clear how these relate to the notion of 'governmentality'. Is bio-power an earlier term for the 'governmental' form of power or merely a specific instance of it? Is the contrast between the 'anatomo-political' and the 'bio-political' (Foucault 1979) the same as the contrast between 'discipline' and 'government' (Foucault 1991)?

This terminological confusion is evident in discussions of the place of 'liberalism' in descriptions of the present. Foucault's analyses suggest that liberal modalities of governing are characteristic of the welfare state (which he terms a 'society of security'). The problem is that 'liberalism', in this usage, is a very broad term that lacks a clear alternative and actually includes political forms that are usually contrasted to it.[7] Thus some writers in this tradition (for example, O'Malley 1996) contrast 'liberal' to 'welfarist', suggesting that the welfare state is not, after all, to be viewed as a liberal state, while others (for example, Rose 1996), contrast 'neo-liberal' policies to welfarist policies, which again implies a welfare/liberal contrast.[8]

The idea of a 'governmentalized state' is also somewhat problematic. Which state is not 'governmentalized' to some degree? How could there be a form of rule that does not engage in the 'conduct of conduct', even if it relies heavily on command and repression to do so? It would seem, therefore, that all states must be more or less 'governmentalized – in the same way that they are all more or less 'interventionist'. The characterization is a matter of degree not of kind. Alternatively, if the defining feature of 'governmentality' is the adoption of a specific set of objectives towards which the 'conduct' of the population is to be 'conducted' (such as health, welfare, prosperity and so on) or of specific techniques and methods of so doing (for example, the 'liberal' style of rule-at-a-distance), then it would seem more appropriate to use terms that evoke these definitive features.

Another potential source of confusion is the use of the term 'governmental' to describe the conduct (and sometimes the status) of a range of authorities who are not part of what conventional political discourse would term the 'state' or 'the government'. The purpose of this Foucauldian usage is clear enough – it serves to emphasize the idea that power is exercised, and conduct shaped, by agencies which are often thought of as 'private' or 'nonpolitical'. As Foucault (1991) stressed, the idea of 'good government' was originally a characteristic of the household or other sub-political organizations, and it became an attribute of statecraft only in the modern period. 'Government' is no more concentrated in the state apparatus than is 'power' – both are dispersed through a multitude of locales and authorities. Nevertheless, the conventional political discourse of the modern period has come to reflect the fact of a 'governmentalized state' – and the concentration of governmental powers and resources that this represents – by using the term 'the government' to refer to the legally constituted rulers of the nation-state. To generalize the idea of 'governmental' to refer to all sources and locales that exercise social power inevitably invites confusion.

Governmentality writers have, for similar reasons, rejected what they see as the confounding distinction between state and civil society, arguing that modern forms of government 'combine action by political and non-political authorities' (Barry *et al.* 1993: 2) or link together 'public and private security' (Rose 1996: 37). But, against this, one might observe that the conventional distinction between state and civil society, or between 'public' and 'private', is not intended to mean that any particular practice or policy will operate exclusively in one or other of these realms. Most sociological analyses stress the interaction and mutual dependency of state and non-state practices, just as most policy analysis depicts the relays that must run between public and private action if government policy is to be effective in bringing about its intended effects.

Nor is the distinction between 'state' and 'non-state' merely an analytical one that can be jettisoned at will. To be demarcated in public law as a state agency is to be afforded special access to legal, economic and military resources, as well as to a special form of authority and a network of supporting organizations. In a stable, constitutional democracy, where the rule of law operates, such resources make a large difference to the capacity of an agency to exercise power and to govern effectively. It is not surprising that the attempt to avoid these important, socially operative distinctions frequently results in circumlocutions that say the same thing in less transparent ways, as when Rose talks about 'the formal political institutions' (Rose 1996: 54) or Burchell refers to 'the authorized governmental agencies' (Burchell 1996: 29).

An Incomplete Genealogy

Foucault's genealogies of the mentalities of government that arose in the seventeenth or eighteenth centuries were not attempts to establish their historical meaning or to understand how they functioned in the Early Modern period. His concern was to identify rationalities and technologies that were instrumental in forming our present, either because they still function in the contemporary period, or else because they gave rise to problems and solutions which do. But unlike his work on the prison, the asylum or on sexuality, he never completed his genealogical account of governmental reason nor published a major book on the topic. His analyses are suggestive rather than substantive. The genealogical threads trail off before they reach the present. There is no detailed account of how particular ways of governing today depend on these lines of descent and are structured by them. So, whereas his genealogical studies of the prison or of sexuality were quite specific in their focus and undeniably relevant to our understanding of current practices, the studies of governmentality do not grasp present-day practices with the same precision or revelatory clarity.

One might agree that Christian pastoralism, or sixteenth-century 'police' or eighteenth-century 'liberalism' all resonate with the practices of modern welfare states, but it is not clear how these genealogies change our understanding in any significant way. We might accept that modern society manifests a 'triangle of sovereignty–discipline–government' but, without very much more specification, this is merely a plausible typology to be set alongside other typologies of power, some of which are more dependably contemporary in their range of reference. Foucault's own work in this field offers analytical suggestions and proposes lines of research – some of which have already been taken up and developed. It is not a compelling history of the present, and certainly not a completed one (if such a thing is imaginable). To engage with this work is not to find a set of ready-made analyses, but to respond to its invitation to take up specific lines of research in order to address certain problems in our present.

Governing through Freedom

One of the recurring motifs of the governmentality literature is the idea that we are 'governed' through, and by means of, our 'freedom'. This is a typically Foucauldian paradox and sounds at once critical and revelatory, particularly in entrepreneurial, consumerist societies in which choice and individuality are dominant cultural themes. The conventional idea of freedom contrasts sharply with the notion of being dominated or being ruled. To suggest that we are ruled 'through our freedom' – that what we cherish as our autonomy, our individuality and our independence of power relations is precisely the basis for our being governed by others – sounds analytically audacious and devastating in its political implications. If the governmentality literature has a central critical claim, then this is undoubtedly it.

However, on closer inspection, this claim turns out to be less interesting than it first seems. When used in respect of 'neo-liberal' practices of government, the idea of 'governing through freedom' is a misleading characterization of the phenomenon. When used in respect of the formation of free persons, it turns out to be very close to certain sociological accounts of individual socialization.

Underlying the claims about 'governing through freedom' and the notion that 'power presupposes freedom' is a punning conflation between two ideas which are actually quite distinct: the concept of *agency*, and the concept of freedom.[9] These two concepts are being run together here as if they were the same thing, when in fact they are significantly different.

The idea of 'agency' refers to the capacity of an agent for action, its possession of the 'power to act', which is the capacity to originate such actions on the basis of calculations and decisions. Agency is a universal attribute of (socialized) human beings, as well as of human organizations and corporate entities. The exercise of directive power in the social sphere is, as Foucault suggests, dependent on this human capacity for action, as are the various techniques of rule-at-a-distance, which depend on the calculative actions of dispersed decision-makers.

Freedom, on the other hand, generally refers to a capacity to choose one's actions without external constraint.[10] Freedom (unlike agency) is necessarily a matter of degree – it is the configured range of unconstrained choice in which agency can operate. The truth is that the exercise of governmental power, and particularly neo-liberal techniques of government, rely on, and stimulate, *agency* while simultaneously reconfiguring (rather than removing) the *constraints* upon the freedom of choice of the agent.

Making up Free Subjects

The phrase 'govern through freedom' is also used to refer to the 'making up' of persons, whose preferences and durable dispositions are oriented towards a set of objectives that coincide with those promoted by governing authorities. (Examples would include the active citizen, the consumer, the enterprising subject, the psychiatric outpatient, and so on.) Precisely because these preferences and objectives have been internalized, they have the experiential quality of being 'freely chosen' by the individual. But, as the governmentality literature points out, authorities and experts and powers of various kinds play a large part in 'making up' the persons in these ways, as do the technologies of the self and conceptions of personhood that these authorities promote.

I find no fault with this analysis, although it must be said that there is nothing particularly original in it. The socialization processes whereby cultural practices interact with developing individuals (who possess the evolved potentialities of the human organism) to produce individuated social agents, capable of intentional, meaningful action, is one that is very familiar to readers of sociological textbooks. So, too, is the paradox, pointed out by Nietzsche (1956) – but better analysed by Durkheim (1973) or Mead (1934) – that to become 'free' (by which he means capable of willing and directing our own conscious action) we must first be subjected to the controls and disciplines and learning experiences of socialization.[11]

Moreover, the Foucauldian approach tends to focus on the identification and analysis of 'technologies of the self' and their relation to broader governmental strategies, and it has little to say about the question of how particular personal styles come to be adopted by particular social groups, or the psychological processes involved in embracing an individual self-conception. The governmentality literature doesn't tell us much about who 'chooses' particular identities and why, or about the process of 'choosing' and the limits of choice. Nor does it have anything to say about the durability of these internalized dispositions in the absence of the external rituals and processes that sanction and reinforce them. It thus abandons these questions at a point where sociological and criminological research might want to begin.

Rationalities and Technologies as Ideal Types

The anatomization of rationalities and technologies is one of the strengths of the governmentality approach. But it would be a mistake to focus on the structure of conceptual and technological assemblages at the expense of an analysis of the pragmatics of use. There is a need to study the way in which these knowledges and techniques are put to use and the meanings they acquire in context. We need to examine the extent to which they are implemented, their corruption in practice, the unforeseen consequences that they produce and the relation they establish with the field that they seek to govern. This point is regularly made within the governmentality literature, and writers such as Nikolas Rose (1996) and Colin Gordon (1991) take great care to stress that governmental programmes are never perfectly realized in practice. But this warning is frequently ignored because of a certain bias that affects this style of scholarship. There is, in Foucault's methodological approach, a textual and philosophical bias which uses the evidence of historical documents to identify and reassemble systems of thought or principles of governing. The overweening concern is to reconstruct these systems – to establish their positivity, their detailed characteristics, their complete anatomy.

Despite Foucault's explicit concern with power and practices and the history of the present, there remains in his work – and in the work of his followers – the traces of his previous incarnation as an 'historian of systems of thought' and an archaeologist whose concern is to uncover and differentiate *epistemes*. In other words, there is a tendency to use historical materials *philosophically* to demonstrate that there are different ways of knowing, rather than asking, as a sociologist or historian might, 'how did these things function?' and 'what did these things mean?'. The result is the analytical reconstruction of what are, in effect, historically grounded ideal types. The rationalities and technologies are presented in an abstracted, perfected, fully formed way. They are compared one to the other, and their contrasts are taken to suggest the contrasts between different historical periods or social arrangements. But as Weber (1985) makes clear in his methodology of ideal types, the creation of such abstractions is not an end in itself but rather an heuristic step in the process of empirical analysis. The abstracted entities ('the spirit of capitalism', 'formal-rational law' ... 'neo-liberal rationality') allow the analyst to investigate the messy realm of practices and relations and the compromised, corrupted, partial ways in which these entities inhabit the real world. Ideal types – or reconstructed rationalities – are a basis for empirical analysis, not a substitute for it.

There are, of course, circumstances in which the reconstruction of abstracted rationalities and technologies is a perfectly legitimate end-point for scholarship – for example, when the project is that of the 'history of systems of thought'.[12] And Rose and Miller (1992) defend this focus when they counterpose their 'nominalist' approach to the study of government to what they term the 'realism' of most historical sociology. In so doing, however, I believe they confuse the procedure for genealogical analysis which allows one to analyse a historical entity in a non-historical manner (see Castel

1994), with the procedure for analysing the present. In the case of the latter, it makes little sense to analyse abstracted entities without proceeding to analyse how they actually function in context.

A genealogical enquiry can legitimately isolate an entity such as Bentham's Panopticon, or the seventeenth-century Christian confession, without asking how it 'really functioned' at that time or what its significance was in its original context, because the 'historian of the present' is concerned to understand the present not the past, and the technology in question is identified as one that still functions today. But, if it is acceptable to neglect the question of how such entities functioned or signified in the past, there can be no avoidance of this question as it relates to the present! On the contrary, it becomes essential to explore the real practices and processes in which these programmes and rationalities and technologies are selectively and sometimes unexpectedly used, with all of their compromise formations and unintended effects.[13]

To take a recent penological example, it might be supposed that the re-establishment of the prison service in England and Wales as an executive agency is a good example of a neo-liberal rationality in operation. In 1993 the prison service was re-established as an autonomized agency, operating at arm's length from the state, enjoying devolved budgets, managerial autonomy and a quasi-private sector ethos, apparently transforming it into an illustration of what Rose describes as the 'degovernmentalization' of the state. But, in fact, the pattern of interaction that occurred between the government home secretary and the director of prisons in the first few years of the agency's existence was more a matter of command and control by the government minister than an instance of responsibilized autonomy for the prisons. As often happens, the legal structures of governance of the organization turned out to be a poor guide to the real organizational dynamics.[14] If we want to understand what is happening in the penal field, we need to study the pragmatics of programme implementation and the processes through which rationalities come to be realized (or not) as actual practices.

Programmes and Problems

The governmentality literature takes it as axiomatic that government is a problem-solving activity – a way of programming the social world to correct problems that emerge there. Indeed, the chief concern of this approach is to specify how authorities come to understand and manage their relations to the problematized field, and the forms of power, knowledge and technology necessary to these activities. However, the literature tends to conceptualize these problems and fields through the perceptual grid of the programmes and rationalities that the authorities generate to deal with them. There is no concern to establish an independent analysis of its own. Consequently, there is no attempt to measure the authorities' analysis against an alternative, avowedly more realistic, account, different from that of the programmers. This seems to me to be a weakness, particularly in relation to the analysis of crime control.

For example, in recent work I have been investigating how the British state problematized and rationalized its crime-control policies in the 1970s and 1980s (see Garland 1996, 1997). This investigation focuses on how the problem was viewed from the vantage-point of the various state agencies, how it was to be known, what powers were to be exercised, how malfunctioning institutions were to be reformed, how inefficiencies were to be corrected and so on. It seems to me to be crucial in this work to understand the authorities' own analysis of the situation, since this played a key part in imposing the 'regimes of truth' that now shape institutional reality. But, alongside this knowledge of the authorities' knowledge, I also want to be able to propose a different reading of what causes crime, why controls are failing, and why penal–welfare measures no longer seem adequate. I want to be able to offer an account of the dynamics of the social field, or of the life-world that is to be governed, that may be at odds with that of the governing authorities.

My view is not that state discourses and programmes disguise their true meaning and have to be read obliquely or contextually to uncover their concealed purposes and objectives – although this is sometimes the case (see Garland 1985). Most of the time, the claim that the authorities would like to reduce crime, protect citizens, do justice, uphold the rule of law and so on can be taken at face value. I agree with the Foucauldians that programmatic social policy objectives are usually just what they say and not some devious cover for capitalist class interests, the reproduction of patriarchy, or some other system function. But because programmers are usually candid in their concerns doesn't mean that they are correct in their analysis. It is precisely because the authorities' analysis can be incorrectly based on false assumptions about how the world works, how 'the crime problem' is created, how punishments have their effects, and so on that one wants to generate alternative accounts. Moreover, these alternative analytical accounts are crucial if one wants to explain not just the nature of programmes but also the impact that they have in the fields that they govern.[15] A history of the present should do more than anatomize the governmental programmes that are brought to bear. It should also seek to explain the pattern of their effects, including their failures and unanticipated consequences.

The 'history of the present' that I am suggesting here is neither a history of systems of thought nor a philosophical account of how subjects have been governed by their relation to truth. It is a grounded social analysis that tries to make sense of a field as it actually operates and as it is experienced by those who inhabit it. The nominalism suggested by Rose and Miller makes sense if one is undertaking an analysis of 'rationalities' – in other words, if one's project is to reconstruct the epistemological grounding of the exercise of power or the forms of thought that emerge in the realm of governmental projects. But, for a history of the present, it is only one (static) element in a dynamic situation. The story of penal policy is one of compromise and accommodation, of ambivalence and poorly implemented policy. It is necessary to look at the whole configuration of practices, and not just the rationalities, or programmes or even the selected practices that best instantiate them.

Such an approach must concern itself with struggles and conflicts and low politics – phenomena that don't involve the invention of new problematizations or the transformation of rationalities, but do bring about shifts in balances of power, changes in opinion, new alliances, and new hierarchies of credibility. It must address the cultural domain, the psychedynamic realm of the symbolic, the shaping of sensibilities and, above all, the popular–political register in which crime control and penal discourses operate.[16] For instance, if we wish to understand why the 'economic' rationality tends to be displaced at certain points by a very different 'rationality' which asserts the need to punish and to protect the public, whatever the cost (see Garland 1996), we must pay heed to the ways in which public fears and anxieties about crime are taken up in the political realm and represented there by populist discourses and 'expressive' measures of a punitive or incapacitative kind. The process of switching between rationalities, or moving from one discursive register (the economic–administrative) to another (the populist–political), is very much a *political* process, structured by conflicting interests *within* government departments and the office of state and motivated by all sorts of exigency, political calculation and short-term interest. The practices that make up the field of crime control may be structured by governmental rationalities but, in its detailed configuration, with all its incoherence and contradictions, the field is also a product of a rather more aleatory history of political manoeuvres and calculations.

Non-Instrumental Rationalities of Government

The governmentality analysis is carefully attuned to technical and knowledge-based rationalities, but tends to neglect the expressive, emotionally-driven and morally-toned currents that play such a large part in the shaping of penal policy. Foucault's work tended to avoid what other theorists refer to as the 'ideological' aspects of government (see Cousins and Hussain, 1986). It focused on the techniques and practices that directly shape subjectivity and action, rather than on the symbols and values which, if they influence action at all, do so through the medium of representations and actors' consciousness. In a similar vein, the governmentality literature also focuses on instrumental rationalities to the neglect of what Weber would term 'value-rational' frameworks of action.

Value-rational conduct tends to be poorly theorized but strongly emotive and expressive. Its logic is absolutist not strategic. Its heavily symbolic discourse is grounded in values rather than knowledge, and its dynamic force is collective emotion rather than instrumental calculation. As I have argued elsewhere (Garland 1990), penal policy is partly shaped by forces of this kind, and it is a failing of the Foucauldian approach that it tends to neglect these, or else to translate them into forms of instrumentality such as the 'sovereign' mode of exercising power.[17]

An example of this tendency is contained in Feeley and Simon (1992). Following the logic of the governmentality analytic, the authors describe the field of penality as being dominated by a new rationality – the 'New Penology' – which is characterized as actuarial, managerial, and control-oriented. They contrast this to the 'Old' (clinical, individualized, rehabilitation-oriented) approach, and argue that the trends and dynamics which characterize the field may be understood in terms of a move from the 'old' rationality to the 'new'.

This analysis conveys very well the importance of these new developments and does an excellent job of rendering them intelligible by contrasting them with older ways of thinking and acting. But, against Feeley and Simon, it is arguable that these two rationalities have, despite their well documented differences, a number of important similarities and are, in many respects, continuous and mutually supportive rather than in conflict. *Both* the 'Old' and the 'New' penologies, so described, are neutral, knowledge-based, purpose-rational approaches, sponsored by social science professionals. Although they differ in their characteristic technologies and forms of reasonings and in the particular professional groups that they privilege, *both* 'penologies' offer 'rational', 'technical' solutions to the problem of punishment. To the extent that they now coexist – and there is no doubt that they do – they represent two *adjacent* positions in a common field of instrumental penality. By concentrating on the *differences* that distinguish the one from the other (differences that are no doubt important both to the professionals involved and the offenders with whom they deal) Feeley and Simon tend to miss a phenomenon which is of great importance to our understanding of the overall configuration of the field. That phenomenon is the *conflict* between this tradition of instrumental rationality (with both its contemporary variants) and its non-instrumental other – the very different tradition of expressive punitiveness that is embedded in the thoughtways of large sectors of the public and is taken up by populist politicians who seek to (re)present this cultural current and put it to political use.[18]

Nor is this expressive populism merely a matter of empty political gestures or symbols without substance. As Bottoms (1995) and Garland (1996) argue, it is a political force that has shaped recent penal practice in the UK, the USA and elsewhere. Indeed, it seems plausible to suggest that populist and 'governmentalized' politics are actually twinned, antithetical phenomena – the first provoking the second as a kind of backlash against the rule of experts and the dominance of professional elites. The facility with which politicians in the 1990s are able to sideline expert opinion by appealing directly to (their representations of) 'what the people want' strongly suggests a level of popular antagonism to a professionalized system that is experienced as failing. It also indicates a decline in the organized power of professional groups such as social workers, psychologists and criminologists who staff that system. Contemporary populism expresses the discontents of a governmentalized state. It invokes a set of political forces hostile to the professional establishment that, until recently, dominated penal policy-making.

Governmentality and Sociological Analysis

The criticism that an approach 'doesn't deal with everything' is not a particularly damaging one. All analytical frameworks are partial, and there is much to be gained by specificity and the targeting of enquiry. My argument has been that an effective history of the present must go beyond the reconstruction of abstracted rationalities and enquire about the ways in which the rationalities and technologies of government are instantiated in the actual practices and discourses that make up a field. My discussion of ideal types, programmes and problems, and non-instrumental rationalities has tried to show that governmentality research inevitably begs a series of sociological questions as soon as it moves away from an archaeological stance towards an attempt to make sense of the present. Governmentality studies do pose a distinctive set of research questions. But in pursuing these questions, they inevitably raise a series of more familiar sociological problems the resolution of which is important to the results of the enquiry. Rather than viewing governmentality research as an autonomous mode of enquiry, it should be developed in conjunction with the sociological tools necessary to it.

The methodological arguments of some governmentality writers give the impression that 'sociology' as such is somehow incompatible with their style of analysis. But it would be more accurate to say that some forms of sociological analysis are incompatible with governmentality research, while others are not. Foucault's own analyses make no attempt to locate his own positions vis-à-vis contemporary sociology. His is the voice of a strong author who has set aside 'the anxiety of influence' (Bloom 1973). The work of other governmentality writers – notably Rose and Miller (1992), Mitchell Dean (1994) and Colin Gordon (1991) – does discuss their relation to sociology, but the overall impression created by these discussions is that governmentality studies raise quite different questions than do sociological enquiries and are conceptually and epistemologically incompatible with sociological approaches. There is also a rejection of systematic generalization and theory-building, which reinforces the tendency to distinguish governmentality studies quite sharply from all forms of sociological analysis.[19]

It is, of course, true that there are many forms of sociological theory and that some of them – notably the state-centred, Marxism-influenced social control theories of the 1970s (to which the governmentality writers frequently refer) – are indeed at odds with the assumptions, methods and analytical claims of the governmentality work. But, to many sociologists, that brand of Marxist theory was always decidedly unsociological, and it can hardly be said to exhaust the analytical range of sociological work. Indeed, the inordinate stress which that approach gave to the powers of the state and its recasting of the idea of 'social control' to mean state control, were actually at odds with the original and abiding mainstream concerns of sociology, which generally focused on the effects of power structures and spontaneous social controls in non-state organizations, such as closed institutions, communities, families, workplaces and professional settings.

Many sociologists will have little trouble accepting the Foucauldian claim that power is dispersed throughout society as well as being concentrated in the state, and that power operates through networks of action that traverse the legal–constitutional divisions that supposedly separate the state from civil society. Nor will this view upset the standard assumptions of historical sociology, which have generated many studies of the reformation of morals, of religious movements, of mass mobilization and of the social history of total war. In that sociology, many of the positions developed by the late Foucault have long been the orienting premises of research. Similarly, the Foucauldian rejection of the idea of a unified, totalized conception of 'society' in favour of a more open-ended, pluralist account of social relations and institutions is actually well established in parts of the sociological literature – not least the tradition that stems from the work of Max Weber (see also Hirst and Wooley 1982; Mann 1986).

In the light of this, it would seem unhelpful to regard governmentality studies and sociological analysis as mutually exclusive undertakings.[20] The idea of 'rationalities of rule' – and the analysis of the ways of thinking and acting that they entail – is a major contribution of the Foucauldian approach, and has already produced a corpus of substantive research. There is no reason why studies of governmentality cannot be extended and enhanced by drawing on sociological analysis, or at least on those forms of sociology which, like Foucault, reject the idea of a unified category of 'society' and adopt a pluralist conception of social relations and forms of power. As I have tried to demonstrate here, recourse to more conventional historical and sociological scholarship will be necessary if the aim of the analysis is to understand a field of practices, such as crime control. This does not mean that those working on governmentality must give up what they do and retrain as historians or empirical sociologists. But it does mean that a more fruitful dialogue might be encouraged between these forms of work. Theoretical criminology has much to gain from, and perhaps something to offer to, a dialogue of this kind.

Notes

1   This chapter is an edited version of a longer paper originally published as D. Garland (1997), '"Governmentality" and the problem of crime: Foucault, criminology, sociology', *Theoretical Criminology*, **1** (2), 173–214.

2   To talk of a style of practical reasoning as a 'rationality' is perhaps to imply more analytical coherence than it actually possesses. Specific rationalities tend to emerge following the success of particular modes of problem solving. They become exemplars, and are the subject of imitation and analogous application. The actors who develop these ways of thinking and acting rarely articulate them in a coherent form. Instead, they become habits of mind and of action which are only later articulated as an explicit framework. Inevitably, then, there is much room for argument about the veracity of such post hoc reconstructions.

3   One effect of this, of course, is to facilitate recourse to a simplified moral discourse about crime and punishment. If crime is a matter of simple rational choice, then we can 'understand less and condemn more' as Prime Minister John Major put it in 1993.

4   This points up an important contradiction in contemporary criminal justice. The legal framework, which dominates current sentencing practice, assumes the truth of the fiction that individuals who are not mentally ill are therefore 'responsible' and proceeds to deal with them on this basis. The prison authorities, on the other hand, recognize that many offenders lack the learned capacity for responsible action and put into action a machinery for creating and reinforcing this absent capacity – a machinery which no doubt fails much of the time. The responsible offender is thus conjured in and out of existence by the different working ideologies of criminal justice agencies.

5   I discuss the agency–freedom distinction in more detail later in this chapter. Note that I am here describing a *form of address* and a *practice of subjectification* aimed at individual prisoners. The question of how prisoners engage with these practices, and the ways in which these practices do or do not actually shape prisoners' subjectivity and behaviour, is a separate issue of great importance. Technologies of the self are not guaranteed in their effects nor singular in their possible uses. It is highly likely that prisoners engage with these procedures in a manner which is at odds with that intended

by the authorities, putting them to their own uses or using them as a lever towards their own ends.

6   Simon (1993) provides an excellent analysis of how US parole officers try to introduce a measure of structure and routine into the 'disorganized' lives of their (workless) clients.

7   Occasionally, writers in the governmentality literature counterpose liberalism to 'police' but the latter seems too archaic and too schematic. The contrast should probably be between liberal and totalitarian.

8   Analysis might be clarified by distinguishing social policy objectives from the political arrangements for their delivery and governance, as in the concept of a 'liberal welfare state'. See Gordon (1991) for a clear and powerful discussion of the relationship between 'liberalism' and 'societies of security'.

9   What makes this pun possible is the nineteenth-century idea of 'free will' which characterized human beings as 'free agents' as opposed to 'causally determined' non-agents. Neither Foucault nor subsequent writers on governmentality subscribe to this crude conception, but its familiarity allows the agency-freedom conflation.

10   It would be a true paradox to claim that a person can be governed through freedom if 'freedom' is defined in this conventional way. It would amount to saying that the realm of the unconstrained is constrained. Any such freedom would be an illusion. Dahl and Lindblom long ago discussed the ability of 'manipulative' forms of power (such as advertising) to create this illusion by their ability to 'simulate feelings of "free choice" and evoke enthusiasm and initiative' (quoted in Wrong 1988: 28).

11   See Hunter (1996) and Hindess (1996) for lucid analyses of this paradox in the context of research on governmentality.

12   However, see Skinner (1969) on the dangers of assembling 'systems' that no living person ever actually 'thought'.

13   On the importance of 'compromise formations' in analysing the relationship of programmes and techniques to practices, see Garland (1985). Since particular techniques and devices are often compatible with a variety of different political rationalities, the contingent historical processes whereby one becomes linked up to another are obviously of great importance to analysis. This is precisely the work of 'genealogies' are intended to do.

14   See the almost daily news reports and commentary in the *Guardian*, October 1995.

15   There is, of course, no innocent or privileged extra-theoretical access to 'how things really are'. The alternative analytical account proposed here will depend upon sociological and historical positions that may themselves be challenged. But this alternative account has the benefit of being free of the particular political and institutional commitments that anchor the analysts of programmers and officials, and its own commitments (to the disciplines of sociology, to the field of academic discourse, to its institutions and politics) and its own methods may be such as to provide it with a better claim to social understanding and explanation.

16   O'Malley (1996) argues for a more 'political' approach to the study of governmentality.

17   Politicians and others may, of course, engage in the politics of expressive justice for instrumental reasons. See Anderson (1995) for a case study.

18   I should immediately add that the authors subsequently note this omission and seek to remedy it (Simon and Feeley 1995). My point is that the governmentality analytic tends to create this kind of blind spot.

19   The rejection of theory-building seems to flow from the anti-essentialist and anti-totalizing pluralism of Foucauldian analysis (and has echoes of old battles against theoretical Marxism). But the wish to avoid dogma in its reductionist or universalizing

forms need not mean that analytical conclusions must be limited to local studies and instant cases. Generalization and theory-building (which are fundamental aspects of scientific enquiry) should be limited only by the characteristics of the field under study and the scope it offers for legitimate generalization across different cases, not by *a priori* considerations. Theoretical work need not aim to produce 'grand theory' or totalized accounts of 'society' and its (singular) 'history'.

20   Note that Foucault's own work – which often drew heavily upon the historical sociology of the Annales school (see Foucault 1977: 75–6) – neither proposed nor adhered to a rigid demarcation of this kind. It is also worth bearing in mind that some of the questions and problems developed in the Foucauldian literature have also been addressed – albeit from different theoretical starting points and assumptions – by sociological scholars. Durkheim (1973), Mead (1934), Cooley (1920) and Elias (1978, 1982) analyse the social moulding of subjects capable of self-directed, intentional conduct. Each of these writers argues that social controls ('government') operate in and through the individual, rather than against individuality. Like Foucault, they view individuality, in its various forms, as an expression of social and cultural routines, not as an escape from them. The link between strategies of governing others and technologies for governing selves is, of course, addressed by Weber (1985) and, rather differently, by Elias (1978, 1982). Philip Selznick (1969, 1992; Nonet and Selznick 1978) analyses the potential and problems of what Foucauldians call 'governing-at-a-distance'. His work has influenced that of Teubner and Luhmann, whose systems theory research addresses related problems of regulation and self-regulation from a rather different theoretical starting point.

References

Adams, J. (1995), *Risk*, London: UCL Press.

Anderson, D.C. (1995), *Crime and the Politics of Hysteria*, New York: Times Books.

Audit Commission (1991), *Going Straight: Developing Good Practice in the Probation Service*, London: Audit Commission.

Audit Commission (1993), *Helping With Enquiries: Tackling Crime Effectively*, London: Audit Commission.

Audit Commission (1996), *Misspent Youth: Young People and Crime*, London: Audit Commission.

Barry, A., T. Osborne and N. Rose (1993), *Economy and Society: Special Issue on Liberalism and Governmentality*, London: Routledge.

Barry, A., T. Osborne and N. Rose (eds) (1996), *Foucault and Political Reason. Liberalism, Neo-Liberalism and Rationalities of Government*, Chicago: University of Chicago Press.

Bayley, D. (1994), *Police for the Future*, New York: Oxford University Press.

Beck, U. (1992), *The Risk Society: Towards A New Modernity*, London: Sage.

Becker, G. (1968), 'Crime and Punishment: An Economic Approach', *Journal of Political Economy*, **76**, 128–47.

Bloom, H. (1973), *The Anxiety of Influence*, New York: Free Press.

Bottoms, A.E. (1995), 'The Philosophy and Politics of Sentencing and Punishment', in C. Clarkson and R. Morgan (eds), *The Politics of Sentencing*, Oxford: Clarendon Press.

Burchell, G. (1991), 'Peculiar Interests: Civil Society and Governing the System of Natural Liberty', in G. Burchell, C. Gordon and P. Miller (eds), *The Foucault Effect: Studies in Governmentality*, Chicago: University of Chicago Press.

Burchell, G. (1996), 'Liberal Government and Techniques of the Self', in A. Barry, T. Osborne and N. Rose (eds), *Foucault and Political Reason*, Chicago: University of Chicago Press.

Castel, R. (1994), '"Problematization" as a Mode of Reading History', in J. Goldstein (ed.), *Foucault and the Writing of History*, Oxford: Blackwell.

Clarke, R. and D. Cornish (1986), 'Introduction', in R. Clarke and D. Cornish (eds), *The Reasoning Criminal: Rational Choice Perspectives on Offending*, New York: Springer-Verlag.

Cook, P.J. (1986), 'The Demand and Supply of Criminal Opportunities', *Crime and Justice*, **9**, 1–27.

Cooley, C.H. (1920), *Social Process*, New York: Scribner.

Coser, L.A. (1982), 'The Notion of Control in Sociological Theory', in J. Gibbs (ed.), *Social Control: Views from the Social Sciences*, Beverley Hills: Sage.

Cousins, M. and A. Hussain (1986), 'The Question of Ideology: Althusser, Pecheux and Foucault', in J. Law (ed.), *Power, Action and Belief: A New Sociology of Knowledge*, London: Routledge.

Dean, M. (1991), *The Constitution of Poverty: Towards a Genealogy of Liberal Governance*, London: Routledge.

Dean, M. (1994), *Critical and Effective Histories: Foucault's Methods and Historical Sociology*, London: Routledge.

Dean, M. (1996), 'Foucault, Government and the Enfolding of Authority', in A. Barry, T. Osborne and N. Rose (eds), *Foucault and Political Reason*, Chicago: University of Chicago Press.

Durkheim, E. (1973), *Moral Education*, New York: Free Press.

Elias, N. (1978), *The Civilizing Process: Volume 1 – The History of Manners*, Oxford: Basil Blackwell.

Elias, N. (1982), *The Civilizing Process: State Formation and Civilization*, Volume 2, Oxford: Basil Blackwell.

Feeley, M. and J. Simon (1992), 'The New Penology: Notes on the Emerging Strategy of Corrections and its Implication', *Criminology*, **30**, 449–74.

Feeley, M. and J. Simon (1994), 'Actuarial Justice: The Emerging New Criminal Law', in David Nelken (ed.), *The Futures of Criminology*, London, Sage.

Ferrant, A. (1997), 'Containing the Crisis: Spatial Strategies and the Scottish Prison System', PhD dissertation, Geography Department, University of Edinburgh.

Foucault, M. (1977), *Discipline and Punish*, London: Allen Lane.

Foucault, M. (1979), *The History of Sexuality: An Introduction*, Volume I, London: Penguin.

Foucault, M. (1991), 'Governmentality', in G. Burchell, C. Gordon and P. Miller (eds), *The Foucault Effect: Studies in Governmentality*, Chicago: University of Chicago Press.

Garland, D. (1985), *Punishment and Welfare*, Aldershot: Gower.

Garland, D. (1990), *Punishment and Modern Society*, Oxford: Clarendon Press.

Garland, D. (1995), 'Social Control', in A. Kuper and J. Kuper (eds), *The Social Science Encyclopedia*, London: Routledge.

Garland, D. (1996), 'The Limits of the Sovereign State: Strategies of Crime Control in Contemporary Society', *British Journal of Criminology*, **36** (4), 445–71.

Garland, D. (1997), 'The Punitive Society: Penology, Criminology, and the History of the Present', *Edinburgh Law Review*, **1** (2), 1–20.

Gemmell, M. (1993), *The Monitoring and Evaluation of the Sentence Planning Initiative: Interim Report*, Edinburgh: Scottish Prison Service.

Giddens, A. (1994), *The Constitution of Society*, Cambridge: Polity.

Gordon, C. (1991), 'Governmental Rationality: An Introduction', in G. Burchell, C. Gordon and P. Miller (eds), *The Foucault Effect: Studies in Governmentality*, Chicago: University of Chicago Press.

Heimer, C. (1985), *Reactive Risk and Rational Action: Managing Moral Hazard in Insurance Contracts*, Berkeley: University of California Press.

Heydebrand, W. and C. Seron (1990), *Rationalizing Justice*, Albany: SUNY Press.

Hindess, B. (1996), 'Liberalism, Socialism and Democracy: Variations on a Governmental Theme', in A. Barry, T. Osborne and N. Rose (eds), *Foucault and Political Reason*, Chicago: University of Chicago Press.

Hirst, P. and P. Wooley (1982), *Social Relations and Human Attributes*, London: Tavistock.

Hunt, A. and G. Wickham (1994), *Foucault and Law*, London: Pluto Press.

Hunter, T. (1996), 'Assembling the School', in A. Barry, T. Osborne and N. Rose (eds), *Foucault and Political Reason*, Chicago: University of Chicago Press.

Janowitz, M. (1975), 'Social Control and Sociological Theory', *American Journal of Sociology*, **81** (1), 82–108.

Litton, R.A. (1990), *Crime and Crime Prevention for Insurance Practice*, Aldershot: Avebury.

Mann, M. (1986), *The Sources of Social Power*, Cambridge: Cambridge University Press.

Mead, G.H. (1934), *Mind, Self and Society*, Volume 1, Chicago: University of Chicago Press.

Nietzsche, F. (1956), *The Genealogy of Morals*, New York: Anchor Books.

Nonet, P. and P. Selnick (1978), *Law and Society in Transition: Towards Responsive Law*, New York: Harper & Row.

O'Malley, P. (1992), 'Risk, Power and Crime Prevention', *Economy and Society*, **21** (3), 252–75.

O'Malley, P. (1996), 'Risk and Responsibility', in A. Barry, T. Osborne and N. Rose (eds), *Foucault and Political Reason*, Chicago: University of Chicago Press.

Pasquino, P. (1991), 'Theatrum Politicum: The Geneology of Capital – Police and the State of Prosperity', in G. Burchell, C. Gordon and P. Miller (eds), *The Foucault Effect: Studies in Governmentality*, Chicago: University of Chicago Press.

Peters, A.A.G. (1986), 'Main Currents in Criminal Law Theory', in J.I. van Dijk *et al.* (eds), *Criminal Law in Action*, Arnhem: Gouda Quint.

Rose, N. (1996), 'Governing "Advanced" Liberal Democracies', in A. Barry, T. Osborne and N. Rose (eds), *Foucault and Political Reason*, Chicago: University of Chicago Press.

Rose, N. and P. Miller (1992), 'Political Power Beyond the State: Problematics of Government', *The British Journal of Sociology*, **43** (2), 172–205.

Ross, E.A. (1901), *Social Control*, Boston, MA: Bacon.

Selznick, P. (1969), *Law Society and Industrial Justice*, New York: Russell Sage Foundation.

Selznick, P. (1992), *The Moral Commonwealth*, Berkeley: University of California Press.

Shearing, C. and P. Stenning (1985), 'From the Panopticon to Disneyworld: The Development of Discipline', in A. Doob and E. Greenspan (eds), *Perspectives in Criminal Law*, Aurora: Canada Law Book Co.

Simon, J. (1987), 'The Risk of Risk: Insurance, Law and the State', *Socialist Review*, **95**, 61–89.

Simon, J. (1993), *Poor Discipline: Parole and the Social Control of the Underclass, 1890–1990*, Chicago: University of Chicago Press.

Simon, J. and M. Feeley (1995), 'True Crime: The New Penology and Public Discourse on Crime', in T. Blumberg and S. Cohen (eds), *Punishment and Social Control*, New York: Walter de Gruyter.

Skinner, Q. (1969), 'Meaning and Understanding in the History of Ideas', *History and Theory*, **8**, 3–53.

Stenson, K. (1993), 'Community Policing as a Governmental Technology', *Economy and Society*, **22** (3), 373–89.

Tuck, M. (1991), 'Community and the Criminal Justice System', *Policy Studies*, **12** (3), 22–37.

van Dijk, J.J.M. (1994), 'Understanding Crime Rates: On the Interactions between the Rational Choices of Victims and Offenders', *British Journal of Criminology*, **34** (2), 105–21.

Walker, S. (1993), *Taming the System: The Control of Discretion in Criminal Justice, 1950–1990*, New York: Oxford University Press.

Weber, M. (1985), *The Protestant Ethic and the Spirit of Capitalism*, London: Unwin Paperbacks.

Wrong, D. (1988), *Power*, Oxford: Basil Blackwell.

3 Crime Control, Governmentality and Sovereignty

Kevin Stenson

This chapter reviews the relationship between Foucaultian conceptions of government, the more or less rational attempts to conduct conduct, with particular reference to issues of crime control. It attempts to clarify the meanings of, and relations between, the key concepts of governmentality and sovereignty. Furthermore, it contests the proposal to absorb governmentality studies into any one social science discipline, favours an eclectic use of methodologies and argues that the main focus of governmentality studies should be the shifting technologies of liberal rule. Liberalism is defined as a tension between an ongoing critique of government and a set of reflections on, and technologies of a form of rule which requires constant vigilance about the limits of and separation between state governmental powers (Dean 1997). Moreover, one of the hallmarks of liberal politics is that they facilitate myriad agendas of governance in the commercial and voluntary sectors and new social movements, beyond the terrain of state and municipal agencies. At root, governmentality studies should be seen as both a product and instrument of liberalism. Governmentality refers to the range of governmental rationalities and practices, associated with liberal rule, by which populations are rendered thinkable and measurable for the purposes of government (Foucault, 1980, 1991). However, beyond this general definition, two meanings of governmentality are distinguished. One emphasizes the mentalities of liberal government, particularly as manifested in textual discourses; these are analysed as archives, using the methodologies of the history of the present. The second meaning involves a recognition that mentalities also operate within oral discourses and social practices, which can be investigated using a range of methodologies, including ethnography. These conceptions of governmentality and the appropriate methodologies for investigating them should be integrated.

It is argued that there is a need to overcome diachronic–sequential conceptions of technologies of rule by focusing on the synchronic–contemporaneous linkages between technologies. This revised methodology enables us to identify and study the great complexity of strategies of governance within liberal societies. Among the key topics is the decline of broadly inclusive 'social' strategies of government, which has been accompanied by the new focus on local, targeted, partnership governmental institutions and practices under the banner of crime control. The new agenda should also include strategies of governance from below, initiated by ethnic, religious, criminal and other social groupings and networks. The elaboration of a more synchronic and less archaic conception of sovereignty, as it functions within the sphere of governmentality, is developed through four examples. These include: first, a critique of David Garland's emphasis on the use of emotive punitiveness as a political instrument to shore up the myth of sovereignty; second, a critique of Jonathan Simon's discussion of the erosion of legal sovereignty in the operation of juvenile justice; third, a brief critique of Malcolm Feeley and Jonathan Simon's theory of actuarial justice; fourth, a discussion of the tensions between sovereign aspects of policing in public spaces, aligned with local community strategies, operating in conjunction with the particularistic governing practices of an ethnic–religious minority.

Finally, the chapter integrates these elements of sovereignty within a broader framework. The operation of local strategies and practices of sovereign rule, working through a variety of linkages, must be viewed within an international context. Sovereign rule is reinforced through the mutual relations between clusters of nation-states, which redistribute their powers both upwards to international institutions and downwards to regional and local organizations. Their ability to perform this governmental redistribution depends on their continued ability to govern and retain the support of relatively immobile populations, which remain largely confined to the nation-state. Given the uncertain power of inclusive, 'social–welfare' strategies of government, there is likely to be, in the struggle to maintain the sovereignty which underpins liberalism, a continued reliance on harsh, despotic technologies of rule to bring government to areas and groups deemed to be most troublesome.

Absorbing Governmentality Studies Into Sociology?

Despite Foucault's scathingly critical view of the scientific pretensions of criminology (Foucault 1980), many commentators have used his insights in attempting to make sense of changes in patterns of crime control. Foucault analysed the shift in European societies in the nineteenth century from body-focused penality, symbolizing the reliance of the old monarchical regimes on coercive forms of sovereign power to secure control over geographical territory, to forms which attempted to create docile bodies, cogs in the wheels of prisons, factories and other great social machines of the new industrial nation–states (Foucault 1977). The aim of the utilitarian reformer was to change mentalities and behaviours through the use of surveillance-based disciplinary controls, underpinned by the social sciences and new modes of expertise. Foucault's analyses provided a stimulus for studies of the new community-based strategies of crime prevention and corrections in the advanced democracies of the mid- to late twentieth century (Cohen 1985). Notwithstanding cautionary critiques (see Bottoms 1983), this critical work elaborated modern theories of the state and domination around the metaphor of society as a punitive city or prison – a dense network of disciplinary controls, interrupted by sporadic, vain resistance from heroic defenders of human freedom.

However, more recent Foucault-inspired intellectuals – usually referred to as the 'governmentality' school – have shifted their focus to the emergence of new forms of governance (Rose 1989; *Economy and Society* 1993; Barry *et al.* 1996). In the field of crime and justice, the new topics of interest include: the introduction of commercial practices of audit and management into the police, criminal justice and other public sector agencies; a redistribution of the tasks of government across the boundaries of statutory, voluntary and commercial sectors; and those strategies and technologies which have emerged to prevent and control crime through an activation of citizen and community involvement in policing (O'Malley 1992; Stenson 1993b, 1996a; Garland 1996; Pavlich 1996; O'Malley and Palmer 1996; Shearing 1996; Hughes 1996). This new agenda for research was developed partly in reaction to an exaggerated emphasis by radical critics on the use by the state of violent repression and disciplinary controls and in recognition of the emphasis in neo-liberal regimes on the need to move beyond welfarism, discourage dependent docility and foster individual and group *self-regulation* and creative enterprise. In these conditions, it was argued, state ministries in the liberal democracies developed technologies of governance which shifted away from 'top down' disciplinary and repressive controls to more indirect and persuasive controls, or *action at a distance*, from the sites of individual and group activity, which the central bureaucracies hoped to influence and shape. In essence, this approach emphasizes the need to *steer* rather than *row* the ship of governance. These central ministries, moreover, have to compete not simply with 'resistance' by heroic or disgruntled malcontents, but also with a host of agendas of governance emanating from multiple sites, from commercial firms to ethnic, gender-based, environmental, religious groups and movements. Hence, in the work of the governmentality school, images of the advanced liberal democracies as dark prisons, bristling with closed circuit TV and other sophisticated security technologies, give way to visions of society as inherently plural – as more open, fluid and organic.

This narrative about change is not necessarily comfortable nor complacent, since it entails a recognition of the profound risks associated with the declining effectiveness and fiscal health of welfare states, the growth of inequality and the perceived inability of state governments to meet the rising demands for environmental, physical and social security. Nevertheless, against the backcloth of the sweeping changes brought in by the Reagan, Bush, Thatcher and Major neo-liberal administrations in the USA and Britain (and similar regimes in Australia and New Zealand) and the collapse of communism during the 1980s, there is, I suggest, in this corpus of work, an implicit celebration of the resilience, creativity and triumph of liberal rationalities and strategies of governance.

In this context it is therefore significant that David Garland has recently recommended that the work of this school could usefully be absorbed, or at least enter, into closer dialogue with, the mainstream of sociology (Garland 1997; cf. Hunt and Wickham 1994), particularly in the (non-normative) Weberian tradition. In its grant-funded forms, this corpus of social science is viewed by senior policy-makers as a respectable adjunct to the (liberal) governmental process within the advanced democracies. But with what aim should there be a *rapprochement* with sociology? The assumption seems to be that we are all scholars united by a common goal in seeking the truth and that some of the concerns of the governmentality school have long been part of the sociological agenda. While there is, in technical terms, a degree of truth in this and there is much to be learned from particular sociological studies and theorists, I argue that the governmentality school should resist seductive offers of wholesale incorporation from sociology, or any other given social science discipline, for two main reasons.

First, governmentality studies are not simply another theory in a non-normative, supposedly objective social science (Dean 1994). It is one of the strengths of this movement that two of its most creative intellectuals, Colin Gordon and Graham Burchell, are not employed as academic social scientists nor subject to its career disciplines. The search for universal or generalizable accounts of power or government, and the attendant analyses of the management of human risks for all human societies or for whole epochs, form elements of the agendas of what could be termed the 'high theorists' of sociology (for example, Mann 1986; Giddens 1990). Even the sociologists who modestly aim to develop grounded, middle-range theory through empirical research still try to generate tools of analysis which can be generally applied to the study of human behaviour (Silverman 1993). Conversely, Foucault emphasized that he was not concerned to develop a *universal* theory of 'power' – and, one might add, 'government' (Foucault 1982). In that sense we are not dealing with simply another theory within political science or sociology. Scholars in the governmentality school have, refreshingly, created a discourse which enables them to cross-fertilize ideas and methodologies across careerist disciplinary boundaries from accountancy to criminology. This fruitful cross-fertilization reinforces what many of us involved in this movement have long felt: the supposed radical differentiation of social science disciplines and their individual imperialist claims are ill-founded and it is liberating to don a pirate's hat and plunder, promiscuously, the range of theories and methods of the human sciences, even if we have to sail with particular flags of disciplinary convenience to survive within the turbulent seas of academia. This happy promiscuity is likely to be seen by the elders of particular disciplines and by the senior civil servants and politicians who influence the commissioning of research as subversive. How many of us, when writing our reports, have been gently advised by these gatekeepers of knowledge to 'go easy on the theory, especially that Foucaultian stuff'?

Second, the force and influence of the governmentality school derives from its radical, critical edge, even if it is sometimes obscured by the fog of academic politics which shrouds most of us. Garland's suggestion of a *rapprochement* with sociology is surely ironic given that earlier generations of radical social scientists had sought inspiration from neo-Marxist and feminist conflict theorists and from Foucault, precisely in order to escape what was seen as the inadequacies of a science, whose principal rationale – at least in its mainstream respectable forms – was to provide usable knowledge for state policy-makers. For radicals of many hues, the political, judicial, military and civil service elites, on behalf of dominant corporate interests in the liberal capitalist societies, had denied freedoms and opportunities to perceived oppressed groups and, despite the lip service paid to constitutional rights, were prepared to suppress with ruthless violence those who presented a serious challenge to state power (Scraton 1987; Davis 1990, 1993; Scraton and Chadwick 1991). The main concerns of the policy-makers were seen to be the attempt to control the lives of the poor and working classes and other subordinated groups and make the world safe for well-heeled neighbourhoods and populations, even at the expense of creating physical and symbolic barriers between the neighbourhoods of the poor and the better off. This political strategy was, and still is, seen as particularly sensitive to the needs of the diminishing numbers who vote and are reluctant to support political parties who allegedly tax and spend too much in an effort to redistribute resources to poorer citizens and neighbourhoods (Galbraith, 1993).

However, if governmentality research has not entirely broken with its critical roots and is not simply another theoretical school in sociology or political science, then what is it? Is it just a subversive state of mind or a rigorously developed body of critical theory and methods of research? I would hope it could be the latter. In the remainder of this chapter, I wish to delineate more clearly the key concepts and contribute to mapping out the research agenda for this field of critical work.

If the principal object of analysis is not the general field of social relationships, as in sociology, then it can also be distinguished from the objects of other bodies of critical theorizing. The objects of Marxist-based political economy are class relationships within the exploitative process of capitalist accumulation, for feminists, the workings of patriarchy, for anti-racists, institutionalized racism and so on. For governmentality researchers, I suggest, it is predominantly liberalism. However, it is vaguely and ambiguously theorized and is sometimes, for example, distinguished from welfare states (Garland 1997: 194). I wish to refer to liberalism in a broader sense, which would include the political rationalities and practices of the welfare states as well as those of the early nineteenth-century buccaneer, *laissez-faire* capitalist regimes and the more recent neo-liberal regimes which have developed since the late 1970s (Stenson 1998). Hence, by contrast with those of the sociologists and political scientists, the Foucaultian agenda was, and remains, more modest. It focuses on the succession of forms of rule that emerged in European societies – though taken up elsewhere – which culminated in liberal ideas and practices, constructed different forms of subjectivity and made possible new modes of resistance to rule (Foucault 1982). As I have argued elsewhere (Stenson 1996a and b), without developing a rigorous empirical research methodology with explanatory and predictive power, which can be transferred to a range of settings, there is a danger that the governmentality literature will be viewed as convoluted jargon which redescribes familiar events and deservedly elicits scorn from hostile observers. In building theory, albeit for studying a restricted range of socio-historical settings, there is a need for explanatory parsimony. In other words, without retreating into crude forms of reductionism, this body of theory should build in a predisposition to highlight the role of particular social relations and factors. I argue here that one predisposing factor in the governmentality explanations should be an emphasis on *the establishment and maintenance of sovereign control over territory* as a core principle of liberal rule, rather than a decaying survival from ages past.

Liberalism as Critique and Rule

Academic debates about liberalism have been dominated by normative philosophical issues: for example, the meaning of the neutrality of the state; issues of distributive justice, including the relative priority given to equality and liberty; how to resolve the tensions between individualism and collective or communitarian interests; how to balance the rights of minorities and the majority, and a recognition of plural values with the need to establish consensual ground rules and values; and how to include a proper recognition of the role of the passions and coercion in social life (Berlin 1969; Rawls 1973; Mouffe 1993). By contrast, the concerns of the governmentality school are not narrowly philosophical in the normative and generalizing senses. According to this perspective, it is important not to confuse liberalism simply with *ideas*, with moral and political philosophies of the middle ground, the obverse of absolutism. Rather, it involves ideas made governmentally technical and practical and operates on two levels.

At the first level, liberalism is conceptualized as an ethos and body of critical tools. The mentalities or rationalities of liberalism, before and after it takes on a governmental form, embody styles of thinking which are self-scrutinizing, vigilant and involve attempts to define and set limits to the powers of authorities (Gordon 1991: 15; Dean 1997). While, as in any other critical work, existing social conditions are judged against normative standards, these standards are not timeless visions of, for example, socialist, non-sexist or non-racist utopias. More modestly, they are grounded, competing values and principles. These evolve in interaction with the shifting problem spaces which open up in the attempt to govern our lives. I suggest that the governmentality literature itself is, like neo-liberalism, part of the logic of liberal critique; it is a product and instrument of liberal political rationalities and a motor for immanent critique and, perhaps, resistance against tyranny in whatever form.

On the second level, with the triumph of liberal movements and the establishment (to varying degrees in the nineteenth and twentieth centuries) of liberal democracies, liberalism was transformed into a body of reflections about, and techniques of, rule. It includes a range of connections between political rationalities, programmes, strategies and technologies of rule (Gordon 1991; Rose 1993; Barry *et al.* 1996). In its governmental form, liberalism has disaggregating, centrifugal tendencies. In weakening centralizing, despotic ambitions, liberal rationalities mobilize political resources in denoting and constituting a range of relatively autonomous and self-regulating spheres outside the 'political' sphere of the state. These include, for example, a designated economic field of market relations, codes of generally applicable law, the family and self-governing professions. Hence, drawing on the later work of Foucault, the governmentality school is, despite internal tensions, somewhat agnostic about the reality of, and distinction between, civil society and the state in their traditional senses. The state is not viewed as a unitary complex of institutions, which performs predictable, dominating functions. Rather, it is a shorthand term which applies to technologies of rule and should not foreclose investigation of the way in which rule operates in a multiplicity of sites, way beyond those normally classified as the province of the state (Foucault 1991; Rose and Miller 1992; Shearing 1996).

Governmentality and the Social as Centripetal

The fragmentary tendencies of liberalism generated new problem spaces and the key question of emerging nineteenth-century social science in the wake of the dislocations associated with *laissez-faire* markets: how is social order possible if the state is not to control every corner of life? Governmentality can be seen as a centripetal, unifying tendency, the sum of the attempts, since the early nineteenth-century, to create the conditions to make possible a field of self-regulated, differentiated spheres of life and to create light, but effective, indirect controls 'at a distance', which foster self-regulation in forms which harmonize with collective goals. It refers to the range of ways, from censuses and public health programmes, to social work with individuals and families, in which the population is made thinkable and measurable for the purposes of government at both collective and individual levels of intervention (Barry *et al.* 1996).

By the late nineteenth-century, in the broad terrain of governmentality, new 'social' forms of government had emerged (Procacci, 1997). These were manifest, for example, in the reappraisal of *laissez-faire* reliance on markets in Gladstone's new socially sensitive liberal administrations in Britain and in the rise of the solidarity movement in France, within which Durkheimian sociology played a key role (Donzelot 1991). These explicitly fostered a solidaristic, inclusive citizenship by employing collectivist and nationalistic rhetorics and the new actuarial technologies for taming chance (Stenson, 1993a). I suggest that 'social' technologies operate at five levels. First, they involve the provision, through philanthropic, state and juridical endeavour, of drains, water supplies, schools and other instruments of infrastructure on which markets and populations rely. This first level of social technology, however, also developed in Fascist and Stalinist societies and so cannot be viewed as an intrinsically liberal form of sociality. Second, social technologies involve the mobilization of public sentiment and the fostering of self-directing, disciplined forms of subjectivity or habitus which are deemed to underpin a liberal order (Elias 1982; Rose 1989). These contrast with images of selfless 'Soviet man' or obedient, valiant warriors of the Reich, which were constructed in Stalinist and Fascist regimes. Third, they involve the management, through the use of actuarial technologies, of collective and individual risks related, for example, to social insurance against poverty, crime, ill-health and unemployment (Donzelot 1991). Fourth, they involve attempts to extend, through social work and other educative strategies, the rights and social and subjective capacities of individuals and families who are deemed to lack the competencies to participate in a liberal order (Stenson 1993a). Fifth, at the heart of the early development of the social was the construction – through rational policing and criminal justice systems, parks, boulevards, sports grounds, provision of social housing and public transport systems – of safe public spaces within which people could gather in a mutually policed way. This enabled social forms of citizenship to be affirmed and celebrated (Johnston 1992; O'Malley 1992; Stenson 1993b).

Moreover, as liberal rule mutated into welfare 'social' states, it spawned new constituencies and sites of power, particularly the powerful professions and bureaucracies of welfare, which, operating from essentially liberal premises, made possible internal criticisms of liberal rule. In addition to the state's agencies, radical critics created their own sites and circuits of power within the world of the social – for example, in the universities, professional associations, the feminist, environmentalist and other new social movements and left-wing local authorities with strong labour unions (Minson 1985; Stenson 1991). These sites provide fields for the construction and defence of orthodoxies, rooted in liberal rights discourses, which can, like other complexes of power and knowledge, acquire authoritarian tendencies, establish vested interests and hierarchies of victimhood, foreclose debate and adjudicate on truth claims about the operation of power. I would strongly emphasize that these orthodoxies are not sacred. Hence, in principle, and in the name of continually developing liberal values, liberal critique can target established critical orthodoxies created by feminists. Marxists, environmentalists, anti-racists and other offspring of liberalism, as well as the discourses of the economic and (big) political elites (Minson 1985).

Ambiguity of Governmentality

Foucault argued (1991) that, in modern liberal societies, strategies of governmentality (and, we might add, the sphere of the social within it) coexisted interdependently with sovereign (coercive and juridical) and hierarchical, disciplinary technologies of rule, with sovereignty viewed as a residue of the style of monarchical governance and discipline a residue of the Prussian-style administrative–absolutist states. However, in illustrating these key concepts in historically sequential terms, Foucault left us a misleading and ambiguous methodological legacy. It is a weakness of the governmentality literature that these early programmatic formulations have not been rigorously developed. Moreover, to list the technologies of governmentality as separable from discipline and sovereignty is to make a categorical mistake; they are not equivalent entities. It is more useful to see governmentality as a broad framework of governance, within which discipline and the sovereign control of territory operate simultaneously, are transformed, updated, realigned and supplemented by new techniques. Hence, these concepts shift from being time-anchored descriptions of methods of rule dominant in particular historical periods – a *diachronic*, or sequential reading – to acquiring the status of heuristic analytic devices which are best understood and used *synchronically*, to analyse simultaneous, interdependent social relations (Stenson 1996a, 1996b).

Despite areas of agreement among scholars, Foucault's original statements were sufficiently ambiguous to generate alternative, even conflicting, interpretations of these issues and what may count as acceptable research agendas, analytical tools and permissible sources of evidence. I will try to identify these ambiguities and suggest a clearer way forward, by distinguishing – with the purpose of integrating – two meanings of governmentality for the purposes of empirical investigation. I also highlight the centrality of the attempts to maintain sovereign power, through, for example, the strategies and technologies of crime control, and the need to embrace a wider range of evidence, permitting contemporary and synchronic analyses in order to complement the more diachronic focus of 'histories' of the present.

Government as Mentality and Practice

The first meaning of governmentality highlights the role of mentality, rationality and general programmes and strategies. The second highlights the role of grounded practices, including those in face-to-face experiential settings in which oral modes of discourse may be as significant as, and are not reducible to, those which assume a textual form (Ong 1982; Stenson 1993a). In the first model the focus is on reflexive *ideas* about government: the self-scrutinizing arts of government and its appropriate limits; the proper boundaries between designated 'public' or statutory agencies; commercial institutions and practices; and 'private' family and communal spheres. However, to reiterate a point, we are not dealing with ideas in the narrowly philosophical or theological senses, but rather with those which are operationalized or rendered into a technical form for the purposes of scientific investigation, policy formation and implementation (Rose 1993). Certainly we have here a recognition of complex forms of articulation between general rationalities and visions and a range of interests, apparatuses, persons and networks of social relations.

Moreover, there is here an emphasis on the inherently political character of techniques and their connection with the development of systematic forms of expertise, grounded in professional networks, which evolve criteria and rituals for authorizing what counts as truth and who is authorized to speak and write it (Barry *et al.* 1996). This seems to provide an agenda for strictly grounded, empirical avenues of investigation of how governing practices at the 'molecular' level (in schools, prison cells and so on) connect to the 'molar', organizing level in strategic centres such as state ministerial offices. This is in sharp contrast to earlier, more narrowly philosophical, interpretations and uses of Foucaultian ideas and also to the more programmatic, universalizing and abstract theorizing of the aforementioned sociologists. Furthermore, it also seems to distinguish itself from the more conventional realist epistemologies of mainstream, empirical sociological investigation of 'real' social institutions, such as police organizations, definable in terms of their social functions or material social effects. By contrast, in much of the governmentality literature the objects of knowledge, even if formally inclusive of practices, are viewed through the prism of *discourses*:

> ... the limits of the political are not defined in terms of the boundaries of an apparatus – the state – or in terms of the fulfilment of certain necessary functions – repressive and ideological state apparatuses – but as themselves *discursive* [my emphasis] ... politics has itself to be investigated genealogically, in terms of the ways of coding and defining or delimiting the possible scope of action and components of an apparatus of rule, the strategies and limits proper for rulers, and the relations between political rule and that exercised by other authorities. (Barry *et al.* 1996: 13–4)

Furthermore, this methodological formula underpins the view that a history of the present and text-oriented investigation uncovers the *condition of possibility* for more prosaic or less visible fields of social practice. Put in another way, according to this methodological position, the 'mentalities' embedded in policy programmes and practices are analytically separable from surface, everyday practices and can be discovered through the analysis of texts.

Transcending Histories of the Present?

I suggest that, while this first meaning of governmentality as discourse is not reducible to its narrowly linguistic sense and embraces practices of various kinds, there is a bias in favour of selecting forms of evidence about practices which take on systematic textual forms. There are two main reasons for this. First, an emphasis on the *history* of the present predictably favours the use of archival data on which historians mainly rely and much of which is found in textual, documentary forms (maps, books, White Papers, reports, prison records, guides to etiquette and so on) which were overwhelmingly produced by the small, literature and numerate populations of past societies. This approach silences or downplays the voices of the inarticulate or less literate – usually low-status groups in the population. For example, Garland's subtle historical analysis of the interplay between strategies of penality, welfare and social insurance in Victorian and Edwardian Britain necessarily relies on available textual sources which were weighted towards the thinking of elite players of the educated and influential classes and institutions (Garland 1985). Much less is known about the oral discourses of the elites and of the poor people who were the main targets of this governmental work and whose experiences of, and adaptations to, well-meaning strategies may have been very different from the intended aims.

Second, the focus on the techniques involved in producing and validating professional expertise tends to highlight the more institutionalized forms of professional knowledge which have been assembled and authorized within professional networks and are manifested in a variety of respected, accredited texts. Hence, this first version of governmentality could be viewed as archaeological in flavour. By this I mean that the elements of discourse could be viewed as *statements*, in the way that Foucault defines the term. That is, they are elements of knowledge which rise above the ephemera of everyday chatter and action, acquire a broader historical significance and are systematically related to each other through the medium of thematic cognitive procedures, made possible by text-based, literate mentalities and cultures (Ong 1982). These systematic knowledge forms, or discursive formations, attain a status which is relatively independent of the more immediate practical settings in which they are produced (Foucault 1972; Dreyfus and Rabinow 1982: 56–71).

I suggest that this position amounts to a form of textual determinism and that it is not always clear where claims about the 'conditions of possibility' of practices can be distinguished from empirical claims about the description and explanation of visible social practices. This methodological ploy echoes the claims of the structuralist school of the 1960s, that there is a deep grammar of social rules which makes possible and generates the surface level of social practice (Piaget 1968). Moreover, this argument provides a warrant for leaving the messy job of undertaking primary empirical research, which involves talking to living human beings and observing their actions – if indeed the exercise is worth the bother – to other intellectual under-labourers. In opposition to this, I argue that mentalities of rule are embodied in texts and also in orally transmitted discourses – through the flux of individual and shared cognitions. Clearly, when investigating the past we cannot observe or interview the dead, so we must use whatever archival fragments we can obtain to reconstruct past cultures, including heuristic models of how oral cultures worked. However, we *are* able to observe and interview the living as well as examine their textual and other material products.

Reliance on textual sources, including archival data from the past, has other drawbacks in addition to a neglect of views and experiences of non-elite people. First, there may be a tendency to exaggerate the continuing influences of past discourses and practices, at the expense of current influences and conditions. Second, programmatic statements can perform a variety of functions. Some of them amount to self-serving rhetoric – for example, for police officers and urban bureaucrats. They therefore need sceptical decoding, particularly since they may not always be implemented in accordance with programmatic visions. It is a cliché of social policy research that there may be – so to speak – many a slip betwixt cup and lip and we need the research tools to enable us to identify the gaps and tensions between textual representations and the practices of everyday life, in which talk interacts in complex ways with texts and embodied actions.

Putting Humpty Together Again

To illustrate this point substantively, as indicated at the beginning of the chapter, recent analyses of shifts in crime prevention and policing, have identified, with some national variations, international trends towards the introduction of neo-liberal managerialist techniques of audit, decentralized budgetary control, goal-setting and so on, allied with the introduction of governmental strategies oriented towards particular population groups, rather than 'social' conceptions of an inclusive national citizenry. With the solidaristic glue of social strategies crumbling away, there is a need to find other means to reassemble the elements of the social body, just as in the period which preceded the rise of the social. Using the analogy of the nursery rhyme figure of Humpty Dumpty, the shattering of Humpty's social body provides a problem space which is almost a reprise of the search in late nineteenth-century Europe for new ways to create a solidaristic nationhood. What will reassemble the social body in some form, at the local 'community', if not national, level? One of the key new epistemological principles – a core element of the mentalities of the new governing discourses – is the notion of 'partnership'. Partnership rhetoric, with is communitarian connotations, emphasizes how policing tasks and the provision of security should be reallocated between public sector, voluntary–communal groupings and commercial organizations – all under the banner of making citizens more responsible for the tasks of crime prevention and control and reducing the immediate responsibilities and fiscal burdens of the central state and the taxpayer (Stenson 1993b, 1996a; Garland 1996; O'Malley and Palmer 1996; O'Malley 1996b; Pavlich 1996; Hughes 1996). The sources of evidence for these developments tend to be mainly what are selected by analysts as key texts, including government White Papers, legislation, party manifestos and other policy documents, and speeches made by key players such as police chiefs and government ministers.

Oral and Textual Discourses

This body of work has made significant advances in our understanding, and there is an important role for analyses which discern trends, perhaps amounting to new discursive formations in a range of settings. These would remain invisible if we confined ourselves to tightly drawn, narrowly idiographic analyses in small-scale settings. However, where possible, we need to supplement and enrich these text-dependent analyses with the results of empirical research which focuses on direct observation and interviews, to uncover that which texts tend to conceal or smooth over. For example, there is a body of empirical research on the workings of multi-agency partnerships for crime prevention in the UK. This involved, in addition to the examination of texts, extensive interviewing of key players, observations of committees in action and the everyday practices and oral and textual legitimations and stories constructed by and through professional agents. Research – for example, by Adam Crawford in the south of England – revealed the limits to which partnership schemes and committee practices permitted contentious issues to reach the agenda and how 'communal' groupings and interests were excluded or enrolled into the game within the constraining terms set by the police or other key players. These were gatekeepers to material and political resources and could, in comparison with other players, be disproportionately influential in determining who was authorized to speak for communal interests, particularly those of the least powerful populations. The incorporation of groups deemed to be troublesome or at the edge of democratic respectability was achieved in such a way that it was likely that many would remain outside the community of acceptable political voices in the local multi-agency policy (Crawford 1994; Crawford and Jones 1995). These processes involved considerable creative adaptations in particular settings, including the anticipation of conflict and the devising of tactics to work around it, and also the tactic of avoiding conflict through non-decision-making. These processes cannot be decoded or predicted from official policy documents alone. Nor will they be from such documents for future researchers when we are dead and can no longer give testament.

My point here is not to undermine the claims of more textually grounded analyses, but rather to point to my second interpretation of the concept of governmentality. This places greater emphasis on the complexity of the linkages between the more general and abstract ideas of government, including textual representations of technique and the messiness, tensions and ambiguities of everyday practices, many of which may barely be represented in formal texts – with the major exception of the reports of empirical investigations relying on interviews and observations of practice. In other words, under the auspices of the second model of governmentality, we need to go beyond a *formal* recognition of the great complexity of governmental techniques and accelerate the development and appropriation of a range of research tools, which will enable us to realize the rich research agenda which has been laid out. It is essential to supplement text-based analysis with this kind of empirical research, including ethnographic explorations of the lives of both elite players and those whose efforts to govern their lives and those of others are rarely filtered through the researcher-friendly medium of texts. Surface social practices are not simply epiphenomena of textual discourses (Silverman 1993).

Hence, in addition to a *history of* the present, we need to plunder methodologies drawn from anthropology, geography, psychology and other disciplines, using a variety of data sources from official statistics to ethnographic studies. Through this we may, for example, discover in detail the ways in which neo-liberal programmes and strategies of corporate governance and relations with client populations are interpreted, translated, excluded or appropriated by key actors and what impact this has on everyday practices. I also suggest that it would be useful to integrate both of the meanings of governmentality in this endeavour.

Government from Below

The groups which are acknowledged as governmental usually include agencies and networks in state, philanthropic, religious, educational, professional, party-political, media-oriented social movements and commercial sectors. However, they compete with a range of other social groupings whose agendas, networks and working practices may barely surface within the researcher-friendly world of formal texts (Stenson 1993b; Stenson and Factor 1994). These groupings often operate within clandestine, largely oral, cultural worlds which rely as much, or more, on word of mouth than texts, as methods to store and transmit information and values. These may include: organized crime and other illegal economic networks, gangs and subcultural networks of young men on the streets (Stenson and Watt 1995; Watt and Stenson 1997), paramilitary groups such as the IRA and UDA in Ireland and the Basque separatists in Spain which for operational reasons need to maintain cellular modes of organization and keep documentation to a minimum, and warlords in the ex-Yugoslavia and other trouble-torn regions – particularly in ex-Soviet societies. In these areas, the authority of the institutions of the nation-state have weakened and the dense, relatively autonomous provinces and practices of liberal institutions have yet to develop, or struggle with, a variety of authoritarian political movements and social practices (Voronin 1996).

More prosaically, governing bodies may also include a range of groupings characterized by varying degrees of formal organization, which claim to speak for and govern ethnic, religious minority and other ethically particularistic groups within advanced democracies, that have more stable state institutions and juridical forms (Stenson and Factor 1994, 1995). While 'official' governing agencies may have recently shifted towards governing at the level of 'communal' sites, this has long been the case for ethnic and religious minority networks, from aboriginal peoples to Irish priests, rabbis and imams, to The Nation of Islam in the USA and Britain. These groups wish to shore up and perpetuate particularistic values and identities, while having to adapt their knowledges and practices to the shifting dominant styles of state governments, which operate in their changing environments. It may not be possible to characterize their governing projects and structures of knowledge in terms of concepts such as discursive formation, yet that does not diminish their importance or effectiveness within their limited domains, and they may enrol and be enrolled by other, more formal, legally respectable professional governing agencies (O'Malley 1996a). The lesson here is that a failure to recognize the significance of these groupings as governmental in their own right, is to risk lapsing back into a 'top down', even implicitly state-centred view of government – a view from above the common people.

Sovereignty and Archaism

Mindful of the extraordinary complexity of governance within liberal societies, this final part of the chapter will try to provide a more useful elaboration of the concept of sovereignty within governmentality research. Foucault's diachronic and historically periodized concept of sovereignty referred to at the beginning of this chapter represented the centralizing tendencies of the newly ascendant, post-medieval, absolutist monarchical states. The weapons employed to subdue the myriad clashing feudal groupings were many and varied, and perhaps not yet fully understood. Yet the rhetoric used to authorize these powers increasingly took on the centralizing and unifying juridical form of rights which were seen to transcend sectional interests. By contrast with the later subtle and positive politics of governmentality, power, Foucault argued, was exercised negatively, mainly through prohibition, restraint, interdiction and sanction (Foucault 1991). This view of sovereignty comes close to Hobbes's and Weber's traditional conceptions of the role of the state. Hence, as a mode of power, he tended to view it in its contemporary operation as an archaic form, explicable principally in terms of its early origins (Hunt and Wickham 1994: 59). This 'archaic', or diachronic view of sovereignty recurs also in the work of more recent Foucauldian scholars. But what current relevance is there for us in an understanding of the crystallization of sovereign powers in the seventeenth and eighteenth centuries and the totalizing police/disciplinary powers which developed in their wake – that is, in a diachronic analysis of sovereignty? The answer is little, if we view sovereign powers as discrete, time-anchored and archaic remnants from the past. In this final section I will illustrate the need to supplement a diachronic analysis with a synchronic analysis of the shifting interpenetrating relations between sovereignty and the technologies of discipline and governmentality, with four examples.

Authoritarian populism

Garland (1996, 1997) has recently argued that modern states are finding it increasingly difficult to fulfil the original Hobbesian promise to provide physical security for citizens. In Britain, for example, there has been a retreat in the face of these pressures, from the old utilitarian belief in the rehabilitation of offenders and measures to tackle the (hypothesized) underlying causes of crime. This retreat is linked with an atavistic attempt to shore up the myth of sovereignty through the use of exaggeratedly punitive policies and, we might add, the exercise of political pressure on judges, harried also by a bloodthirsty, vengeful tabloid press, to impose longer custodial sentences. Garland is correct to emphasize that governmentality research has been overly concerned with investigating rationalities based on systematic knowledge forms and modes of expertise, at the expense of morally- and emotionally-driven influences on policy and practice. In recent years draconian punishment and the scapegoating of criminals have been used by politicians to manipulate public emotions of fear and insecurity. Garland even draws links between the display of monarchical might manifest in the spectacular torture and execution of the eighteenth-century would-be regicide Robert Damiens and the 'tough on crime' stance of the UK Prime Minister John Major (Garland 1996: 460)! This atavistic reliance on emotionally manipulative, irrational sovereignty through punishment is contrasted with the social science knowledge-based, administrative rationality of the civil service policy-makers and professionals in the criminal justice system, whose authority is based on scientifically established expertise. The volatility of this irrational, authoritarian populist politics, responding to the fluctuations of opinion polls, further weakens the (alleged) traditional 'social' commitment to the rehabilitative ideal of the old penal–welfare complex (Garland 1997: 202–3).

While having some sympathy for this narrative, my main misgiving is that it too neatly counterposes politicians, allied with a reactionary public, as the emotionally manipulative villains of the piece, with the civil servants and professionals implicitly cast as Platonic or Fabian/liberal guardians, trying to preserve what they can of civilized values and stable, knowledge-based welfare and crime reduction strategies. But, to what extent did penal and crime control practice ever match lofty civil service and professional rhetoric? There are powerful critical counternarratives, drawing on views from lower down the social scale, which challenge the notion that there is a neat differentiation between rational and ruthless, sovereign coercive governing practices. Surely both penal–welfare and sovereign strategies and practices can be rational, and goal-directed? After all, retribution, including new technologies of execution, and genocide, can be, and have been, pursued through the use of eminently well organized and thoughtful scientific means. Those fighting to review miscarriages of justice, challenge police malpractice and investigate brutal prison conditions, would baulk at the notion that civil servants in the British Home Office and their largely compliant, grant-funded clients in the universities are a bastion of rational penal enlightenment. Within these counternarratives, in the UK, for example, civil servants are depicted as chameleons, changing colours in order to adapt to the political environment of the day. According to this view, they have, in effect, endorsed the deep reluctance by the senior judiciary to review manifest miscarriages of justice and the perceived damage that such reviews may do the majesty and authority of sovereign law. They have also been quite prepared to maintain, for example, a brutalized prison service, indifferent to the emotional and medical needs or civil and legal rights of prisoners – and all this during the supposed golden years of the penal–welfare complex (Scraton 1987; Sim 1987, 1990, 1991, 1994). In addition, as I shall argue, there is more to sovereignty than the supposedly archaic punitiveness which Garland highlights.

In the name of the father ...

The diachronically-oriented view of sovereignty as an archaic survivor also surfaces in an otherwise path-breaking paper by Jonathan Simon. This analyses the decline of the welfare-oriented juvenile court in the USA in terms of the shift away from a legal form of sovereignty inherited from English law, echoing the old claims of kings to be protective fathers of the nation (Simon 1995). Although nineteenth-century US jurists had struggled to create a republican form of law for citizens rather than for subjects, removing legal representations of the sovereign, a compromise was reached in the case of juveniles who were deemed to be still in need of paternal care and authority. The principle of *parens patriae* (rule in the name of the (state as) father) traded a diminished conception of the citizenship rights and legal subjectivity of the young defendant for protection from the full rigours of adult sentencing tariffs. This mode of sovereignty, which we could argue remains a core juridical component of the penal–welfare complex, is now on the wane, albeit unlikely to disappear. The toughening attitudes towards young offenders, in effect, reduce the differentiation of their status in relation to adult offenders (Singer 1996).

The subtleties of Simon's analysis constitute a significant advance in our understanding of sovereignty. Nevertheless, it should be noted that, as it operates within governmentality, sovereignty in the juvenile court would hardly be recognized by the absolutist Stuart kings of England, since it involves a complex interplay with the disciplinary knowledge and expertise of welfare professionals, who remain central players within the juvenile justice systems of the liberal democracies, particularly in the application of a combination of welfare-oriented approaches and risk management policies for dealing with young offenders (Pratt 1989; Pitts 1992). Furthermore, against the backcloth of the diminution of the legal differentiation of young from adult offenders and a shifting away from softer dispositions for young offenders, Simon identifies the repressive practices of the police and prisons in relation to young men in the ghettos as providing a contrasting example of an 'archaic' form of sovereignty – the heavy hand of the 'bad father' (Simon 1985: 1419). But why archaic? This kind of sovereignty involves the use of force, symbolic representations of force and juridical authority and, as such, is a sophisticated feature of current social reality. This is reinforced by the use of advanced physical policing technologies, including CCTV systems and new computer systems for investigation, crime pattern analysis, new command and control training routines and methods for public order policing (Waddington 1991). The doubtful implication of Simon's analysis is that all this belongs to an earlier historical period than do more recently evolved penal and policing powers.

New penology and sovereignty

This leads into my third example. In a rightly celebrated thesis, rooted in the governmentality literature, Feeley and Simon argue that the technologies of the new penology (in a sphere of governmentality) target the population, rather than the individual offender, constructed as an individual case, for the purposes of disciplinary control. Furthermore, the newly dominant technologies of actuarial justice and risk management – for example, incapacitation, preventive detention and the construction of drug courier profiles – cut across the liberal–conservative divide in an attempt to create knowledge about and contain population aggregates and categories assessed and measured as dangerous (Feeley and Simon 1994). However, while it is admitted that these new technologies do not simply displace the technologies of the old penology, the very terms 'new' and 'old' convey the misleading view that these technologies are time-anchored and that the technologies of discipline and sovereignty are somehow 'survivors' from earlier eras.

To reinforce the point made in the last section, this 'archaic' dimension of sovereignty, with its continually updated repertoire of new repressive hardware for crowd control and police command and control technologies in the governance of geographical territory, lies at the cutting edge of rule. These technologies of rule operate, flexibly, in a multiplicity of sites, from the attempts to recolonize, for sovereign law, perceivedly crime-ridden housing projects, to the defence of locations of key symbolic significance for the state, such as the environs of the White House in Washington DC, Trafalgar Square in London and the centre of Belfast in Northern Ireland. Moreover, they work in conjunction with disciplinary surveillance technologies and work hand-in-glove with – and, indeed, shade into – what Feeley and Simon describe as actuarial justice in its aggressive danger management mode (cf. Jefferson 1990). In fact, it would be more useful to describe these technologies as rooted in a particular interaction between sovereignty and actuarial justice. This is particularly apposite given that Feeley and Simon include the attempt by the Israelis to contain Palestinian resistance as an example of actuarial justice in danger management mode. This is, surely, *par excellence*, not only an example of the struggle for sovereign control over geographical territory but also a setting where clashes on the street between agents of the state and young men who claim allegiance to a different sovereignty can have enormous geopolitical significance. In turn, these technologies could be seen as playing a central role in producing and maintaining the well documented increasing geographical and social segregation of groups, differentiated by wealth, occupation and ethnicity (Davis 1993).

Ethnic government

My fourth example is drawn from my ethnographic study of a large, noisy and long-running street scene of young (largely) Jewish people in North London, together with strategies developed to govern the young people in both constraining and protective ways. These were negotiated between Jewish community organizations and city-wide and local police departments, under the auspices of community policing policies (Stenson and Factor 1994). In this setting, communal organizations were concerned to protect, through the activities of youth workers and semi-legitimized adult volunteers, young Jewish people from a range of moral and physical dangers – in part, guided by an underlying concern to bolster Jewish identity and foster marriage within the fold. This included protection from groups perceived to be hostile – notably, working-class, white skinheads and young Afro-Caribbean males who were accused, respectively, of anti-Semitic abuse, and 'muggings', drug trading and intimidation.

The volunteers, described by some sceptics as vigilantes, enjoyed a comfortable relationship with the Metropolitan Police, which included some joint training for street regulation. The adult volunteers recruited a body of young people from the street scene in their mid- to late teens, to assist in the surveillance and protection of younger children on the street. They were provided, in local synagogues, with training in self-defence, including psychological training for conflict avoidance and dispute resolution and also classes on Jewish history and identity. While open confrontation was discouraged, some of the young men, away from the tutelary eyes of the adult volunteers, did perceive this to be their role and there were some violent clashes, especially with young black men. The volunteers were perceived by many of the young black people to be engaged in attempts to exclude them from the street scene, partly through helping the police to gather evidence leading to arrest and prosecution. This was despite their popularity with sections of young Jewish people, and despite the fact that, by contrast with the governance of mass private property such as Disneyland and shopping malls (Shearing and Stenning 1985), the street scene took place in public spaces. Regulation of this scene involved a subtle (though at times, vigorously physical) interplay of disciplinary controls, the fostering of self-regulation and Jewish identity and the attempt to contain or exclude, on territorial and actuarial justice principles, categories of youth defined as undesirable and, crucially, 'out of place'. This took place in predominantly affluent neighbourhoods which included substantial, though not exclusive, Jewish settlement.

The official state police mandate to maintain a transcendent sovereign control of, and protection within, public spaces for the generality of citizens interacted uneasily with a complex agenda of (particularistic) government by organizations and networks within a politically well resourced and well connected minority. The targets of these local governmental initiatives were largely young people drawn from other, less well resourced minorities, including lower-class, young white men from nearby housing projects. Their parents were *not* involved with the police in attempting to regulate the street scene. In turn, the struggle for sovereignty through policing and voluntary initiatives was largely occasioned by the vigorous struggle for territorial dominance over 'turf' by groups of young men. Sovereignty here involved containing within, or ultimately excluding some groups from, public spaces.

Significantly, while this research was being conducted, a few miles away in Tottenham, the police were engaged in a different, if related, struggle to reassert sovereignty at Broadwater Farm, a poor area of social housing, with a large proportion of black residents and a highly developed illegal economy of drug trading. This had been the scene, in 1985, of a major riot, during which a community police constable was brutally murdered. This incident had left deep emotional scars among rank and file Metropolitan Police officers about what they perceived as a major defeat in what had become widely seen as a 'no go area'. Waddington describes how one later, expensively resourced, operation to arrest drug dealers took on deep significance for officers. In the words of the local police commander, this was viewed as a means of 'retaking ground', in effect, from groups who were seen to have displaced sovereignty with their own illegal technologies of governance (Waddington 1998).

Synchronic Model of Sovereignty

In moving beyond diachronic, archaic models of sovereignty, we should recognize that it has never been reducible to monopolistic control within a given territory – an *inward territorial* view of sovereignty which Foucault and his followers have tended to share with a range of more orthodox thinkers. From its inception in seventeenth-century Europe, and, arguably, coincident with the early origins of liberalism, the modern state's novel claims to exclusive political control within a territory resulted from agreement between clusters of states to provide mutual recognition of these claims and their respective jurisdictions (Hirst and Thompson 1995: 171).

This core, synchronic feature of nation-state government and law has remained throughout the twists and turns of the rise of, and shifting relationships between, liberal democracies. It also highlights the essential hybridity of government, in that liberalism never exists in a pure form, but usually in alliance with modes of nationalism (Gellner 1983; Dench 1986).

In opposition to the fashionable theories of globalization, which predict the decline and perhaps disappearance of the state amidst the proliferation of competing modes of governance, thus dissolving the traditional boundaries between nation-states, it has been argued that the liberal-democratic, nation-state has retained a central role in redistributing elements of sovereign power and national jurisdiction (Hirst and Thompson 1995: 192). A major reason for this is the increasing concern to limit mass migration of poor people into the richer democracies, especially given the diminishing demand for unskilled labour and the current paucity of frontier destinations for the emigrant, equivalent to the American West or Australia in previous generations. Hence, apart from an internationally mobile elite, the bulk of modern populations in the advanced democracies remain largely landlocked within the linguistic, cultural and increasingly well guarded spatial boundaries of the nation-state which must retain primary responsibility for the government of its citizens (Hirst and Thompson 1995: 181). Many of those who manage to penetrate the defences of the richer countries tend to join populations who have been economically and culturally marginalized from the mainstream economy and polity and, in effect, have been denied the full privileges of citizenship. They are also more likely to become constructed as candidates for the more stringent sovereign–juridical and disciplinary technologies of population management. These include tougher legal controls over asylum-seekers and ethnic minority populations within the Western cities (Cook and Hudson 1993). We should expect a reliance on actuarial and self-regulatory technologies for the majority to coexist with a reliance on despotism for governing significant proportions of the population (Valverde 1996).

The legitimated redistribution of sovereign powers is seen as moving upwards to: new international bodies such as the international police organizations and networks which have developed in the wake of concern about international fraud, money-laundering, drug trafficking, and other forms of organized crime (Sheptycki 1995) as well as to such organizations as the European Union, NAFTA and NATO. It is also seen as moving downwards to regional and more local spheres of government and governance, such as aforementioned multi-agency crime control partnerships. Hence, establishing and maintaining the sovereignty of the state remains of crucial significance within liberalism in order to provide legitimacy for these redistributions of sovereign powers, especially given the reduced significance of nationally inclusive, 'social' welfare-governing practices and the attendant growth of inequality. If the integration of the social body cannot be achieved through persuasion, it must ultimately be guaranteed by force.

Conclusion

The great complexity and rapidity of the redistribution of the tasks of government between statutory, voluntary and commercial agencies and between local, regional, national and international levels of organization, creates new problem spaces for (public forms of) government. While the role of public authorities remains crucial, with the new multiplicity and polycentricity of power centres, there is some loosening of the linkage between government and territory. Put simply, despite their pivotal role, state governments have much more competition over who exercises governance within a particular territory (Hirst and Thompson 1995: 171, 183–4; Shearing 1996). In these conditions, one of the key tasks of government is to stitch together the linkages between statutory, voluntary and commercial sector agencies and spatial levels of governance (Watt and Stenson forthcoming). This is fraught with difficulties and I have elsewhere, for example, argued that the new shared forms of sovereignty within Europe can create uncertainties about legitimacy within a nation state (Stenson 1998).

This has particular relevance for police and multi-agency crime control organizations in their efforts to integrate local, diverse, particularistic, communal concerns with the wider, transcendent, integrative concerns of sovereign law. Imposing order is always a local exercise, but is conducted in the name of a wider leviathan, or integrative social body. In Britain, for example, with the old union of the United Kingdom under pressure from Celtic nationalism and other forces, in which name do the police enforce the law? It is not always clear whether the collectivity should be represented by the monarch, the nation state, parliament, the European Union or other Continental authorities.

Consequently, the struggle to establish and maintain a legitimated sovereignty is functionally central to liberal rule. It is emphatically *not* an archaic residue from the past and usually operates in complex synchronic assemblages of technologies of rule (Dean 1996). These stretch from disciplinary, to actuarial, to self-regulatory practices. In this chapter I have tried to chart a clearer framework for examining liberal governmental practices and have encouraged the use of a wider range of methods in this endeavour. This is not simply a dry objective project; we are engaged human subjects, acting within the reality we are observing. *Our vocation as critical liberal intellectuals is to be sentinels of freedom*, to chart how these technologies operate together and to what extent their operation remains compatible with liberal values and the separation and balancing of powers. One of the principal casualties of a reliance on despotism, on behalf of the majority, may be the key liberal injunction to tolerate vulnerable minorities. We should also recognize that the struggle for sovereignty at every level, despite the ubiquity of feminist critiques, continues to rely on, and reproduce, violent constructions of masculinity to enforce it and also, therefore, the violence which underpins the word of sovereign law. In addition, as indicated in my example of policing in London, and as applicable to newly liberal societies like South Africa, the attempt, in mature liberal democracies, to reassemble the shattered Humpty Dumpty of the social body through diverse local, community or communitarian strategies can be destabilizing. It can, unintentionally, foster feuding and violent conflict as endemic features of liberal societies. This is because the roles of the police and justice system, as representative of universalizing, transcendent sovereign force, tend to be compromised to the extent that they become implicated in the particularistic concerns of local neighbourhoods and sectional interests, thus constraining their core liberal role as brokers between groups in conflict (Stenson 1993b, 1996a)

Acknowledgements

An earlier version of this chapter was prepared as a paper for the Symposium on New Forms of Governance, at the Centre of Criminology, University of Toronto, October 1996. I am grateful to Clifford Shearing, Pat O'Malley and Gordon Hughes for comments.

References

Barry, A. *et al.* (eds) (1996), *Foucault and Political Reason, Liberalism, Neo-Liberalism and Rationalities of Government*, London: UCL Press.
Berlin, I. (1969), *Four Essays on Liberty*, London: Oxford University Press.
Bottoms, A. (1983), 'Neglected features of contemporary penal systems', in D. Garland and P. Young (eds), *The Power To Punish*, London: Heinemann.
Burchell, G., C. Gordon and P. Miller (eds) (1991), *The Foucault Effect: Studies in Governmentality*, Chicago: University of Chicago Press.
Cohen, S. (1985), *Visions of Social Control: Crime, Punishment and Classification*, Cambridge: Polity Press.
Cook, D. and B. Hudson (eds) (1993), *Racism and Criminology*, London: Sage.
Crawford, A. (1994), 'The Partnership Approach to Community Crime Prevention: Corporatism at the Local Level?', *Social and Legal Studies*, 3 (4), 497–518.

Crawford, A. and M. Jones (1995), 'Inter-agency Co-operation and Community-based Crime Prevention', *British Journal of Criminology*, **35** (1), 17–33.

Davis, M. (1990), *City of Quartz: Excavating the Future of Los Angeles*, London: Vintage.

Davis, M. (1993), *Beyond Blade Runner: Urban Control, the Ecology of Fear*, New York: The New Press.

Dean, M. (1994), *Critical And Effective Histories: Foucault's Methods and Historical Sociology*, London: Routledge.

Dean, M. (1996), 'Putting the Technological into Government', *History of The Human Sciences*, **9** (3), 47–68.

Dean, M. (1997), 'Neo-Liberalism As Counter-Enlightenment Cultural Critique', Paper presented to the Symposium on the Displacement of Social Policies, University of Jyvaskyla, Finland, January.

Dench, G. (1986), *Minorities in The Open Society: Prisoners of Ambivalence*, London: Routledge & Kegan Paul.

Donzelot, J. (1991), 'The Mobilization of Society', in G. Burchell, C. Gordon and P. Miller (eds), *The Foucault Effect: Studies in Governmentality*, Chicago: University of Chicago Press.

Dreyfus, L. and P. Rabinow (1982), *Michel Foucault: Beyond Structuralism and Hermeneutics*, Brighton: The Harvester Press.

Economy and Society (1993), special issue on liberalism and governmentality, **22** (3), August.

Elias, N. (1982), *State and Civilization*, Oxford: Basil Blackwell.

Feeley, M. and Simon, J. (1994), 'Actuarial Justice: the Emerging New Criminal Law', in David Nelken (ed.), *The Futures of Criminology*, London, Sage.

Foucault, M. (1972), *The Archeology of Knowledge*, New York: HarperCollins.

Foucault, M. (1977), *Discipline and Punish: the Birth of the Prison*, London: Penguin.

Foucault, M. (1980), 'Prison Talk', in C. Gordon (ed.), *Michel Foucault, Power/ Knowledge – Selected Interviews and other Writings 1972–1977*, Brighton: The Harvester Press.

Foucault, M. (1980), *The History of Sexuality. Vol. 1: An Introduction*, New York: Vintage/Random House.

Foucault, M. (1982), 'The subject and power', in L. Dreyfus and P. Rabinow, *Michel Foucault, Beyond Structuralism and Hermeneutics*, Brighton: The Harvester Press.

Foucault, M. (1991), 'Governmentality', in G. Burchell *et al.* (eds), *The Foucault Effect: Studies in Governmentality*, Chicago: University of Chicago Press.

Galbraith, J.K. (1993), *The Culture of Contentment*, Harmondsworth: Penguin.

Garland, D. (1985), *Punishment and Welfare: A History of Penal Strategies*, Aldershot: Gower.

Garland, D. (1996), 'The Limits of the Sovereign State: Strategies of Crime Control in Contemporary Society', *The British Journal of Criminology*, **36** (4), 445–71.

Garland, D. (1997), '"Governmentality" and the Problem of Crime: Foucault, criminology, sociology', *Theoretical Criminology*, **1** (2), 173–214.

Gellner, E. (1983), *Nations and Nationalism*, Oxford: Blackwell.

Giddens, A. (1990), *The Consequences of Modernity*, Cambridge: The Policy Press.

Gordon, C. (1991), 'Governmentality Rationality, An Introduction', in G. Burchell, C. Gordon and P. Miller (eds), *The Foucault Effect: Studies in Governmentality*, Chicago: University of Chicago Press.

Hirst, P. and G. Thompson (1995), *Globalization in Question*, Cambridge: Polity Press.

Hughes, G. (1996), 'Strategies of Multi-agency Crime Prevention and Community Safety in Contemporary Britain', *Studies On Crime and Crime Prevention*, **5** (2), 221–44.

Hunt, A. and G. Wickham (1994), *Foucault and Law, Towards a Sociology of Law as Governance*, London: Pluto.

Jefferson, T. (1990), *The Case Against Paramilitary Policing*, Milton Keynes: Open University Press.

Johnston, L. (1992), *The Rebirth of Private Policing*, London: Routledge.

Mann, M. (1986), *The Sources of Social Power*, Vol. 1, New York: Cambridge University Press.

Minson, J. (1985), *Genealogogies of Morals, Nietszche, Foucault, Donzelot and the Eccentricity of Ethics*, London: Macmillan.

Mouffe, C. (1993), *Return of The Political*, London: Verso.

O'Malley, P. (1992), 'Risk, Power and Crime Prevention', *Economy and Society*, **21** 93), 252–75.

O'Malley, P. (1996a), 'Indigenous Governance', *Economy and Society*, **25** (3), 310–26.

O'Malley, P. (1996b), 'Policing, Postmodernity and Political Rationality', paper presented to the Law Society Association (USA) Conference, University of Strathclyde, Glasgow, 10–13 July.

O'Malley, P. and D. Palmer (1996), 'Post-Keynesian Policing', *Economy and Society*, **25** (2), 137–55.

Ong, W. (1982), *Orality and Literacy*, London: Methuen.

Pavlich, G. (1996), 'Governance and Crime Prevention: "Social" versus "Community" Regulation', paper delivered to the Law Society Association (USA) Conference, University of Strathclyde, Glasgow, 10–13 July.

Piaget, J. (1968), *Structuralism*, London: Routledge & Kegan Paul.

Pitts, J. (1992), 'Juvenile Justice Policy in England and Wales', in J.C. Coleman and C. Warren-Adamson (eds), *Youth Policy in the 1990*, London: Routledge.

Pratt, J. (1989), 'Corporatism: The Third Model of Juvenile Justice', *British Journal of Criminology*, **29** (3), 236–54.

Procacci, G. (1997), 'Poor Citizens, Social Citizenship and the Crisis of Welfare States', paper presented to the Symposium on the Displacement of Social Policies, University of Jyvaskyla, Finland, January.

Rawls, J. (1973), *Theory of Justice*, London: Oxford University Press.

Rose, N. (1989), *Governing The Soul: the Shaping of the Private Self*, London: Routledge.

Rose, N. (1993), 'Government, Authority and Expertise in Advanced Liberalism', *Economy and Society*, **22** (3), 283–99.

Rose, N. and Miller, P. (1992), 'Political Power Beyond the State: Problematics of Governments, *British Journal of Sociology*, **43** (2), 173–205.

Scraton, P. (ed.) (1987), *Law, Order and The Authoritarian State*, Milton Keynes: Open University Press.

Scraton, P. and Chadwick, K. (1991), 'The Theoretical and Political Priorities of Critical Criminology', in K. Stenson and D. Cowell (eds), *The Politics of Crime Control*, London: Sage.

Shearing, C. (1996), 'Public and Private Policing', in W. Saulsbury, J. Mott and T. Newburn (eds), *Themes in Contemporary Policing*, London: Policy Studies Institute.

Shearing, C. and P. Stenning (1985), 'From the Panopticon to Disney World: the Development of Discipline', in A. Doob and E. Greenspan (eds), *Perspectives in Criminal Law*, Aurora, Ontario: Canada Law Books Inc.

Sheptycki, J. (1995), 'Transnational Policing and the Makings of a Postmodern State', *British Journal of Criminology*, **35** (4), 613–35.

Silverman, D. (1993), *Interpreting Qualitative Data: Methods for Analysing Talk, Text and Interaction*, London: Sage.

Sim, J. (1987), 'Working for the Clampdown: Prisons and Politics in England and Wales', in P. Scraton (ed.), *Law, Order and The Authoritarian State*, Milton Keynes: Open University Press.

Sim, J. (1990), *Medical Power in Prisons: the Prison Medical Service in England 1774–1989*, Milton Keynes: Open University Press.

Sim, J. (1991), '"We are not Animals, we are Human Beings": Prisons, Protest and Politics in England and Wales, 1969–90', *Social Justice*, **18** (3), 107–29.

Sim, J. (1994), 'Reforming the Political Wasteland? A Critical Review of the Woolf Report', in E. Player and M. Jenkins (eds), *Prisons After Woolf: Reform Through Riot*, London: Routledge.

Simon, J. (1995), 'Power without Parents: Juvenile Justice in a Postmodern Society', *Cardozo Law Review*, **16** (3), 1363–419.

Singer, S. (1996), *Recriminalizing Delinquency, Violent Juvenile Crime and Juvenile Justice Reform*, New York: Cambridge University Press.

Stenson, K. (1991), 'Making Sense of Crime Control', in K. Stenson and D. Cowell (eds), *The Politics of Crime Control*, London: Sage.

Stenson, K. (1993a), 'Social Work Discourse and the Social Work Interview', *Economy and Society*, **22** (1), 42–76.

Stenson, K. (1993b), 'Community Policing as a Governmental Technology', *Economy and Society*, **22** (3), 373–89.

Stenson, K. (1996a), 'Communal Security as Government – the British Experience', in W. Hammerschick (ed.), *Jahrbuch für Rechts und Kriminalsoziologie*, Baden: Nomos.

Stenson, K. (1996b), 'Youth, Crime and Governmentality', paper delivered to the Law Society Association (USA) Conference, University of Strathclyde, Glasgow.

Stenson, K. (1998), 'Displacement of Social Policy Through Crime Control', in S. Hanninen (ed.), *The Displacement of Social Policy*, Jyvaskyla: SoPhi.

Stenson, K. and Factor, F. (1994), 'Youth Work, Risk and Crime Prevention', *Youth and Policy*, **45** (1), 1–15.

Stenson, K. and Factor, F. (1995), 'Governing Youth – New Directions for the Youth Service', in M. May and J. Baldock (eds), *The Social Policy Review no. 7*, London: The Social Policy Association.

Stenson, K. and Watt, P. (1995), 'Young People, Risk and Public Space', paper delivered to the Youth in 2000 Conference, University of Teeside, July.

Valverde, M. (1996), 'Despotism and Ethical Governance', *Economy and Society*, **23** (3), 357–72.

Voronin, Y.A. (1996), 'The Emerging Criminal State: Economic and Political Aspects of Organized Crime in Russia', *Transnational Organised Crime*, **2** (2/3), 53–62.

Waddington, P.A.J. (1991), *The Strong Arm Of the Law*, Oxford: Oxford University Press.

Waddington, P.A.J. (1998), *Policing Citizens*, London: UCL Press.

Watt, P. and K. Stenson (1997), 'It's A Bit Dodgy Around Here: Safety, Danger, Identity and Young People's Use of Public Space', in T. Skelton and G. Valentine (eds), *Cool Places, Geographies of Youth Culture*, London: Routledge.

Watt, P. and K. Stenson (forthcoming), 'Governmentality and "The Death of The Social?": A Discourse Analysis of Local Government Texts in the South East of England', *Urban Studies*.

4 Criminalization and Gender: The Changing Governance of Sexuality and Gender Violence in Hawai'i

Sally Engle Merry

In Foucault's analysis of the development of the art of government since the sixteenth century, he notes a shift in the significance of the family (Foucault 1991: 98–101). As governmentality increasingly focuses on populations, the family disappears as a model of government. Instead, it becomes an element within the population and a fundamental instrument in its governance, a transition Foucault dates to the mid-eighteenth century (ibid.: 99). But, in response to particular cultural configurations and processes such as capitalist transformation, colonialism, and globalization there have been significant variations within this pattern since that time. Moreover, it appears that, recently, in advanced capitalist societies, the family as a sovereign unit of governance is being effaced and individuals are coming more directly under state systems of governance, particularly within subordinate class groups. This chapter compares two moments of transition, both effected by the law as it criminalizes certain practices of family life. These examples illuminate historical variations in the way the governance of the family is embedded in the governance of the state.

These moments of transition are historically and culturally specific, occurring in the same town 150 years apart. Both represent the legal construction and reconstruction of family relationships through the criminal law. One occurred in the mid-nineteenth century in Hilo, Hawai'i; the other in the late twentieth century in the same town. The first, during the 1840s and 1850s, redefined all sexual relations outside the marriage bond as crimes. The second, in the 1990s, redefined acts of violence against women within

75

marriages as crimes. These are both moments in which practices which had been commonplace, and to some extent tolerated or even condoned, were criminalized.

In the first instance, strategies of governance created a private, legally inviolable sphere of the family under the sovereign control of the father/husband. In the second, this legally private sphere is pierced by the policing of domestic violence and thus opened to further practices of inspection and management by the state. Under the former regime, a husband exercised sovereignty over the private sphere of his wife and children; under the latter, governance of individuals is further detached from family units. This change expanded the governance of populations now less encapsulated within family bonds.

Although both are examples of criminalization, the cultural discourse surrounding each, as well as the political economy of the region, was vastly different. The first moment of criminalization represented an effort to transform the marriage practices and family lives of native Hawaiians under the influence of New England protestant missionaries and jurists. Its goal was to construct an enduring form of marriage which was not easily terminated, to circumscribe sexual relations to this marriage and to allocate to women the task of managing the household and raising the children under the protection and control of their husbands. The second was part of a feminist movement to protect women from violence in the home, if necessary by breaking apart the marriage and providing women with social and legal supports for living separately from batterers. Because those brought to court and allocated to treatment programmes for battering are almost all from the lower social classes, subordinated women are emancipated from the control of subordinated men, and both men and women are inserted into an expanded regime of societal discipline. Men's authority over their wives and children is diminished but this applies only to marginally employed, lower-status men who are pulled into the legal/service system. Thus, demands for the protection of women increase women's safety but, at the same time, serve as the basis for increased control and surveillance over economically and socially marginal populations.

The first moment of criminalization was part of the 'civilizing project' of nineteenth-century colonialism. The disparity between the cultural practices of family life of the native Hawaiians and the notions of the bourgeois family of the colonizing Americans and Britons was particularly sharp. Although nineteenth-century Hawai'i was an independent kingdom, by 1850 its governmental system and legal apparatus had been largely adopted from the US and Britain. After conversion to Christianity in the 1820s, the Hawaiian *ali'i nui*, (high chiefs) gradually adopted a constitution, a system of courts, a bureaucratic system of governance and a set of laws proposed by

American legal scholars and missionaries. One of the early missionaries, William Richards, spent several months in 1839 teaching the *ali'i nui* the principles of political economy. They subsequently adopted a Declaration of Rights based on European models and a constitution. In 1850 the Kingdom of Hawai'i adopted a penal code based on a Massachusetts penal code proposed in 1844.

In some ways, the *ali'i nui* accepted the goal of transforming the everyday practices of the native Hawaiian population expounded by New England missionaries and British visitors. This transformation was framed by a discourse of innate character: the new institutions were to reform the 'indolent' and 'licentious' character of the 'Hawaiian' in the essentializing singular. Creating an enduring, sexually circumscribed family was understood by both the New Englanders, and probably the *ali'i nui*, as fundamental to forming a 'civilized' society recognizable as entitled to sovereignty in Europe and therefore immune from imperialist desires.

Today, Hawai'i is a post-colonial society in a globalizing world. In the mid-nineteenth century, Hawai'i experienced the transformation from mercantile capitalism to an industrial capitalism based on sugar plantations. In 1893 a military coup against Queen Liliou'okalani, led by American settler sugar planters, brought the Kingdom to an end, and, in 1898, it was annexed by the United States as a colony. In 1959 the residents of the Territory voted for statehood, decolonizing the islands politically but not economically. Despite a far more varied ethnic make-up than most other parts of the USA, its citizens are fully incorporated into the US governmental and legal system. The 1980s and 1990s movement against gender violence was inspired by feminists from the US mainland who galvanized local women into pressing for legislative reforms, the creation of new forms of treatment for batterers and better enforcement of laws against domestic violence by the police and judiciary. After describing both instances of criminalization, I will compare the changing relationships between the family and the art of governance.

Adultery and Fornication in Nineteenth-Century Hawai'i

The lower courts of the Kingdom of Hawai'i in the 1840s and 1850s were full of cases of adultery and fornication. Together with lewd and lascivious behaviour, these offences constituted almost half of the case-loads of the lower courts in Honolulu, the principal town, and Hilo, a smaller port town. In 1853, for example, 44 per cent of the cases heard by the court in Hilo concerned adultery, fornication, lewdness or prostitution.[1] Adultery and prostitution were major concerns in the 1850s and 1860s, but declined precipitously as a focus of court surveillance. In 1853, 44 per cent of all 123 cases concerned adultery or prostitution, in 1863, 28 per cent of all 137 cases, but by 1873, only 6 per cent of the 240 charges were for adultery or prostitution. By 1883, only 2 per cent of the 409 cases were adultery cases, by 1893, 1 per cent of 379, and by 1903, 2 per cent of 280. Almost all the defendants were Hawaiians. Penalties were severe: a $30 fine for each party, or four months' or even eight months' hard labour. Indeed, some contemporaries reports claim that adulterers built the Hawaiian road system. After the 1860s, however, such cases disappeared from the courts. There were 54 in 1853, 38 in 1863, only 14 in 1873, seven in 1883, three in 1893, and six in 1903, even though court case-loads increased dramatically during this period.

Arrests were typically made by constables who, until the 1870s, received a portion of the fines for successful prosecutions. American-born judges in Hilo sentenced adulterers to heavy fines or eight months' hard labour, usually building roads. Everyday forms of sexual interaction that had been approved, or at least tolerated, became the object of legal censure and surveillance. The defendants were mostly suppliers of food, sex, and other services for merchant exchanges with visiting ships or were self-sufficient farmers outside the global market.

Most of the adultery and fornication cases in the records of the lower court in Hilo concerned relations between Hawaiian couples. They commonly described situations in which a couple had been more or less regularly cohabiting or engaged in a love relationship. The cuckolded husband, constable or both would spy on the couple, seeking to catch them in the act of sexual intercourse. In some cases, they followed couples into the coffee fields, in others they peered through the hatch of a house or broke into a house in the middle of the night. Several cases indicated that these couples were living together in a way that would have been acceptable in the past.

For example, on 26 April 1853, Kilioi and Kanowina were charged with adultery and pleaded not guilty. The woman's brother testified that:

Kilioi and Kanowina have formed a situation of husband and wife according to Hawaiian fashion. The woman and myself live in the same house. Kilioi visits there often – he has always been trusted as one of the family. Last Saturday Kilioi visited there and stayed overnight. On going to bed the defendants lay in different places apart from each other. In the morning when I awoke I saw the defendants locked in each others arms in the same bed. It was the woman that left her place and went to where the man was. I did not see anything amiss before that. The defendants were asleep locked in each others' embrace. It is a long time that defendants have been connected in this Hawaiian fashion.

The case record does not explain why the brother testified against his sister unless he sought to break up the relationship. After considerable further testimony including evidence that Kilioi had neglected his wife for some time, the woman admitted that she was guilty of adultery. The judge, a fairly recent arrival from New Zealand, convicted them and sentenced each to pay a fine of $30 and, in default of payment, to be sentenced to eight months' hard labour. In this cash-poor town, in which only a total of a few hundred dollars were in circulation at this time, such a fine represented a staggering burden.

This case is typical in its presentation of the offence as part of accepted Hawaiian kinship patterns. Early Hawaiian marriage was, according to virtually all sources, casual, marked with little formality at its initiation, and easily broken (Linnekin 1990: 121; Ellis 1969; Handy and Pukui 1972). Young people were initiated early into sex and continued to be sexually active throughout their lives. During certain periods of life, particularly for young people and for chiefly men and women after their first children were born, sexuality was relatively unconstrained. There was clearly a different economy of the body and desire among the Hawaiian population than among the New England missionaries.

The flood of cases concerning extra-marital sexuality reflected the New England Calvinist missionaries' harnessing of the legal system to the project of containing the Hawaiian body – swathing it in clothing, containing desire within the bonds of a lifelong marriage, restricting sexual behaviour to private spaces. They sought to constrain desire and confine sexuality to the regulated space of the marriage bed. In the words of Anna Goodhue, a *kanaka maoli* (native Hawaiian) woman born on the rural island of Molokai'i in 1918, testifying at the People's International Tribunal Hawai'i 1993:

> When the white man came, the first thing he did, he destroyed our religion, our religious beliefs, and foisted their own religious beliefs upon us. They were fanatics, their religion steeped in self righteous bigotry. He taught us to be ashamed of our bodies and clothed us in Mother Hubbards, clothing unsuitable in our mild climate. Today, we go about suitably clothed while they display their unclothed bodies without shame, without respect for themselves or others (Molokai'i Testimony, *Ka Ho'okolokolonui Kanaka Maoli: 1993 The People's International Tribunal Hawai'i Mana'o* (transcript, p. 84).

Although the missionary rhetoric of the early nineteenth-century constantly referred to the evils of prostitution and the detrimental moral effects of visiting sailors, their primary concern seems to have been marriage. There were surprisingly few cases of prostitution in the courts of Hilo, even though it was a port town visited by large numbers of whaling ships during the 1840s and 1850s. Of the 55 cases concerning sexuality heard in the Hilo police court in 1853 none were for charges of prostitution, one was for pimping and one was for keeping a disorderly house. In the latter case, only the Hawaiian owners, not the foreign clients, were punished. The Honolulu case-loads were similar. Despite the justification that women needed protection from the immoral influences of sexually deprived sailors, it seems that the principal concern of both the police and the courts was to contain sexuality within the confines of a bourgeois form of marriage.

As the missionaries sought to contain sexuality within the bonds of the family, they developed a rich discourse of licentiousness and degradation to describe their difficulties and frustrations. This is illustrated by the answers to a series of questions posed by the government of Hawai'i to 11 missionaries in 1846 in which many waxed eloquent on the theme of licentiousness and vice among Hawaiians.[2] In these commentaries, foreign seamen and their temptations are named as the chief evil, but, as we have seen in Hilo, such concerns were of secondary importance in the courts to the maintenance of a certain form of marriage (see also Grimshaw 1989).

For example, a missionary stationed in the main port city, Honolulu, who arrived from Pennsylvania in 1832 and sired 10 children (Piercy 1992) wrote that, by far the most ruinous form of vice was licentiousness, both among married and unmarried, but more among the latter. He maintained that it was by idleness, living in small miserable houses without partitions, the debased state of moral feelings, and 'the licentious conduct of many foreigners who tempt Hawaiian females to the commission of crime, by money and other enticing articles. In the year 1846, 164 cases of adultery were brought before the courts in Honolulu; and it has often been said that a large portion of the money taken in the shops of this town – say three-fourths – is the wages of licentiousness'. He advocated some change in the laws current at that time because the previous penalties which comprised a fine of a few dollars or prison work was 'but a feeble check', in that the fine was easily collected from friends and, once paid, the parties were ready for a new transgression. Working on the road or in the prisons was 'not dreaded at all scarcely', and, in his opinion, prison discipline was far too lax.

The native Hawaiians, he argued, needed to learn early habits of industry to supply their wants, to 'make their homes comfortable and remove the temptation to wander about and commit crime in order to get money or fine dress'. Moreover, an entire change in the 'odious' land system existing on the islands would help, to give them land in fee simply to get them engaged in agriculture. People also needed to be restrained from travelling from remote areas to seaports, especially Honolulu and Lahaina, the major ports for whaling ships stopping to refit their ships and recuperate their crews with food, rest, and women.

Multitudes resort to these places for the most trivial reasons, fall into temptation, become diseased and go back to their homes, only to scatter death around
them and be a curse to their friends. Much licentiousness too is practiced on
small vessels going to and from these central towns (Kingdom of Hawai'i 1846:
32–33).

Another missionary added that licentiousness was the prevailing vice of
the district, as it was of the entire islands:

More married persons than unmarried are guilty of this sin, thus adding adultery
to uncleanness. Of late, I have not heard of very many cases, still they occur
often enough to cause me to tremble for the nation; for 'sin' and no sin more
perhaps than this, 'is the reproach' and ruin 'of any people'. (Green in Kingdom
of Hawai'i 1846: 31)

As causes of this sin he listed the haste and thoughtlessness with which
people entered into marriage, often with no genuine affection, leading eventually to mutual disgust and cold feelings or quarrels and subsequent infi-
delity. Idleness was also considered to contribute to the problem, 'especially
the idleness of the female portion of the community. They are not "keepers
at home", but wandering about, fall into the society of the profligate, and as
is often the case, become tempters of others' (Kingdom of Hawai'i 1846:
31). Bishop (Kingdom of Hawai'i 1846: 33–5) also maintained that the
most prominent vice was licentiousness, although it was 'much diminished
from its former universal prevalence. During the first years of my residence
on these islands, it was shocking to witness the entire want of decency, both
of feeling and action, among all classes'. The problem, he concurred, was
idleness: women and children had scarcely any employment and women
were 'given to gossiping or absolute idleness, and the latter [children] of
both sexes are left to grow up untaught in all kinds of work'. Children were
permitted to run at large, with little family discipline or family instruction.

Yet, by 1848 the missionary community was willing to report signs of
improvement in practices of marriage and control of sexuality to its support-
ers and donors back home in Boston. The terms of this improvement are
themselves revealing. For example, in its General Letter on the state of the
mission to Rufus Anderson, assessing the state of improvement since 1820,
the missionary authors noted that the people now ware clothes, whereas,
before, even high chiefs would swim and walk from house to beach naked.
Now all ware some foreign clothes, especially to church (Houghton Library,
Harvard University, 1848).

In 1820 none of the relations of domestic and social life were regarded as
sacred and binding. As these missionary authors put it:

... both men and women could have as many partners as they wished – a man as many as he could feed, a woman as many as she could entertain, and both could turn the spouses out as suited their convenience and pleasure, or husbands might leave a wife if they desired and women could leave men as they desired. The king had five wives – one was a widow and one the daughter of his deceased father – and each had her particular day of service when she followed her lord with spit-dish and fly-brush. There was no such thing as conjugal affection, no domestic concord, and no such thing as parental authority.

There were no stated laws which defined the duties of parents towards children and of children towards parents; they regarded parental authority if they were quite at leisure to do so, and only so far as suited their convenience. No obligations were felt on the part of parents to take care of their children, nor on the part of children to obey their parents, and they often destroyed their children before or after birth in order to be released from the trouble of taking care of them. Such are a few of the facts which belonged to the generation of 1820. The present generation are in a different position in these respects. The facts are altogether of a different character. There is scarcely a single feature of that generation discernible in the present in regard to their habits of civilization and in their social arrangements. Then there was no law; nothing to regulate society. Now all the natural social and domestic relations are respected – the duties of each in some measure respected, and regulated by good and wholesome laws; and a neglect to perform the duties attached to these various relations is punishable by fine, imprisonment or other disabilities. Parents and children, husbands and wives, masters and servants, are recognized in laws and on any delinquency in the performance of the duties of their respective relations, they are answerable to the laws of the land.

Several strategies were devoted to creating this form of marriage. First, marriage could only take place under the control of the state and its representatives, such as clergymen.[3] Missionaries retained the right to question marriage applicants about their own religious affiliations, forbidding non-Christians from marrying their converts (Linnekin 1990). Marriages had to be registered and conform to the conditions established by the state.

Second, divorce became very difficult. It required lengthy and expensive legal proceedings. A man's absence of four years entitled a woman to divorce. A person could also be granted a divorce as a result of his or her partner's adultery. However, in the early years of Western influence, an adulterer was not permitted to remarry as long as the cuckolded person remained alive. In 1840, one high chief, eager to remarry but forbidden to do so while his wife lived, poisoned her. He was freed to remarry but hanged for the murder (Gutmanis 1974).

Third, women who deserted their husbands were returned to them. The early laws on family and divorce from 1841, which were based to some extent on Hawaiian practices, allowed separation for quarrelling and living in fear of one's spouse, but subsequent laws dropped the provision that violence was a reason for leaving a husband. Indeed, women who fled violent spouses were routinely sent back to their husbands by the courts in Hilo throughout the nineteenth-century. Between 1853 and 1913, 181 cases involving women who deserted their husbands were brought before the Hilo district court. In the court records, women often expressed a desire to visit their families or travel, which was opposed by their husbands. Virtually all were returned to their husbands, or the case was dropped after they agreed to return even though there were indications of violence in a minimum of one-quarter of the cases. Women who refused to return were sentenced to hard labour in prison. In one particularly egregious case, a woman had been to court many times complaining of her husband's violence. The judge, who had heard most of the previous cases, finally agreed to allow her to petition for divorce. After the petition was refused, the husband beat her again. Many of these cases involved Hawaiian women married to Portuguese, Caucasian or Chinese men. The latter two groups, in particular, tended to arrive without women and bring with them a far more authoritarian understanding of the family and gender inequalities.

During the same period, there were 487 wife assault cases. Only if the weapon were severe, the witnesses unambiguous and the injury significant was the man convicted. But penalties were much lighter than for adultery, with a fine of $6 the usual penalty for a conviction. Quite often, a woman would go to court several times about a man's beating her and would then finally desert him. The court, under these conditions, usually returned the woman to the husband. A comparison of wife-battering and desertion cases indicates that the court was far more likely to find the deserting wife guilty than the violent husband. This differential reflects not only the preference for the permanency of marriage; but also the significant differences in the evidentiary problems posed by these two kinds of cases. A deserting wife was easily proved to have left; the only question was whether the couple had married in the first place. On the other hand, the courts demanded at least one eye-witness to an unambiguous blow; a pull of the hair or a scream for help typically was not sufficient to convict.

A fourth strategy promoting the creation of the bourgeois form of marriage involved the redefinition of women as legal minors under the control of their husbands. In 1845, the Kingdom of Hawai'i adopted the law of coverture (Gething 1977). The common law principle of coverture, brought from England to the USA and from there to Hawai'i, redefined the relations between husband and wife and greatly increased the subordination of women to their husbands. The principle of coverture in effect in Massachusetts in 1835 specified that, at marriage, the husband and wife became a single legal person and, in effect, the husband was that person. He acquired virtually full legal responsibility for, and control over, his wife. She could not own property; any property which she owned in her own right became his on marriage as did any property she acquired through inheritance or her work. She could neither sue nor be sued nor could she make contracts. The husband was responsible for her support and her torts. She was, in the eyes of the law, 'civilly dead' (Gething 1977: 192, n. 22). Since the husband was responsible for his wife, he was entitled to discipline her so long as he did not kill or seriously injure her. He was legally responsible for the support of his children and, on divorce, was awarded their custody. Because of the woman's inability to make contracts, she was impeded in business activities and was thus relegated to the role of wife and mother.

Clearly, this new position was vastly different from that within Hawaiian society in which women of rank exercised enormous power. Gething (1977: 197) notes that the Constitution of 1840, which included a good deal of Hawaiian law, was considerably less sexist than the subsequent constitutions. As Gething says, by 1845 the legal status of women in Hawai'i and New England was very similar, except that women in Hawai'i had more political freedom (ibid.: 204). In 1850 a new elections law denied women the vote and excluded them from many other public activities that depended on being a qualified voter (ibid.: 210). Women were not allowed to serve on juries or run for office, even though many of the most powerful *ali'i nui* over the previous 30 years had been women. In 1888 the Married Women's Property Act somewhat ameliorated the control of men over their wives' property, again following similar legal changes in the USA during the preceding decades (ibid.: 211). Thus, laws passed in 1845 and 1850 dramatically transformed gender relationships, reconstituting the family as a single, private unit outside the scope of the law and under the sovereign control of the husband.

This new form of family was sharply different from Hawaiian family systems. Although it is difficult to be certain of the facts about native Hawaiian marriage practices, particularly before the missionaries arrived in 1820, most sources agree that, among commoners, marriage was easily entered and not marked by ceremonies.[4] Ellis, a British missionary who lived in Hawai'i in the 1820s, reported that parents of women received no gifts, nor was a dowry given to a wife. Ceremonies solemnizing marriage were few (Ellis 1969: 434–5). In 1854 a Hawaiian testified in court: 'In the old days, before the custom of marriage became general, it was moe aku, moe mai [sleep there, sleep here]' (Linnekin 1990: 121). Missionary writers in the 1840s complain about the mobility of Hawaiians, the numbers of young women arriving at the ports during the shipping season, and their patterns of moving from place to place to visit relatives (Kingdom of Hawai'i 1846). Hawaiian women went to the ports to earn cash during the shipping season while substantial numbers of Hawaiian men worked on merchant ships and whalers, travelling around the world.

Kamakau, a mission-educated Hawaiian writing in the 1860s, distinguished between cohabitation, the most frequent type of attachment, and 'the binding form of Hawaiian marriage', called *ho'ao pa'a* (Kamakau 1961: 347; Handy and Pukui 1972: 52; quoted in Linnekin 1990: 123). The former involved many wives or many husbands. The latter could not be dissolved and involved ceremony and reciprocal exchanges between the families, while children born to the couple sealed the relationship between the two families. Kamakau, as a Christian convert, disapproved of the loose form of marriage, although this is generally described as the typical form, on the grounds that it was a cause of trouble and brought on quarrelling. On the other hand, the custom of *ho'ao pa'a* was the custom of the chiefs, the first-born children of prominent people, and children who were family favourites.

Linnekin relies on these written sources as well as court documents produced during the Mahele, a major division of land occurring in 1848–50, for her analysis of marriage at the mid-nineteenth century (1990). She argues that binding unions occurred when they were important to a family's destiny. Marriages involving high-ranking women were more lasting then those of other women, even if male chiefs had to use some coercion to prevent some of the *ali'i* women from initiating other relationships. Among the commoners, first-born children of prominent people and chosen favourites were most likely to become family leaders and consequently to have more binding unions. For the young, for junior siblings who could not move into leadership positions and for most Hawaiian commoners, cohabitation was the norm. This was the pattern for the vast majority of the Hawaiian population, in which women were free to leave when they wished (Linnekin 1990: 58). In commoner families, although a person might leave his local kin group for marriage, it was often only temporary. Despite considerable mobility in the short-term, over the long run a set of cross-sex siblings constituted the core of the family unit, with dependents attached to them. As Linnekin notes, given the fragile and ephemeral nature of marriage, affines were 'structurally extraneous members of the household, people who could always return to their natal ma, the land where they belonged' (Linnekin 1990: 145).[5]

Linnekin questions whether *ho'ao pa'a* was a recognized social practice in pre-Christian times but, if so, this indicates that some relationships were expected to create a bond between families and were marked by feasting and exchanges, while casual relationships were not. It was the birth of children that held relationships together: births were marked by extensive ceremonies and, according to Kamakau, 'sealed' the relationship between the families. They also secured the family's continuity and succession on the land, as grandchildren were seen to replace the grandparents. Thus, the more enduring commoner marriages created household groups within and between *ahupua'a*, landholding districts (Linnekin 1990: 125).

There was a major difference between the family lives of commoners and chiefs. Chiefly marriage was politically important, and the sexual behavior of *ali'i* women was hedged with restrictions. Although chiefly women had liaisons and secondary unions, they could not do so with impunity, especially if they had high *kapu* rank or politically critical relatives (Linnekin 1990: 60). Some chiefs were jealous of their consorts' sexual liaisons, such as Kamehameha over Kaahumanu, and some placed a *kapu* on daughters or wives. The sexual and social lives of high-ranking women were sometimes closely guarded (Malo 1898). Linnekin notes that, although women flocked to the ships in large numbers to make alliances with the newcomers, chiefly women gave material gifts while only the commoners provided sex (Linnekin 1990: 56). Both commoner and chiefly women, however, lived in separate spheres from men and enjoyed considerable autonomy. Gender relations appear to have been fairly egalitarian (ibid.: 114).

Transforming such family relationships into the model of the bourgeois family with enduring husband–wife bonds, female subordination to male sovereignty and exclusive sexual relationships, at least for women, was not easy. Although they are difficult to discern in the remaining documents and court records, there are hints of resistance. The missionaries constantly bemoaned the inability of the 'Hawaiian' – as the people were called in the essentializing singular – to follow the path of correct conduct and to achieve conversion in the heart as well as on the surface of behaviour. As the capitalist transformation of the islands into sugar plantations proceeded after 1876, the number of adultery and fornication cases in the Hilo court case-load dropped precipitately, falling to a small percentage of all cases and a dribble of absolute numbers. Even as the proportion of the population of native Hawaiian ancestry fell, the majority of defendants continued to be native Hawaiians. The effort to reconstitute the marriage relationship was never expended upon immigrant plantation workers from China, Japan, Portugal, Korea or Puerto Rico, since these groups did not fall within the colonizing, missionizing project. They were interpreted as alien and dangerous, but not heathen. Moreover, they brought with them understandings of marriage more similar to that of the modernizing bourgeoisie of Hawai'i, most of whom were of American or British ancestry.

By the end of the nineteenth-century, when Hawai'i was annexed to the USA as a colony, the project of transforming the Hawaiian family had apparently succeeded. The number of prosecutions for sexual offences and violations of the marriage bed had diminished significantly, both absolutely and in comparison to other kinds of cases, such as labour violations. It was generally accepted that marriage had to be certified by the state, and divorce was difficult. At the same time, in more rural and isolated pockets of the islands, Hawaiian kinship practices which were centred on the bilateral extended network of relatives, the *ohana*, persisted as subjugated knowledges. In these places, siblingship remained important as well as marriage (Handy and Pukui 1972).

The new family form was part of the project of creating a modern society and system of governance in Hawai'i. The New England missionaries subjected themselves to the same family form and sexual restraints, defined by a legal system already in force in New England in the eighteenth and early nineteenth centuries (Grimshaw 1989). The sovereign male subject was given dominion over female subjects who were understood as less capable of self-governance. The public sphere was constituted by agreement among equals while the private sphere, outside the law and different in kind, was the realm of emotions, desires, needs and cultural traditions in which inequalities were understood as the result of naturalized differences and capacities, such as those based on gender (Collier, *et al.* 1995: 8).

This family form was fundamental to the rule of law in the modern liberal state. The rule of law claims universal rule outside the preserve of the subject's free action (Fitzpatrick 1992: 168). This private space is the family. Fitzpatrick (1992: 180) notes that modern law claims universal applicability but marks out a free, private realm of the family within which the subject engages in self-governance subject to the forms of self-discipline and policing embodied in the microtechnologies of power of the modern period. The creation of a private space of the family beyond law is fundamental to the constitution of the modern liberal legal order. This space is externally structured by law which regulates marriage, divorce, property rights and inheritance, but its internal governance is vested in the sovereignty of the husband over the wife and the father over the children. In other words, the state constitutes this private space but cedes its authority inside the space to the father/husband. The interior space is outside the law, subject only to the sovereignty of the husband while the external shape of the family is constructed by the state in durable and intractable terms.

Establishing a new family form among the native Hawaiian population pre-dated the significant capitalist transformation of Hawai'i. Not until two decades after the major effort to control sexuality and contain sensuality within the bonds of marriage (at the same time that other sensual activities such as the hula and surfing were also under attack) did the native Hawaiians become a significant part of the plantation labour force. Although they had earlier worked as sailors and providers of food for whalers and traders and the women had provided sexual services, they were not part of the labour force of the sugar plantations until the late 1860s and 1870s. Court records indicate that, at this time, the number of convictions for labour violations began to increase sharply. Thus, the creation of the modern subject grew first out of the redefined gender and sexual relationships and only later out of work and time discipline. The bourgeois family, with its contained sexuality and ideology of masculine self-governance and family sovereignty, was thus a precondition to the creation of a capitalist economic order based on wage labour and individual responsibility for production.

In sum, with the introduction of American court systems and legal codes, the conditions of family life were fundamentally transformed. Marriage became a more durable relationship; divorce became virtually impossible. At the same time, violence and fear of violence were defined as irrelevant to ending the relationship. Women who deserted in fear were returned to their husbands, sometimes with penalties. Thus, changing this relationship to a more permanent tie increased women's vulnerability to violence. With the advent of laws of coverture which persisted from 1845 until the late nineteenth century, the woman lost the right to the joint property which they formed together (Gething 1977). Within the family, the sovereignty of the husband dominated all relationships. The woman was expected to remain in the house performing domestic tasks rather than wandering more broadly – visiting, farming and keeping ties with other kin (Grimshaw 1989). This cultural transformation subjected women to a kind of isolation and the authority of their husbands. The transformation in the family from the open *ohana* system to the circumscribed and contained bourgeois family, with a private core protected from the intervention of the state or public scrutiny of any kind, made women far more vulnerable to gender violence within these relationships than they had been before.

Gender Violence in the 1990s

The 1990s has witnessed another example of the criminalization of family and gender practices in the campaign against gender violence.[6] In Hawai'i, a series of legal and procedural reforms during the 1980s significantly increased the scope of punishment, the severity of the criminal justice response and the availability of treatment programmes for wife-battering. Case-loads for civil restraining orders and criminal convictions increased enormously in the early 1990s in Hilo, as well as in Honolulu. Earlier police reports and case records stretching back to the mid-nineteenth century suggest that gender violence is at least as old as the bourgeois form of marriage, but only recently has the law been willing to intervene severely. This is a second moment of criminalization dedicated to changing family and gender relationships, 150 years after the first.

Since the late 1970s, an activist feminist movement in Hawai'i has produced a gradual change in the law's stance towards domestic violence in Hawai'i, as it has throughout the USA. Laws have targeted wife-battering and penalties have become more stringent. A law passed in 1973 distinguished domestic violence from other assaults but did not immediately produce significant numbers of arrests and convictions. During the 1980s it was augmented by stronger sentences, longer cooling-off periods, more energetic police arrest policies, and more diligent prosecution. A 1985 addition to the statute required all convicted batterers to attend a treatment programme for battering. In the town of Hilo, local feminists started a shelter in 1978 (Rodriguez 1988) and in 1986, working with the activist local judiciary, developed a violence control programme which offered training for batterers, and a women's support group.

Case-loads mushroomed in the late 1980s and early 1990s as more and more women went to court for restraining orders and to prosecute their batterers.[7] During the 20-year period from 1974 to 1994, the population of the County of Hawai'i almost doubled, but the number of calls to the police concerning domestic violence more than quadrupled (County of Hawai'i, 1994). The number of requests for civil protective orders, commonly called temporary restraining orders (TROs), has increased dramatically since the early 1970s. Between 1971 and 1978, there were seven TROs issued in Hilo for domestic violence. By 1985, however, the year in which the new spouse abuse law came into force, the numbers were much larger. I could not find data for the period from 1979 to 1984, but in the ten years from 1985 to 1995, the number almost doubled, increasing 182 per cent. The most spectacular increase has been in criminal cases: during the 16 years between 1979 and 1995, the number of criminal wife-battering cases increased 25 times from a very small initial number to almost 800 out of a population of 135 000. In 1993 there was one call to the police for every 58 residents and one charge of 'Abuse of a Household Member' for every 183 residents in the county. In 1994 domestic violence cases formed about 30 per cent of the active probation case-load of the criminal court.

The increase in civil TROs suggests that women are more inclined to turn to the legal system for help. The even greater increase in criminal cases indicates that the police are more energetic in making arrests and prosecutors in pressing charges. By 1995 this increase began to level off and the courts handled approximately the same number of civil as criminal cases. I interpret these statistics as indicating that wife-battering has long existed as a social practice but that, as public consciousness increased during the 1980s, more women turned to the courts for help. As courts became more attuned to this problem, a higher proportion of cases were prosecuted. However, the fact that calls to the police for help have increased more slowly than criminal prosecutions suggests that the change is not the result of more wife-battering but the victims' greater willingness to turn to the law for help and for police, prosecutors, and judges to take their complaints seriously.

The sharp increase in criminal cases is partly the result of a decision by the police to arrest all perpetrators of abuse in a household relationship, not just those who resist leaving, who come back before it is over, or who inflict serious injury. I was told by a public defender that this policy change occurred in 1989. There has also been an expansion of the victim/witness programme which endeavours to encourage women to press charges, particularly during the last three years. At the same time, the victim/witness programme has developed a more cooperative working relationship with the established women's shelter, which facilitates prosecutions. These changes are even more marked in more urban areas, such as Honolulu. A bill presented to the House of Representatives for the 16th Legislature, HE No. 364, S.D. 1, claims that, on Oahu, arrests for domestic violence increased from 128 in 1986 to 1 400 in 1988, while restraining orders issued by the family court on Oahu increased from 164 in 1980 to 918 in 1988.

Over the last 20 years, there has been a sea change in the legal system as police, prosecutors and judges have become willing to take domestic violence seriously and to arrest and prosecute the perpetrators. At the same time, women have become far more active in asking for the help of the legal system in wife-battering situations. The recent levelling-off of numbers is intriguing. I think that there has been a massive, one-time movement of wife-battering cases into the courts. Most, but not all, of the defendants are men and the victims are women. They are going to court for behaviour which, 20 years ago, was taken for granted as a part of male authority.

These cases have long appeared in court in small numbers, but rarely received severe penalties. An examination of the case records for the lower court of Hilo from 1853 to 1913 indicates that the courts heard 473 cases involving domestic violence over these 60 years, averaging about eight per year in a fairly stable pattern. Only eight had female defendants and 13 male and female defendants. Of the total 96 per cent were male defendants. Of these, 48 per cent whose plea is recorded plead not guilty. The court convicted 76 per cent of these, but of those convicted, 88 per cent were given a fine under $100, generally $6. There was no further penalty or treatment for batterers during this period.

In the 1980s batterers' treatment programmes became the cornerstone of the local judiciary's increasingly assiduous attack on domestic violence. All convicted batterers and many of those subject to restraining orders, particularly for contact restraining orders, were mandated by the court to attend a violence control programme. Judges sometimes required women to attend the women's support group. Over a three-year period from 1990 to 1993, 400 men were referred to this programme. According to the intake forms filled out by these men and their partners, this was a disproportionately poor, uneducated, unemployed group of people (Merry 1995).

The batterers' training programme teaches men to manage their anger and provides them with new beliefs about gender privilege. Leaders of the programme say that their principal concern is with women's safety but, because the government was interested in rehabilitating men, they offered training for batterers. By monitoring the violence of the men in the batterer's programme, they give added protection for women while the men are in the programme. Programme staff believe that batterers should be offered education and will respond when they are ready, although they have limited hopes for reforming men who batter.

Thus, through this programme and the legal system in which it is embedded, feminist advocates are endeavouring to construct new gender identities by means of law. The women are told that they do not deserve to be hit no matter what they do and the men are told that they can win love, trust, and affection through negotiation and collaboration instead of force. The men are taught how to control their violence and rethink their beliefs about male–female relationships, while the women are offered support in negotiating the legal system and put into contact with other women who have experienced violence.

Comparative Criminalization

How are these two instances of criminalization similar and different? Both use the authority and sanctioning power of the law to redefine gender and marriage relations, imposing relatively severe penalties on commonplace, widely accepted, forms of behaviour. Both reforms were dedicated to a new vision of family life and gender relationships framed in a larger social–religious theory brought by reformers from the outside. Both were designed to protect women, but the first sought to protect women morally and sexually by placing them under the authority of their husbands while the second endeavoured to protect them from the physical and emotional abuse of their husbands.

In both cases, those whose behaviour became the object of court surveillance were primarily from the lower social classes. Because chiefly native Hawaiians in the 1850s already practised a more permanent form of marriage, it was primarily the commoners who ended up in court, charged with adultery and fornication. The men brought into the courts and batterers treatment programmes in Hilo in the 1990s and the women attending the support groups were also largely poor and uneducated. In both cases, the objective of the criminalization process was to construct an autonomous, choice-making rational subject within this class segment. In the nineteenth-century, this was a male subject who was to assume authority within the family. In the present period, men are encouraged to take responsibility for their violence and to see it as a choice which harms their relationships with wives and children rather than an inner force they cannot control. Women are encouraged to leave partners who batter and to prosecute their batterers. If they fail to leave or to testify against their partners, they are sometimes seen as troublesome and difficult even though legal action subjects them to danger from an angry spouse and risks alienating their relatives.

Both increase surveillance and control over men in the name of protecting women. In the first instance, women were to be protected from their husbands' adultery; in the second from their husband's violence. Yet it is unclear whether the women's situation has been significantly improved by either intervention. Locking women into permanent marriages under husbandly authority diminished their mobility and economic autonomy and reduced the importance of kinship linkages to siblings and others in the extended kin network or '*ohana*. Providing women legal means of separating from their husbands does not help them if they lack the resources to set up a separate household and care for their children.

Indeed, in both cases law had a rather limited effect. The penalties were as irregularly and uncertainly imposed in the nineteenth-century as they are now, and resistance and evasion by local police, prosecutors, judges and the general public was commonplace. Resistant practices are alluded to in the historical records but are much easier to observe through ethnography in the contemporary period. Men argue with the judges who impose TROs, pointing out that the problem is the woman's provocative behaviour. They fail to attend the treatment programme or attend sporadically, offering excuses, evading demands to return, until their period of probation is over. Alternatively, they sit in treatment programmes and say nothing, resisting participation and refusing to accept the new definition of how to be a man. Many joke about how they control women, thus undermining the message of the programme facilitators (see, further, Merry 1995).

There are, of course, numerous differences in these two moments of criminalization. The first sought to place women more clearly under the control of husbands in a private sphere beyond the law while the second invited the law into the family to protect the woman, even if this meant sacrificing the marriage. Separation and prosecution are understood as the only realistic way to protect women from violence.[8] The first intervention was not interested in creating more gender equality while the second was. The missionaries brought notions of a Christian family with a submissive wife busy in the domestic sphere; the feminists bring a secular vision of an egalitarian gender regime organized by mutual respect between autonomous individuals who can separate if abuse takes place. The first vision privileges the maintenance of the nuclear family, the second the maintenance of the autonomous subject. Both, of course, promote the self-governing subject but, in the recent criminalization, women as well as men are considered candidates for this subjectivity.[9]

These moments of criminalization emerged in very different social and cultural contexts. In the mid-nineteenth-century there were wide differences between the kinship practices of native Hawaiians and Christian Americans. These differences were conceived by Americans in the discourse between primitive and civilized – an opposition which legitimated efforts to transform the so-called primitive way of life. The resistance to the new family form among native Hawaiians was such that it was necessary to pay constables a proportion of the fine to trackdown offenders despite the avid support of the churches. Many of the adultery cases were discovered by constables who spied on known *moekolohes'* (literally 'rascally sleeping') the term the missionaries invented to describe adultery. Disgruntled displaced partners also enlisted constables to help them spy on offenders. In contrast, the campaign against gender violence relies largely on the initiative of victims who call the police for help or go to the family court requesting a TRO.

Each moment of criminalization grows out of a distinctive understanding of race and gender identities. The missionaries and jurists interpreted native Hawaiian family life through their lens of the Hawaiian 'character', understood as licentious and indolent, and the apparent incapacity for self-governance of the Hawaiian people. They conceived of the Hawaiian women as degraded and subjugated by the looseness of family life. The feminist criminalization of gender violence tends to see men as inherently violent and women as not violent, thus essentializing gender identities. However, the missionaries had a self-preoccupation and cultural obliviousness which is not at all characteristic of the feminist movement against gender violence.

These reforms occurred within very different economic situations. The first reform facilitated the transition to agrarian capitalism and the second to the post-industrial service economy. Missionary teachings of literacy, industry, nuclear family life, conserving resources within the nuclear family rather than sharing with the *'ohana*, plus restrictions on games and recreations, travelling around, surfing and the hula clearly predisposed native Hawaiians to enter the capitalist labour market or to work as entrepreneurs. As Kame'eleihiwa (1992) points out, commercial enterprise fitted with Hawaiian cultural practices far better than these ideas which were precursors of industrial capitalism. The second reform encourages more conciliatory approaches to conflict and penalizes male violence. It teaches men to be more flexible and negotiative and helps them move into the new jobs that are opening up in construction and tourism. Those who cannot fit into the new service economy are encouraged to cool out.

Finally, these two moments of criminalization occurred within very different systems of governance and discipline. The first was part of a major effort to transform the social order of native Hawaiians in accordance with nineteenth-century European notions of social governance, family governance and self-governance. As we have seen, the family, imagined as a husband, wife and children, engaged in farming a plot of land and preserving and storing the food, constituted a fundamental unit of governance. Its durable outside guarded significant internal autonomy. In the second moment, the court was connected to a vast disciplinary system of social services such as batterers' treatment programmes, alcohol programmes, shelters, parenting classes, welfare payments and so on. The woman who refuses to leave her batterer, for example, risks losing her children to the Child Protection Services. Thus, the contemporary system of governance relies on many forms of regulation from welfare to child protective services to regulations of licensing and insuring cars to zoning. These systems target individuals rather than families. The new reform dismantles the bourgeois family in which the woman is controlled by her husband but replaces it with new disciplinary mechanisms directed at her and her husband as individuals. The boundary between the law and social services is blurred and even effaced. It is likely that this expansion of disciplinary systems has diminished opportunities for evasion and resistance.

From a broad perspective, these two moments occurred in the context of very different social and economic transitions. The first embodied the expansion of modernity; the second the twilight of modernity and its replacement by a globalizing post-modernity. The 1850s criminalization formed part of the effort to construct modern subjectivity and to bring Hawaiians into a world governed by core Enlightenment values such as universal law and morality, rational thought and objective science (Harvey 1989: 12–13). The 1990s criminalization took place after the residents of Hilo had been fully incorporated into the social and economic arrangements of modernity and the global economy. As the plantation economy, the engine of capitalism in Hawai'i, crumbled under competition from the global economy, a two-tiered economy of salaried professionals and marginally employed people working in temporary jobs and carrying out subsistence activities emerged in Hilo. In the new post-plantation economy, the men brought to the courts of wife-battering are typically on the fringes of the new service economy, working in poorly paid and unstable jobs, if at all. They are often 'discarded' workers doing temporary work or surviving on welfare and subsistence-hunting and food-gathering.

Thus, a wide variety of historical and contextual factors determine the relationship between family governance and governance of the state. Efforts to reshape the family are critical to the tactics of governmentality, but particular approaches vary between the expansion of modernity and the emergence of post-modernity and its demand for flexible, negotiative workers. There are clearly continuities in the use of law to engineer the transformation of gender relations but there appears to be a significant shift in modernity from the family as the unit of governance and the explosion of that unit so that the individual him or herself becomes the subject of knowledge and control by systems of discipline.

Postscript: Intervention and Cultural Imperialism

Are these instances of legal intervention to promote change examples of cultural imperialism? This comparison has proved very troubling for me. I have continually wanted to deny the obvious parallels between the missionary assault on sexuality and the feminist assault on gender violence. They re-emerge, and I try again to find ways in which they are different. My desire to find them different is moral and political: while I am offended at the missionaries' perspective on Hawaiians and their sexual mores that led them to attack this behaviour, I support feminist efforts to reduce violence against women. The first seems deeply intrusive and disrespectful of Hawaiian culture while the latter conforms to my commitment to gender equality. Are they really the same? What are the differences between them? And, perhaps more importantly, can the world of the 1990s be compared with that of the 1850s, or are there fundamental differences that change the meaning and implications of transferring ideas about family life through the law from one place to another? I think that there are.

The main form that the critique of both of these forms of intervention has taken, and continues to take today as human rights becomes a global language, is that it is ethnocentric. The critique is that the spread of human rights is like imperialism: it is a Western concept which is being imposed on cultures which are quite different and do not share similar ideas about rights. China made this argument forcefully in Vienna at the World Congress on Human Rights. Any claims to universal standards for moral behaviour violate cultural differences and, like imperialism, represent acts by the West to reshape the rest in its own image. I think the analogy between nineteenth-century imperialism and late twentieth-century human rights is fundamentally wrong.

I will begin to explain why I think so by telling a story. A few years ago a nagging back pain drove me to the office of a local chiropractor. He quickly diagnosed my problem as a backbone out of line and recommended frequent visits over a period of months in which he would straighten my backbone and hold it in place. As he put it, 'It is like orthodonture: you have to put the bones in the right place and hold them there until they stay there themselves'. I dutifully submitted to a few weeks of unhelpful chiropractic visits, then turned to a physical therapist who found a cure to what turned out to be a muscle problem. This experience led me to consider the power of the analogy that the chiropractor had offered me to think about my back. Are spines like teeth? Is the process of straightening a backbone in fact analogous to orthodonture? Is the relationship between the backbone and its surrounding tissue the same as that between teeth and the bone which holds them? It is clear that this analogy makes no sense. Yet the power of the analogy held me for several weeks.

This experience is relevant to the present comparison. There are clear analogies between the missionary efforts to control Hawaiian sexuality in the mid-nineteenth-century and the introduction of mainland feminist efforts to reduce domestic violence in the late twentieth-century. But, there are also substantial differences. One of the most important is that the world is not the same. In the nineteenth-century, there were sharp cultural differences between the missionaries and the Hawaiians. Although the Hawaiians had experienced 42 years of contact with Western traders before the missionaries arrived, they had not experienced a sustained effort to reshape their family and community life. The Hawaiians did not share the notions of law, of government, of religion, of family, of sexuality that the missionaries brought.

In the late twentieth-century, the globalization of culture means that the cultural world of Hilo is in some ways different, but in other ways deeply similar, to that of the rest of the USA. There are not separate and distinct cultures into which feminist ideas intrude. Instead, there are local communities with some variations in cultural traits, but they are not mapped out as distinct cultures with sharp boundaries. Each group has repertoires of cultural meanings and practices which overlap with those of other groups but are in some ways distinct. The concept of culture, in the classic anthropological sense, is misleading in this context. There are not distinct, bounded groups sharing integrated and cohesive sets of practices and world-views. Instead, there are multiple, overlapping, communicating communities which share some ideas and contest others and others where different groups make different interpretations of the same symbols.

The situation was different in the contact zone of the mid-nineteenth-century. The notion of a bounded, isolated and static culture was still not accurate, of course, since Hawaiian culture itself had changed and developed over the centuries of residence on the islands and had experienced massive transformations during the period of disease and death following contact. Nevertheless, the missionaries arrived into a complex, hierarchical, ancient cultural space, armed with a clear agenda of cultural transformation accompanying religious conversion, a denigration of Hawaiian culture and a desire to make these 'savages' civilized. They helped the settlers create private landownership and wage labour with the belief that these moves toward capitalism would benefit the Hawaiian people, hoping even to stem the dying by giving Hawaiians land of their own to work. This is the classic imperialist situation, replicated throughout Africa, Asia and the Pacific.

Cultural relativism emerged in response to this kind of imperialism. Malinowski and early proponents of relativism used the argument to challenge the cultural transformation project. He argued that cultures needed to be understood in their own terms, that customs should be evaluated by internal standards of social functioning rather than the norms of European civilization. In *Argonauts of the Western Pacific* (1922), he argued that the Trobrianders actually had an economic system and the capacity for rational thought. The apparently irrational *Kula* exchange was no more bizarre than the British worship of the Crown Jewels when understood as a complex, integrated system. Ironically, the defence of local cultures against nineteenth- and early twentieth-century imperialism produced the static, bounded, cohesive vision of culture that now burdens our efforts to understand the fluidity and globalization of culture in the current period.

Cultural relativism, in the anti-imperialist form that it took in the wars against imperialism in the early twentieth-century, is no longer adequate as a moral position in the late twentieth-century nor is the concept of culture on which it is founded an accurate description of the world. Tolerance for differences is insufficient in a world in which the institutions of capitalism and Western culture have penetrated to virtually all segments of the globe and are being reappropriated and mobilized in various ways as forms of resistance. Cultural relativism grew out of an artificial imagining of cultural distinctiveness and boundedness – an imagining that provided useful fodder for resisting colonialism. But, just as the analogy of orthodonture is inaccurate and misleading for thinking about backbones, so is cultural relativism and the notion of separate and contained cultures inaccurate and misleading as a moral guide in the late twentieth-century.

The communities now experiencing the new influences of the West, such as the criminalization of gender violence or the dissemination of concepts of human rights, are already participating in social worlds that have, by and large, been shaped by capitalism and by Western law and its concepts of rights. These ideas have been, and are still being, seized, appropriated and redeployed in moments of resistance. A close analogy is the spread of the labour movement from Britain to the cities of Africa and from California to the docks and plantations of Hawai'i. This is not the same mode of imperialism as the missionary introduction of Christianity to Hawaiians. Instead, the spread of unions followed the spread of capitalism, and they emerged in Africa as they did in Europe in response to similar conditions of capitalist labour. This is a different process to that of imperialism because the societies receiving the labour organizers already have a culture which includes capitalist labour relations. European nationalism, defined in linguistic and ethnic terms, has similarly been seized upon in many parts of the formerly colonized world.

The Hawaiian sovereignty movement is another parallel process of introducing apparently 'foreign' ideas into Hawai'i. Although many of the leaders are Hawaiian, they have typically been educated in Western conceptions of rights, sovereignty and political struggles. Many are women as well (Trask 1993). While the men engaged in electoral politics, the women pursued a more radical course, charting a demand for self-determination rather than simply participation in the electoral process. However, the form taken by this self-determination was the creation of a constitution, an electoral system and an assembly, one body including the religious leaders of pre-contact Hawai'i. Is this an example of Hawaiians borrowing a Western form? I think not. The Western form of government was introduced to Hawai'i in the 1840s, under considerable duress. But, 150 years later, Hawaiian activists, drawing on various facets of their culture in order to construct a new order, find this form of government part of their own tradition, tailored in the constitution of Ka Lahui to a Hawaiian framework. In other aspects of its activity as well, the sovereignty movement has drawn on law to make demands for reparations, to try the US government for its crimes against the Hawaiian people and their culture, to demand the right to sue over the misuse of Hawaiian Homelands. This recourse to law is not to a 'foreign' cultural repertoire; on the contrary, it is a turn to concepts of law and rights which have become part of Hawaiian social organization for almost 150 years. As these concepts were absorbed, they were also adapted and appropriated to the Hawaiian context.

In the current movement, the concept of law itself is being redefined as both global and local, rather than national. The areas of contest between cultural meanings cannot be thought of simply as that between distinct cultures; instead they are among various groupings within cultures, such as those based on race, class, gender, region, history, occupation and so on.

Thus, the claim that the global spread of feminism or ideas of human or indigenous rights replicates nineteenth-century imperialism is wrong. Arguing that cultural relativism is a barrier to global interventions in behaviour viewed as offensive by some groups, does not recognize the nature of globalization or the character of post-modern society.

Notes

1 In order to chart the shifting case-loads of the courts of Hawai'i, I recorded and tabulated the texts and characteristics of all cases in the Hilo district court at ten-year intervals from 1853 to 1903, a total of 2325 cases. For each case, I recorded the charge, plea, conviction, disposition, presence of an attorney, and gender and ethnicity of the defendant. I also collected the texts of cases involving interpersonal relationships at ten-year intervals. I also recorded the texts and the characteristics of all domestic violence and wife desertion cases from 1852 to 1913 – a total of 683 cases. These records are housed in the Hawai'i State Archives in Honolulu. The minute books have been preserved in a virtually complete set from Hilo from the 1850s until 1913, but subsequent records were destroyed. This laborious work was done by Erin Campbell and Marilyn Brown. For half of this period, court records were in Hawaiian; the rest were in English. These records have been ably translated by Esther Mookini, an experienced translator of nineteenth-century Hawaiian court records.

2 I am grateful to June Gutmanis for providing me with a copy of this document.

3 Collier, Maurer and Suarez-Navaz (1995: 1–2) use the term bourgeois law to refer to the legal concepts and practices developed in Europe since the eighteenth-century, a term which emphasizes the link between this form of law and the possession of property within capitalist economic relations.

4 Sources are often Hawaiians who have been trained in missionary schools and consequently interpret Hawaiian kinship through the highly critical lens provided by the missionary, intent on reformulating the Hawaiian approach to marriage and sexuality.

5 The term in general use for the bilateral local household group is '*ohana*, from Handy and Pukui (1972: 5), which they use to refer to the true family, differentiated from unrelated dependents and helpers. Linnekin, following Sahlins, advocates the concept of *ma* instead for the bilateral household group, while Handy and Pukui refer to *ma* as 'and family'. In Linnekin's view, it represents the associates at a particular time, not necessarily a longstanding or permanent group (1990: 137).

6 The term 'gender violence' emphasizes that the violence occurs in cultural defined gender relationships which privilege male authority and control and, to some extent, legitimate violence as discipline.

7 In Hilo, the number of requests for TROs has increased dramatically since the early 1970s. Between 1971 and 1978, there were seven TROs issued in Hilo for domestic violence situations. In 1985 there were 250; in 1991, 320; in 1992, 404; in 1993, 451; and by the middle of 1994 there were 252. The number of criminal cases of domestic violence has increased even more, from 31 in 1979, nine in 1980, to 291 in 1990 and 551 in 1991.

8 Her safety is not something to work out together but needs to be attached to a criminal penalty, and the batterer's behaviour needs to be monitored.

9 Remnants of the nineteenth-century image of the family persist in some of the counselling programmes developed by evangelical Christian churches which are rapidly expanding in this community in the 1990s: for example, scriptural counselling promotes the continuity of the family while seeking reconciliation and forgiveness.

References

Collier, Jane, William Maurer and S. Suarez-Navaz (1995), 'Introduction to Special Issue on Sanctioned Identities', *Identities: Global Studies in Culture and Power*, **2** (1–2), 1–27.

County of Hawai'i (1994) *1994 Data Book*, Hawai'i: County of Hawai'i Department of Research and Development.

Ellis, William (1969), *Polynesian Researches: Hawai'i*, (new edn), Rutland, VT and Tokyo, Japan: Charles E. Tuttle.

Fitzpatrick, Peter (1992), *The Mythology of Modern Law*, London: Routledge.

Foucault, M. (1991), 'Governmentality', in G. Burchell, C. Gordon and P. Miller (eds), *The Foucault Effect: Studies in Governmentality*, Chicago: University of Chicago Press.

Gething, Judith (1977), 'Christianity and Coverture: Impact on the legal status of women in Hawai'i, 1820–1920', *The Hawaiian Journal of History*, **11**, 188–220.

Gordon, Colin (1991), 'Governmental Rationality: An Introduction', in G. Burchell, C. Gordon and P. Miller (eds), *The Foucault Effect: Studies in Governmentality*, Chicago: University of Chicago Press.

Grimshaw, Patricia (1989), *Paths of Duty: American Missionary Wives in Nineteenth Century Hawai'i*, Honolulu: University of Hawaii Press.

Gutmanis, June (1974), 'The Law ... Shall Punish All Men Who Commit Crime', *Hawaiian Journal of History*, **8**, 143–5.

Handy, E., S. Craighill and Mary Kawena Pukui (1972), *The Polynesian Family System in Ka-'u, Hawai'i*, Rutland, VT: Charles E. Tutte.

Harvey, David (1989), *The Condition of Postmodernity*, Cambridge, MA: Blackwells.

Houghton Library, Harvard University (1848), *ABCFM*, 13 (10–12), General Letter to Rufus Anderson from Missionaries Thurston, Hitchcock, Paris and Comee, 2 June.

Kamakau, Samuel M. (1961), *Ruling Chiefs of Hawai'i*, Honolulu: Kamehameha Schools Press.

Kame'eleihiwa, Lilikala (1992), *Native Land and Foreign Desires*, Honolulu: Bishop Museum Press.

Kingdom of Hawai'i (1846), *Answers to Questions: Proposed by His Excellency R.C. Wvllie, His Hawaiian Majesty's Minister of Foreign Relations, and addressed to all the Missionaries in the Hawaiian Islands. May 1846.*

Linnekin, Jocelyn (1990), *Sacred Queens and Women of Consequence: Rank, Gender and Colonialism in the Hawaiian Islands*, Ann Arbor: University of Michigan Press.

Malinowski, Branislaw (1922), *Argonauts of the Western Pacific*, London: Routledge & Sons.

Malo, David (1951), *Hawaiian Antiquities (Moolelo Hawai'i)*, (2nd edn), trans. Nathaniel B. Emerson, Bernice P. Bishop Museum, Special Publication 2, Honolulu, HI: Bishop Museum Press.

Merry, Sally Engle (1995), 'Gender Violence and Legally Engendered Selves', *Identities: Global Studies in Culture and Power*, **2** (1–2), 49–73.

Piercy, LaRue W. (1992), *Hawaii's Missionary Saga: Sacrifice and Godliness in Paradise*, Honolulu: Mutual Publishing.

Rodriguez, Noelie Maria (1988), 'A Successful Feminist Shelter: A Case Study of the Family Crisis Shelter in Hawai'i', *Journal of Applied Behavioral Science*, **24**, 235–50.

Trask, Haunani-Kay (1993), *From a Native Daughter: Colonialism and Sovereignty in Hawai'i*, Monroe, ME: Common Courage Press.

5   Preventing Crime: 'Social' versus 'Community' Governance in Aotearoa/ New Zealand

George Pavlich

For much of the twentieth-century, images of 'social control' have dominated liberal modes of regulation. However, recent decades have yielded a rival community-based order that has challenged and fragmented the very foundations of social rule. Under the guise of local communities wresting power from the social welfare state, this order promised an 'empowering', less coercive and more cost-effective political regime (see Cohen 1985: 115 ff.). Community policing, community psychology, community justice, community corrections, community work and so on soon became entrenched 'realities' of everyday social relations. Advocates heralded an amorphous concept of 'community' as an arena where stability could be achieved and individual freedom enhanced (see, for example, Etzioni 1993). If notions of autochthonous community control appealed to more radical political thinkers, promises of cost-effectiveness alongside nostalgic echoes to an earlier time engaged conservative thinking. With respect to the latter, an extremely influential neo-liberal framework articulated narrow visions of 'the community' and thereby diluted the anarchic and democratic formulations of radical thought. In the process, promises of greater grassroots 'community control' has come to appear much more ominously like 'control through communities' (Cohen 1985; Pitch 1995).

The following analysis examines the governmental logic of one aspect of this unfolding political arena – namely, community crime prevention.[1] Its overall thesis is that the rise of community crime prevention is not just a slight adjustment to political technique; rather, the very notions of who is governed, who governs and what governance entails are in the process of significant revision. That is, the political logic underlying community crime prevention measures derives from an 'advanced' neo-liberal discourse that has substantively eroded the previously dominant 'social welfare' governmental rationales. To locate my argument in wider debates, this chapter begins by situating the concept of 'governmental rationality' within Foucault's work and offering a cursory look at the genealogy of liberal governmental rationales out of which neo-liberal discourses have emerged. This discussion prefaces an attempt to show how liberal social welfare governmental rationales in Aotearoa/New Zealand authorize a very particular conception of crime prevention. Then, focusing on an influential New Zealand Treasury document which explicitly delineates a blueprint for neo-liberal governance, the following section indicates some key challenges directed at the social welfare rationales. These challenges license a different governmental logic that promote an alternative version of 'community crime prevention'. After examining the measures and logic associated with the latter, the analysis concludes by highlighting the possible dangers of emerging community crime prevention patterns in Aotearoa/New Zealand.

Background Considerations: Liberal Governmental Rationalities

Any attempt to carve a narrative path through the quagmire of contemporary modes of regulation is bound to equivocate, especially when venturing into relatively uncharted discursive territories. It is thus useful, even if by way of schematic reference, to point to a framework from which the ensuing analysis derives. In particular, I have found Foucault's work on 'governmentality' useful in context precisely because of its attempts to analyse contemporary power relations without assuming that the 'state' is necessarily at the heart of all regulation (1979, 1982, 1988). This permits an examination of 'power outside the state' and allows one to explore the extremely diverse measures that can be, and often are, mobilized to fashion, direct, shape or manage the actions of oneself and others (Pavlich 1996; Gordon 1991; Miller and Rose 1990). It also encourages one to scrutinize the rationales – the 'mentalities' – that render particular governmental measures both conceivable and implementable (Rose 1996). In tandem, these scattered references to a growing body of literature defer to notions of government,

> ... as a more or less methodical and rationally reflected 'way of doing things', or 'art', for acting on the actions of individuals, taken either singly or collectively, so as to shape, guide, correct and modify the ways in which they conduct themselves. (Burchell 1993: 267)

Here, Foucault's (1979) neologism 'governmentality' is useful precisely because it intimates the inextricable association between measures of governance and the rationales through which these are discursively enunciated and deployed.

It is this insight that I wish to develop in relation to the rise in community crime prevention measures in Aotearoa/New Zealand. As I see it, crime prevention initiatives involve political measures, or techniques, that aim to regulate anticipated (as opposed to actual) offending patterns. Such measures are rendered conceivable by governmental rationales that proclaim their importance, or necessity, and condition their eventual deployment. But what do we mean by 'governmental rationalities'? Following Gordon, it seems useful to define these as

> ... a way or system of thinking about the practice of government (who can govern; what governing is; what or who is governed), capable of making some form of activity thinkable and practicable both to its practitioners and to those upon whom it is practised. (Gordon 1991: 3)

Using this formulation as a base, my analysis will focus on the emerging governmental rationales through which crime prevention measures are deployed in Aotearoa/New Zealand; that is, it will examine the 'mentalities' that project images of who is governed, who/what is licensed to govern, and what governance entails. Such rationales are persuasive, or not, within particular discursive horizons. The political rationales that have enunciated community crime prevention techniques in context are framed by a commitment to neo-liberal, public choice philosophies (see below). As such, the rationales are traceable to a (largely Western) liberal political ethos; the 'emergence' of the logic relies upon 'lines of descent' within a broadly liberal tradition of governance. To clarify the point, let us here briefly allude to different approaches within the tradition at hand.

Traditions of liberal governance are sometimes said to have introduced techniques of power that limit direct state action. In this sense, the focus of its governance is different from, but nevertheless related to, medieval images of a 'law and sovereign' model of state power (Hunt and Wickham 1994; Hunt 1993, 1996a; Rose and Miller 1992). In the latter, the strength of a state was measured by its wealth, territorial control, military strength, laws, sumptuary decrees and so on (Hunt 1996b). But such images were diluted by liberal governmental discourses that urged the importance of a population's 'good order' to achieving a strong state (Foucault 1979; Burchell 1991). These discourses explored a certain 'art of government', noting the significance of 'pastoral' political techniques that could (metaphorically) be linked to images of a shepherd leading a flock (Foucault 1981d, see Pavlich

1996a: 107–10). The overriding image of this pastoral power is not coercive intervention, but that of a caring, nurturing leader (the pastor) who attends to the minutiae of each singular life to secure the well-being of all (the congregation). The political logic of pastoral power solicits actions that promote the happiness of each individual as a means of advancing the welfare of all. Such pastoral visions have proved to be enduring and have come to comprise a *leitmotiv* of liberal governmental rationales, authorizing measures that grant, 'in an essential paradox, as much value to a single lamb as to an entire flock' (Foucault 1981d: 239). This logic pervades 'reason of state' and later 'police science' discourses of sixteenth-century Cameralist thought where a certain 'art of government' is heralded as an efficient means of securing order (Foucault 1979; see also Steinmetz 1993; Squires 1992; Raeff 1983). The point of such control is to preserve the 'freedom' of constitutive units within a totality, and to mobilize this freedom in regulatory efforts that reinforce the integrity of the collective. This is taken to be an important means of dealing with the contingencies – the unknown futures – which all political units inevitably face. In this framework, governors are deemed more akin to the 'helmsman' than to the sovereign, for their role is one of 'preserving ship and passengers from the hazards of reef and storm' (Gordon 1991: 9).

Early (eighteenth-century) liberal discourses of governance extended this pastoral 'problem space' by enunciating rational individuals as choosing agents who constitute the singular units of a collective 'population' or 'civil society' (Burchell 1991, 1993; Gordon 1991). Notions of individual freedom and its essential nature were viewed as primordial to, and as the driving force of, democratic state action and prudent economic activity. In this context, nurturing a particular form of individual liberty was deemed crucial (rather than antithetical) to the effective regulation of populations, and thus to achieving the security of all the state's citizens. In other words, the strength of state was seen to be enhanced, rather than threatened, by allowing appropriate versions of individual liberty to flourish. In one of his lectures, Foucault captures the point succinctly by arguing that:

> ... liberty is registered not only as the right of individuals legitimately to oppose the power, the abuses and usurpation of the sovereign, but also now as an indispensable element of governmental rationality itself. (Cited in Gordon 1991: 19–20)

Later nineteenth-century liberalism elaborated on the pastoral problem of seeking to pair individual liberty and collective security by evoking different images of the one and the many. Now, the flowering of individual freedom was to be preserved in democratic rights, and collective notions of 'population' or 'civil society' became overshadowed by a growing emphasis on a 'social' domain (Steinmetz 1993; Donzelot 1979, 1988, 1991; Deleuze 1979). By the end of this century, the 'social' arena had become a focal point in the rising popularity of (social) welfare patterns of governance (Burchell 1991; Squires 1992). Here, one finds a concerted quest for 'social government' which Gordon describes as 'a government which can elicit for itself, amid the contending forces of modernity, a vocation and functionality anchored in the troubled element of the social' (1991: 23). Even though social welfare liberalism marked a shift from early liberal governmentality, it too clung to the theme that emphasized the well-being of each individual as crucial to the welfare of the whole 'society' (hence the call for public assistance or national insurance schemes and the like). This logic continued to expand and develop through the early twentieth century, with notable increases in the volume of state interventions directed at preserving this social domain, thereby weakening the discursive integrity of 'populations' or 'civil society'. In the process, a new series of political problems arose – most notably, how the social welfare state could continue to rely on a purportedly spontaneous domain of liberty (society) that it increasingly controlled and structured. As both Gordon (1991) and Donzelot (1991) point out, it is sociology – at least in its objective 'science of society' incarnation – that takes on the role of 'expertly' indicating both the true nature of society and the state interventions that are therefore required.

By the 1960s there was a well entrenched unease with the promise of social welfare liberalism and a growing acceptance of what Squires (1992) describes as 'anti-social' rationales. This decade witnessed the expansion of 'neo-liberal' rationales of government which challenged the very bases of social welfare liberalism's concept of what it is to rule (Burchell 1993; Rose and Miller 1992: 198). As Bell puts it:

> Against a back-drop of welfarism, neo-liberal discourses appeal against too much government intervention, poses 'the market' as the solution, and befriends the family, suggesting it has been downtrodden by welfarism and needs to become both independent and responsible once more. (Bell 1993: 395)

Adding to this, Rose (1996: 61) distinguishes the 'brief flowering' of transient neo-liberal rhetoric from the ways in which the very foundation of what it is to govern has shifted. As such, he usefully speaks of an emerging ethos in which the 'problematics' of government are different, and where questions on what it is to rule in an 'advanced liberal way' become paramount (1996: 53–61). Whether the insight requires one to withdraw allegiances to the term 'neo-liberal' is debatable but, for my purposes, the more important point is this:

Although strategies of welfare sought to govern *through society*, 'advanced' liberal strategies of rule ask whether it is possible to govern without governing *society*, that is to say, to govern through the regulated and accountable choices of autonomous agents – citizens, consumers, parents, employers, managers, investors – and to govern through intensifying and acting upon their allegiance to particular 'communities'. (Rose 1996: 61)

Against the backdrop of a shift from social welfare to neo-liberal rationales of government, one can better understand the significance of community crime prevention measures in Aotearoa/New Zealand.

Social Welfare Liberalism and Crime Prevention in Aotearoa/ New Zealand

Some have argued that liberal welfare governance was not part of early colonization efforts in Aotearoa/New Zealand:

Early New Zealand history shows that the first settlers did not bring with them any striking new theory of social security or community welfare, though new political, economic and social thoughts were already emerging in Europe. (New Zealand Yearbook 1972: 1015)

Even so, the formation of liberal social welfare government is traceable to late nineteenth-century pension provisions, 'charitable aid' schemes and national insurance schemes (McCarthy 1971: 495–501; McIntyre and Gardiner 1971: 186–95, 232–4). By the early twentieth-century, one finds a series of ad hoc welfare provisions directed at various categories of people, although welfarist rationales of government are by no means abundant (New Zealand Yearbook 1972; McIntyre and Gardiner 1971: 212–4; Sinclair 1969). Undoubtedly, the defining moment for the formation of social welfare governance in Aotearoa/New Zealand occurred after the depression of the early 1930s when the first Labour government introduced the Social Security Act of 1938. This legislation enacted a remarkably comprehensive welfare package and demarcated the boundaries of a 'social' domain (McIntyre and Gardiner 1971: 337–43). The Act, in its preamble, noted government's role to safeguard people from 'disabilities' relating to age, sickness, widowhood, unemployment and so on. Good government would provide social and medical benefits for all at a level that was 'necessary to maintain and promote the health and general welfare of the community'. Welfare governance thus aimed at redistributing wealth to the extent of securing normal, healthy, non-poverty-stricken *individuals* free from grossly disabling *social* (and economic) restraints. In this logic, individual liberty is deemed to be directly proportionate to the general welfare of 'society'; a symbiotic state where liberty exists through relative social equality is considered a prerequisite for 'social security'.

Within these rationales of governance, discourses on crime prevention are neither common nor explicit. However, they do appear as supplements to a more general attempt to preserve the integrity of 'society'. Here, the prevention of crime is tied to notions of 'preventive treatment' as expressed in two distinct ways. First, there is the concept of 'treating' individual offenders to 'prevent' them from offending in the future. This logic enlists various disciplinary measures to correct (rehabilitate) 'deviant' behaviours and/or dispositions; treatment must reform deviant individuals to enable them to live normal (non-criminal) lives in society. Thus, as the Controller-General of Prisons reports in 1935–36,

> The year under review has witnessed several improvements in prison conditions, all of which have been designed, without burdening the taxpayer, to make imprisonment more effectively fulfil its real purpose – namely, that it should as far as practicable be corrective and reconstructive (Prisons Department 1936: 3).

The 'improvements' he notes include better classification measures and psychological services allowing prisoners to be treated according to diagnosed maladies. Disciplinary techniques are complemented by such technologies as the indeterminate sentencing, borstals, probation, parole and after-care programmes. All are mobilized to correct deviance and secure a normal society (Cohen 1995; Foucault 1977). They seek to prevent crime from being committed in society, either by incarcerating 'habitual offenders' (preventative detention), or rehabilitating deviant individuals to an assumed normality. A central thrust of these preventive measures is the attempt to normalize 'juvenile delinquents' (Simon 1995); the point here is to reform youth before deviant patterns of life are established. Within the logic of this framework, one can understand why the creation of Borstals is enacted as The Prevention of Crime (Borstal Institution Establishment) Act of 1924 (s. 20), or why its preamble announces:

> An Act to make Better Provision for the Prevention of Crime and the Reformation of Young Offenders and for those Purposes to Provide for the Establishment of Borstal Institutions.

The implicit logic of crime prevention is coterminous with the social welfare problem space that dominates Aotearoa/New Zealand governmental discourses well into the 1970s. Indeed, in 1973, the logic continues to be reiterated by the Department of Social Welfare:

... in any preventive programme our main aim must be to deal with offenders earlier ... it would clearly be an advantage to offer help when the first indications of pre-delinquent behaviour appear. Many offenders before becoming delinquent have developed differently from normal children. (Department of Social Welfare 1973: 32)

Again, the early and extensive deployment of disciplinary measures aimed at 'juvenile delinquents' is lauded as a key crime prevention strategy.

The second concept follows the logic that crime can be prevented by reforming society to 'treat' structural maladies; social security legislation aimed at alleviating *social* problems is one example of such a strategy (see, for example, McCarthy 1971). This rationale suggests that a relatively equal society will 'prevent' people from being tempted to commit crime. The social is deemed pertinent because of its role in creating crime, in that criminals are 'part of society, and in some ways a product of it' (Department of Justice 1968: 397). The *Report on Crime in New Zealand* (1969: 19) echoes the tenets of this logic by suggesting that prevention initiatives lie squarely within the realm of building a secure society:

In the main preventive measures in the sense of all the influences that go towards building a stable and happy society lie outside the scope of Police and Justice Administration.

In both versions of crime prevention, the governmental aspirations of the state amount to a vehement defence of 'normal society'. The logic echoes a pastoral theme by seeking to reconcile individuals and society around notions of the 'normal'. It is by normalizing deviant individuals, or aberrant social orders, that functioning order is deemed possible. The reconciliation of individuals and society works in both directions: deviant individuals are to be disciplined, regressed to the norm, while problematic 'social' orders are to be reformed. Crime prevention is achieved when these strategies are successful. As such, the logic of social welfare governance isolates deviant individuals (especially juveniles) and problem societies as the main focus of is efforts at crime prevention. These objects are regulated in institutions of correction (for example, prisons, psychiatric hospitals and so on) that are spatially separated from, but expressly designed to fortify, 'normal society'. The reconciliation of individuals in society is delegated to numerous normalizing governors (such as penologists, criminologists, psychologists, sociologists) and to bureaucrats who run the institutions. In general terms, the expertise of the normalizing judge encapsulates what is deemed appropriate governance: defining, categorizing and correcting behaviours that deviate from shifting and amorphous normative limits. The flexible reconciliation of individual and society through normalization involves vast power–knowledge formations that propagate mechanisms of discipline to work simultaneously on each and all (see Foucault 1977, 1981d).

As noted, such liberal welfare rationales of governance remain dominant well into the 1970s; indeed, in 1971, a Royal Commission on Social Security '... did not detect any widespread desire for radical change' to current social security arrangements (McCarthy 1971: 4). Subject to minor reforms, the commissioners endorse the view that Aotearoa/New Zealand's 'categorical social security benefits and supplementary assistance is in tune with the social and economic realities of the 1970s' (McCarthy 1971: 14).[2] As entrenched as the reconciliation of normal individuals and society is for this decade, the next was to unleash a neo-liberal 'experiment' which challenged the very auspices of social governance (Kelsey 1995; Peters and Marshall 1988). Here, 'community crime prevention' discourses achieve greater prominence, and the quest to isolate factors that will predict criminal behaviour is pursued with vigour (see, for example, Mitchell 1973; Finlay 1973; McKissack 1973). In the process, crime prevention discourses drift from their conceptual orbit around notions of pathological individuals and societies and begin to settle around precepts more akin to the rising neo-liberal rationales of governance.

The Neo-Liberal 'Prince': Managing Government and Preventing Crime

It is beyond the scope of this chapter to detail the expanse of the neo-liberal vision that placed itself within a wider 'public choice' theoretical framework (Hayek 1976) and which took root in Aotearoa/New Zealand during the 1980s (see Kelsey 1993; Peters and Marshall 1988). However, the genealogy of such governance may be traced to a key document in which the New Zealand Treasury enunciated its (neo-liberal) rationale for effective governmental measures. Such rationales have woven at various times, and rates, new patterns of governance into the very fabric of Aotearoa/New Zealand's associative patterns (Kelsey 1995). In a key document entitled 'Government Management: a Brief to the Incoming Government', the Treasury offers clear advice to its incoming 'prince'. As the title implies, management principles underlie the approach to effective governance; its vision directly contradicts, and seeks to undermine, the 'social welfare government' that had erected an extensive 'social' domain. Here we focus on four related aspects of the document used by recent governmental rationalities of crime prevention.

First, it directs an attack on social rationales of government by overtly rejecting the claim that the 'social' domain is an ontological reality. The document argues, by contrast, that the 'social' is 'imaginary construct':

It is sometimes suggested that there is some wider society which is greater than the sum of the people in it and social benefits are felt by this society even though none of the people may comprehend the gain ... we would have some difficulty in deriving policy from an imaginary construct of that type. (The Treasury 1987: 448)

The emphasized point is that collectives do not exist independently of the entities that constitute them (ibid.: 429). In this sense, the social is not a primordial, objective fact. This is not to deny that we do speak of 'societies', but only to say that this is a residual, abstracted concept. Since no independent, innate 'social structures' exist, questions of equity cannot be redressed at the levels of social redistribution, or through Rawlsian 'social justice' (ibid.: 406–26). The social is then considered to be a marginal, subordinate category.

This relates to the second orientating feature of neo-liberal rationales of government: the 'well-being of individual people' is taken to be a 'logical starting point' for social analysis (1987: 405). Here, the Brief emphatically rejects the notion that 'groups in fact do decide and organise the lives of individuals in a deterministic way' (ibid.: 430). Rather, the individual is proposed as the most basic, primordial construct for all social analysis. Mill's and Bentham's utilitarian precepts are seen to be flawed, but their 'main beauty' lies in attempts 'to arrive at a collective view while building from individual concerns and positions' (ibid.: 421). In general, the document describes the individual as a being who is naturally 'rational, altruistic and opportunistic' (ibid.: 431). It is important to clarify what I take to be a key distinction: these 'individuals' are not the same as those fashioned through social government's disciplinary techniques. If liberal welfare notions of 'society' are fragmented and unhinged by neo-liberal discourse, so too is the 'individual'. In neo-liberal visions, the emphasis is placed not on bodily comportment to be corrected, or rehabilitated, but on conceptions of a *homo economicus* who is capable of 'rational choice' (Cohen 1985). In this, one detects a significant shift: notions of 'selfhood' assume a central role in the emerging governmental rationale. Now, the rational, enterprising, freely choosing, responsible self is placed at the centre of a regulatory arena that isolates factors which can predict the lifestyle choices specific selves are likely to make. The singular liberal entity is that of a rational, choosing 'self', and more especially the enterprising self who is prudent in making risk assessments in a 'self-interested' way (see Pavlich 1996b; Rose 1990, 1992). The view of selves using their reason for self-interested opportunism is said to be tempered by their capacities for altruism (1987: 413). As such, people are not simply self-interested opportunists, but also beings with an altruistic 'drive', 'a care for others', as enunciated by 'socio-biology' (ibid.:

413–5). From such auspices, the Treasury Brief argues that 'social' policy ought to deploy measures that sanctify individual choice and reduce dependency on the state; it must permit selves the voluntarism to choose actions which they perceive to be in their self-interests and yet fulfil their basic altruistic aspirations (1987: 122, 429–31).

Third, and following from the (socio-biological) idea that these selves are always located in kin contexts surrounded by immediate community groups, the Brief emphasizes 'families, voluntary social groups, ethnic and tribal affiliation, and other communities' (ibid.: 434). In this formulation notions of community and family loom large as collective concepts that explain individual action. Most starkly, the unity of the social is fragmented into a heterogeneous, second-order concept; it becomes the catch-all 'community of communities'. The primordial self is located in family and community contexts:

> We know that people value their connections to their kin and community. We also know that community structures can withstand non-altruistic behaviour. The purpose of advice in social policy is to try to explore which community structures will be most successful in mobilizing the (often non-altruistic) behaviour of individuals for the collective good of all people. (1987: 435)

Three important points are contained in this quotation: 'community structures' are invoked to replace erstwhile 'social structures'; the behaviour of 'individuals' (selves?) is reconciled not with 'society' but the 'collective good' of all people; and, it is the community which must assume the responsibility of dealing with the non-altruistic (for example, criminal) behaviours of individuals. As we shall see, such reasoning clearly guides the rationales for 'community-based' crime prevention strategies.

Fourth, the Treasury Brief argues that appropriate 'government' must maximize efficiency, equity and liberty (ibid.: ch. 1). As such, its policies ought to reconcile self-interest with wider community interests. An effective way to achieve this, so it is argued, is through a 'minimalist' state that devolves, or decentralizes, its functions to local authorities, community programmes and voluntary associations:

> The main advantage offered for decentralising control to local bodies is the likelihood that better solutions will result if those making decisions are close to the problems being addressed. (39)

Consonant with this view, and echoing public choice theory, an influential think-tank for neo-liberal ideas calls for the development of an 'enterprise culture' and argues that 'an excessive government role, with its inevitable costs, crowds out the private sector (including personal and community initiatives) and leads to poorer economic and social outcomes' (New Zealand Business Roundtable 1996, 3–4). Such views implicitly evoke images of local empowerment in which selves located in communities have increased 'freedom' to make choices in the absence of the constraints of majority interests. However, despite the rhetorical appeal to such images, the discourse is later elaborated such that – as Kelsey correctly notes – devolution has come to mean 'the government retaining power over essential resource and policy decisions, while delegating delivery to the voluntary or private sector' (Kelsey 1993: 78–9). The relationship between government and 'service providers' is now seen as a 'partnership'; the key instrument by which the former exercises directional control over the latter is through accounting, financial and management procedures.

In these four areas of the Treasury's discourse one can identify a significant challenge to notions of 'deviant individuals' and the 'social' as objects of governance. No longer is the dominant image one of erecting and protecting a normal society that offers security for individuals; now the state is placed in relation to the problem of nurturing (creating) locally-based (family or community) regulatory arenas to foster the 'natural' freedom, opportunism and altruism of selves in communities. This neo-liberal governmental rationality has cleared the way for a flurry of community crime prevention discourses in Aotearoa/New Zealand. The latter see themselves as different from previous approaches: 'Up until now, society's main focus on crime has taken place after the event through the criminal justice system' (Crime Prevention Unit 1994: 4). By contrast, the spirit of the new neo-liberal governmental rationality applying itself to 'crime' is enshrined in a document produced by the Crime Prevention Action Group (CPAG).[3] Influenced by community crime prevention strategies overseas (see, for example, Hope and Shaw 1988; King 1988), and in local police reports (for example, New Zealand Police Department 1985), CPAG enunciates a knowledge base that provided a rationale for establishing, in 1993, a Crime Prevention Unit within the Department of the Prime Minister and Cabinet. Its mission is explicit: 'to enhance community safety and security through crime prevention' (Crime Prevention Unit 1994: 1). The 'community' emerges as a key regulatory object in which the Unit – echoing the Treasury's Brief – seeks to coordinate the formation of 'community partnerships'. Here, it seems appropriate to outline key neo-liberal crime prevention measures that have been deployed by the Crime Prevention Unit, before examining the governmental rationales that render these both conceivable and practicable.

After Discipline: Neo-Liberal Crime Prevention Measures

The current community crime prevention regime in Aotearoa/New Zealand is an outcome of early community policing initiatives and a 1991 Safer Communities Pilot Programme. Amongst the latter programme's varied aims was the promotion of 'public interest' in crime prevention in the four cities of its operation (see Gray 1993; New Zealand Police Department 1985). The perceived success of these Safer Community Councils has fuelled their formidable expansion, assisted to some degree by the above-mentioned Crime Prevention Unit. This Unit is mandated to: advise the state on crime prevention; plan, coordinate, monitor and advise on the implementation of prevention strategies; and ensure that 'there is a co-ordinated and co-operative approach between central Government, government departments, iwi,[4] local government, Pacific Peoples' [*sic*] and other community groups' (NZMJ 1996: 10). In practice, the chief crime prevention strategy is an ambiguous and complex one. Safer Community Councils are meant to ascertain what sorts of prevention programmes are 'needed', and must then apply to the Crime Prevention Unit for central government funding (although, the Councils can apply for funds from other bodies). The responsibility for researching local crime patterns and assessing 'need' is largely shifted onto Safer Community Councils, although ongoing liaison with the Crime Prevention Unit does occur.

No doubt there are several variations on the above theme, but the Crime Prevention Unit locates Safer Community Councils alongside legally recognized 'sponsors' (for example, local bodies, such as city councils, iwi groups and so on). Safer Community Council Coordinators receive support from 'sponsors', often in the form of office space. Sponsors administer funds and are accountable for their use. Having conducted a crime prevention 'needs assessment' within a more general 'community profile', the Safer Community Councils are mandated to spend the funds on areas of 'need' in their 'communities' (see Hawtin *et al.* 1994). Such profiles vary from place to place, but they should include information on community composition, levels and common types of crime, known offenders and crime prevention activities already in place. On the basis of the profile, Councils must highlight 'gaps in service delivery and where, to and by whom interventions need to be targeted' (NZMJ 1996: 11). This then serves as a 'community plan' and is used to support funding requests (see, for instance, Manukau Safer Community Council 1995). The 'purchased' programmes vary, but most reflect priorities outlined in a document produced by the Crime Prevention Action Group. For example, the report prioritizes programmes that seek to redress problems associated with 'at risk youth' (for example, video/CD-ROM schemes in schools, youth resource centres, initiatives to deal with truancy and so on) and family violence (such as radio campaigns and 'healthy homes' programmes).

In these governmental measures, what counts as a 'community' and indeed a 'partnership', is significantly shaped by specific protocols established by the Crime Prevention Unit (Crime Prevention Unit 1994). Moreover, the actual deployment of particular Safer Community Councils is monitored by the accountability (and accounting) requirements which this Unit places upon the Safer Community Councils and service delivery agents. It is chiefly through management techniques in the context of neo-liberal (corporate) visions of government (such as devolution, accountability, central control of funding, coordination and centralized strategic planning) that the crime prevention measures are deployed in local 'community' contexts. But what, one may ask, is the governmental rationality – the conceptual grid – that renders such measures thinkable? In addressing the latter let us recall Gordon's (1991) previously noted scheme to analyse the governmental rationality involved. To reiterate, this neo-liberal logic does not only provide justifications for the above-noted crime prevention measures; they also help to create, or make practicable, the subjects (who is governed?), the governors' roles and the governmental actions considered appropriate to 'conduct the conduct' of others.

Emerging Preventive Governmental Rationales

Who, or what, is governed?

The CPAG report notes that:

> ... who should be targeted and how that targeting should be done are important questions which need to be resolved by careful and thorough analysis in relation to any of the detailed plans developed within a crime prevention strategy. (CPAG 1992: 81)

In line with its neo-liberal auspices, the CPAG views the main problem as one of balancing the 'mutual rights of the individual and community' (ibid.).[5] In this formulation, crime prevention must be 'comprehensive' and so include all 'criminal activities' (as defined by law), including family violence and white-collar crime.[6] As such, it locates several targets for preventive measures and urges that groups 'at risk' of offending need to be targeted (ibid.: 40). Recognizing that risk determination is not exact, the CPAG nevertheless relies on selected studies to identify the 'known characteristics' of particular offenders and offending types (ibid.: 20). Using what it considers to be relevant evidence from the field, the report identifies young men (13–25 years) as the principal at-risk group, and singles out Maoris aged between 13–16 years in particular (gender and ethnicity being identified above others). 'Migrants' too are automatically placed into the at-risk group.[7] Furthermore, the CPAG claims that, when two or more key factors are present, the 'likelihood' of offending increases significantly. These factors include, we are told, certain psychological states (for example, low self-esteem, depression and psychosis); poor relational skills; 'lower socio-economic status'; living in a 'dysfunctional family'; having a parent with a criminal record; gender; age; living in an urban area; belonging to a minority ethnic group (ibid.: 31–2).

The document separates two classes of offenders within at-risk groups: 'opportunistic youth offenders' (or 'casual offenders'); and 'persistent of-fenders' (ibid.: 6). It also focuses on 'at-risk families', in particular a so-called 'multi-problem' family (ibid.: 70). Since, at risk self-identities are said to be created by 'dysfunctional families' (ibid.: 32), the latter are targeted as needing comprehensive and coordinated support programmes (for example, ante-natal parenting education, support for children with 'significant behavioural problems' and so on). In addition, the CPAG targets 'victims' and 'potential victims', aiming to educate people about ways to reduce the risk of becoming victims, whilst supporting those who are vic-timized. The interventions are intended to encourage communities to feel secure when responding to, and thus providing necessary participation in, programmes to prevent crime.[8] Finally, the report argues that 'communities' must 'own' the crime prevention strategies which they deploy.

In tandem, the neo-liberal rationale isolates specific objects of govern-ance. On the one hand, no longer are 'deviant individuals' isolated as targets for corrective disciplinary action. Neo-liberal governance has a weak alle-giance to notions of both the 'disciplined individual' and the disciplining of offenders. It is perhaps instructive here to call on Deleuze who suggests, 'Individuals have become "dividuals"', no longer located within a body, but dispersed within a 'code' that provides access to information (Deleuze 1992: 5, 7). In other words, notions of the criminal offender have shifted from the behaviour of the 'deviant individual' to a collection of abstract 'factors' that define the 'dividuals' who are either considered at risk of offending or not. If at risk, then the 'dividuals' are targeted for appropriate community programmes. On the other hand, the selves are deemed to be located with 'dysfunctional families' or 'communities' in need of preventive intervention. As noted, here images of community are defined by a relation-ship to legally constituted local sponsors (such as city councils). In most cases, the community is defined by a Safer Community Council, and is presented as both instrument and target of crime prevention strategies.

The Governors

In the managerial ethos surrounding neo-liberal crime prevention measures, funders, managers, and coordinators of programmes emerge as governors. To begin with, managers and coordinators of the Crime Prevention Unit report to the Cabinet and take, 'the lead in developing a strategically co-ordinated and managed approach to the problem of crime' (CPAG 1992: 9). Under the Unit's leadership, a pastoral image of local community control over crime-related problems is deployed, and a 'comprehensive' strategic response encouraged. In the process, a diverse array of 'community governors' are rationalized as agents of crime prevention. There are, for example, the 'sponsors' charged with organizing, accounting for and coordinating all community crime prevention initiatives. Typically this involves a manager within the sponsoring agency (for example, a local municipal government) who accounts for funds within Safer Community Councils. Local council coordinators are important governors who are instrumental in developing profiles, applying for funding and coordinating programme initiatives.

Consequently, the central players in this regulatory field are not the social science experts, or the bureaucrats, of liberal social welfarism, but the managers and coordinators who extend neo-liberal public management principles to new regulatory environments. The Safer Community Councils are also enlisted as corporate governors. Even though their composition varies across time and place, membership does not entail formal elections. Yet as 'representatives' of a given 'community' they are responsible for drafting a 'profile' of that 'community', and also for contracting the services of community crime prevention programmes. This implicates another series of governors at the level of local implementation – the community-based programme 'providers'. These constitute the last link in a convoluted and not clearly defined relay of accountability (see Pavlich 1996a: 142–5). The relays turn back on themselves through evaluation activities which assess the degree to which levels of responsibilities, contractual obligations and such like are being met. As such, evaluators form the last of the governors; they report on the formation, processes and outcomes of deployed control activities. They provide the knowledge deemed necessary for management decisions to maximize the 'efficiency, economy and effectiveness' of the regulatory environment. This diverse assemblage of governors has replaced the bureaucrats and experts of social welfarism; they are rationalized as the caring face of a neo-liberal strategy which

> ... implies that the whole community needs to work towards reducing anti-social behaviour by those 'at risk', helping men to reduce their expressions of

violence and ensuring that all young people are brought up in a safe and caring environment. (CPAG 1992: 85)

One further governor is identified through this rationale – the victim. In the CPAG crime prevention strategy, the victim is charged with assuming a dual responsibility: that of reporting criminal activities (to amass reliable information for community crime profiles); and for governing environments (including their homes, themselves and so on) to reduce the number of 'situational' factors promoting crime. All the governors are united in a very particular vision of 'community' and are cast as the 'owners' and 'implementors' of a crime prevention strategy. By its close association with the strategy, this 'community' is thought more likely to feel committed to the overall success of the initiative (Crime Prevention Unit 1994).

Theoretically, it is significant to observe that the crime prevention governors in Aotearoa/New Zealand are justified through a wider neo-liberal commitment to the extension and deployment of an 'enterprise culture' (see New Zealand Business Roundtable 1996). What is important for our purposes here is the recognition that the regulatory focus is no longer with the creative fashioning of normal, socialized 'individuals' (with the attendant sense of 'public responsibility') through the disciplinary techniques of social governance. Rather, the advanced liberal quest for an enterprise culture stresses self-interest and (economically) 'rational' choice, placing much greater emphasis on techniques of self-formation, where the very aspirations of selves are aligned with consumptive and entrepreneurial concerns of 'free markets' (Pavlich 1996b; Rose 1990, 1992). The divisions between 'government of self', the 'selves that govern', and 'self-government' is increasingly blurred as governmental techniques seek to fashion enterprising selves in communities that formulate, coordinate and deploy strategies and programmes in a market-driven regulatory environment. As such, the governors are increasingly cast as responsible, prudent, enterprising and consuming self-identities who fall into 'low risk' categories. These selves are enlisted as governors in the quest to prevent crime by virtue of a 'common' self-interest in preventing crime in their communities.

Governance and Crime Prevention

Having now given some sense of what is governed, and by whom, we now turn to neo-liberal formulations of governance. In developing an overarching political logic that associates the governors and the governed, the Crime Prevention Unit takes as its first task the formation of a particular kind of 'space' (physical and conceptual) within which governance is to occur – the 'community'. This idea is underscored by Prime Minister Bolger in the introduction to a Crime Prevention Unit strategy document:

> Good government provides the community with support to extend a helping hand to those who need its care and protection. (Crime Prevention Unit 1994: 3)

Echoing the view of the Treasury Brief, this statement portrays good government as limited and indirect. The state must nurture the 'community' to enable the latter to protect and care for those 'in need'. The appeal to a pastoral image of spontaneous community care, of reconciling those in need with their communities, is clearly in evidence. But what is equally evident is the degree to which the Crime Prevention Unit is involved in deploying – from the top down – a particular image of 'community'. The Unit's community liaison agents promote and guide the formation of Safer Community Councils. In this important role, together with the protocols that must be followed for establishing Councils, lie the seeds of governmental actions concerned with creating the 'community' that is to govern and to be governed. Within this created domain, community agents are granted a 'freedom' to chose from amongst prioritized crime prevention programmes. Here, a dubious managerial 'freedom' is granted to both governors and the governed; they are invited to locate themselves in 'communities' and to choose crime prevention programmes they deem appropriate. This freedom is practically 'managed' through devolution, or decentralizing crime prevention initiatives to a fragmented 'community' space, whilst retaining control over important funding decisions and monitoring the entire process through protocols, accountancy and evaluation.

Yet, the Crime Prevention Unit does not only govern by deploying such 'communities', it also relies on new political technologies. Perhaps the most important of these, and which has attracted some attention in the literature, is that of 'risk management' (O'Malley 1996, 1992; Castel 1991; Simon 1987). Risk management incorporates an actuarial logic that departs from erstwhile concerns with 'dangerousness', and may even deploy a form of 'actuarial justice' (Feeley and Simon 1994). As Ewald puts it:

> Rather than notions of danger and peril, the notion of risk goes together with those of chance, hazard, probability, eventuality or randomness on the one hand, and those of loss or damage on the other – the two series coming together in the notion of accident. (Ewald 1991: 199)

No doubt an actuarial logic of risk was associated with social welfarism, particularly in its attempts to spread risks across society through national (collective) insurance and accident compensation schemes. However, in the neo-liberal crime prevention arena, this logic has been significantly modified (Crawford 1995, 1996a). That is, the very precepts of a socially oriented actuarialism have been privatized, as risk is managed through 'private' programme providers competing in a quasi, free market regulatory environment. O'Malley (1992: 261) succinctly describes this 'major revision' as 'a construct of governance which removes the key conception of regulating individuals by collective risk management, and throws back upon the individual the responsibility for managing risk'. He refers to this shift in risk management as 'prudentialism' (see also ibid.: 199–201).

As perceptive as O'Malley's concept is, it is important to issue a caveat for its use in the context of Aotearoa/New Zealand. Here, the demand for prudentialism within crime prevention governance does entail transferring to the 'victim' the dual responsibilities noted above. However, the main thrust of its 'prudentialism' is placed squarely within the confines of predefined 'communities' (for example, via Safer Community Councils and their sponsors), and the enterprising selves deemed to comprise these (Crime Prevention Unit 1994; see also Rose 1990, 1992). If this implies a differently nuanced version of 'prudentialism', it is one that dovetails with Castel's argument that neo-liberal challenges to the social domain involve a move away from disciplinary procedures directed at individuals (see also Crawford 1996b). Thus, as Castel notes, the neo-liberal 'projection' (rather than imposition) of order through risk management '... is no longer obsessed with discipline; it is obsessed with efficiency' (Castel 1991: 295). It may then be that techniques of self, rather than discipline, are crucial to deploying the 'enterprise culture' that lies at the heart of neo-liberal prudentialism.

Thus conceived, prudentialism's actuarial logic, as applied to crime prevention, implies several issues. First, crime risks are no longer calculated on the basis of, and spread within, the confines of a social (public) arena. Instead, this social arena is fragmented into a series of local 'communities', each charged with calculating where they are most vulnerable to (or, more precisely, at risk of) criminal activities. Then the enterprising selves who constitute communities are invited to 'purchase' the services of privately-competing programmes to manage the risks in question. Prudentialism is thus demanded of the selves – in the name of self-interest – within the deployed environment of the 'communities' created by neo-liberal crime prevention strategies. The Crime Prevention Unit (1994) may enunciate the priorities for Safer Community Council strategies, but the implementation and interpretation of these is issued as the responsibility of Councils (see, for instance, Manukau Safer Community Council 1995).

Second, identifying and governing the profiled 'risks' of crime within the community is not designated as a state responsibility. Instead, it is selves within the 'community' who must plan their own security, and deploy privately contracted services to prevent crime. In the process, the rationale for isolating regulatory spaces to be infiltrated by private security measures is in place. The dramatic rise of private (or quango) governance (for example, private policing) may have taken root elsewhere (Shearing 1992; Johnston 1992), and its expansion in Aotearoa/New Zealand seems imminent. To speculate further, the state may well continue to maintain its authority to license private initiatives (mainly through accounting and management protocols over funding), but might only be involved remotely in the provision of services. Even now, its contact with such services is often mediated through evaluators. In any case, out of its actuarially-based analyses, the CPAG (1992) report notes how communities might govern two main classes of potential offenders through crime prevention strategies. On the one hand, strategies aimed at the 'occasional (casual) offender' should be 'situational', enlisting the services of programmes that aim to remove opportunities for committing offences (for example, improving street lighting). On the other, 'persistent offenders' require any number of long-term measures that need to be well planned and coordinated in a series of programmes targeted at the factors which are seen to increase the likelihood of offending. In both cases, though, the provision of service occurs through programmes that are located outside the state; the state's gaze is focused on fostering selves who are prudent and able to coordinate local 'community' cells and their crime prevention strategies. In such an ethos, governance assumes the form of management by accountancy in which calculable spaces are deployed and where 'calculating selves are enmeshed in networks of calculation, as objects and as active participants' (Miller 1992: 75).

In sum, then, governance in the context of Aotearoa/New Zealand's crime prevention rationales is centred round the deploying communities as the regulatory space within which technologies of risk management are deployed to reduce the likelihood of criminal offending. The connection between governors and at-risk groups is made through the strategies of prudent, enterprising selves in deployed communities, who manage the risks of crime through programme interventions. It is such patterns of association which constitute the basis of a neo-liberal governmental rationality of crime prevention in Aotearoa/New Zealand.

Concluding Reflections

Through the lenses of our interpretation of Foucault on governmentality, we have traced the genealogical lineage of a neo-liberal governmental rationality to the pastoral concerns of early liberal, and then later, social welfare mentalities regarding what it is to rule. In the context of Aotearoa/New

Zealand, we have explored the transformation of crime prevention measures licensed by governmental rationalities associated with 'social welfarism' as opposed to those deployed through a prudentially-oriented 'neo-liberal' political logic. The discussion indicates that, along with altering governmental rationalities come changes in the objects of governance (abnormal individuals in society versus prudent and 'at-risk' groups or victims in the community), and who governs (individual social science experts as opposed to rational, responsible, managerially focused, enterprising, prudent selves). Finally, the very notion of what it is to govern is recast, and the emphasis on corrective disciplinary techniques is shifted with the rise of actuarial technologies and techniques of self that seek to 'manage' risk in the 'self-interests' of predefined communities.

With this discussion in mind, one may well ponder the possible dangers of neo-liberal measures and their rationalities, not as a defence of erstwhile welfare measures but as a means of taking seriously the assumption that all power–knowledge formations embrace dangerous effects. A possible task for critical inquiry may be to diagnose perils in a relentless pursuit of 'alternatives' to specifically oppressive limits that constitute our historical forms of being (Foucault 1984). It should be insisted, however, that the limits to neo-liberal regulation are not clearly defined, for traces of social welfarism continue to remain intact. The intersections and cleavages between these governmentalities requires further analysis; here, I have focused on their differences. In any case, let us allude to three pressing dangers that seem particularly pressing as a result of neo-liberal crime prevention initiatives.

First, there are important dangers associated with the postulated 'objects' of regulation. By focusing on the 'at-risk' entities prioritized, neo-liberal governance seeks to replace the 'abnormal' individuals targeted by 'social' with 'at-risk' groups identified through actuarial calculations. In such an ethos – and here is a key danger – regulatory measures and rationales single out groups purely on the basis of their possessing factor combinations. For instance, as we have seen, if Deleuze's dividual is a migrant, has a parent with a criminal record and is a young male (especially if identified as Maori), then there are sufficient risk factors present to intervene with some sort of crime prevention measure. The commission of an offence is no longer an issue – or, at least, is an issue only to the extent that it pertains to increasing the risk of future offending. Such preventive measures could help create groups of 'risky dividuals' who become singled out for programme intervention, not for committing an offence but for committing the actuarial sin of accumulating too many of the factors that are taken to predict criminal offending. This may not be greeted with hostility by people in search of programme intervention, but it is likely to produce a category of 'risky dividuals' who become vulnerable, regardless of what they may or may not have done, to the planned expansions of programme entrepreneurs. This undoubtedly suggests the yokes of a coercive tendency that is masked by neo-liberal rhetoric around freedom and empowerment.

Second, there are several dangers associated with locating the governance of crime prevention strategies within the 'community' as spatially defined by the Crime Prevention Unit (no doubt compromising the very idea of a 'partnership'). Crawford (1995, 1996b) indicates that local-level politics often create 'oligarchies' that deploy undemocratic and unrepresentative networks of special interest. The prioritized 'at-risk' groups are seldom represented on such local bodies, which are often constituted through uneven selection processes. There are several dangers intrinsic to such an ethos, including those of 'parochialism', exclusionary practices and the denial of differences within the postulated 'communities'. To begin with, Crawford notes that community crime prevention environments foster a certain parochialism which not only risks the formation of vigilante groups, but also has the consequence of shifting the problems of crime, 'into areas and onto people who are less well organized, poorly resourced, already more socially disadvantaged, and with little political leverage' (1996a: 253). Moreover, he notes that community politics of this kind sets up an 'us versus them' ethos in which the targeted 'at-risk' groups are viewed as 'outside' the community. The constitution of 'at-risk' groups as the 'other' creates actuarial exclusions that marginalize in a largely unaccounted way. Furthermore, in some cases – as in the case of CPAG's identification of 'migrants' as 'at risk' – such tendencies have the potential to encourage racism, or at least the view that those at risk of offending are not really part of a community.[9] Lastly, the image of a singular concept of community via a Safer Community Council over heterogeneous and socially fragmented geographical areas can only be deployed at the cost of imposing the 'consensus' of a contrived 'common' community concern. There is much that is hypostatized in speaking of 'the community' as though it were a united, homogeneous entity whose members necessarily share common interests and views on crime prevention objectives. No doubt current power formations will define the character of any postulated 'consensus', allowing dominant subject positions to silence those in oppressed and unequal social locations.

Finally, as a form of remote control, the Crime Prevention Unit's crime prevention strategy does not set up hierarchical bureaucracies, but fosters a complex assemblage of networks between government, sponsors, Safer Community Councils and their coordinators, programme implementors and evaluators. In such networks, decisions do not necessarily follow a chain of command; 'partnerships' are defined through technologies of accountancy, management and evaluation. These permit Crime Prevention Unit decisions to affect decisions of, say, Safer Community Councils through alliances that are formed

> ... not only because one agent is dependent upon another for funds, legitimacy, or some other resource which can be used for persuasion or compulsion, but also because one actor comes to convince another that there problems or goals are intrinsically linked, that interests are consonant, that each can solve their difficulties or achieve their ends by joining forces or working along the same lines. (Miller and Rose 1990: 10)

An important danger associated with this control pattern is to encourage an emphasis on the technocratic, managerial, accounting and coordinating dimensions of deploying a crime prevention strategy to the conspicuous exclusion of discussions about the justice of its precepts. Such an all-encompassing concern with the efficiency of Crime Prevention Unit operations might incur the wider cost of demeaning critical investigations into the perverse effects of the 'system' in operation. Excluded here are all-important critical formulations that defer to logics (such as morality or ethics) other than those offered by management principles.

In these and other dangers, we glimpse some perilous outcomes associated with neo-liberal crime prevention measures and rationalities. However, let us not forget that the quest for 'community' alternatives to liberal social control were alluring precisely because of the atrocities involved in separating 'criminal' individuals from 'society' for 'treatment', or technocratic 'social reforms'. This mode of control also exacted its costs and perils. However, the promise of community crime prevention does appear to have vanquished its rhetoric of community control in favour of a quest to control through communities. It is difficult to see how the neo-liberal reliance on enterprising, prudential and egotistic selves can be reconciled with their postulated altruism in technically engineered and managed 'communities'. This is especially the case in regulatory environments that nurture parochialism and exclusion rather than compassion and reconciliation, and which rely upon entrepreneurial self-interest for their very operations. In all this, one may legitimately ponder the plight of justice.

Acknowledgements

The author wishes to thank Warren Moran, Nick Lewis and Greg Blunden for their very helpful comments on an earlier draft of this chapter.

Notes

1   This chapter focuses on neo-liberal crime prevention initiatives in Aotearoa/New Zealand, but on the assumption that there are clear parallels with commensurate 'community policing' initiatives within the country (New Zealand Police Department 1985), international community crime prevention initiatives (Hope and Shaw 1988; Rosenbaum 1989; Bright 1991; O'Malley 1992; Crawford 1995, 1996a, 1996b) and other forms of community control (Pavlich 1996a; Stenson 1993; Leibrich 1992, etc.).

2   It is instructive to note that here the commissioners continue to articulate the view that social security measures should, 'continue to give effective support to the changing needs of an evolving society' (McCarthy 1971: 33).

3   This group was established by the New Zealand government Cabinet in 1992 to formulate a crime prevention strategy, and to report on how to achieve this practically (see CPAG 1992: 1).

4   A traditional-based tribal grouping.

5   Again, however, a close reading of the document underscores that the regulated 'individual' is not commensurate to that of social welfare rationales. Rather, that it is the responsible, prudent, consuming, enterprising self which dominates here.

6   Even if they are ideally to be included as 'at risk', characteristics of 'white-collar' and 'family violence' offenders prevents an easy identification of who comprises this 'target group' at this time.

7   Ominously, this document notes that Pacific Island people and other 'ethnic minorities' only comprise a small proportion of offenders and prisoners, but adds 'as migrant communities they fall into the "at risk" group' (CAPG 1992: 5).

8   The CPAG does note that crime prevention strategies should avoid the situation where victim outrage encourages the 'public' to demand 'short-term palliatives which could undermine the concept of a longer-term strategy' (CAPG 1992: 75).

9   See Crawford's congruent conclusion (1996a: 253).

References

Beck, Ulrich, Anthony Giddens and Scott Lash (1994), *Reflexive Modernization: Politics, Tradition and Aesthetics in the Modern Social Order*, Cambridge: Polity Press.

Bell, Vicki (1993), 'Governing Childhood: Neo-liberalism and the Law', *Economy and Society*, **22** (3), 390–405.

Bright, J. (1991), 'Crime Prevention: The British Experience', in K. Stenson and D. Cowell (eds), *The Politics of Crime Control*, London: Sage.

Burchell, Graham, Colin Gordon and Peter Miller (eds) (1991), *The Foucault Effect: Studies in Governmentality*, Chicago: University of Chicago Press.

Burchell, Graham (1991), 'Peculiar Interests: Civil Society and Governing "the System of Natural Liberty"' in G. Burchell, C. Gordon and P. Miller (eds), *The Foucault Effect: Studies in Governmentality*, Chicago: University of Chicago Press.

Burchell, Graham (1993), 'Liberal Government and Techniques of Self', *Economy and Society*, **22** (3), 267–82.

Butler, Nancy (1990), 'Gender Trouble, Feminist Theory, and Psychoanalytic Discourse', in Nicholson, Linda J. (ed.), *Feminism/Postmodernism*, New York: Routledge.

Cain, Maureen (1988), 'Beyond Informal Justice', in R. Matthews (ed.), *Informal Justice?*, London: Sage.

Castel, Robert (1991), 'From Dangerousness to Risk', in G. Burchell, C. Gordon and P. Miller (eds), *The Foucault Effect: Studies in Governmentality*, Chicago: University of Chicago Press.

Cohen, Stanley (1984), 'The Deeper Structures of Law; or Beware the Rulers Bearing Justice', *Contemporary Crisis*, **8** (1), 83–93.

Cohen, Stanley (1985), *Visions of Social Control: Crime Punishment and Classification*, Cambridge: Polity Press.

Crawford, Adam (1995), 'Appeals to Community and Crime Prevention', *Crime, Law and Social Change*, **22** (2), 97–126.

Crawford, Adam (1996a), 'The Spirit of Community: Rights, Responsibilities and the Communitarian Agenda', *Journal of Law and Society*, **23** (2), 247–62.

Crawford, Adam (1996b), 'The Local Governance of Crime: Whither Accountability and Social Justice?', paper presented to the Australian and New Zealand Society of Criminology Conference, Wellington.

Crime Prevention Action Group (1992), *Strategy Paper on Crime Prevention: Report on the Preliminary Stage of Analysis*.

Crime Prevention Unit (1994), *The New Zealand Crime Prevention Strategy*, Wellington: Crime Prevention Unit.

Dean, Mitchell (1994), *Critical and Effective Histories: Foucault's Methods and Historical Sociology*, London: Routledge.

Dean, Mitchell (1996), 'Foucault, Government and the Unfolding Authority', in A. Barry, T. Osborne and N. Rose (eds), *Foucault and Political Reason*, Chicago: University of Chicago Press.

Defert, Daniel (1991), '"Popular Life" and Insurance Technology', in G. Burchell, C. Gordon and P. Miller (eds), *The Foucault Effect: Studies in Governmentality*, Chicago: University of Chicago Press.

Deleuze, Gilles (1979), 'The Rise of the Social', Foreword in Jacques Donzelot, *The Policing of Families*, New York: Pantheon Books.

Deleuze, Gilles (1992), 'Postscript on the Societies of Control', *October*, **60** (1), 3–7.

Department of Justice, New Zealand (1968), *Crime in New Zealand*, Wellington: Government Printer.

Department of Social Welfare, New Zealand (1973), *Juvenile Crime in New Zealand*, Wellington: Government Printer.

Diamond, Irene and Lee Quinby (eds) (1988), *Feminism and Foucault: Reflections on Resistance*, Boston: Northeastern University.

Donzelot, Jacques (1979), *The Policing of Families*, New York: Pantheon Books.

Donzelot, Jacques (1988), 'The Promotion of the Social', *Economy and Society*, **17** (3), 395–427.

Donzelot, Jacques (1991), 'The Mobilization of Society', in G. Burchell, C. Gordon and P. Miller (eds), *The Foucault Effect: Studies in Governmentality*, Chicago: University of Chicago Press.

Etzioni, Amitai (1993), *The Spirit of Community: The Reinvention of American Society*, New York: Touchstone.

Ewald, François (1991), 'Insurance and Risk', in G. Burchell, C. Gordon and P. Miller (eds), *The Foucault Effect: Studies in Governmentality*, Chicago: University of Chicago Press.

Ewald, François (1991), 'Norms, Discipline and the Law', in R. Post (ed.), *Law and the Order of Culture*, Berkeley: University of California Press.

Feeley, Malcolm and Jonathan Simon (1994), 'Actuarial Justice: the Emerging New Criminal Law', in David Nelken (ed.), *The Futures of Criminology*, London: Sage.

Finlay, A. Martyn (1973), *Prediction in the Prevention, Detection and Treatment of Criminal Offenders*, Wellington: Price Milburn.

Foucault, Michel (1977), *Discipline and Punish: The Birth of the Prison*, New York: Vintage.

Foucault, Michel (1978), *The History of Sexuality: An Introduction*, vol. 1, New York: Pantheon Books.

Foucault, Michel (1979), 'Governmentality', *Ideology and Consciousness*, **6** (Autumn), 5–21.

Foucault, Michel (1980), *Power/Knowledge: Selected Interviews and Other Writings, 1972–1977*, Brighton: Harvester Press.

Foucault, Michel (1981a), 'Foucault at the College de France I: A Course Summary', *Philosophy and Social Criticism*, **8** (2), 235–42.

Foucault, Michel (1981b), 'Foucault at the College de France II: A Course Summary', *Philosophy and Social Criticism*, **8** (3), 351–59.

Foucault, Michel (1981c), 'Sexuality and Solitude', *London Review of Books*, 21 May–2 June: 3–6.

Foucault, Michel (1981d), 'Omnes et Singulatum', in S. McMurrin (ed.), *The Tanner Lectures on Human Values*, vol. 2, Cambridge: Cambridge University Press.

Foucault, Michel (1982), 'The Subject and Power', in H. Dreyfus and P. Rabinow (eds), *Michel Foucault: Beyond Structuralism and Hermeneutics*, Chicago: University of Chicago Press.

Foucault, Michel (1984), 'What is Enlightenment?', in P. Rabinow (ed.), *The Foucault Reader*, New York: Pantheon Books.

Foucault, Michel (1988), 'Technologies of the Self', in L. Martin, H. Gutman and P. Hutton (eds), *Technologies of the Self: A Seminar with Michel Foucault*, Amherst: University of Massachusetts Press.

Foucault, Michel (1989), *Foucault Live (Interviews 1966–1984)*, New York: Semiotext.

Gordon, Colin (1987), 'The Soul of the Citizen: Max Weber and Michel Foucault on Rationality and Government', in S. Lasch and S. Whimster (eds), *Max Weber, Rationality and Modernity*, London: Allen & Unwin.

Gordon, Colin (1991), 'Governmental Rationality: An Introduction', in G. Burchell, C. Gordon and P. Miller (eds), *The Foucault Effect: Studies in Governmentality*, Chicago: University of Chicago Press.

Gray, Alison (1993), *An Evaluation of the Safer Communities Council Pilot Scheme*, Bound Report.

Hawtin, Murray, Geraint Hughes and Janie Percy-Smith (1994), *Community Profiling: Auditing Social Needs*, Milton Keynes: Open University Press.

Hayek, F. (1976), *The Mirage Foucault Social Justice*, London: Routledge & Kegan Paul.

Heelas, Paul and Paul Morris (eds) (1992), *The Values of the Enterprise Culture: The Moral Debate*, London: Routledge.

Hope, Tim and Shaw, Margaret (eds) (1988), *Communities and Crime Reduction*, Home Office Research and Planning Centre, London: HMSO Publications.

Hunt, Alan (1993), *Explorations in Law and Society: Toward a Constitutive Theory of Law*, New York: Routledge.

Hunt, Alan (1996a), 'Governing the City: Liberalism and Early Modern Modes of Governance', in A. Barry, T. Osborne and N. Rose (eds), *Foucault and Political Reason*, Chicago: University of Chicago Press.

Hunt, Alan (1996b), *Governance of the Consuming Passions: A History of Sumptuary Law*, New York: St Martin's Press.

Hunt, Alan and Gary Wickham (1994), *Foucault and Law*, London: Pluto Press.

Johnston, L. (1992), *The Rebirth of Private Policing*, London: Routledge.

Kelsey, Jane (1993), *Rolling Back the State: Privatisation of Power in Aotearoa/New Zealand*, Wellington: Bridget Williams Books.

Kelsey, Jane (1995), *The New Zealand Experiment: A World Model for Structural Adjustment?*, Auckland: Auckland University Press/Bridget Williams Books.

King, Michael (1988), *How to Make Social Crime Prevention Work: The French Experience*, London: NACRO.

Leibrich, Julie (1992), 'Against the Odds: Community Based Care and Psychiatric Disabilities in New Zealand', in P. Close (ed.), *The State and Caring*, London: Macmillan.

Mabbot, J. (1993), 'The Role of Community Involvement', *Policy Studies*, **14** (2), 27–35.

McCarthy, Thaddeus P. *et al.* (1971), *Report of the Royal Commission of Inquiry: Social Security in New Zealand*, Wellington: Government Printer.

McIntyre, W. David and W.J. Gardiner (1971), *Speeches and Documents on New Zealand History*, Oxford: Clarendon Press.

McKissack, I.J. (1973), 'An Overview of Delinquency and its Prevention', in *Symposium on the Prevention and Treatment of Delinquent/Anti-Social Behaviour in Children and Adolescents*, edited by D.R. Mitchell, Hamilton: University of Waikato.

Mahood, Linda (1995), *Policing Gender, Class and the Family: Britain, 1859–1940*, London: UCL Press.

Manukau Safer Community Council (1995), *Manukau: a Safer Community Plan, 1995–2000*, Report.

Miller, Peter (1992), 'Accounting and Objectivity: The Invention of Calculating Selves and Calculable Spaces', *Annals of Scholarship*, **9** (1/2), 61–86.

Miller, Peter and Nikolas Rose (1988), 'The Tavistock Programme: The Government of Subjectivity and Social Life', *Sociology*, **22** 93), 171–92.

Miller, Peter, and Nikolas Rose (1990), 'Governing Economic Life', *Economy and Society*, **19** (1), 1–30.

Mitchell, D.R. (ed.) (1973), *Symposium on the Prevention and Treatment of Delinquent/Anti-Social Behaviour in Children and Adolescents*, Hamilton: University of Waikato.

New Zealand Business Roundtable (1996), *Moving in the Fast Lane*, manuscript/pamphlet.

New Zealand Ministry of Justice (NZMJ) (1996), *Justice Matters*, Issue 1.

New Zealand Official Yearbook (1972), 'Evolution of Social Security in New Zealand', Wellington: Department of Statistics.

New Zealand Police Department (1985), *Community Initiated Crime Prevention*, manuscript with mimeos of readings.

O'Malley, Pat (1992), 'Risk, Power and Crime Prevention', *Economy and Society*, **21** (3), 252–75.

O'Malley, Pat (1996), 'Risk and Responsibility', in Barry, A., T. Osborne and N. Rose (eds), *Foucault and Political Reason*, Chicago: University of Chicago Press.

Pasquino, Pasquale (1978), 'Theatrum Politicum. The Genealogy of Capital – Police and the State of Prosperity', *Ideology and Consciousness*, **4** (Autumn), 41–54.

Pavlich, George C. (1995), 'Contemplating a Postmodern Sociology: Genealogy, Limits and Critique', *Sociological Review*, **43** (3), 548–72.

Pavlich, George C. (1996a), *Justice Fragmented: Mediating Community Disputes Under Postmodern Conditions*, London: Routledge.

Pavlich, George C. (1996b), 'The Power of Community Mediation: Government and Self-Formation', *Law and Society Review*, **30** (4), 707–34.

Peters, Michael and James Marshall (1988), 'Social Policy and the Move to "Community"', two submissions to *Future Directions: Associated Papers*, for The Royal Commission on Social Policy, *Appendix to the Journals of the House of Representatives of New Zealand*, 1987–90, vol. XV, Wellington.

Pitch, Tamar (1995), *Limited Responsibilities: Social Movements and Criminal Justice*, London: Routledge.

Prisons Department (1936), *Report, 1936*, New Zealand Appendix to the Journals of the House of Representatives, vol. iii, H-20.

Raeff, Marc (1983), *The Well-Ordered Police State: Social and Institutional Change Through Law in the Germanies and Russia, 1600–1800*, New Haven: Yale University Press.

Report on Crime in New Zealand (1969), Wellington: Government Printer.

Rice, Geoffrey (1992), 'A Revolution in Social Policy, 1981–1991', in G. Rice (ed.), *The Oxford History of New Zealand*, Auckland: Oxford University Press.

Richards, Raymond (1994), *Closing the Door to Destitution: The Shaping of the Social Security Acts of the United States and New Zealand*, Pennsylvania: Pennsylvania University Press.

Rose, Nikolas (1990), *Governing the Soul: The Shaping of the Private Self*, London: Routledge.

Rose, Nikolas (1992), 'Governing the Enterprising Self', in P. Heelas and P. Morris (eds), *The Values of the Enterprise Culture: The Moral Debate*, London: Routledge.

Rose, Nikolas (1994), 'Expertise and the Government of Conduct', *Studies in Law, Politics and Society*, **14**, 359–97.

Rose, Nikolas (1996), 'Governing "Advanced" Liberal Democracies' in A. Barry, T. Osborne and N. Rose (eds), *Foucault and Political Reason*, Chicago: University of Chicago Press.

Rose, Nikolas and Peter Miller (1992), 'Political Power Beyond the State: Problematics of Government', *British Journal of Sociology*, **43** (2), 173–205.

Rosenbaum, D. (1989), 'Community Crime Prevention: A Review of What is Known?', in D. Kenney (ed.), Police and Policing: Contemporary Issues, New York: Praeger.

Shearing, Clifford (1992), 'The Relation Between Public and Private Policing', in M. Tonry and N. Morris (eds), *Crime and Justice: Annual Review of Research*, vol. 15, Chicago: University of Chicago Press.

Simon, Jonathan (1987), 'The Emergence of a Risk Society: Insurance, Law and the State', *Socialist Review*, **95** (2), 93–108.

Simon, Jonathan (1995), 'Power without Parents: Juvenile Justice in a Postmodern Society', *Cardozo Law Review*, **16** (3), 1363–1419.

Sinclair, Keith (1969), *A History of New Zealand*, Harmondsworth: Penguin Books.

Squires, Peter (1992), *Anti-Social Policy: Welfare, Ideology and the Disciplinary State*, London: Harvester Wheatsheaf.

Steinmetz, George (1993), *Regulating the Social: The Welfare State and Local Politics in Imperial Germany*, Princeton, NJ: Princeton University Press.

Stenson, Kevin (1993), 'Community Policing as a Governmental Technology', *Economy and Society*, **22** (3), 373–89.

The Treasury (1987), *Government Management: Brief to the Incoming Government*, Wellington: Government Printing Office.

6 Governmentality, Neo-Liberalism and Dangerousness

John Pratt

In the mid-1990s a man in the United States gained extensive fame and attention: he was sentenced to life imprisonment for stealing a pizza. In fact, he had become one of the first and most notorious 'victims' of the State of California's 'Three Strikes and Out' legislation. These laws, which have swept across the United States, provide that two previous offences for sexual or violent offending followed by a third for a felony render the offender 'out' (using a baseball analogy) and thereby liable to mandatory terms ranging from 25 years to life imprisonment. However, such dramatic insistence on the punishment of persistence is currently by no means confined to the United States. Similar initiatives can be found across other English-based jurisdictions – for example, the Western Australia Crime (Serious and Repeat Offenders) Sentencing Act 1992. This was aimed at *'high risk juvenile offenders'*, and provided for the possibility of their indefinite detention: 'serious offences' were to include *'burglary, arson and stealing a motor vehicle aggravated by reckless or dangerous driving'*; a 'repeat violent offender' is one appearing for sentence on his/her fourth 'conviction appearance' in 18 months for a listed violent offence or the seventh for a listed serious offence with the last being for one of the listed violent offences (including resisting or preventing arrest, various assault offences, wounding, robbery, sex offences and homicide) (Broadhurst and Loh 1993: 2 [emphasis added]).

In Britain, the Conservative government proposed to introduce a form of 'Two Strikes' life imprisonment for those who commit 'serious violent or sexual offences' and furthermore 'burglars convicted three times would be subject to a minimum sentence yet to be fixed' (*The Independent*, 13 October 1995). The purpose of these measures, it was claimed, was to 'send shock waves through the criminal community ... [and to] put honesty back at the heart of sentencing and it will build a safer Britain' (ibid.). In addition, the government planned to introduce 'secure training centres' for juvenile offenders aged 12 to 14 years, 'who have committed one imprisonable offence whilst subject to a supervision order, and have committed two similar offences'. In such cases, sentencers would be 'asked to consider whether or not the offences are serious enough for such an order to be made' (see Hagell and Newburn 1994). In New Zealand the introduction of a form of 'reviewable sentence' – as proposed in the English Report of the Committee on Mentally Abnormal Offenders 1975 but not followed up at the time – has been considered (Law Commission 1994). This would be able to deal with 'a small number of people who pose a serious danger', drawing on the example of the Washington State Community Protection Act 1990 which 'authorizes a judge or jury to determine that an offender who is about to be released or has been released is a "sexually violent predator"'. If, after the offender has been evaluated by a professional, a judge or jury determines that the offender is a 'sexually violent predator', the offender is committed to a secure facility of social and health services. Again, persistence is the key, except that, in this case, the suggestion is designed to *prevent* repeated offending.

In addition to such specific proposals to punish persistence *per se*, there are also converging anxieties over a range of other apparently ungovernable groups whose very way of life becomes a threat to the well-being of the rest of the population: these include beggars and vagrants, mentally disordered offenders who, having been disowned by an asylum are left to roam the streets, and the homeless, particularly those now carrying some form of communicable disease. In one way or another, the penal measures or proposals against all these groups envisage an increase in the use of imprisonment. In some of these countries, this is already taking effect, with further huge increases predicted for the future. In New Zealand, for example, the prison population has increased by around 80 per cent over the last 10 years and is projected to increase by another 33 per cent over the next decade (Ministry of Justice 1995). In California, it has been estimated that its Three Strikes law will necessitate the building of 20 new prisons and that it will force the state to incarcerate 275 621 more inmates over the next three decades (Skolnick 1995).

As such, these new provisions and plans would seem to represent important points of departure from penal trends of the last 20 years or so. First, they indicate a broadening of the concept of 'dangerousness'. This penal status had been introduced to most Western penal systems in the early part of the twentieth century: although it was a rather loosely used term, it nonetheless referred to those criminals whose repeat offending endangered the rest of the population to such an extent that 'special measures' of protection were needed to control them. In other words, they were 'ungovernable' within the existing penal framework. Despite their repeat offending, they were manifestly not insane and could not be detained under those provisions in the criminal law but, as sane offenders, the only sanctions available to the court were finite terms of imprisonment which, as their repeat offending seemed to testify, had no effect. Hence the introduction of indefinite imprisonment as the only appropriate modality of governing them. Again, over the last two decades in virtually all these countries, this form of sentence had been narrowed and confined almost exclusively to recidivist violent and sexual offenders (particularly rapists). Indeed, in England, there had been a shift away from 'persistence' as a sentencing criterion altogether. In *R* v. *Queen*, the court of Appeal stated that 'the proper way to look at the matter is to decide on a sentence *which is appropriate for the offence* for which the prisoner is before the court' (1981, 3 Cr App Rep (s) 245 emphasis added). Furthermore, the extended sentence provision (a form of lengthened prison sentence specifically for those with records that demonstrated 'persistence') had been abolished by the Criminal Justice Act 1991, leaving the option of moving beyond the existing tariff framework only for those whose persistence made them dangerous. Initially, those judged to be dangerous largely consisted of small-time habitual property criminals, they were joined in the 1930s by certain groups of sex criminals – most notably the North American 'sexual psychopaths'. Nonetheless, these characters had more or less disappeared from the dangerousness framework by the mid-1960s, and it then came to be populated – at least until these recent developments – by a much narrower band of recidivist sexual and violent offenders (see Pratt 1995, 1996).

Second, such a tendency would also seem to mark a retreat from the principle of bifurcation as one of the dominating features of contemporary penality (see Bottoms, 1995). Bifurcation insisted on a quite rigid line of demarcation between the 'serious offender' (which, in contemporary usage was most likely to mean those who committed offences against the human body) for whom prison was essential and the non-serious (usually property) offender for whom some form of community-based sentence was more appropriate. If applied correctly, it was thought, prison populations would be reduced, affording a valuable saving to the state in both economic and human terms. Indeed, in the 1970s, a high prison population was considered to be a source of shame, to use the expression of the then British Home Secretary Roy Jenkins. Although the aim of lower prison populations as a result of this strategy was not really achieved there has undoubtedly been a qualitative shift in the nature of prison populations during the bifurcation era – in particular, a growing concentration of younger, more violent offenders (on Britain, see Morgan 1994; on New Zealand, see Braybrook 1992). With these new initiatives and the broadening of the concept of dangerousness itself, however, prison is clearly intended to be much more generally available. Instead of a dangerous few, we seem to be moving towards the idea of a dangerous many, which can include minor property offenders and so on.

Why then are these penal developments emerging – in direct contrast to the general direction of penalty of the last two decades? I suggest that, behind this shift in the governance of the dangerous, lies a merger between:

1   a continuing and overarching theme of modern penalty itself: that is, the onus on modern states to protect its citizens from 'the dangerous' – in other words, those whose persistent offending is thought to constitute a risk so great that the only way to control it is to move beyond the usual penal parameters and introduce 'special measures' (that is, the indefinite/indeterminate prison sentences that figure so prominently in current penal agendas); and

2   the way in which the shift in political rationalities – from welfarism to neo-liberalism – across these societies to a greater or lesser extent during the 1980s and 1990s has both mediated and reformulated the nature and extent of this 'right to protection', involving, *inter alia*, the creation of new risk groups and new strategies of risk management.

The Right to Protection

It has now become commonplace for the 'Three Strikes' laws and the like to be justified by reference to their embodiment of what has come to be regarded as a 'right' that citizens expect their governments to provide. This is clearly illustrated in the New Zealand parliamentary debates on the dangerousness issue during the 1980s. For example: 'the [Criminal Justice] Bill tries to achieve two separate purposes. *They are, first, that people have the right to be protected from violent crime and violent criminals and they expect the House to take a severe attitude towards violent crime*' (New Zealand Parliamentary Debates [NZPD] 1985, vol. 464, p. 5833, emphasis added). Similarly, draft Canadian legislation of 1993 was aimed 'at repeat, high-risk sex offenders ... there is clear consensus among Canadians that the government must have the power to keep these violent offenders in custody as long as their release poses a serious threat to society'. In 1996 the British government published a White Paper entitled *Protecting the Public*, in which it not only reaffirmed this commitment but also extended it into new areas, as indicated above (Home Office 1996).

This inscribing of the right to protection from those whose 'riskiness' seemed so great that they were regarded as 'dangerous' begins with the initial crop of such laws in the first decade of the twentieth-century. The English Prevention of Crime Act 1908 seems to have been the first to write this concept on to the statute book, and it clearly underwrote the laws that were then being introduced in corresponding jurisdictions. In New Zealand, for example, the then justice minister stated that:

... the object of keeping the habitual in the place of confinement to which I have referred is not so much for the purpose of punishment as for the protection of society ... the first object we must have in dealing with the criminal is the protection of life and property and the security of society as a whole ... I make the protection of society paramount and the reformation of the criminal secondary. (NZPD 1910, vol. 150, p. 348)

At that time, such initiatives were also in line with a broader series of developments indicative of the way in which risk management was then being established as an accepted part of the programme of government of the modern state: it was increasingly thought that the government had a duty to manage risks which had hitherto been thought to be natural phenomena, or which individuals were judged to have brought on themselves by their own lack of prudence – such as ill-health, poverty and unemployment – and risks that were posed by those who persistently broke the law. Thus, using the British legislation of the period as an example, we find action to provide protection against: the consequences of unemployment – the Unemployed Workmen's Act 1905; similarly, accidents at work – the Workmen's Compensation Act 1907; poverty in old age – the Old Age Pensions Act 1908; and unscrupulous employers – the Employers and Workmen Act 1875 and the Coal Mines Regulations Act 1887. A further series of initiatives introduced sets of minimum standards below which the ordinary conditions of human existence would no longer be allowed to slip, as, for example, in relation to housing conditions (Housing of the Working Classes Act 1905). However, in return for offering such protection against risk, the modern state also assumed increasing powers of administration and control over the lives of its subjects: to ascertain the extent of risk that individuals both posed and were threatened by, each individual by the same token had to become 'knowable' to the state through bureaucratic procedures of one kind or another. Indeed, in the case of *R* v. *White and Shelton* ((1927) 20 C App Rep 61), it was 'the accused's silence on his life' between two convictions that was the telling factor in proving persistence (or 'habituality', as it was then referred to) and thereby rendering him to preventive detention.

Furthermore, to give protection against risk, new powers were made available to the state: indefinite prison sentences to control persistent offenders were one such innovation. Yet, despite being designed to give public protection, these new penal measures were by no means universally popular when first introduced. We know through historical analysis of pre-modern societies that the relationship between law enforcement, punitiveness and the general public was much more fragile than seems to be the case today (Hay *et al.* 1975). What tends to be neglected though is the way in which this fragility continues into modernity itself. Thus, as we see detailed by Radzinowicz and Hood (1986) and Wiener (1990), a number of the early attempts to introduce laws against persistent offenders in the latter part of the nineteenth-century came to grief because of politicians' fears that the public would be very *hostile* to such measures. At that time it was clear that the relationship between state and citizen, the scope of protection that this entailed and the ways of enforcing this was perceived in much narrower terms than today: there was, it seems, a great deal of suspicion of state power and the way in which this might be used.

Such hostilities continued into the twentieth-century, as we see in the 1910 New Zealand case of the convict Joseph Pawelka. He had escaped from custody three times while awaiting sentence for offences of burglary and committed further offences of burglary and arson while a fugitive. He was also alleged to have killed a policeman. On his final recapture he was sentenced to three consecutive terms of seven years imprisonment and also sentenced to the equivalent of preventive detention – to be served thereafter. And yet, despite his crimes, public sentiments seemed very much on his side. Petitions against the *severity* of the sentence were sent to parliament. *The New Zealand Times* (9 June 1910) protested that

> ... from Pawelka expiation was due to society for many offences against the law. From society which shared so heavily in this man's guilt something was due to him, and the least of this was that he should have been given opportunity to atone for his sins. Has he been afforded this by a sentence declaring him a habitual criminal and sending him to gaol for so many years that on release he will be approaching fifty? It is impossible to think so.

These sentiments would be remarkable today. There may well be occasional cries for leniency in exceptional cases (for example, pregnant women, pensioners or again, reflecting changing values and sensitivities, abused women who defend themselves), but generally the mood is one of 'populist punitiveness ... this concept is rather different from "public opinion" pure and simple; instead, it is intended to convey the notion of politicians tapping into, and using for their own purposes, what they believe to be the public's generally punitive stance' (Bottoms 1995: 40). This then translates itself into a demand for more and fiercer punishment. Nonetheless, the Pawelka case is indicative of the historicized nature of the demand for public protection. It has *not* been a permanent feature of modern societies. Indeed, the last formal record of such opposition to special measures against the dangerous that I have been able to find appears in the English Report of the Committee on Sexual Offences Against Young Persons (Home Office 1925). Here, it was argued that preventive detention should be made available to the courts to sanction such offenders, notwithstanding the unpopularity amongst the public of such measures:

> ... we consider that special action is called for in cases of repeated sexual offences [against children] ... *we are aware that the public mind is distrustful of any kind of indeterminate sentence*, but we believe that a period of prolonged detention in a special institution might occasionally effect a cure. In any case it would protect the public more effectively than many short terms of imprisonment. (ibid., 25, emphasis added)

Thereafter, it seems that public opinion on these laws is regarded as unproblematic, as in the next official English commentary on these provisions, the *Report of the Departmental Committee on Persistent Offenders* (1932). As evidence of this shifting relationship between individual and the state that welfarism engendered, not only did it come to be assumed that public protection was now expected from governments, but the public insisted on this as a matter of right. Hence the continuous references to these rights and expectations in dangerousness discourse throughout the remainder of the welfare era: in Canada the 1938 Archambault Report claimed that 'we believe we are on safe ground in stating that no system can be of any value if it does not contain as its fundamental basis, the protection of society' (Archambault 1938: 140). And in the subsequent Canadian legislation – the 1946 Criminal Code Amendment Act s 75(b) – the criteria for preventive detention included three convictions for an indictable offence, leading a persistent criminal life and that the offender is 'one whose criminal habits and mode of life require a special type of detention for the protection of the public'. Section 21(2) of the English Criminal Justice Act 1948 states that 'if the court is satisfied that it is expedient for the protection of the public that [the offender] should be detained in custody for a substantial period of time'. In New Zealand, the Department of Justice (1954) declared that 'hardened criminals should be placed in custody for a long period of time in order that the community may be protected from them, and in order that they themselves may realise the futility of their criminal activities' (Department of Justice 1954: 6). The English 1967 Criminal Justice

Act made provision for the imposition of the extended sentence (replacing preventive detention for dangerous offenders) 'having regard to his antecedents and the need to protect the public'.

Of course, as outlined above, this commitment has since continued despite the shift to neo-liberal political rationalities of the 1980s and 1990s. But that it should become established at some point around the late 1920s, as the English reports suggest, is not without significance, since it was around this time that the sources of information on which we assess risk were being transformed. This did not *suddenly* happen in the late 1920s. More likely, this period represents a kind of crossover point in the predominance of different forms of risk assessment: that of early modern societies, in which risk assessment was still largely based on discussion with neighbours or kin, gave way to the risk assessment processes of modernity which rely on far more abstract sources of information – the mass media rather than neighbours, for example. In this way, the presentation of the risks and threats from the phenomenon of crime today have become both more globalized and more localized (Giddens 1990) As is well known, the way information about crime is presented makes it appear to be 'everywhere' and at the same time localizes its particular threat to us, however unequally the *real* threat of crime is distributed across the population – and however great the variation is the threat of *particular* crimes (Skolnick 1995). The popularization of the mass media, with its emphasis on crime stories towards the end of the nineteenth-century began this process. It then accelerated in the first half of the twentieth-century, with the expansion of the popular press, the growth of popular weeklies, cinema newsreels and so on. Then, in the postwar period, mass communication first proliferated and diversified and then underwent a technological revolution: this not only introduced us to new sources of information (for example, e-mail, the Internet, satellite television) but they also became a constant presence in our lives. At some point in this process – perhaps in the late 1930s[1] – the official crime statistics started to be regularly brought to the attention of media consumers as being the yardstick against which crime risks were to be assessed. Moreover, during the last 20 years, these statistics themselves have had to compete with a number of other sources which claim to represent truer measurements of crime and more accurate yardsticks of risk. These new sources include university-organized crime surveys, independent victim surveys, self-report studies, surveys conducted by telephone, those organized by sections of the media and so on – all of which claim to represent the reality of crime (albeit a different version of this reality) and a good many of which tell us that the world is an even scarier place than we thought it to be. Consequently, one of the more recent lines of criticism of the official crime statistics is that they minimize the crime risks faced by particular sections of the population (Young 1994).

Now it is not the authenticity of such surveys and reports that is the point here, nor do I wish to contest the very real levels of fear that some of them indicate. What I do want to suggest, though, is that these disparate 'regimes of truth' about crime risk are likely to have a dual effect. They do not simply tap into, and report back, hitherto unexpressed or unacknowledged fears and risks, they may also enhance fear, encourage its growth and add to the sense of uncertainty through their generalizing and localizing effects. Indeed, the self-protection and security industry has a vested interest in ensuring precisely these effects (Stanko 1990). Not surprisingly, the end result of the popularization of such truths is that they are accepted as such; and they become truths with effects such as the following, regarding womens' fears of sexual attack

> ... violence traps women in a web of fear. Women feel virtual prisoners in their homes after dark and want harsher punishments for sex offenders, including the return of capital punishment, a national survey of women's attitudes shows. A report compiled from 2 250 postcards from women reveals that they feel 'like outsiders, marginalized in a violent society, where they have little influence'. (*The Australian*, 18 May 1994)

This in turn – although by no means unproblematically – [2] feeds back into the sentiments of populist punitiveness and its demand for special measures of protection to the point where, today, this has become an inescapable duty of governments to provide. To retreat from this principle becomes politically unacceptable for any government, whatever the shade of party political opinion it claims to represent: hence the continuity of the dangerousness laws themselves, as part of the umbrella of protection from such risks that the state is expected to provide.

Changing Political Rationalities: from Welfarism to Neo-Liberalism

This remains the case despite the shift in political rationalities from welfarism to neo-liberalism that has been, to a greater or lesser extent, characteristic of all these societies during the 1980s and 1990s and which has correspondingly informed the strategies, tactics and objectives of government. In essence, this has involved moving the general burden of risk management away from the state and its agencies and on to the self, in partnership with non-state forms of expertise and governance. What has been needed to effect this task is a complete reorganization of the forms of economic and social life that existed under welfarism. Now, under neo-liberal rule,

... the well being of both political and social existence is to be ensured not by centralizing planning and bureaucracy, but through the 'enterprising' activities and choices of autonomous entities – businesses, organizations, persons – each striving to maximize its own advantage by inventing and promoting new projects by means of individual and local calculations of strategies and tactics, costs and benefits. (Rose 1992)

In addition to an intrinsic electoral popularity of many aspects of the programmes and ideology of neo-liberalism itself, it was helped to political dominance by a sustained economic and cultural critique of welfarism. In terms of economics, it appeared, during the 1970s, that the welfare state itself was no longer economically sustainable in the sense of overstretching government borrowing requirements to meet public expenditure and the high levels of personal taxation that were needed to sustain it. In addition, the services that it provided were increasingly thought to be inefficient, overbureaucratized and geared to the interests of their employees rather than consumers, except when, paradoxically, the 'scroungers and bludgers' that welfarism was thought to encourage received assistance (Dean and Gooby 1992). In addition, the security which these services and programmes were meant to bring seemed to be of dubious value. Taxation had progressively increased to sustain these programmes.[3] However, as apparent proof of welfare inefficiency, there was a steady growth of unemployment during the 1970s: in the United States, from 1971 to 1980, unemployment increased from 5.9 per cent to 7.1 per cent; in the United Kingdom from 3.5 to 7.4; in New Zealand from 0.3 to 2.9, and in Australia from 1.9 to 6.1. Meanwhile, to again offset perceived deficiencies in welfarism, this period witnessed the beginnings of what has subsequently become a huge growth in private health insurance: in Britain, membership of such schemes more than doubled between 1971 and 1983 (Gooby 1985); in New Zealand, around 45 per cent of the population are now covered by health insurance; in Australia, the figure is 34 per cent.

In effect, if welfarism, by the mid-1970s, had been able to raise living standards and alleviate some of the old pre-welfare risks associated with homelessness, squalor, pauperism and disease (thus downgrading the riskiness of some of the earlier dangerous criminals, particularly the petty thieves and property offenders), it was also creating a new set of risks which it no longer seemed able to govern. For example, it was increasingly unable to meet the social expectations that it had raised over the course of the century. Public health services had made a huge contribution to these raised expectations, but by this time were seen as being increasingly unable to maintain them – hence the growth of interest in private sector services. But instead of even more welfare being perceived as the solution, what was now needed, it was thought, was a general recasting of the relationship between the individual and the state (as set out in neo-liberal ideology) as a solution to the dilemmas that welfarism was now posing. The more it tried to guarantee security and minimize risk, the more it fostered dependency and established new risks – risks that were perceived as both the product of its own inefficiencies and its entrapment of its subjects. In contrast, neo-liberalism was prepared to release the entrepreneurial energies of its hero, 'the enterprising individual':

> ... in every country, a tiny minority sets the pace, determines the course of events. In the countries that have developed most rapidly and successfully a minority of entrepreneurs and risk-taking individuals have forged ahead creating opportunities for imitators to follow, have enabled the majority to increases its productivity. (Friedman 1980)

In effect, neo-liberalism claimed to offer a new sense of freedom – freedom from the supposed restraints and debilitating consequences of welfare – and an altogether new set of possibilities designed to maximize the potential of human existence. No longer the dependent subjects of welfare, satisfied with security and the safeguards that guaranteed their minimum conditions of existence, the enterprising individuals of this post-welfare period

> ... see the world as full of opportunities for making things happen; they do not hang back and wait to see what others will do before committing themselves to action; and they regard problems as there to be solved or overcome – not as objects of contemplative fascination, nor as occasions for self-doubt or dismay. Finally, enterprising individuals are keen to pursue the rewards that come from success in a competitive world. (Keat and Abercrombie 1991: 6)

Indeed, in further support of the enterprising individual (and thereby sustaining its own electoral popularity), neo-liberalism was prepared to penalize those subjects who seemed to find favour under welfarism by cutting state benefits, policing welfare applicants, toughening eligibility for state assistance in various ways and attacking crime (Taylor 1981); and it ensures that enterprise is rewarded by shifting the burden of taxation. This has meant a lowering of base rates of tax[4] and an increase in indirect levels of taxation – giving, it is claimed, individuals greater freedom in deciding how their money is to be spent. This does not mean, of course, that the neo-liberal state does not have minimum conditions of existence for it subjects any more; rather, it is as if the threshold of what the state is prepared to guarantee its subjects has been lowered – above this, individuals would be allowed to determine their own levels of existence. For all practical purposes, individuals will be allowed to reap the rewards of their own success to a greater extent than before, while at the same time, taking responsibility for risk management themselves, at least to a greater extent than in the heyday of post-war welfarism.

As such, the place and role of the state in the differing modalities of governing under welfarism and then under neo-liberalism can be contrasted as follows. On the one hand, Howard Jones, writing at a time which proved to be the apotheosis of welfarism, commented that:

> ... *the amelioration of social conditions is accepted in almost every civilized country as a proper function for governments to assume.* Though there is still more poverty about than some are willing to admit, the Welfare State has brought about a transformation of our national life, cured many social evils, and achieved a greater degree of social justice as between different classes in society than has ever been possible before. (Jones 1965: 150, emphasis added)

On the other hand, and in contrast, the purpose of government for Frederick von Hayek, one of the doyens of neo-liberal thought, was expressed as follows:

> ... rules of conduct ... are not designed to produce particular benefits for particular people, but are multi-purpose instruments developed as adaptations to certain kinds of environment because they help to deal with certain kinds of situations ... once we see that, in the absence of a unified body of knowledge of all the particulars to be taken into account, *the overall order depends on the use of knowledge; possessed by individuals and used for their purposes it becomes clear that the role of government in that process cannot be to determine particular results for particular individuals or groups, but only to provide certain general conditions whose effects on the several individuals will be unpredictable.* (von Hayek 1976: 5–13, emphasis added)

For Jones, reflecting welfarist rationality, the purpose of government is to determine what the outcome of the contests it makes possible will be. For von Hayek, however, the purpose of government is only to make the rules and to then let the contest be played out. But, as von Hayek also indicates, neo-liberalism does not mean that individuals will be 'ungoverned'; rather, to a greater or lesser degree, the state makes a range of withdrawals to the parameters of everyday existence and instead allows the rational, responsible subjects of its discourse to make choices for themselves concerning health, education and the like.

Here, then, is a new modality of governing under neo-liberalism. This is no longer exercised primarily through the state but is likely to be channelled through a plurality of mechanisms. Some areas, such as defence, still have the state at the epicentre of control; and in certain other respects, to ensure that its objectives are not undercut or challenged, or that the rules it sets in place are not subverted by bodies or institutions with vested interests or differing political agendas, the neo-liberal state has paradoxically been prepared to centralize more power in itself by, for example, setting national objectives and standards for organizations such as the universities, as well as the criminal justice bureaucracies (Bottoms 1995).

But, elsewhere, we find a model of government wherein individuals 'make their choices' about the course of their lives, but are guided by new forms of expertise that exist outside of the state apparatus. This does not mean that the state fades from view: it presides over these new ways of governing to give them authority (Donzelot 1979), while still being prepared to intervene should they break down or function inadequately. Yet it is more likely to police the parameters of these new domains of everyday existence, constituting a form of 'government at a distance' (Miller and Rose 1990). And to effect such a model of government the relationship between subject and state has to be recast: the dependent subject of welfarism, shielded from risks, and on whose behalf the state will intervene, is replaced by the juridical subject of neo-liberalism, now granted rationality and responsibility – free to decide for his/her self, as it were. Previous guarantees from the state have accordingly been reduced and replaced with 'rights' of various kinds that individuals may enforce against other citizens or former, but now usually corporatized or privatized, state institutions.

Governmentality, Dangerousness and Neo-Liberalism

Nevertheless, as we have seen, one right at least that the state owes to its subjects still lives on – the 'right to protection' from the dangerous. Even so, this reaffirmation from the state regarding its responsibilities in this area was to be modulated through a series of themes and issues specific to neo-liberalism – ensuring that the form and extent of state protection was both more refined and sharper than during the welfare era. Thus, post-1970, the dangerousness laws became much more tightly drawn. They became specifically targeted against sexual and violent offenders – particularly the rapist. If this served to ensure that the right to protection from the dangerous would thus be continued, it also demonstrated the changing nature of dangerousness itself and the new set of risks on which it fed post-1970 – the way in which concepts such as 'freedom', 'choice' and 'responsibility' were allowed to find expression in matters of personal morality. When then combined with increasing affluence and leisure they produced as their end-product the consumerized human body – the subject of a range of discourses designed, on the one hand, to maximize its potential as a source of pleasure and self-expression and, on the other hand, to alert us to the new dangers that this very process would lend itself to.

State protection against this more restricted group of dangerous offenders was thus to continue. Here again, though, the neo-liberal state was prepared to 'set the rules' in advance to safeguard its own values and interests from those organizations and interests that might stand in the way. This was evident in the subsequent New Zealand parliamentary debates on this matter:

> ... the list of offences to which preventive detention now applies has been doubled in the [Criminal Justice] Bill. The list not only includes sexual offences, as was the law, but a range of violent offences ... *there is simply no merit in the argument that the sentence should be extended willy-nilly.* It should be extended only so far as the research by the Department of Justice explains, and that shows that a connection between the committing of serious crimes of violence and the committing of crimes of a sexual nature such as rape. (NZPD 1987, vol. 481: 9535)

Indeed, the powers of the judiciary have thus been significantly curtailed and restricted to ensure that 'dangerousness' is applicable to those whom the state has already decided are likely to be dangerous. At the same time, this strategy undercuts one of the main bulwarks of opposition to the indeterminate sentence – the judiciary, which, throughout its history has generally been reluctant to use it (Morris 1951; Pratt 1997), primarily because, it would appear, the social defence principles which the indeterminate sentence incorporates have run so counter to the judicial *Weltanschauung*. As the English Court of Appeal stated in *R* v. *Sullivan*:

> ... it was necessary in the interests of the prisoner that very watchful care should be exercised by this court and also by those who preside over trials in which a prisoner is charged with being a habitual criminal [and thereby liable to preventive detention], to see that the prisoner's interests are jealously safeguarded, because ... he stands in a peculiar position, which is, to say the least of it, not a favourable one, when the trial of the particular matter takes place before the jury; that is to say, he is first of all convicted of the offence for which he is indicted, then he is put upon trial as an habitual criminal, and consequently, it is enough to say that one must be scrupulously careful to protect him when this particular question whether he is a habitual criminal or not is put to the jury. ([1913] CCA 205)

Furthermore, in the post-war period, indeterminate sentences were too closely associated with totalitarian societies – the only countries in which they had been used to any significant extent (Ancel 1965). Although for much of the nineteenth and twentieth centuries judges had been given a broad spectrum of sanctions to apply to given offenders as they saw fit, the neo-liberal state increasingly 'set the rules' in a form of 'systemic managerialism' (Bottoms 1995). The judges were told who and when they might send to prison and who they might not, as well as what kinds of persistent law-breaking constituted dangerousness and what did not.

At the same time, the specification of dangerousness by the state would also curb a tendency that ran in the opposite direction from the parsimonious use of these laws by suspicious judges: that is, the likelihood of psychological experts to *over-diagnose* dangerousness and thus unnecessarily waste expensive penal resources. In the United States case of *Baxstrom* v. *Herald* ([1966] 383 US 107), it was revealed that psychologists had been overpredicting dangerousness. This led to the mass transfer to civil state mental hospitals of large numbers of so-called dangerous inmates held in secure custody in the New York state institutions following the successful challenge to the legal basis for such commitments by the US Supreme Court. 'Few of the 992 inmates transferred were found in fact to require secure custody, and a substantial number were in very short order released altogether or continued as voluntary patients' (Price 1970: 41). In England, such a tendency posed a major ethical problem for the *Report of the Committee on Mentally Abnormal Offenders* (1975: 74):

> ... doctors and others who have responsibility for violent offenders are likely to err on the side of caution in deciding on their discharge and there can be little doubt that, as a result, some people continue to be detained who, if released would not commit further offences.

If, at the entrance to the penal system, the power of the judges has been undercut by legislation undermining their autonomy, so too, at its exit, the power of psychological experts to assess who should be released on parole has come to be eroded. Although there are clear differences of emphasis between jurisdictions, actuarial methods seem to hold the key towards more certain determinations of future offending, which is increasingly seen as the most important criterion in the decision to release dangerous offenders.[5] In New Zealand, a recent move towards actuarial calculation has been justified as follows:

> ... until now the [Parole] Board has approached its task in a clinical fashion. It has attempted to obtain the best available information about the individual seeking parole – the offender's background, prior offending, the present offence, behaviour and treatment during sentence, the offender's understanding of the causes of the offence and post-release plans – to assist in deciding if or when the

inmate ought to be released ... however, the Parole Board has a continuing obligation to seek to improve the quality of its decision making. To that end, it has examined the use of structured decision making instruments (SDM's) and policy guidelines by parole authorities in North America and has concluded that its adoption of similar systems would enhance the quality of its decisions. (Department of Justice 1996)

The result of these trends was that, by the early 1990s, a quite coherent picture of the way in which dangerousness was to be governed by the neo-liberal state was evident. First, notwithstanding the realignment of insurance mechanisms and provisions that had been set in place, the neo-liberal state was committed to protect its subjects from dangerous offenders. However, *simply* being 'repeat offenders' would not in itself suffice at that point to bring the dangerousness classification into play (O'Malley 1994). This was because dangerousness had become more streamlined and focused, with new forms of expertise being drawn on to sustain this intent, while the power and influence of those who might counterveil this tendency was restricted. At the same time, the concentration of dangerousness around sexual and violent offending – to the exclusion of earlier dangerous characters such as persistent petty offenders – expressed the changing nature of risk itself at this time. In terms of taking retributive action, the state put more value on the human body, particularly that of a women or child, than property. Crimes against the body constituted irreparable damage (Ewald 1991) whereas property could be replaced, compensated for by means of private insurance, designed out through a commitment to defensible space architecture, kept under surveillance and control by the formation of Neighbourhood Watch groups and so on; but essentially, it was expected that management of such crime would not be the responsibility of the state alone. Instead, an assortment of arrangements between state organizations, citizens' groups, insurance firms, the voluntary sector and so on has been brought into play.

Furthermore, those committing such offences were largely downgraded in penal importance and severity of sanction to be applied to them. Towards the end of the welfare era a new set of provisions had been envisaged for some of these criminals (in Britain it was to consist of state-provided homes, hostels and day training centres) in accordance with their new classifications as inadequate rather than dangerous – what risks they had once posed had now become manageable and insurable. However, such plans were largely discontinued by the neo-liberal state: providing such expensive resources for the harmless did not fit its programme of government – they would be expected to manage their own lives with minimal interest or support from the state.

At least, this was the position up to the early 1990s. Why has the concept of dangerousness been so significantly broadened through the provision of 'Three Strikes' laws and the like since then?

The Resurgence of Risk

To answer this question, let us first remind ourselves that, while the case of the pizza thief received considerable and understandable publicity, these measures, for the most part, are still aimed primarily at recidivist violent and sexual offenders: here, they confirm existing trends, reformulating them as appropriate or, as with Britain, realign the law in this area where there had been departures from these standards. But, beyond this, these new policies and laws can also be seen as a response to the new risk groups which have been created by neo-liberalism itself. If the space for this political rationality was created out of the failure of welfarism to respond to the risks that had been created by its very successes (Beck 1992), we see the same processes now taking place under neo-liberal rule. In particular, the subjection of economies to market forces and the cutting back of welfare programmes of assistance has led to the re-creation of risks which welfarism had alleviated – poverty, unemployment and the formation of a new indigent class of vagrants, beggars, the homeless, the mentally ill with criminal tendencies who now find themselves left to roam the streets, holding conversations with imaginary colleagues: an assorted collection of 'social junk' (Box 1987). Here, perhaps, is the sum of the cuts to welfare budgets and services which neo-liberalism had demanded.

But what is it, then, that turns 'junk' into danger? Perhaps the reason why these particular characters can now seem so risky is not so much that they have become 'unknowable' to the state, in the same way that the earlier class of dangerous offenders were: on the contrary, it would appear, from the various attempts that have been made to massage politically sensitive statistics such as the unemployment figures (which reveal the extent to which neo-liberalism has undercut welfarist assumptions and expectations), the state would prefer that they remain unknowable. Instead, their riskiness is assessed more perhaps on the basis of the affront and sense of menace that they create in public space – as if they pollute the glittering allure of the affluence that neo-liberalism has fostered there. It is as if they have become an intolerable reminder of the dark side of neo-liberalism. Thus the following letter to the *Washington Post* in 1994:

> What is so complicated about taking out a huge pile of trash? The pile, which is situated on Virginia Avenue, opposite the beautiful, new Western Presbyterian

Church at 24th Street, NW has been there for at least five months. The mound includes a big canvas tent, broken chairs, filthy blankets, large boxes and plain garbage. Inhabiting this is a vagrant who can be intimidating to those going to the Watergate to shop or to the Kennedy Center for a show. (Cited in Kress 1995)

Shopping, promenading, making the most of the affluence that neo-liberalism has given many of its subjects, is tainted by the visual reminders of the social cost that has accompanied with this. In these respects, then, perhaps it is the sheer dereliction of this new group – the beggars, vagrants, the mentally ill, the petty thieves and other likely targets of the broadening-out of dangerousness – which offends the sensitivities encouraged and developed by some two decades or so of neo-liberal rule and thought that now creates the offensiveness – sensitivities framed around the pleasures and plenitude that one can enjoy as an individual, rather than concern that the minimum conditions of existence for the population as a whole are being undercut by the neo-liberal programme of government.

What of the proposals against younger offenders and juveniles? Irrespective of the immediate and precipitating background of these measures,[6] it is as if the group of younger offenders at which they are aimed constitutes a residual category that had hitherto been governed by welfarist penal measures and thereby largely excluded from responsibility for their actions: the crop of measures against them effectively brings the modality of governing them more into line with neo-liberal trends. They represent something of a fine-tuning and updating of the neo-liberal dangerousness matrix. Instead of being 'exempted' by virtue of their age from the consequences of law-breaking, the rights and sanctions available to them are to be brought more in line with those available to the rest of the community: young people have in effect been given the right to be made criminally responsible for their actions. Or they demonstrate unpredictability and uncertainty in terms of the menace they pose: these permanently unemployed groups of youngsters who have nothing to lose from repeatedly committing crime and are not subject to any other normative controls or, alternatively, still manage to place themselves outside of the new systems of governance that the neo-liberal state has introduced to police and manage these aspects of their lives – specifically, perhaps, the UK Manpower Services Commission and its panoply of training programmes, 'education for life' curricula and make-work schemes (Pratt 1993; Finn 1987).

As for the proposed measures against burglars in England, this may reflect a need to bolster existing neo-liberal modalities of governing this area of criminality: in particular, reliance on insurance and self-help measures (with fading interest from the police) are unlikely to be sufficient to assuage public anxieties and sensitivities over such intrusions into personal life. Here, the 1991 proposals of the Home Office (*Crime, Justice and Protecting the Public*), whereby burglars would receive community sentences, were reversed in the 1996 publication, *Protecting the Public*, with its proposals for mandatory minimum terms. In these respects, the subtle but very significant change in title in the two documents is symptomatic of these growing public insecurities. Indeed, it is as if the more pervasive fear becomes, the more it becomes emboldened: now it is not only waiting for us in the darkness outside our homes, but is also beginning to probe the security we have put in place there, trying to find a way in, no longer patiently waiting for us as we tentatively emerge into the public territory which it has already colonized. This, again, would also demonstrate the way in which risk management itself is constantly being negotiated and renegotiated: should one set of strategies – the moves towards self-reliance – begin to appear unsuccessful, it becomes possible for the state to reintervene in this way and impose its own authority, under the guise that it is prepared to extend its assistance in support of a public which it still exhorts to 'take care of itself'.

At the same time, and running alongside the creation of these new risk groups which range from permanently unemployed young people, the diseased homeless, beggars, burglars, thieves and sex attackers, there are the undercurrents of anxieties and insecurities which exist independently of this and which drive penal policy in these new directions – anxieties and insecurities that begin to creep in to everyday life when one experiences the disembedding processes that neo-liberalism has ushered in impermeable anxieties and insecurities, the product of removing welfare structures of dependency and support which had been set in place for around half a century. As a result, everyday life as a whole becomes fraught with tensions. If neo-liberalism had been able to free its subjects from the risks created by welfare policies and programmes, it has also succeeded in carrying out a form of risk regeneration: new possibilities of pleasure, a raising of the thresholds set down for the minimum conditions of existence that its subjects now had a right to expect in these societies through their own efforts – alongside a lowering of the thresholds that the state was now prepared to guarantee – as well as new values associated with one's body, one's appearance and its significance, are continuously counterbalanced by the risks and dangers that these new ways of conducting oneself bring into being. While opportunities for self-fulfilment and indulgence have been increased, risk too has been enlarged.

It is these anxieties which continue to drive penal policy as it targets these new kinds of dangerous individuals or dangerous groups who are represented as undermining the security of everyday life in the sources of information on which crime risk is assessed. Dangerousness owes its existence and new form to them and not to the official crime statistics which have faded further into the background of risk assessment. If these were its sole determinants, we would know that the great explosions of crime rates that took place during the early 1960s through to the mid-1980s have been followed to a large extent by a stabilizing of crime trends and, in some countries a decline, at least according to these sources. However, this is largely obscured by the growing importance of new databases which vie with one another to illustrate that crime is moving in the opposite direction, and which are then brought home to us with growing intensity as mass media technology becomes more sophisticated and pervasive:

> ... fear of crime tends to be higher and rises with publicity. Crime reportage has long been the staple story of the evening news; and the volume of television news has exploded in the past thirty years. Moreover, in the postmodern world of satellite technology, a crime committed in Petaluma, California, frightens the viewers in Poughkeepsie, New York. (Skolnick 1995: 6–7)

Overall, the new laws and formulations of dangerousness can be seen as the product of a number of divergent, but coalescing, trends. These relate to the creation of new risk groups, a further erosion of modalities of governing which bore the imprint of welfarism, and the continuous enhancement of risk in everyday information sources. Nonetheless, once this new collection of dangerous figures has been brought together, then the neo-liberal state, in the last few years, has been prepared to broaden its dangerousness specifications to include them within it.

The Relegitimation of Prison

In virtually all these new cases of ungovernability, the state has promised to meet it with some form of indefinite or quasi-indefinite incarceration, irrespective of the potential that this has for increasing the prison population. Towards the end of the welfare era, high levels of imprisonment were becoming a source of shame in modern societies: as risks had been reduced and security more embedded, overflowing prisons became a sign of the state's inhumanity towards its unfortunates and of its ineffectiveness in its chosen modalities of governing. Those societies with the lowest imprisonment rates, such as the Scandinavian countries and the Netherlands, were regarded as the most progressive – the most important role models for societal development in the West. But now the anxieties that used to be expressed, during the welfare era, by liberal critics, politicians and justice department officials alike about the 'unacceptability' of prison levels above a certain number have largely evaporated from the planning of penal policy. The justice officials find that they can live with higher prison populations – and, indeed, are planning and budgeting for them. For politicians, rather than being a sign of the state's inhumanity towards its unfortunates, a high prison population becomes a symbol of virility in the urgent fight against crime: as with the 'Three Strikes' discourse and the more general commitments to extending the availability of indeterminate imprisonment, it becomes a signifier of the extent to which the state is prepared to guarantee protection from unacceptable risks.

What, then, has made this commitment to increasing prison populations a logistic probability which the neo-liberal state can now accept, it seems, with equanimity? For much of the period from the late 1970s onwards, it seemed that the notion of 'containment' had come to replace rehabilitation as an official prison policy. Prison, it was now claimed, could achieve nothing constructive for its inmates, nor was there any point in it being used as some sort of residual 'home' for the inadequates: this was only another form of welfare dependency. Therefore it should be used as a penal sanction for those who *had to be* incapacitated (Greenwood and Abrahamse 1982) and thereby ensure that its use would be in line with the bifurcation principle. There were, in effect, two versions of what 'containment' might mean. In its liberal–reformist version (King and Morgan 1980), containment was to mean the prison would conform to a fixed set of basic minimum standards which would be legally enforceable (in line with the growing recognition of the legal status of prisoners themselves). In the more sinister version of containment, it meant little more than 'warehousing' (Cohen 1977), with conditions well below the minimum threshold of existence that one would expect to find in Western societies. However, hidden from the rest of the population, such regimes could control their inmates by pacifying them with drugs (Sim 1990) and/or by the introduction of increasingly sophisticated electronic technology. In some jurisdictions, this warehousing aspect of prison has become even more intensified: indeed, as some of the recent North American developments, such as the reintroduction of chain gangs in the state of Alabama illustrate, the mood of populist punitiveness seems to allow penal conditions which a couple of decades ago would have been unthinkable and too 'shameful' to contemplate. Nowadays there need no longer be any coyness about the extent to which prison is again to be made intolerable for its recipients, as states seem to compete with each other to set new yardsticks of inhumanity.

However, what we also find at the present time are some significant moves in the government of prisons and prisoners which run in the opposite direction. These incorporate ideas of changing prisoners' conduct through self-determination – ideas which clearly have more resonance with neo-liberal thinking than mere containment. Whatever the outcome, it allows for the possibility of even the supposedly irrational seeing the logic of rational behaviour, and it conforms to economic priorities regarding the need to maximize state resources, rather than using the prisons as human warehouses to achieve nothing. As Pat O'Malley has suggested,

> ... from an advanced liberal perspective it is this which distinguishes its programme from the earlier approaches [i.e. welfare correctionalism and classic liberalism], for it seeks through the calculus of punishment primarily to press upon the offender (and the potential offender) the model of individual responsibility. Accepting responsibility for one's actions does not imply accepting or obeying any specific set of morals. It implies accepting the *consequences* of one's actions. The individuals may choose, are free to choose, in a way and to a degree never envisaged by normative disciplinarity – but if these choices lead into criminal offending, they must take the burden of their choice. (O'Malley 1994: 14)

In this new model of governance, the prisoner's progress through the penal system is, within certain clear constraints, a matter for them to decide, as is the recognition of their own guilt, shortcomings, problems and ways in which these may be remedied. These principles have been written into what, on the face of it, might appear to be a residue of the rehabilitation era to be found in some prisons. In New Zealand, a 'treatment programme' for a group of prisoners with sexual offences in their history

> ... provides an opportunity for the offender to recognize [treatment goals] and to learn strategies to change his behaviour and beliefs. In particular, distorted beliefs, dysfunctional patterns of emotional responding, and personal and social skills defects are targeted for change. A balance is achieved between an educative approach and process-oriented learning, whereby naturally-arising situations in the therapy groups are explored and utilized *to help the men learn about themselves and develop more appropriate social behaviours and self-concepts.* The ways in which the offender overcame his own, the victim's, and other social restraints to offending, permits comprehensive planning for his future, through adopting a 'life long plan' for avoidance of further molestations. (Department of Justice 1994)

For such regimes of self-help and responsibility to come into effect, prisons themselves must change or, to use Richard Sparks' (1994) term, they must be 'relegitimated'. 'Warehousing' is not only inappropriate for this but is actually counterproductive: it denies the model of the rational, responsible subject prepared to make choices about the course of his/her life, since it denies them any choices in the material conditions of existence it reproduces for prisoners; and it allows prisons as institutions to degenerate to such an extent that they begin to offend sensitivities – those of the public and officials alike. Hence, in Britain, the Woolf Report of 1991, an inquiry into prison disturbances the previous year,

> ... breaks with the assumptions of prior official statements ... all of which regard the maintenance of legitimate authority in prisons as *essentially* unproblematic, albeit *practically* difficult at times. By the same token Woolf has no particular attachment to 'rotten apple' or 'powder keg' theories of prison riots which attribute the existence of trouble to a shared sense of injustice. What flows from this in policy terms is a significant extension of the scope of legal formality in prison management, especially in relation to grievance and disciplinary procedures. (Sparks 1994: 20)

In Woolf, and in coincident documents in New Zealand and Australia (Roper 1989; Kleinwort-Benson Australia Ltd 1989; Kennedy 1988), we find the emergence of a new vision for the prison and a new form of language in which this is articulated: strategic plans and mission statements are being written which refer to matters such as 'quality control' and ascribe to standards of 'excellence'. The internal regime is to achieve these objectives by making programmes, activities and other forms of self-help available to its inmates. By making the appropriate choices from this assortment of possibilities, they are thus to determine their own progress through the institution and the improvements they can make to their life. Such a regime would also be guaranteed by minimum safeguards – hence the emphases in current prison discourse on 'justice', 'legitimate expectations' and so on.

This process of relegitimating the prison is perhaps even more clear-cut in New Zealand – and was presaged by the Roper Report of 1989. Here, too, the old model of prison life (that is, prison as a rehabilitative process) was found irrelevant and inappropriate to the political and social climate of the late 1980s. It was to be replaced, and largely has been, although not exactly in the manner envisaged by Roper, by introducing the concept of 'habilitation' (meaning 'to furnish or equip for life') as the purpose of prison. Essentially, 'habilitating' seems to involve the same process of self-determination and choice within prescribed possibilities, as that envisaged by Woolf. This is to be achieved through the 'case management approach'. Such programmes, 'while having a non-authoritarian atmosphere, demand and cultivate a strong sense of personal discipline in the participants' (Roper 1989: 36). In addition, each 'programme'

> ... must be based on a social learning model rather than a medical model of treatment. That is to say it must emphasise the acquisition of new skills, language and behaviour rather than the curing of an illness. Considerable

emphasis must be placed on the inmate confronting his or her criminal behaviour and on the enforcement of pro-social behaviour. Realistic and socially appropriate problem-solving must be re-emphasised in the programme. The programme must establish a therapeutic or educational culture which is reflected in the quality of the relationship between staff and inmates. The relationship should be positive and challenging rather than negative and punitive. (Roper 1989: 37)

And thus, although the picture is by no means clear-cut, what I have tried to suggest here is that we can see the emergence of a modality of governing prisoners which is broadly in line with neo-liberal thinking, particularly in so far as this is predicated on the prisoners disciplining themselves by means of updated techniques and knowledges. As such, it helps to relegitimate the prison and to make it once more a central feature of the penal universe, rather than something shameful, to be hidden in the shadows and only brought into play as a last resort.

At the same time, these changes in the internal management of prisons are facilitated by the harnessing of other strategies to the building of the new prison – both physically and ideologically. To this end, parole has already been modified to be more in tune with the necessity to calculate the future risk of those prisoners being considered for early release. More generally, the continuous tinkering with its rules for eligibility and the release mechanisms that it can provide results in a faster turnover of bedspace as well as providing for a holding function for increasing numbers likely to be punished for longer because of their persistence in crime. To this effect, while 'truth is sentencing' may have been introduced in some jurisdictions such as New South Wales and in parts of the United States, elsewhere parole itself has not been abolished but refurbished, to bring it more into line with neo-liberal expectations. Introduced in most of these jurisdictions towards the end of the welfare era, when it was thought possible that prisoners reached some optimum point in their response to treatment and should be released accordingly (Home Office 1965), it is now dictated much more by notions of risk to the public (Brown 1994). This, in turn, makes parole a much more heterogeneous strategy, rather than a uniform arrangement that runs across the prison population. As in the case of New Zealand, for those serving relatively short periods of imprisonment, it can come into play at an earlier period than before (in some cases one-third, in others half of the sentence); for those serving longer periods, it can come into play at two-thirds of the sentence, be denied altogether for 'serious violent offenders' against whom the state has decided in advance that the public risk of reoffending would be too great; in the case of those sentenced to indefinite imprisonment, it can become available after a minimum period of 10 years' imprisonment has been served (again, decided in advance by the state; see the Criminal Justice Act 1993), or after a longer non-parole period, stipulated on sentence by the presiding judge, has been served. Here, judges are still allowed some sentencing autonomy, but only in so far as this does not contradict the minimum expectations of the state regarding an appropriate penalty.

Similarly prison privatization is a means to not only cut the cost of prison itself (thereby making it more economically palatable as a sanction), but, by also undercutting the power of public sector employees, it helps to confirm this emerging new image of the prison. In New South Wales, the Kleinwort-Benson Report put the matter as follows '... the private prison could be used as a precedent for introducing an alternative style of management or accelerating change within public prisons' – in addition to its potential as a money saving strategy. Indeed, what we see from such examples is that wholesale privatisation is not needed to achieve the relegitimation of prison: the partial use of privatisation, or even the threat of it, when harnessed to the corporatization of each prison, as in New Zealand, has been sufficient to ensure quite dramatic change in internal management structures. Equally, the new technology and architecture to be found in prison design[7] – perimeter fencing, backed by elaborate close circuit surveillance, surrounding improved and sanitized internal living arrangements – helps in this process of relegitimation.

What these trends point to – both the brutalizing prison warehouse on the one hand and the relegitimated prison on the other – is a new set of tactics which make possible the governance of those now judged to be dangerous. As this category has been reshaped and broadened out to encompass the new risk groups generated by neo-liberal politics, so too do these tactics of government bear the imprint of neo-liberal thinking. We have moved from the attempts to restrict prison use at the start of this period to a position where increased use of prison becomes not only a managerial possibility but a source of political strength and popularity – a way of giving assurances to an increasingly frightened and insecure public.

Acknowledgements

I would like to thank Arie Freiberg for comments made at a seminar given at the Department of Criminology, University of Melbourne, which have since helped to influence the shape of this chapter. An earlier version of it was presented as a paper at the International Conference on 'New Forms of Governance: Theory, Research and Practice' at the Centre of Criminology,

University of Toronto, 25–6 October 1996. I would like to thank the various participants for the helpful comments that were made on that occasion.

Notes

1 In Sutherland's (1950) analysis of the American sexual psychopath laws, changes in the official statistics on sexual offending received significant press coverage in the late 1930s. Other than this, there seems to be no historical analysis of *when* publication of the official crime figures prompted the sensationalized media coverage we take for granted today actually began – although clearly, by 1970, such coverage had become commonplace (see Wiles 1971).

2 By no means all the social movements involved in the demand for protection see this as taking the form of tougher laws.

3 In Britain, in 1979, just prior to the Thatcher success in the election which ensured the commitment to neo-liberalism, basic rates of tax ranged from 25 per cent to 60 per cent of income; in New Zealand, in parallel circumstances in 1984, they ranged from 20 to 66 per cent.

4 In Britain these now range from 20 to 40 per cent; in New Zealand they range from 20 to 33 per cent.

5 The most thorough analysis of actuarialism as a new penal phenomenon is to be found in Simon (1993).

6 For example, the Western Australian legislation was introduced after the death of a pregnant Perth woman on Christmas Eve – she was run down by joyriding teenagers; the English secure training centres were devised in the aftermath of the enormous *angst* produced by the murder of two-year-old James Bulger by two ten-year olds.

7 At least, these are the current trends in prison design in Australia and New Zealand; see, for example, Corrections Corporation of Australia Pty Ltd (1995).

References

Ancel, M. (1965), *Social Defence*, London: Routledge & Kegan Paul.

Archambault, Mr Justice (1938), *Report of the Royal Commission to Investigate the Penal System of Canada*, Ottawa: King's Printer.

Beck, U. (1992), *Risk Society*, London: Sage.

Bottoms, A.E. (1977), 'Reflections on the Renaissance of Dangerousness', *Howard Journal of Penology and Crime Prevention*, 16 (1), 70–96.

Bottoms, A.E. (1995), 'The Politics and Philosophy of Sentencing', in C. Clarkson and R. Morgan (eds), *The Politics of Sentencing*, Oxford: Clarendon Press.

Box, S. (1987), *Recession, Crime and Punishment*, London: Macmillan.

Braybrook, B. and P. Southey (1992), *Census of Prison Inmates*, Wellington: Department of Justice.

Broadhurst, R. and N. Loh (1993), 'Sex and Violent Offenders: Probabilities of Reimprisonment', paper presented to the Australian Institute of Criminology, Canberra, Symposium on Offender Management.

Brown, M. (1994), 'Serious Offending and the Management of Public Risk in New

Zealand', Wellington: Institute of Criminology, Victoria University, unpublished manuscript.

Cohen, S. (1977), 'Prisons and the Future of Control Systems', in M. Fitzgerald *et al.* (eds), *Welfare in Action*, Oxford: Martin Robertson.

Corrections Corporation of Australia Pty Ltd (1995), *Borallon Correctional Centre: Excellence in Corrections and Project Management*, Queensland: Corrections Corporation of Australia.

Dean, H. and P. Taylor Gooby (1992), *Dependency Culture*, London: Wheatsheaf.

Department of Justice (1954), *A Penal Policy for New Zealand*, Wellington: Government Printer.

Department of Justice (1994), *The Kia Marama Programme for Sexual Offenders*, Wellington: Department of Justice.

Department of Justice (1996), *The Parole Board: Structured Decision Making*, Wellington: Department of Justice.

Donzelot, J. (1979), *The Policing of Families*, London: Hutchinson.

Ewald, F. (1991), 'Insurance and Risk', in Burchell, G., C. Gordon and P. Miller (eds), *The Foucault Effect: Studies in Governmentality*, Chicago: University of Chicago Press.

Finn, D. (1987), *Training without Jobs*, London: Macmillan.

Friedman, M. (1980), *Free to Choose*, New York: Harcourt Brace Jovanovich.

Giddens, A. (1990), *The Consequences of Modernity*, Cambridge: Polity Press.

Gooby, P. Taylor (1985), *Public Opinion, Ideology and State Welfare*, London: Routledge & Kegan Paul.

Greenwood, P., and A. Abrahamse (1982), *Selective Incapacitation*, Santa Monica: Rand.

Hagell, A. and T. Newburn (1994), *Persistent Young Offenders*, London: Institute of Policy Studies.

Hay, D. *et al.* (1975), *Albion's Fatal Tree*, London: Allen Lane.

Home Office (1925), *Report of the Departmental Committee on Sexual Offences Against Young People*, London: HMSO, Cmnd 2561.

Home Office (1965), *Adult Offenders*, London: HMSO, Cmnd 2852.

Home Office (1991), *Crime, Justice and Protecting the Public*, London: HMSO.

Home Office (1996), *Protecting the Public*, London: HMSO.

Jones, H. (1965), *Crime in a Changing Society*, London: Penguin.

Keat, R. and N. Abercrombie (1991), 'Introduction', in R. Keat and N. Abercrombie (eds), *Enterprise Culture*, London: Routledge.

Kennedy, J. (1988), *Commission of Review into Corrective Services in Queensland, Final Report*, Queensland: Government Printer.

King, R. and R. Morgan (1980), *The Future of the Prison System*, Farnborough: Gower.

Kleinwort-Benson Australia Ltd (1989), *Stage 1 Report: Investigation into Private Sector Involvement in the New South Wales Corrective Service System*, Sydney, New South Wales.

Kress, J. (1995), 'Homeless Fatigue Syndrome: The Backlash against the Crime of Homelessness in the 1990s', *Social Justice*, **21** (1), 85–103.

Law Commission (1994), *Community Safety: Mental Health and Criminal Justice Issues*, Wellington: Parliamentary paper E31V.

Miller, P. and N. Rose (1990), 'Governing Economic Life', *Economy and Society*, **19** (1), 1–31.

Ministry of Justice (1995), *Forecasting New Zealand's Prison Population*, Wellington: Government Printer.

Morgan, R. (1994), 'Imprisonment', in M. Maguire *et al.* (eds), *The Oxford Handbook of Criminology*, Oxford: Oxford University Press.

Morris, N. (1951), *The Habitual Criminal*, London: Longman.

O'Malley, P. (1994), 'Penalising Crime in Advanced Liberalism', unpublished paper, Melbourne: Department of Legal Studies, La Trobe University.

Pratt, J. (1983), 'Reflections on the Approach of 1984', *International Journal of the Sociology of Law*, **11** (4), 339–64.

Pratt, J. (1995), 'Dangerousness, Risk and Technologies of Power', *Australian and New Zealand Journal of Criminology*, **28** (1), 3–32.

Pratt, J. (1996), 'Governing the Dangerous: An Historical Overview of Dangerous Offender Legislation', *Social and Legal Studies*, **5** (1), 21–36.

Pratt, J. (1997), *Governing the Dangerous: Dangerousness, Law and Social Change*, Sydney: Federation Press.

Price, R. (1970), 'Psychiatry, Criminal Law Reform and the Mythophilic Impulse: On Canadian Proposals for the Control of the Dangerous Offender', *University of Ottawa Law Review*, **4**, 1–61.

Radzinowicz, L. and R. Hood (1986), *A History of English Criminal Law*, Vol. 5, London: Butterworths.

Report of the Committee on Mentally Abnormal Offenders (1975), London: Home Office, Cmnd 6244.

Report of the Departmental Committee on Persistent Offenders (1932), London: HMSO Cmnd 4090.

Roper, C. (1989), *Report of the Ministerial Committee of Inquiry into the Prison System*, Wellington: Government Printer.

Rose, N. (1992), 'Governing the Enterprising Self', in Heelas, P. and P. Morris (eds), *The Values of the Enterprise Culture*, London: Routledge.

Sim, J. (1990), *Medical Power and the Prison*, Milton Keynes: Open University Press.

Simon, J. (1993), *Poor Discipline*, Chicago: University of Chicago Press.

Skolnick, J. (1995), 'What Not to Do About Crime', *Criminology*, **33** (1), 1–14.

Sparks, R. (1994), 'Can Prisons be Legitimate?', in R. King and M. Maguire (eds), *Prisons in Context*, Oxford: Oxford University Press.

Stanko, E. (1990), 'When Precaution is Normal: A Feminist Critique of Crime Prevention', in L. Gelsthorpe and A. Morris (eds), *Feminist Perspectives in Criminology*, Milton Keynes: Open University Press.

Sutherland, E. (1950), 'The Sexual Psychopath Laws', *Journal of Criminal Law and Criminology*, **40** (4), 543–54.

Taylor, I. (1981), *Law and Order: Arguments for Socialism*, London: Macmillan.

von Hayek, F. (1976), *Law, Legislation and Liberty*, London: Routledge & Kegan Paul.

Wiener, M. (1990), *Reconstructing the Criminal*, Cambridge: Cambridge University Press.

Wiles, P. (1971), 'Criminal Statistics and Sociological Explanations of Crime', in W. Carson and P. Wiles (eds), *Crime and Delinquency in Britain*, London: Martin Robertson.

Young, J. (1994), 'Incessant Chatter: Recent Paradigms in Criminology', in M. Maguire *et al.* (eds), *The Oxford Handbook of Criminology*, Oxford: Oxford University Press.

7 Governing the Young

Richard V. Ericson and Kevin D. Haggerty

Society consists of myriad institutions, each with a relatively autonomous system of governance. Governance is organized in terms of risk management technologies that simultaneously identify dangers and help do something about them. A major component of risk management is sorting people into population categories that identify who is at risk and who poses a risk. This 'taming of chance' through construction of population categories has been central to modern liberal governance for two centuries (Hacking 1990; Miller and Rose 1990; Burchell, Gordon and Miller 1991; Rose and Miller 1992). Governance has meant surveillance of populations in order to develop statistical probabilities about them that will assist in judgements of social utility, health and happiness.

While surveillance of institutional populations at risk remains the governing basis of society, there are significant social changes occurring that affect how and why risk management is conducted. It is reasonable to contend that we now live in a 'risk society' because of the perpetual manufacture of new risks, and the extent to which all institutions are therefore driven by demands for knowledge of risk (Beck 1992a, 1992b; Giddens 1994; Beck, Giddens and Lash 1994; Ericson and Haggerty 1997). There are new emergency needs – for example, health risks such as AIDS. Populations are highly mobile, creating new demands on institutions to find better ways of tracing, risk-profiling and trusting them. Science and technology have not only managed risks but created new ones, and these are responded to with even more scientific and technological solutions that generate more risks in an amplifying spiral. Computers represent a technological change of particular significance in that they enable new formats of risk communication and instant dispersal of knowledge of risk to interested institutions. With the swipe of a credit card, passport, library card, driver's licence, health card and so on, local knowledge immediately enters into distant institutional databases. The databases, rather than the individual bureaucrat, become the basis of governance through knowledge. Knowledgeability becomes systemic, operating at institutional more than individual levels (Nock 1993; Gandy 1993; Altheide 1995).

While each institution develops its own peculiar risk management criteria and technologies – credit cards for retail markets, transcripts for educational credentialism, passports for citizenship and national identity and so on – there is also a great deal of risk communication between institutions. For example, as we argue more fully elsewhere (Ericson and Haggerty 1997), the primary role of the police is risk communication to and from other institutions. Through their routine surveillance and reporting practices, the police provide other institutions with knowledge for their own systems of risk management.

In this chapter we examine police collaboration with other institutions in providing knowledge of risk regarding one particular population category – namely, youth. We initially elaborate on the police role in constructing population categories. We next consider why the police pay particular attention to young people, followed by an empirical analysis of three specific programmes in which the police join with other institutions to govern the young. In school-based programmes, police officers function simultaneously as security educators, informant system operators, counsellors and gatekeepers for special programmes that deal with youths at risk. In deselection programmes for high-risk youths, the police rely on their own surveillance systems, along with those of other institutions, to calibrate the degrees to which the chosen few should be excluded from social life. In programmes for tracing missing children, the police also work with other institutions to ensure that all youths are accounted for in risk management terms. Analysis of each of these programmes illustrates how the police operate at the fulcrum of risk communication systems for governing the young.

Population Identities

A directory of social services produced and distributed by a police organization includes the following 'long-range objective': 'To promote a professional police image by demonstrating impartial service to the law, and by offering service and friendship to all members of the public without regard to gender, race, religious beliefs, ancestry or place of origin'. This objective is proper for a public institution officially dedicated to consensus and order. However, like full enforcement of the law and suppression of all crime, it represents one of the 'impossible mandates' (Manning 1977) set for the police. The police are asked to be agents of a cultural coherence that does not exist. They will have no luck in sustaining cultural coherence than did anthropologists who originally devised that notion with reference to the Zande. As it turned out, the Zande peoples had 20 culturally alien groups and eight languages.

In risk society, impartial service to law and community identities is impossible because the police are compelled to work within the identity categories of other institutions and to differentiate in their terms. In order to effect their own forms of risk management, these institutions require, for example, that: young people be treated differently than older people, people of higher financial standing be given different forms of insurance and lines of credit than those of lower financial standing; minority groups be given selected access to institutional resources; and so on. Working within the identity categories of other institutions, the police inevitably reproduce the forms of differentiation within those institutions.

Differentiation is the relentless product of the 'panoptic sort' (Gandy 1993) among institutions in risk society. It creates social group identities for the purpose of differential treatment. While it thereby allows the legitimate needs of particular groups to be met, it also excludes others. Inclusion and exclusion do not necessarily entail prejudice (negative preconceptions) or discrimination (unjust selection), although prejudice and discrimination are often built into the classification schemes of differentiation and thereby become institutionalized.

Institutions are the authorial source of identities. People identify their selves with their institutional categories of risk and the differentiated needs which those categories urge. Individual identity is confirmed within the classification schemes and expert knowledges of institutions. '[A]n individual must find her or his identity amid the strategies and notions provided by abstract systems' of risk (Giddens 1990: 124). Thus individuals are 'inherently non-self-sufficient entities. The individuals so constituted must rely on forces they do not control to gain satisfactory control of themselves' (Bauman 1992a; see also Douglas 1986).

The police author peoples' identities within the terms of established risk categories. Far from being original or creative authors in this work, the police merely fit the person to the categories available in the management systems of external institutions. All police reporting on the actions they have taken offers 'a set of messages about the groups, selves and identities of participants. This is the case regardless of the self-conscious intentions of those involved' (Manning 1980: 96). These messages are 'the primary products of police organizations ... conveying statements to social groups about their moral well-being, their social position (horizontal and vertical rankings), identity, and status' (Manning 1988: 53–4).

Researchers with a structural focus argue that police involvement in processes of differentiation and identity construction is above and beyond what can be observed in their routine work. Differentiation is analysed largely in terms of prejudice and discrimination and inequality is said to be structured 'historically' and at a 'macro' level above and beyond the minutiae of daily policing tasks. This view has been put forward, for example, by Brogden, Jefferson and Walklate:

> This sketch of the profane reality of policework – waiting, watching, serving, form filling, etc. – can obscure what the history chapter has so relentlessly revealed: the bias in police attention towards particular powerless groups ... The patterns of such bias will provide the key to understanding how policework relates to the wider structure of society – its role in relation to society's social divisions – in ways which attention to the most obviously visible and time-consuming feature of police work, the mundane, uncontroversial matters cannot. (Brogden *et al.* 1988: 101)

To the contrary, we argue that the most mundane aspects of police work – routine surveillance, form filling, and indeed the forms themselves – reveal a great deal about how the culture classifies people in terms of their identities and, through the power of risk classification, keeps them in their places.

As Beck (1992a, 1992b; Beck, Giddens and Lash 1994) observes, ascribed identities such as age, race and gender have new political significance in risk society. They are given significance through risk communication systems that make evident, with all the precision of actuarial science, the ascribed categories of social inequality. The new politics of risk identities is manifest in '*ascribed* differences and inequalities of race, ethnicity, nationality, gender, age and so on; second, in new and changing differentiations which arise from reflexivity in the domain of private social relations and private ways of living and identity. Thus, new social lifestyles and group identities inside persistent social inequalities begin to emerge' (Beck 1992a).

One important manifestation of this politics of risk identities is new social movements that focus on victims. People in various ascribed identity categories – for example, women (spousal abuse), children (child abuse), the elderly (elder abuse), and ethnic and racial groups (discrimination) – give voice to their victimization with the assistance of government (Rock 1986, 1990), science (Hacking 1995) and mass media (Chermak 1995). The police have become part of the victims movement through the routine production of risk-relevant data on ascribed characteristics, data that are used by other institutions to address the movements' criteria and claims. In this work the police help other institutions determine which ascribed identities will be granted 'residence permits' and ultimately 'citizenship status' in the land of late modernity, and which ones will be deported (cf. Bauman 1992a). In other words, what is at stake is the policing of symbolic borders that make clear who is one of us and who is the other and, within acceptable boundaries, where those among us should be assigned so that they least disrupt the rational and efficient flow of institutional life. Bauman's observations on ethnic categories are instructive:

> [W]e will accept, after Fredrik Barth, that ethnic categories provide an organizational vessel that may be given varying contents and forms in different sociocultural systems. They may be of great relevance to behaviour, but they need not be; they may pervade all social life, or they may be relevant only in limited sectors of activity; that the continuous existence of an 'ethnic category' depends solely on the *maintenance of a boundary*, whatever are the changing cultural factors selected as the border posts; that it is in the end 'the ethnic *boundary* that defines the group, not the cultural stuff that it encloses'; that all having been said and done, the very identity of that cultural stuff (its 'unity', 'totality') is an artefact of firmly drawn and well guarded boundary, though the designers and guardians of borders would as a rule insist on the opposite order of causality ... Identity stands and falls on the security of its borders, and the borders are ineffective unless guarded. (Bauman 1992b: 678–9)

In what follows we examine the police role in patrolling the borders of youth. The data are derived from a broader research programme on policing and risk communication. We studied risk communication systems in a number of Canadian police organizations through open-focused interviews with police personnel, observation of their work activities and analysis of their documents (for more details, see Ericson and Haggerty 1997).

Attending to Youth

There is substantial evidence that the police give 'overattention' (Brogden *et al.* 1988: 112) to patrolling the borders of youth. For example, in a field study of police patrols in Ontario, Ericson (1982) found that youths in general, and young males of lower socio-economic standing in particular, were disproportionately subject to proactive stops, searches, questioning and contact card reports. Within the police culture the population with these identity characteristics were referred to collectively as 'pukers,' signifying their status as outside the mainstream and therefore in need of extra surveillance. Similarly, a study of police patrols in London, England, revealed that 'younger people were much more likely to be stopped than older people, by a factor of about 11 to 1 in terms of the proportion of people stopped or about 30 to 1 in terms of the mean number of stops per person' (Policy Studies Institute 1983: 95).

There are many reasons for this overattention. First, young people are simply involved in more illegal activity, especially in public places.

Second, a lot of this activity is behaviour that would be deemed legal if engaged in by adults, for example drinking alcoholic beverages, being temporarily absent from an educational institution, driving automobiles and congregating in public places. Consider, for example, the requirement in one police jurisdiction we studied of a special application for a '*Teenage Dance Permit*'. No similar application was required for adults. This application is a risk screening device whereby the police ascertain who is sponsoring and supervising the event and whether a name band will appear that might invite unruly behaviour.

Third, some of his illegal activity is related to the fact that youths are acquiring skill and experience regarding activities in which adults are more accomplished and experienced. For example, youths are a high-risk category as drivers and are targeted accordingly. As explained by an accident data analyst we interviewed, statistical categories are created to target particular problems, such as impaired driving, and particular problem populations, such as youth.

> [D]rinking and driving is basically the young drivers. A lot of the statistics come … from what you [decide to] collect. If you don't have it you don't even know target groups that you've got to give this to. You don't just gear your advertising campaign, if you will, to everybody. Just like a private advertiser doesn't just send his money anywhere. He targets an audience … You have to target people where you get results. And culture is sometimes as important in accidents as in statistics.

Fourth, the wider culture constitutes youth as a symbolic threat. Disorderly youths are an expression of 'respectable fears' (Pearson 1983) about disorder and decline in general. 'If the statistical involvement of youth in crime provides the justification for police attention to them, it would appear to be the *image* of "deviant" youth as *potential* trouble, or symbolic threat to authority, that structures much of police thinking and practice in this area' (Brogden *et al.* 1988: 103). The reality of this image is recognized by the police in their efforts to proactively remove unsightly youth from sites where they pose a risk to peoples' sense of well-being and business enterprise. For example, in a document regarding downtown development prepared by a police crime prevention unit, in collaboration with government, corporate and retail businesses, it was stated that 'street youth' are

> … 'abnormal' users of an environment (Newman 1972). They accentuate the differences between themselves and normal downtown users. These differences may inspire uncertainty and a fear of the unknown in normal users. While these street/youth people may not increase the actual danger in the downtown, there is a marked increase in the perception of danger. Social strategies to assist street

youth/people are an important factor in improving the perception of downtown public safety.

The emphasis here is on '*social* strategies'. The result of police overattention to youth is not heavy criminalization through prosecution and punishment. The vast majority of youths arrested in Anglo-American juris-dictions are cautioned by police and diverted rather than prosecuted in court. For example, in England and Wales in 1990, 72 per cent of juvenile males and 85 per cent of juvenile females arrested were cautioned by police rather than charged and prosecuted in court (Evans 1993: 2–3). In an Ameri-can jurisdiction studied by Meehan (1993), there was little community or police administrative demand for formal processing of juvenile suspects, resulting in 'a shift to surveillance and the development of internal record-keeping as the primary form of control'. Most juveniles are not scathed by formal prosecution and punishment, but marked on police records. These records are kept for possible police uses in the future and for distribution to other institutions. The result is further overattention, as knowledge of the juvenile's involvement with police is selectively moved to health, education and welfare institutions.

School Programmes

An analysis of police programmes in schools illustrates how they join with other institutions in governing the young.

The police have a long history of serving as expert educators in schools. In particular, they visit schools to provide instruction on traffic safety and personal security. Larger municipal police organizations usually have full-time officers dedicated to such education. Their role often extends to over-seeing and evaluating safety patrol units operating within schools.

Police education to school students has broadened in recent years. The cultural obsession with the risks of drugs has placed drug education on school curricula, and the police are brought into the schools as experts. Some police organizations have full-time 'drug awareness' officers who lecture to schools and other interested institutions. These officers have usually acquired their expertise by working as narcotics detectives, but they are expected to stay on top of the latest drug-using habits and risk analyses thereof. A police drug specialist whom we interviewed said that full-time experts were needed be-cause of their expert knowledge of their young audiences.

[T]he experience and background will add to the credibility. When you stand up in a high school with a bunch of kids in there they may be using drugs and they may be a lot more knowledgeable in drugs than that policeman standing up there. They can make it pretty hot and heavy for them if he doesn't know what he is talking about ... [Our instructors] are coming off of drug sections. They've been involved in drug enforcement in the past and it's a matter of taking their drug investigational knowledge, tying it into their presentational abilities, skills, and going out and selling a product.

The police also have an intimate regular presence in schools to help identify high-risk youths and to collaborate in their risk management. A junior school programme studied had four full-time police officers and a social worker who was also a police employee. The social worker was hired initially to help the police gain acceptance in the schools. The original justification of the programme was the need for education about the risk of delinquent activity, especially use of illegal drugs, but the programme expanded rapidly into other areas. A person involved with the programme explained the place of the educational component in relation to broader concerns about risk and security.

Drugs is the medium ... but we've got programmes that talk about self-esteem, problem-solving, peer pressure ... It's [drugs] something that's in the news and in the media and all that kind of stuff, so it's a good way to catch kids attention ... There's this concern in school about violence now ... And I predict that pretty soon the people that make the videos will pick up on that as a medium and develop some good programmes to deal with it ... [but] the underlying message is always the same ... to get the students familiar with the officer who will be in the school ... The real thing that we're trying to do is to be accessible to the students and to the parents and the teachers ... A kid blows up ... calm him down and get him back to the classroom. The teaching staff don't have time to do it.

This respondent estimated that the formal educational component comprised 25–30 per cent of the officer's time in the school, providing something for her to do while students are in classrooms. However, school security functions are also mandated, whether the problem is disruptive children, trespassing by strangers or aggressive parents. Moreover, the key to fulfilling this mandate is risk knowledge production and management.

The first risk assessment was at the level of schools as organizations. 'High needs' or high-risk schools were selected in terms of an epidemiological analysis of a wide range of population health problems such as truancy, nutrition, misbehaviour at school and crime. This panoptic sort of the population of school organizations was followed by a parallel sort, using the same criteria, of individual students. An official publication of the police organization described this risk management approach explicitly, stating that the programme offers police 'outreach services to selected elementary schools ... identifying children (primarily in grades 4, 5 and 6) who are experiencing problems, and assisting with the coordination of a multi-agency effort to help these children and their families'.

High-risk children were identified through a wide range of informants. There was input from officials in health and welfare agencies, schoolteachers and counsellors, and parents. Home visits were sometimes deemed necessary. The children themselves were primary informants, often relating problems that were not school-specific. A programme official stressed that:

[S]tudents and their parents ... can access the officer about anything they want. And they don't necessarily have to let the school know. We've got disclosures of sexual abuse, physical abuse from kids. And we've got parents coming seeking information on marriage separation, wife battering, husband battering ... The officers can make referrals to any community agency ... We advise the [school] principal that we've done that.

Members of the unit refrained from keeping formal intelligence files on children. However, they kept notes on potential high-risk children, and used a student profile form to rate welfare history, school history, special problems, collateral agency contacts, and criminal history of the family. As explained by a programme official:

We've consciously tried to keep away from the officers starting to keep files on kids. That was one of the concerns that the schools have had about, 'Are you here to gather intelligence on students?'. We can say that we don't keep files on kids, and we don't. The officers do, though, keep their notes on kids who they have a concern about ... so they get a picture of kids that they're trying to monitor.

The various knowledges were brought together at case conference sessions involving the school's police officer and staff, as well as invited members of other agencies. The school record was tabled alongside all other records, and higher-risk individuals were identified. The individuals so identified were required to receive counselling by outside agencies or by the school police officer himself. As described by a police member, there was

... counsel in the sense of trying to find out what the problem is. And then get the student and the family to the resource that can best deal with the problem ... There's some students that are more behaviour problems. The student is taken out of class and actually spends time with them [a police officer] one-on-one, playing board games. We've got some officers doing, building models with groups of kids ... who have trouble interacting with their peers ... If these kids can be truly identified at the early stages, and if they can establish some sort of bond with a police officer, maybe they will think twice about the person they might be letting down if they go out and get in trouble.

The three dozen or so most risky individuals were placed into a risk management system set up to track them throughout their school careers.

The police saw their work in this school programme as exemplifying the inter-institutional partnership aspect of community policing. An official police statement on the programme stated that an objective was 'to promote proactive police involvement in the community, and improve police relations through open communication and understanding'. A police officer echoed this statement by observing that '[we are] using the school as a base, it is true community-based policing, it's not reactive at all'.

The official statement also emphasized that 'the officer's effectiveness is enhanced if he/she is viewed as being a member of the school staff'. According to one police official we interviewed, officers in the programme were indeed viewed as school staff.

> [Officers are] part of the staff almost ... get consulted ... participate in the ... School Resource Group ... case conferencing ... [T]he problems can be academic behaviour, whatever ... The officer might have a role to play, an equal role to play in the school. They really have worked their way into more of a, almost a staff position, an extra resource. The resource just happens to wear a uniform and has a different viewpoint.

We also studied a police programme in high schools that had 12 full-time uniformed police officers and a sergeant. Unlike the school programme analysed above, the selection of high schools was not based on those deemed to contain the highest risk populations. Selection on this basis was seen to be too 'political': the school board would have to admit officially that some schools were especially troublesome, which would stigmatize them and affect students' decisions about which schools to attend. School selection was based on population size. Each police officer was stationed in one of the largest high schools, but also visited a smaller high school and/or a junior school in his area at least one day each week. The police office was usually next to the office of the school guidance counsellor, and there was a close working relationship between them.

This programme was in stark contrast to the situation that pertained prior to its implementation. Previously, there were no police officers stationed in the schools and problems were only dealt with reactively. Uniformed patrol officers were prohibited from entering the schools for investigative purposes. They were required to enlist plain-clothes juvenile bureau officers because these plain-clothes officers were the only ones authorized by the school board to deal with cases.

As one respondent remarked, this high school programme exemplifies community policing as total involvement in an external institution. 'They are the only members of the department that face 2 000 citizens day in and day out all under [one] roof ... There's much more of accountability in a school setting to follow up and do everything you possibly can to alleviate somebody's problems or stress level because you're going to see them in the hallway the next morning ... and they're going to be asking.' The programme also illustrates how community policing is set up to facilitate communications policing (Ericson, *et al.* 1993; Ericson and Haggerty 1997). The same respondent stated that 'the whole purpose of this programme was to, in a kind of outreach way, obtain better communication, better attitudes, particularly among young people towards uniform police officers'.

This programme sought communication for the purpose of preventive security and enforcement. The classroom education component was explicitly directed at moral lessons about crime and related evils. Eleven out of 15 'canned' talks focused on serious crimes and the law: the Criminal Code, Young Offenders Act and Charter of Rights and Freedoms; provincial and municipal laws; impaired driving; theft and vandalism; sexual assault and date rape; organized crime and youth gangs; family violence; shoplifting; drugs and alcohol; runaways; and, arrest and the court system. The remaining talks were on driver education, bicycle safety, anger management and suicide, the role of the police and police careers. In addition, the school police officer sought opportunities to integrate police instruction with courses in the academic curriculum. For example, a police traffic management specialist was brought into a mathematics class to show how formulas and measurements are part of practical police work. In keeping with their strong sense of what counts in risk society, the programme members kept accurate records of all of this activity. In a 12-month period they recorded 812 presentations to a total audience of 27 009 students.

These presentations had several purposes and effects. They provided knowledge about legal institutions and processes, helped promote awareness that the police are problem-solvers and stimulated new problems for them to solve. A programme participant related that, after recent presentations on suicide prevention, there were 'now four people we've identified with suicidal problems in those classes and I helped to set straight'.

The classroom was only one of the many contexts in which the school police officer elicited knowledge about risks. The officer worked to establish a trusting relation with individual students that would eventually pay off in the currency the police value most, risk-relevant knowledge. A school programme officer described his knowledge work in this regard:

I want to get involved with the new ones on a one-to-one basis so if they have a need then they'll come to me without being intimidated or scared, or [concerned] that I'm going to publicly announce what they come in to see me about. When they come in to see me I always have my window blind down so nobody can see in. I have to give them that confidentiality when they're with me ... So there's always that stigma attached to it ... [A] student wants to see me behind [closed doors] in my office, confidential matters. I also provide that *service* to them. In fact, just this week I had one, was very startling actually. She had information on a major hydroponic operation in the city and we're dealing with that as an informant.

Another person involved in the programme stressed the significance of having informants, but indicated that there was a fine line between providing a reactive 'service' and proactively recruiting informants.

Our sole function wasn't to go there and develop informants in the school community ... However ... working in the school situation, working anywhere ... you get information. And then being policemen, we're in the information business, so we will take that information. We'll call it intelligence in many cases, and we will channel it to the proper department internally here, or to another agency if required. But we don't recruit informants at the high school level or the junior high school level. But on the other hand, if a kid comes in and wants to pass on some information, we will treat that as confidential information from a confidential informant basically, and then pass it on to the appropriate members or department or agency to deal with it.

At the time of the research there was continuing tension over whether to make the information function more visible and explicit. From its inception the programme was under suspicion of being a guise for a 'narcs' unit, and this suspicion lingered. At the same time, risk society is a knowledge society in which *informing* is promoted as not only legitimate but an act of good citizenship. This positive image of being an informant is fostered by the police and mass media through various electronic wanted poster shows such as Crime Stoppers (Carriere and Ericson 1989), Crime Watch UK (Schlesinger and Tumber 1994) and America's Most Wanted (Cavendar and Bond-Maupin 1993). People are strongly urged to join the police in their suppression of undesirable conduct by reporting anyone or anything suspicious.

Crime Stoppers had some presence through posters placed on school walls. There was a desire by some, however, to have a full-time student-based Crime Stoppers operation. Others argued this approach would make the informant-centred nature of police presence in schools too obvious. A compromise plan was a school watch programme, which a respondent described as helping to

... make the students be responsible for the security of their school. It's similar but not the same as Crime Stoppers. There's no reward for it. If there's something going on in the school that somebody sees, then they'll report it. There's going to be a box set up where they can put the information in a box, slide [us anonymous tips] ... So they will look after the security of the school. And then, if there's something that we can grab and run with it, that's what we'll do. We'll charge somebody or have it ground-out for investigation if it's in the community. One or two of the schools have started it. It started down in Florida and it seems to be working very well.

The community policing idea of making everyone responsible for their own security permeated the school programme. School staff were regarded as security agents, an embodiment of Robert Peel's original community policing ideal that 'the police are the public and the public are the police' (Task Force 1974). A school police officer said of schoolteachers 'They're security guards also, not just for me ... [and] I'm not just a uniform walking around there ... I am a staff member. We're all staff members ... I'm just like you or anybody else ... we all deal with the same problems'.

This conception of security collaboration allows the police to naturalize their role in the educational institution. A school police officer said that his ability to maintain security depended on his ability to blend into the school environment and thereby to cultivate informants. Cultivating informants in turn

A [D]epends on how much visibility you have in the school, and I make a point of walking around, constantly walking the hallways, dropping in on classes just so they know I'm there.

Q You mean dropping in unannounced even?

A Yeah. Staff at the school I work with don't have a problem with that.

Intimate regular presence in the classroom was also sustained by surveillance cameras. The same respondent continued:

If I need a particular problem solved, like camera work or something like that where you were monitoring, I'll go [the School Board Security Supervisor] because that's his job ... Say there was missing money from a classroom or a particular area and can't find it, or can't catch the person, we'll get a camera to monitor it, and just monitor it and see what happens. If the guy continues to show up – take the money out of the 'till' – then we got our guy. But that would be in special circumstances. It's not normal procedure.

This high school police programme was clearly oriented to sorting out those who pose criminal risks and taking action against them. A police officer observed that the high school programme was 'more into interaction with the zone [patrol officers] and with charging kids, and information sharing ... [from] the guys in the school to the guys in the street'. During school holiday periods school officers served as regular officers in the same zone as their school to build relationships with other police officers. In a 12-month period, high school officers recorded 473 official occurrences and undertook 720 other school-based investigations. A school officer whom we interviewed estimated that he handled a monthly average of five criminal investigations, ten trespass warnings and one or two trespass charges. He said that patrolling for trespass was a significant part of his job:

> If we have visitors from other schools, I'll call up the school and then tell the principal that Joe Blow from your school had visited our school, was seen on our property. They will then go to that student and serve a trespass warrant on him for our school and the next time he's there, I'll charge him under the School Act for trespassing. Or they're suspended ... The only time it's legitimate is when a student from another school walks in the door and goes directly to the office. If they're walking around the hallways, that's not legitimate. They're trespassing. If we allow that to happen, students would come to and fro ... Some people with the high jackboots and the shaved head, you know damned well they're not students. So I challenge them and take them down to the office, serve them. Tell them to get out, don't come back ... I do arrest them. I don't fool around at all. Neither does the staff ... The staff are the greatest because they know most of the students. If it's a non-student, usually they stand out like a sore thumb because they're looking around, they're aware that somebody's watching them. So they look suspicious right off the bat.

In criminal matters, the general orientation was to diffuse the problem and to handle it administratively by warnings rather than criminally through prosecution. School administrators were said to be very sensitive about crime-related publicity. There were stories about how school administrators went to great lengths to circumvent media coverage. Sometimes the police were not called at all about a major incident, or a school administrator reported an incident in person at a police station, in order to avoid the possibility that the matter would be picked up by the media on their 'scanner' radios tuned to police frequencies.

School officers said that students were very aware of the diversion practices of youth courts, and that they were more concerned about how school authorities would deal with their transgressions. As articulated by one officer, students

> ... are more afraid of school punishment than they are of punishment from the police so it works to my advantage ... In the court system, you take the person to court on assault, usually not much happens to them anyway. It's an inconvenience to get them to court with all the paperwork and the work involved. Is it

really worth it? ... But being dismissed from school is very serious to the student and if they're sent to the Area Superintendent to either be placed in another school or suspended indefinitely, that's serious, and much further, long-range consequences than going to court.

Long-range consequences in the criminal justice institution are reserved for a de-selected few. A primary orientation of school police officers, in collaboration with other special police units, is to identify the highest risks for more intensive surveillance.

Deselecting Highest Risk Youth

Police involvement in deselection of highest-risk youth is illustrated by a special programme in one jurisdiction studied. An official police publication said that this programme 'was initiated to efficiently control the activities of *high-risk* juvenile offenders' based on the 'ideology' that 'today's young offenders may become tomorrow's hardened criminals'. The programme involved up to two years' intensive, one-to-one contact with police officers, and surveillance extended to the youth's family and their involvement with health, education and welfare institutions. Each of the four police officers in the programme had a case-load of about a dozen youths, and they were supported by a part-time social worker and by citizen volunteers. As stressed in a handbook for volunteers, their functions were to go beyond counselling to surveillance and scheduled reporting:

> You may respect the confidentiality of your client, but you cannot condone the commission of an offence, whether it is a municipal bylaw, provincial, federal or criminal statute. You must report all offenses committed by a young person under your care to police, preferably the youth unit members, so that the individual is held accountable for his actions ... you will be required to report your client's progress monthly in written form to the supervisor.

Persons whose risk profiles were not lowered as a result of being in this programme – a high probability given its surveillance intensity – became candidates for another panoptic sorting process. As stated by a police officer, 'If they're successful, great. If they're not successful then they move on to the other side of the wall with our PAYs'. According to an official statement, the Police Attending Youth Programme (PAY):

> Supports increased efforts by the Youth Justice System to identify PAYs early in their criminal career; to work cooperatively together to investigate and record their activities; to actively disseminate this information on an inter-agency basis;

to prosecute them using vertical prosecution techniques; to sentence them appropriately, and to supervise them intensively in institutions and in the community.

The programme had approximately 100 youths identified as PAYs at a given time. With a programme staff of nine full-time police officers and a full-time civilian analyst, as well as volunteer analysts, this may seem a low number to have under intensive surveillance. However, the heavy staffing was not actually dedicated to direct surveillance, but rather to the risk profiling required to deselect who should be subject to further direct surveillance and who should be given less attention. Direct surveillance was conducted by patrol officers and detectives, and by officials in other agencies. A police manager described PAY officers as knowledge brokers who 'don't really investigate as much as they coordinate between investigators and constables out in the districts'. The PAY officers were fed information from the entire patrol force, who submit contact cards when youths are deemed to be out of place and time. They also received information and dossiers from health, education and welfare agencies, either directly or through related youth units such as the school police programmes.

This 'targeting' did not involve guns but, rather, risk technologies. Candidates for the programme were youths who received demerit points, much like the system that operates for drivers who receive demerit points for driving infractions. Once a youth received a designated number of demerit points, he was subject to a fuller investigation. An officer explained:

> And what that means then is the investigator would go out and would look at the individual, talk to him, talk to the family, Mom and Dad if, in fact, there are two and most times there isn't. Talk to the school, talk to the probation people and so on, and understand who this kid is and decide, based on that investigation, whether or not they were actually serious habitual offenders.

The decision to include the youth in the exclusive group of PAYs was made by an interinstitutional committee composed of representatives from the police, provincial Attorney-General, provincial Solicitor-General, provincial social services, provincial community health, provincial alcohol and drug abuse commission, municipal social services, municipal public school board, municipal Catholic school board, the John Howard Society and the Canadian Bar Association. While the risk profile of the points system provided a guide, the committee had the power to include or exclude youths regardless of their risk score. As stated in a police document on the programme, 'On the recommendations of an Inter-Agency Committee Member and subject to the majority consensus of a Criteria Review Board any young offender may be included or excluded from the efforts of the program'. As expressed in an interview by a police officer, the main aim was to identify the 100 or so worst youths in the city to ensure that they were a target for every risk knowledge system possible:

> We're interested in the kids who commit the most crime. If you listen to the number out of the States, they claim that 4% of their youth commit up to 60% of the crime. That may be here too, but we can't prove that. I wish we could. What we can say here is, at the moment, about 2% of the young offenders [who] we've identified as PAY offenders, are charged with probably between 15% and 20% of the crimes. And that's all we can go on is the charges that we lay. Now we're satisfied that they're responsible for a hell of a lot more than what we charge them for. Especially when you talk to some of them and [they] say, 'Look, you're catching me maybe 10% of the time. The rest of the time I'm getting away with it'. We're confident that they're responsible for a heck of a lot more.

To raise their confidence levels, PAY officers coordinated an elaborate surveillance system on the chosen few. The reach and intensity of this system is exemplified by a police officer's enthusiastic description of how PAYs were traced into the urban geography he policed:

> We have a product called 'Data Map' which runs on a PC. For one area of the city they plotted youth crime with red dots and they plotted known houses of PAYs in another coloured dot. It was an incredible correlation. The red dot and two blue dots around it. A red dot, two blue dots. It shows where the problem is.

In each district police station there was a special bulletin board section devoted to PAYs. The photographs of PAYs who lived in the district appeared on the bulletin board, accompanied by the following statement directed at police officers:

> Familiarize yourself with these offenders and check them whenever possible. The worst or most active offender in each zone has been selected as a 'target'. Make a special effort to:
>
> 1. Check them as often as possible.
> 2. Charge them as often as possible.
>
> Let them know that we will continue until they change their criminal habits or they move.
>
> Be polite, be professional but be pressing.

In addition to such harassment by patrol officers, special surveillance projects were used to entrap particularly troublesome young offenders. For example, in the face of a car theft problem, a decoy car programme was established. The decoy car was a sports model chosen because of its high-risk popularity with car thieves. Youths were enticed into it by leaving it running with the keys still in the ignition. When the youths seated them-selves in the car, the ignition system shut down and a remote control was used to lock the door automatically. Arrests and charges followed.

PAYs were typically on various court orders, such as probation orders, which restricted them in terms of time and place and with whom they could associate. Field stop contact cards submitted by patrol officers were compu-ter-searched to ascertain violations of these restrictions. According to a police officer we interviewed, the policy with respect to any such violation was to 'charge them with breach and throw them back inside again'. A colleague confirmed this approach, stating that the purpose of the pro-gramme was 'a pressure and a scarce tactic to bring the full bear of the system against a habitual before they get that clean slate and turn 18'.

The risk knowledge system was brought to full bear at the point of prosecution. When a PAY was arrested, his prosecution file was stamped PAY. This signalled that one of four prosecutors specially assigned to handle show-cause hearings for the programme would be required. These prosecu-tors were dedicated to PAY in order to help the police bring maximal negative knowledge of the accused before the courts and thereby achieve punitive outcomes. A PAY-appointed police investigator appeared in court. According to a police respondent, this person has

> ... a copy of the 'show cause' in his hot little hands and we can provide the information on that kid from day one, from the first time he was reported missing when he was aged 8 all the way through the gambit. There's often 20 or 30 pages of information that we can provide the court ... It almost becomes a police programme as such in that we've gathered all this information and ... what we're getting is longer sentences and we're getting better terms of release when they are released.

The reference to 'police program' here is an appreciation that – unlike most other instances of interinstitutional involvement where the police are providing knowledge for the purposes of external agencies – in this case, the external agencies are supporting the police in crime fighting. Criminal pros-ecution and punishment of youths is only the very tip of the iceberg, but at least there the police have the full knowledge support of other institutions that risk-profile youths. Another police respondent underscored this maxi-mal prosecution for maximal punishment goal of PAY.

> [We produce] complete and accurate packages for the court – who this person is, how many times they've breached probation ... It's very effective because, in

the past, the system just could not keep track. A guy would come up and it would be his fifth charge. He's been on probation four times. What options has the court got? They don't know any background. They haven't heard what he's done, what the breaches [of probation] involve. Invariably they end up going off with the same thing every time. This and probation. And now what they're doing is they're to the point where some of these kids are being incarcerated almost to the limit of the Young Offender's Act. And they're starting to get a lot more reaction out of the courts. They're starting to get a little stiffer with some of them. They're starting to court order a lot more treatment for them, as opposed to sending them somewhere and see if they can get treatment, that sort of thing. They target the young offenders, these habituals, so that they feel that when they go back out on the street eventually, that there's someone looking over their shoulder all the time.

Still there were gaps. Plans were afoot for a reorganization of the entire police programme on youths at risk to effect better coordination. Under the plan, all youth and school police programmes were to be integrated under one Inspector. Moreover, there was to be a new school police programme at the junior high school level – a level that was previously only served part-time by the high school police. A proponent of this plan said that the goal was 'targeting these kids in essence from day one, although in earlier years obviously we're talking intervention and education and so on, and then a natural progression to deal with the enforcement side of it'. The ambition did not stop there. Fully committed to risk profiling everyone's careers and identities from cradle to grave, a parallel unit for adult habituals was visualized:

We're looking seriously at starting an Adult Recidivist Unit which will take over where our [PAY] program ends ... At the moment when they reach 18 they kind of get thrown back into the mainstream ... [There'll be] better coordination of information and, quite frankly, I suspect it's going to be more kick ass ... a couple of teams of 5 or 6 people with a supervisor who are going to be going out ... What we see is that when these [PAY] kids are on the street they're committing crime. As we speak, probably 40% to 45% are behind bars. When they're on the street within a day or two they're back to a housebreak. So I guess our thought is that when they hit the street in the future we're going to have people following them around and wait for them to do it and we're going to throw them back inside again, you know, as adults at that point. I mean, you look at our statistics on house break-ins and car thefts, we're getting blown out of the water. We suggest that the youth is our problem.

The approach to youths taken by this police organization is consistent with the view that due process is weakening in face of system rights to knowledge for surveillance (Ericson 1994). Due process does not even enter into the picture during the daily routines of surveillance in school police programmes. On the statistically rare occasions when criminal process comes into focus, as in PAY risk profiling, every effort is made to emphasize the need for routine knowledge production over any procedural restrictions. A police document on the PAY programme underscores this system sensibility in no uncertain terms.

> The PAY process represents a system's effort ... PAY implementation leads to the creation of a system response ... The ultimate utility of the program is its ability to produce integrative methods and procedures.

Ronald D. Stephens, Executive Director, National School Safety Center, Pepperdine University, USA, is quoted in support of the free flow of confidential information as the key to system integration and procedural efficiency:

> Responding to the needs of children, particularly juvenile offenders, requires *not only good judgement* but also *good information* ... Confidential information should be shared on a routine, ongoing basis when specific needs warrant such sharing. Too often, juvenile agencies are unaware that they are serving the same at-risk youths. When information is shared appropriately, improved strategies for rehabilitating, educating, and better serving those youths – and for improving public safety – can be developed.

There is no mention of procedural propriety here, only procedural efficiency. It is efficiency in the production and distribution of knowledge of risk that is said to hold the key to improving the system. Elsewhere in the same report, US Justice Department marketing plans for the PAY programme were cited to indicate that this programme is, or should be, the wave of the future:

> Marketing activities and pro-training assessment for six additional PAY sites will begin in late 1989, with training at these sites to begin in the spring of 1990. By that time, the current 18 sites will have produced experienced prosecutors available for training and technical assistance assignments as PAY consultants. In the months and years ahead, an effort will be made to market [PAY] in a way that promotes fundamental change in the relationships among agencies that deal with justice.

Missing Youths

The police invest considerable knowledge resources in registering and tracing people who are reported missing. There are special programmes and knowledge systems in relation to missing children and youths, many of which are coordinated by the RCMP Missing Children's Registry in Ottawa. This Registry was initiated by the Solicitor-General of Canada in 1988, in relation to interest group and mass media concern over child abuse, child abduction and runaways (Nelson 1984; Best 1990; Webber 1991; Hacking 1995). It has an explicit knowledge brokerage function. An official publication describes the Registry as an operation that 'maintains and monitors files on missing children', functions as 'an information and research centre', and provides 'an investigative and consulting service' to other police organizations.

In addition to police officers, the Registry is staffed by a PhD research analyst, and by statistical analysts, including one seconded by Statistics Canada. These police experts consult with other experts on child and youth at risk in the Department of Justice, Ministry of the Solicitor-General and Health and Welfare Canada. They symbolize the fact that the primary role of the Registry is indeed registration, and associated risk profiling of youths who, however temporarily, cannot be accounted for.

At the investigative level, the Registry is primarily committed to identifying youths whose risk is at the hands of separated parents in conflict over child custody and other property rights. They are assisted in this investigation work by three seconded employees of Canada Customs and Canada Immigration. They function primarily as agents of the child and of the stay-at-home parent, seeking to locate the child and to bring it back to where the courts decide it is supposed to be. As indicated in Table 7.1, in 1991 there were 412 such cases recorded for investigation. The *Annual Report on*

Table 7.1 Missing Child Registry Cases 1991

Reason	Cases Entered		Cases Removed	
	N	%	N	%
Stranger Abduction	78	0.1	64	0.1
Accident	60	0.1	34	0.1
Wander off/Lost	783	1.3	746	1.4
Parental Abduction	412	0.7	326	0.6
Runaway	43 786	74.0	40 426	74.1
Unknown	11 863	20.1	10 952	20.1
Other	2 153	3.7	1 967	3.6
Total	59 135	100.0	54 515	100.0

Source: Adopted from 1991 *Annual Report on Canada's Missing Children*.

Canada's Missing Children (RCMP 1991) for that year states that among this number

> ... 168 were abducted in contravention of an existing custody order while 244 had no custody order in effect at the time of abduction. Historically, we have seen a fairly constant level in parental abductions in Canada. This year shows a decline of 5% from the 432 reported in 1990 ... there were a total of 246 reported cases from other countries in which assistance from the Canadian authorities was requested, and it was believed that there was a possibility that the children could be in Canada. The majority of the Registry's case-load is based on international cases such as these.

Table 7.1 makes evident that the vast majority (74 per cent) of unaccounted-for children and youths are runaways. Moreover, abduction by strangers is very rare indeed. Only 78 or 0.1 per cent of recorded cases in 1991 were a result of 'stranger abduction'. Furthermore, the definition of 'stranger' used by the Registry includes close relatives (for example, grandparents, aunts, uncles) and friends who do not have legal custody of the child! The available data do not indicate how many of the 78 recorded stranger abductions turned out to be not strangers at all, but it is reasonable to assume that it was probably most of them. Clearly, stranger abduction is not a substantial problem for the Registry, although it has great symbolic importance.

The Registry employees are mainly knowledge system managers. The main knowledge system is provided through the Canadian Police Information Centre (CPIC). Police organizations across Canada file unsolicited messages to the Registry in the CPIC categories listed in Table 7.1 These messages are sent to enter, alter or remove missing child cases. The Registry uses these data to constantly profile Canada's missing children problem, including a weekly overview that is distributed to police, voluntary agencies and the media.

The Registry has a knowledge brokerage function to police organizations in Canada and abroad. This function includes general CPIC information on the status of a person reported missing, investigative help with parental abduction cases, and legal advice concerning whether a case is a criminal or a civil law matter.

There is a close relationship with voluntary sector agencies, including, for example, the Missing Children Society of Canada, Missing Childrens' Network, Child Find Canada and the Missing Children Locate Centre. Co-operation includes providing these agencies with case-specific information, and receiving information from them in exchange. These agencies supply the police with literature, and with posters identifying high-profile missing children. In turn, they distribute police-produced literature including the *Annual Report on Canada's Missing Children*.

In addition to routine releases to the news media, the Registry has cooperated with the 'child find' version of police reality shows on television, *Missing Treasures*. This show featured high-profile missing children case re-enactments, and solicited public assistance in supplying knowledge relevant to these cases. According to an official, the police worked with the show's producers

> ... very closely in getting them the initial information so they could develop the program. And the 800-number is answered by Canada Customs through their ... training academy ... [I]t depends on what you mean by success. It's been a success in that it's brought forward the information to the public. I don't know of any particular case that we can point to that we found the child because of that ... [but it helps people to] realize that things like this happen and they have to have some protection for their children ... tips for parents ... keep the problem of missing children there in the forefront to the public so they don't forget about it.

The sensibility expressed by this official is characteristic of policing the risk society. While the instrumental effectiveness of police programmes is limited, there is an effort to promote the programme's advertising value because it will induce reflexivity in each and all to be their own risk managers. At the instrumental level of investigations, missing children programmes have very little to do with the problem of stranger abductions, but at the symbolic level this problem remains the primary focus. At the symbolic level the police join with other institutions in promoting education of parents, who in turn educate their children about the problem of stranger abductions. Thus, in spite of its own evidence, the 1991 *Annual Report on Canada's Missing Children* stresses the need to be eternally vigilant about the risk of stranger abductions:

> [B]ecause such high profile is given to any stranger abduction, the public's perception is that this phenomenon is common in Canada. This in fact is not the case. However, it is still prudent for parents to teach their children to be 'street smart' and to be aware of the dangers of our society. Street proofing of children is essential to preventing such tragedies. Many of Canada's police are actively involved in preventative policing and are able to provide tips on personal safety. It is important to remember that the legal definition of 'stranger' is anyone who does not have custody of the child. Therefore, children who are taken by a grandparent, aunt, uncle, or friend of the family would be entered into CPIC under the category of stranger abduction.

In order to prevent children and youths from being unaccounted for, police organizations mobilize 'street-proofing' projects. In some jurisdictions parents are asked to include their children in special registration systems. For example, a police organization ran an 'Operation Child Identification Program' in which a young person's detailed written description, photograph and fingerprints were taken and filed. A brochure produced by a provincial Solicitor-General's office and distributed by police throughout the province urged parents to maintain their own home-based knowledge system for mapping and tracing their children:

> Build a home information centre, which includes a map of your neighbourhood and its play areas, and have your child identify where he will be at all times, and when he will return ... Maintain up-to-date records which include a recent photograph of your child, his height and weight, medical and dental histories, and if you wish, a video tape and fingerprint record.

A police officer we interviewed saw such urgings as part of the 'continual reinforcement' of parents to maintain good records. She saw these records as being of importance when something untoward happens, because parents are usually in an 'emotional state' at such times, and this state interferes with rational, efficient police work. In other words, families are to be like other institutions, providing data that are properly formatted and readily accessible

> They have that information just there, they can hand it to the officer, it saves a hell of a lot of time in the police officer trying to calm them down enough to ask questions so they can get the information from them – details and description. The person wants the policeman to get out right now and go out and find their kid.

Parents are not only to keep detailed records of their childrens' identities, they are also to remain perpetually reflexive about risks. The above-mentioned brochure stresses that the safety tips it offers 'will not completely protect your child, however they will increase the level of awareness'. Indeed, parents are made aware of imagined negative consequences that lurk behind the most mundane aspects of a child's everyday life:

> Avoid clothing and toys which personally display your child's name, because children are less likely to fear a stranger who knows their name ... Know all of your childrens' friends, their families and their phone numbers; insist that your child ask for permission to visit his friends ... accompany your child on door-to-door activities, such as Halloween or school fund-raising.

As indicated by the instruction to avoid labelling a child's property with her name for fear that a stranger might become familiar, many of the lessons in the brochure focus on communication. Community policing as communications policing extends into the home and family-based education of the young. For example, children are asked to manipulate appearances and even lie in the interest of risk reduction:

> When children are home alone, [they are] to tell phone callers that you are there, but you are busy, and cannot come to the phone, and that the caller should call back later ... If a stranger is at the door, teach your child to tell the stranger that you are busy, and he should go away and come back later.

Like the electronic home security alarm system, children are to be given a code to help signal who are trusted insiders and who are to be excluded from any possible contact: 'use a pre-selected code word with your child and those whom you may ask to give your child a ride; where necessary, change the code word with your child after it has been used for a period of time'. No mention is made of the confusion that might ensue for the mother who is trying to remember the codes of the six children she picks up in her stationwagon on the way to their Saturday morning hockey game. The parent is to know everything about the child's communications with other adults. Having secrets is age-graded, and in communications between children and adults who are not close family members confidentiality is to be breached: 'some secrets – like surprise birthday presents – are fun, but a secret that another adult says only the two of you can know is not right – come and tell me'.

Conclusion

Young people are governed through numerous risk communication systems in different institutions. The police have an important role in these systems. Their primary task is the production and distribution of knowledge of risk on behalf of other institutions, more than direct involvement with youths at risk. They have a range of surveillance systems for tracing youths in the urban landscape, including, for example, street-stop recording systems, geographic mapping systems and missing persons registries. The knowledge gained from these systems is routinely fed to health, education, welfare and criminal justice institutions concerned with youths at risk. The police also collaborate in surveillance systems operated jointly with these institutions. In some cases, such as in schools, the collaboration extends to direct participation in the institution and its own surveillance systems. In other cases it entails interinstitutional collaboration, coordinated by the police, in sharing knowledge about high-risk youths who are candidates for more intensive surveillance and possible proactive intervention on behalf of the criminal justice institution.

The analysis suggests that late modern institutions are continuing the early modern quest for governance through risk management of populations. Modern technologies of risk communication are continuously invented to know populations better and to manage their institutional participation more efficiently. These technologies are linked to central state institutions, such as the police, who oversee a system of governance that is otherwise fragmented into relatively autonomous institutions.

The main effort of those who work within risk communication systems is to patrol the borders of population categories, deciding what the categories mean, who should inhabit them and who should be relegated to the margins or excluded altogether. This work requires an extensive surveillance network that is increasingly facilitated by innovations in electronic media, and especially computers. The electronic surveillance media allow institutions to engage in a perpetual panoptic sort of where each individual is situated on the continuum of risk or imprecise normality.

The risk society is also a 'transmission society' (see Castel (1991) who refers to a two-speed society) because it registers peoples' social utility in terms of significant accomplishments and failures, credentials and demerits, routines and accidents experienced in the life course. Some are selected for the motorway, others relegated to the highways with speed limits, and still others to local roads with speed humps. The police spend a great deal of time and energy helping other institutions regulate traffic in the transmission society. Some youths are deselected early as high-risk, and gradually excluded from full participation in many social institutions. Most youths eventually graduate to obtain drivers licences, credit cards, frequent-flyer cards and other accoutrements of mobility in the utilitarian culture of risk society.

References

Altheide, D. (1995), *An Ecology of Communication: Cultural Formats of Control*, New York: Aldine de Gruyter.

Bauman, Z. (1992a), 'Life-World and Expertise: Social Production of Dependency', in Stehr, N. and R. Ericson (eds), *The Culture and Power of Knowledge: Inquiries into Contemporary Societies*, Berlin and New York: Walter de Gruyter.

Bauman, Z. (1992b), 'Soil, Blood and Identity', *The Sociological Review*, **40** (4), 675–701.

Beck, U. (1992a), *Risk Society: Toward a New Modernity*, London: Sage.

Beck, U. (1992b), 'Modern Society as Risk Society', in N. Stehr and R. Ericson (eds), *The Culture and Power of Knowledge: Inquiries into Contemporary Societies*, Berlin and New York: Walter de Gruyter.

Beck, U., A. Giddens and S. Lash (1994), *Reflexive Modernization: Politics, Tradition and Aesthetics in the Modern Social Order*, Cambridge: Polity Press.

Best, J. (1990), *Threatened Children*, Chicago: University of Chicago Press.

Brogden, M., T. Jefferson and S. Walklate (1988), *Introducing Police Work*, London: Unwin Hyman.

Burchell, G., C. Gordon and P. Miller (eds) (1991), *The Foucault Effect: Studies in Governmentality*, Chicago: University of Chicago Press.

Carriere, K. and R. Ericson (1989), *Crime Stoppers: A Study in the Organization of Community Policing*, Toronto: Centre of Criminology, University of Toronto.

Castel, R. (1991), 'From Dangerousness to Risk', in G. Burchell, C. Gordon and P. Miller (eds), *The Foucault Effect: Studies in Governmentality*, Chicago: University of Chicago Press.

Cavendar, G. and L. Bond-Maupin (1993), 'Fear and Loathing on Reality Television: An Analysis of "America's Most Wanted" and "Unsolved Mysteries"', *Sociological Inquiry*, **63** (3), 305–17.

Chermak, S. (1995), *Victims in the News: Crime and the American News Media*, Boulder, Col.: Westview Press.

Douglas, M. (1986), *How Institutions Think*, Syracuse: Syracuse University Press.

Ericson, R. (1982), *Reproducing Order: A Study of Police Patrol Work*, Toronto: University of Toronto Press.

Ericson, R. (1994), 'The Royal Commission on Criminal Justice System Surveillance', in M. McConville and L. Bridges (eds), *Criminal Justice in Crisis*, Aldershot: Edward Elgar.

Ericson, R. and K. Haggerty (1997), *Policing the Risk Society*, Toronto: University of Toronto Press.

Ericson, R., K. Haggerty and K. Carriere (1993), 'Community Policing as Communications Policing', in D. Dölling and T. Feltes (eds), *Community Policing: Comparative Aspects of Community Oriented Police Work*, Holzkirchen: Felix-Verlag.

Evans, R. (1993), *The Conduct of Police Interviews with Juveniles*, Research Study Number 8, The Royal Commission on Criminal Justice, London: HMSO.

Gandy, O. (1993), *The Panoptic Sort: A Political Economy of Personal Information*, Boulder, Col.: Westview Press.

Giddens, A. (1990), *The Consequences of Modernity*, Cambridge: Polity Press.

Giddens, A. (1994), *Beyond Left and Right: The Future of Radical Politics*, Cambridge: Polity Press.

Hacking, I. (1990), *The Taming of Chance*, Cambridge: Cambridge University Press.

Hacking, I. (1995), *Rewriting the Soul*, Princeton: Princeton University Press.

Manning, P. (1977), *Police Work: The Social Organization of Policing*, Cambridge, Mass.: MIT Press.

Manning, P. (1980), *The Narc's Game: Organizational and Informational Limits on Drug Law Enforcement*, Cambridge, Mass.: MIT Press.

Manning, P. (1988), *Symbolic Communication: Signifying Calls and the Police Response*, Cambridge, Mass.: MIT Press.

Meehan, A. (1993), 'Internal Police Records and the Control of Juveniles: Politics and Policing in a Suburban Town', *British Journal of Criminology*, **33** (4), 504–24.

Miller, P. and N. Rose (1990), 'Governing Economic Life', *Economy and Society*, **19** (1), 1–31.

Nelson, B. (1984), *Making an Issue of Child Abuse*, Chicago: University of Chicago Press.

Newman, O. (1972), *Defensible Space: Crime Prevention through Urban Design*, New York: Macmillan.

Nock, S. (1993), *The Costs of Privacy: Surveillance and Reputation in America*, New York: Aldine de Gruyter.

Pearson, G. (1983), *Hooligan: A History of Respectable Fears*, London: Macmillan.

Policy Studies Institute (1983), *Police and People in London: Vol. III: A Survey of Police Officers*, London: Policy Studies Institute.

RCMP (1991), *Annual Report on Canada's Missing Children*.

Rock, P. (1986), *A View from the Shadows: The Ministry of the Solicitor-General of Canada and the Making of the Justice for Victims of Crime Initiative*, Oxford: Oxford University Press.

Rock, P. (1990), *Helping Victims of Crime: The Home Office and the Rise of Victim Support in England and Wales*, Oxford: Oxford University Press.

Rose, N., and P. Miller (1992), 'Political Power Beyond the State: Problematics of Government', *British Journal of Sociology*, **43** (2), 173–205.

Schlesinger, P. and H. Tumber (1994), *Reporting Crime: The Media Politics of Criminal Justice*, Oxford: Oxford University Press.

Task Force on Policing in Ontario (1974), *The Police are the Public and the Public are the Police*, Toronto: Solicitor-General of Ontario.

Webber, M. (1991), *Street Kids: The Tragedy of Canada's Runaways*, Toronto: University of Toronto Press.

8 Consuming Risks: Harm Minimization and the Government of 'Drug-users'

Pat O'Malley

In 1987, the Australian federal government launched its new harm minimization programme with a major ministerial document *National Campaign Against Drug Abuse: Assumptions, Arguments and Aspirations* (NCADA 1987). One of the most striking features of this document is that the terms 'addict' and 'addiction' were hardly mentioned in the text of the document. In 1992 'The National Campaign Against Drug Abuse' changed its name, further reduced its reference to 'Drug Abuse' and became 'The National Drug Strategy' (Task Force 1992). A few years later, in the Victorian Drug Strategy 1993–1998, a state-based programme formally operating within this federal rubric of harm minimization, not only 'addiction' and 'drug abuse', but even drug 'misuse' had given way to discourses of 'drug use'. While opposition to such developments in the United States is intense, this shift in Australian governing discourses cannot readily be dismissed as a particular social democratic or 'liberal' political platform, for at the time the respective federal and (Victorian) state governments were Labour and (Neo) Liberal. Nor is it an isolated national policy, for similar trends can be detected in the governmental projects, plans and policies of other nations which are adopting harm minimization strategies with respect to illicit drugs (for example, the Netherlands, Germany, Canada and Britain) (Fischer 1995; Fischer *et al.* 1997).

Nevertheless, this move toward harm minimization runs against a strong contemporary practice of governing illicit drugs through discourses of addiction and abuse. These two key concepts represent two ends of an imagined continuum of the will. At one end are images of drug-using subjects compelled by forces beyond their will – most especially pathologies such as the 'addicted personality', or the irresistible 'addictive' power of drugs. Set against these compelled and determinist imageries is that of the wilful 'drug abuser' – a category developed by retributivists and others to counter the implication that addicted drug-takers have an attenuated free will and thus are not fully subject to criminal law (Matza and Morgan 1995). Despite their almost polar oppositions in this respect, models of 'addiction' and 'abuse' both accept that the activity of drugtaking is a moral and/or medical pathology, and formulate 'a narrative of inexorable decline and fatality' for the drug-taker, requiring prohibition and regimes of treatment or correction (Sedgwick 1993).

Overshadowing discourses of addiction and abuse in harm minimization programmes, new governmental categories have emerged, organized around the label 'drug use'. Instead of blanket imageries of addictions and abuses, there emerges a spectrum of qualified conditions and forms of 'use', ranging from 'dependent' and 'harmful' through 'excessive' and 'inappropriate' to 'informed', 'controlled' and even 'responsible'. 'Drug use' in this discourse, it appears, has nothing *inevitable* or *absolute* attached to it: it does not appear necessarily as a pathology and can no longer be subjected to universal descriptors or evaluations. By implication, if drug use can be excessive, it can also be not excessive; if harmful then it can also be not harmful; and if inappropriate then it can be appropriate. It even becomes possible to sustain, at state level, governmental imageries of 'healthy drug related behaviour' distinct from 'abstention' (HCS 1993). The clear implication emerges that drug consumption is being understood in much the same way as any 'normal' activity and, like such an activity, can be performed in a variety of ways. As with any 'normal activity', it seems that there is some preferred range behaviours and actions (by implication, 'informed', 'responsible', 'healthy', 'controlled' and so on). Like normal activities it can – but need not – take forms such as 'excessive', 'dependent' or 'inappropriate' that may benefit from expert or other intervention. Both the drug-users, and their relationships to drugs are being re-imagined.

This chapter sets out to explore the emerging discourse of governing drugs through harm minimization. It examines this development not so much in terms of how far the changes are being implemented or resisted in practice – an important but separate issue – but rather in terms of the way in which government plans and blueprints effect a re-imagination of what it is to govern drug consumption. To borrow a phrase from the governmentality literature (for example, Miller and Rose 1990), drug-taking is being rendered 'thinkable in new ways' – that is, discursively transformed and thus made subject to new techniques of governance. This chapter examines a series of questions in order to map out this emerging governmental framework: what kinds of drug-taking subject are being thought into existence to displace the 'addict' and the 'drug abuser' in these discourses? How are the drugs and their effects being recast as problems for rule? How is the relationship between drug and drug user being imagined? How are the drugs and the drug-taking subjects to be governed? What techniques are to be deployed in relation to such modes of governing? Why and how is it believed that these changes will govern drug consumption 'better' than existing regimes?

The Consumption of Risk: Normalizing the Drug-taker

The National Drug Strategy, endorsed by all federal, state and territory governments in Australia, defines harm minimization as:

> An approach that aims to reduce the adverse health, social and economic consequences of alcohol and other drugs by minimising or limiting the harms and hazards of drug use for both the community and the individual without necessarily eliminating use. (Commonwealth Department of Human Services and Health 1994)

This summary statement makes clear the nexus between official discourses on governing the drug problem in terms of 'drug use', and the current ascendance of models of risk management and 'actuarialism' as technologies for government (see, for example, Reichman 1986; Simon 1987; O'Malley 1992; Feeley and Simon 1994). Risk managerial models focus on governing through the calculation of risks and the distribution of harms. They concern themselves far more with the effects or consequences of problematic actions, and with the mitigation or prevention of these effects, than with the more overtly disciplinary techniques that attempt to eliminate problems through locating and eliminating their causes. They are less concerned with individuals *per se*, whether with correcting them or understanding why they create problems, and are more focused on the patterns and characteristics of aggregates and distributions. Where individuals are considered, it is almost always in terms of their membership of risk categories, their relationship to risk factors and their performance of risk-bearing behaviours, rather than in the more familiar disciplinary sense of the biographical individual in need of correctional intervention (Cohen 1985; Castel 1991). It is clear that such risk managerial technologies have become increasingly influential throughout the criminal justice systems of many nations (for example, Feeley and Simon 1992, 1994; O'Malley 1992). Given this ascendance, it is therefore at least superficially intelligible why the movement towards harm minimization in the governance of drugs has become so prominent, for the risk managerial framework of such programmes is explicit enough (Mugford 1993). As the *Victorian Drug Strategy 1993–1998* (HCS 1993) describes itself:

> ... (t)he specific objectives of the Drug Strategy focus on changing behaviours and reducing other risk factors which have been shown to increase the potential for drug related harm ... There is a strengthened commitment to the principle of harm minimization in its broadest sense. All objectives are defined in terms of risk factors linked to specific harms, with emphasis on prevention wherever possible and on minimising the negative impact of drug use problems where they occur.[1]

Risk management or harm minimization places an analytic and governmental grid across the social terrain it seeks to govern that does not necessarily correspond to the grid laid down by other governmental technologies, such as that of prohibitory laws. For harm minimization, the legal–illegal categorization of drugs and drug-taking is of only subsidiary importance, especially where the governmental risk calculus is concerned with, for example, health, social or economic harm. Harm minimization programmes either refuse to recognize the functional distinction between licit and illicit drugs, or distinguish between the licit and illicit drugs specifically in terms of the distinctive risk profile created by legal prohibition. In other words, where they do deploy the licit–illicit distinction, the latter term is used largely as a shorthand for a socially defined range of substances, rather than – as in prohibitory legal discourses – to denote intrinsically harmful substances. Almost without fail, harm minimization documents stress that 'it is important to recognise that illicit drugs are, in functional terms, the same as legal drugs' (PDAC 1996). While they recognize 'the devastating effects that illicit drug use can have', they do so in the context of observations that align them with licit drugs, for example: 'alcohol and tobacco cause by far the most harm to society' and 'the misuse of pharmaceuticals is a major cause of ill health and reduced quality of life for many thousands' (HCS 1993; see also DSEV 1995; PDAC 1996; Blewitt 1987).

In this way, by rendering licit drugs problematic and rendering it comparable (in some ways unfavourably) with illicit drugs, illicit drugs are normalized. More precisely, they are regarded as one aspect of the much broader set of drug consumption, which as a whole is to be understood as made up of risk-taking behaviours that are a normal – if not necessarily desirable – characteristic of modern society. Thus the Victorian programme stresses that: '(d)rug use and the risks associated with use affect almost all Victorians ... (w)e live in a drug taking society in which legally available substances still cause major problems and in which illegal substances continue to be supplied and used' (HCS 1993). Likewise, at the federal level, the Minister for Health noted that harm minimization makes '(n)o utopian claims to eliminate drugs, or drug abuse, or to remove entirely the harmful effects of drugs, merely to minimize the effects of drugs on a *society permeated by drugs*' (Blewitt 1987: 2, emphasis added).[2]

In addition, this strategy normalizes illicit drug use in the sense that it *subordinates* criminal law, with its exclusionary, coercive and denunciatory techniques to the inclusionary 'technical' and ostensibly amoral techniques of harm minimization. These disrupt law's claims to sovereignty and moral domain, and render it merely an expendable administrative option. For example, illegal behaviour may be thought of as governmentally substitutable for actions not proscribed by criminal law where the former represent lower health and social risks.

> Petrol sniffing has been observed worldwide among adolescent indigenous people and has been reported as a serious health problem in many remote Aboriginal communities in Australia. In most cases the habit ceases when the young person becomes old enough to gain access to alcohol. Arguably, alcohol is less harmful to young people than inhaling leaded petrol. Should the communities concerned permit their young people access to alcohol at an earlier age to reduce the dangers of solvent abuse. (Commonwealth Department of Human Services and Health 1994)

Likewise, issues and practices of law enforcement are patterned and shaped not by the dictates of law but rather by pragmatic principles of risk management, even where these give rise to official actions contrary to legal prescription and proscription. Thus as part of the Victorian Drug Strategy.

> Victorian Police will support the needle-syringe exchange program by, where appropriate, sharing information and developing complementary strategies including non-enforcement of possession offences in the vicinity of exchange outlets and provision of information on exchange programs to drug users. (HCS 1993)

Ultimately, legal prohibition itself is regarded in harm minimization terms as merely one available administratively dividing practice, being considered for inclusion as 'part of a harm minimization policy, but only if it can be demonstrated to contribute to the overall aim of reducing the harms associated with drug use' (PDAC 1996).

Here, the subordination of law to the dictates of normalization becomes an explicit governmental aim. One of the major concerns of harm minimization policies is the capacity of prohibition's exclusionary categories and procedures to 'demonise' illicit drug-users, and thus – in the terminology of the sociology of deviance – to 'amplify' the harms of such drug use. The observation is also made that this legal exclusion of drug use creates resistance to programmatic intervention, for compulsion and coercion create resistance among the very drug-using subjects upon whom the programme is intended to have its effects (see, for example, PDAC 1996; Task Force 1992). The strategy of harm minimization, therefore, is to 'emphasise voluntary treatment rather than punishment of users and minimise the stigma of criminalisation of drug users' on pragmatic grounds (Blewitt 1987: 4). Indeed, later, the focus on treatment itself becomes qualified for similar reasons:

> Not only is treatment no longer seen as the prime focus of alcohol and other drug interventions, but also the conception of what constitutes effective treatment has undergone radical reformulation ... Current research indicates that brief interventions, delivered by skilled workers and over short periods of time, provide the best evidence of treatment effectiveness for the majority of persons considered at risk of, or even moderately debilitated by, harm related to alcohol and other drug use ... (A)doption of this approach nationally can successfully address many of the issues surrounding alcohol and drug use in ways that do not necessarily stigmatise or marginalise users. This approach avoids the unproductive exercise that targets alleged alcohol and other drug abusers without proper attention to the total user environment. (Task Force 1992)

Thus, in contrast to the Foucaultian sense of normalization as bringing deviant subjects into conformity with a constructed norm (licit drug use or no drug use), 'normalization' in the lexicon of harm minimization takes on the meaning of rendering illicit drug-taking subjects normal subjects of government. This is to be achieved through 'the gradual shift from disease and criminal models', precisely because of an awareness 'that "drug addicts" and "alcoholics" can bear the brunt of problems in our community and can be the scapegoats of more severe social ills' (Task Force 1992). The object of normalization in this sense is to render illicit drug use a *self-governing* activity not usually requiring expert intervention, but even then on a voluntary basis (PDAC 1996; Blewitt 1987). As this suggests, normalization is undertaken precisely in order more effectively to govern drug-users, to align the wills of such subjects with the project of harm minimization, and to align the distribution of risks and harms with the objectives of government programmes.

The Probability and the Locus of Risks

In harm minimization discourses, the governmental status of any behaviour is determined by the aggregate level of risk that it generates. In this mode of framing the questions of how to rule, harms enter a field of abstract equations in which not only issues of legality, but even the identity of a risk is erased almost altogether. Issues of substantive 'conventional' legality and morality appear to be substituted by an amoral technology in which the distribution of efforts and resources is geared to the measured potential for harms. Thus, in one governmental briefing paper, the question of how harms and risks may be 'assessed and weighted in comparison with each other' suggests that:

> ... if we had the ability to measure the harm with precision in terms of the severity, prevalence and the nature of the affected populations, we would be more able to appropriately tailor harm minimization strategies. When comparing ... types of harm a common framework is required: estimates of the economic costs of different harms to the community can be made to compare and prioritize different types of harm, or measures such as 'person years of life lost' can be derived. (Commonwealth Department of Human Services and Health (1994)[3]

Thus we begin to see that, governmentally, all social phenomena can be (or are already) aligned according to their *relationship to risk*. Problems for government therefore appear objectified and reified, identified and prioritized scientifically and intersubjectively rather than in terms of the value commitments and arbitrary moralities of some political regime. Implied in this is a second move, to which we now turn, identifying the location of risk in probabilistic 'risk factors'.

In discourses of addiction and abuse, the problem of drug consumption lies largely in determinist accounts, either in terms of the given properties of chemicals and/or in terms of the characteristics of certain users. In consequence, conventional discourses of drug governance focus on the presence or absence of 'free will' (Sedgwick 1993). In models of abuse, the problem of government is to punish the juridical subject, who of their own free will, breaks the law. In discourses of addiction, the problem is to restore to addicts a healthy or free will (Valverde 1998). In these essentially binary models, the subject is, or is not, a wilful law-breaker, is, or is not, an addict and consequently is, or is not, a subject of rule. However, by regarding drugs as part of the generalized issue of risk management, harm minimization operates within a statistical and irreducibly probabilistic model that erodes the binary of free will and determinism (Hacking 1991; Ewald 1994). Whether with reference to alcohol, tobacco, pharmaceuticals or 'illicit drugs', harm reduction involves 'a recognition that drug use involves varying degrees of risk for the user' (DSEV 1995; see also Commonwealth Department of Health 1987). The drug-user is understood to be variably free or variably constrained. But, as this also suggests, risk implies that the locus of harm creation lies neither in the properties of drugs, nor in the characteristics of the user, but in the *variable yet calculable relationships between them*.

It is for this reason, among others to be discussed now, that the governance of drug use is almost always expressed in terms such as 'drug *related* behaviours', 'drug *related* problems', 'drug *related* harms' and even '(d)rug related critical incidents' (DSEV 1995). The governmental categorization of types of drug use and drug-user is structured in terms of the probabilistic, risk-based understanding of how drugs and users are brought together. The core principle of harm minimization is that these probabilities may be calculated and thus known and governed. There is an attenuation of concern with the properties of drugs or the free will of users, and increased stress on the user's relationship to an array of risk factors. Thus:

> The minimization of harm may involve a range of outcomes including abstention from drug use, reduced or controlled use, safer behaviours associated with drug use, or reduction of harmful consequences of drug use for the community. Inherent in this approach is the recognition of a continuum of risk for each drug, from high risk to low risk, along which the user can move. Drug use involves a complex set of social behaviours that need to be viewed in terms of the individuals involved, the physical, social and economic environment in which they live, and the drug itself. To formulate strategies to minimise harm effectively is necessarily to take all three factors into account and to acknowledge that all behaviours occur in a social context. (DSEV 1995)

Likewise the Victorian Drug Strategy

> ... promotes an integrated model of harm minimization which takes into account the relationships between people, the drugs they use and the environments in which they use them ... Depending on the individuals and environments concerned, effective outcomes may include abstinence or prevention of drug use, reduced or controlled drug use, safer drug administration, or reduction of other harmful consequences of drug use for the community. (HCS 1993)

Government in terms of risk, in other words, requires that we recast the ways in which drugs and users are considered as being related to each other – not simply as causally linked by ties of will or its impairment, or of the properties of drugs, but in terms of a theoretically much wider array of possible 'factors', all of which may bear on the question of minimizing 'drug-related' harms. These factor-related, probabilistic understandings in turn shape the nature of the emergent governmental categories of drug use or user.

Excessive Use and Polydrug Use

The starting point here is close to, but distinct from, the traditional approaches to drug governance. In harm minimization discourses, the governmentally relevant biochemical and psychodynamic effects of certain drugs – to produce hallucinations, to slow the pulse rate or to suppress respiration and so on – are clearly acknowledged, but are invariably linked to the volume and frequency of use. Management of the risks associated with 'the properties' of drugs, in other words, lies in the (self) government of their use – so that, for example, 'excessive use' or 'problematic use' rather than 'use' *per se* emerge as sites of possible intervention (PDAC 1996). But how is 'excessive use' to be defined? For most of the modern era, this has been done in behavioural terms – for example, with respect to the inability of individuals to perform certain tasks – or with respect to a certain state of the will (Valverde 1998). In harm minimization discourses, the answer is almost invariably given in terms of actuarial rates (for example, rates of brain damage or motor coordination impairment related to levels of drug intake), on the basis of which a level is drawn up beyond which use is 'excessive'. In other words, government in terms of harm minimization, even where concerned with the effects of drugs on the body, moves us away from an emphasis on the fixed biochemical properties of drugs, towards their actuarial rates of risk production, and thence to the government of risk-informed patterns of use.

What is particularly significant is that the level at which use is defined as 'excessive use' varies according to the risk in terms of which it appears as a 'factor'. In some cases this may be straightforward as, for example, with respect to 'safe' levels for the long-term health of the user or for the purposes of driving a motor vehicle. In other cases, however, the risks factoring may become more complex. In Victoria, while the general level of use defining safe levels for driving is a blood alcohol content of .05 per cent, for drivers in their first three years of licensed driving the figure is zero. This is based on the relationship between the risk factor associated with drug consumption and a second risk factor associated with accident rates for new or young drivers. In other words, the definition of problematic drug use in this context is produced socially by the articulation of two discrete risk factors, one of which has no intrinsic connection with drug use.

Here, the discussion has strayed into the territory occupied by a second category, *inappropriate use*, which will be considered later. For the moment it is only important to note that 'inappropriate use' includes that class of 'excessive use' that warrants state intervention, identified by the point at which the consequences of excessive use are represented as creating significant risks for others. By and large, however, the category of excessive use *per se* remains in the domain of self-government. The role of state governmental programmes is primarily advisory: to establish and broadcast the so-called 'recommended safe levels of usage', founded on expert evaluations of actuarial data, so that responsible users may moderate their risk-bearing behaviours in line with an officially endorsed risk calculus.

This issue of the calculability of risk becomes particularly acute where 'polydrug use' is considered. Unlike 'excessive use', polydrug use emerges as a category for governance precisely because of is unpredictable nature. The combination of varying numbers of drugs, and in varying volumes, ratios and sequences of usage, creates incalculable risks. Here the displacement of drug effects by drug-related risk in the centre stage of government is brought into sharp focus, for polydrug use – like excessive use – is regarded as 'high-risk', so much so that there is no recommended safe level of polydrug use (PDAC 1996). But if the categorization of 'excessive' use as 'high-risk' is a tautology, for the actuarial risk level is used to define what is excessive; it is the *unpredictability*, and thus the ungovernability, of polydrug use by techniques of 'the taming of chance' that is deployed to determine the governmental status of polydrug use.

In both examples it is the risk-bearing practices of the users – their mode of deployment of the drug rather than the given effects of drugs – that is identified as that which is to be governed. Ultimately, this extends to factors that are extrinsic to *any* property of the drug. These include, in particular, the conditions whereby drugs are obtained, administered and experienced (see, for example, PDAC 1996). Thus an enormous amount of attention has been given to the mechanics of drug administration. The provision of needle and syringe exchanges, bleach sachets and education programmes on low-risk modes of drug administration all highlight the fact that, for harm minimization, some of the most crucial drug-related risks have nothing to do with properties of drugs or users. Beyond this, there is considerable interest displayed in the social setting of drug use and its role as a risk factor. Emphasis on the importance of avoiding drug use in 'high-risk' settings, such as rave parties, also bring to the fore the ways in which the risks to be governed are environmental or situational.

Finally, one of the most crucial issues considered by harm reduction is that the chemical effects of the drugs also are often regarded as less important than the risks of collateral harms. Again, while some of these relate to risk factors associated with properties of drugs (for example, driving under the influence), others do not – most notably harms associated with crime, corruption and violence. It is partly for this reason that prohibition and law enforcement are understood not simply as expendable risk managerial techniques, but as risk factors themselves, for they contribute to the generation of black markets, drug adulteration and disrespect for the law (PDAC 1996).

Thus, the probabilistic framework of harm reduction, coupled with its identification of the key risks as existing outside the drug or the user, distance it from models of drug abuse and addiction and, in some respects, allow an attenuation of the concern with free will and determinism. What emerges instead is an understanding of drug-users as subjects who are variably constrained by an environment of risk factors. In this way of thinking, this conditioning of freedom and constraint emerges in the form of a subject who must make choices from among a limited range of alternatives. The drug-user as *choice-maker* becomes the key form of subject through which government of drugs proceeds.

Responsible Users: Choice and Self-Government

Government through choice-making subjects begins with what will, in the shadow of the war on drugs, appear a series of striking propositions. Consider the following view from the Victorian drug education programme for schools:

The principles of harm minimisation include:

*an understanding that many students have used, currently use, and will use drugs
*a recognition of the rights of students not to use drugs
*a recognition that non-drug using students are subject to potentially harmful situations by the behaviour of drug using people
*a recognition that drug use provides varying degrees of risk for the user
*an acceptance that drug use by young people is a personal choice that is not within the control of teachers or schools

… A harm minimisation approach acknowledges that many young people will use drugs at some stage in their life, making it critical that students acquire knowledge and skills that will assist them in making informed decisions about their drug use and so minimise any harmful effects associated with that use. (DSEV 1995)

Drug users have been rendered choice-makers whose consumption choices not only cannot be governed by direct means, but arguably should not be so governed. This programme for secondary schools not only 'respects other's rights to make their own decisions', but more importantly, deploys such freedom of choice as the key element in the self-government of 'responsible' users and potential users:

A key premise of the strategy is that all Victorians should have access to accurate information and education programmes relating to drugs and drug use, *on the basis that informed, skilled individuals are able to make better choices which help prevent drug problems.* (HCS 1993, emphasis added)

Buried in this governmental proposal is a series of key assumptions. The first is that the freedom of the individual as a choice-maker is established and facilitated. The second is that these choice-makers can be assumed to make rational decisions that accord with the aims of government, providing they are given 'accurate' information and the skills required to make choices. The third is that the role of government is to provide access to the necessary skills and information. As might be anticipated, the skills and the information to be presented are understood as relating to risks. Thus the *Get Real* drug education package describes itself thus:

*It provides accurate and meaningful information
*It provides a framework for understanding the forces that shape choice
*It develops an awareness of risk situations
*It develops skills to avoid situations of risk and to manage them when they arise
*It encourages open discussion about drug use
*It is open to young people's views and experiences
*It does not encourage, condone or condemn the use of drugs by young people
*It develops skills that enable young people to influence and change their environments
*It helps students understand that drugs perform many useful functions in our society. (DSEV 1995)

Built into this array are a series of carefully developed strategies for ruling at a distance, through shaping the choice-making of users. The emphasis on providing accurate and meaningful information follows from the assumption that government is intended to work through the actions of choice-makers. But examination of the texts of harm minimization policy indicates another layer to this strategy of self-government. It is noted frequently in the literature that provision of biased or incomplete information aimed at deflecting people from drug use has been found to be counterproductive (see, for example, PDAC 1996). Information that distinguishes between illicit and licit drugs on the basis of the harmfulness of the former, for example, is found to limit the credibility of drug education, particularly among young people. Information that provides distorted and alarmist accounts of illicit drug use, such as tales of the inevitable slide from marijuana use into opiate addiction, is likewise found to discredit the programme because it can be refuted by experiences of users. The provision of 'accurate information' is preferred, therefore, partly because it is understood to govern more effectively.

However, it is also clear that provision of accurate information alone is not regarded as sufficient, for evidence is produced to show that, by itself, it does not reliably reduce risk-taking behaviour (PDAC 1996; Commonwealth Department of Health 1987). It is at this point that responsible choice-making users are to be *created* by government, for such programmes are to provide 'skills' as an essential adjunct to information. The *Get Real* education package, for example, provides potential users with 'a framework for understanding the forces that shape choice. It develops an awareness of risk situations. It develops skills to avoid situations of risk and to manage them when they arise' (DSEV 1995). In particular, these risk managerial skills include the building of self-esteem, recognition of the importance of peer group influence on choice-making, and skills for managing such pressures. These skills are targeted on the basis of evidence indicating their role in reducing risky behaviour. Put another way, the choice-makers are being given skills to render them more *autonomous*. But, at the same time, this autonomy is given a particular form or alignment that renders the subjects more able to isolate themselves from pressures which may lead in directions other than those sought by harm minimization.

Finally, it is also the case that public and school programmes themselves are shaped in their format by evaluation research, once more in order to facilitate the alignment of drug-takers' choices with harm minimization goals. Thus, for example, educational programmes formerly included travelling information teams, including ex-drug-users as well as drug educators and police. These programmes were found often to be counterproductive, with drug use or risk-related behaviours sometimes increasing after visits. Likewise, programmes which were integrated into the school curriculum, but were stand-alone drug education courses, were found wanting. Currently, preferred models emphasize building the drug education programme into the normal curriculum (for example, as part of the 'Life Skills' or 'Health Education' streams), with teachers who are part of the normal establishment of the school. These programmes are found to 'work better', thus cementing the process of government through normalization, but in a carefully tailored process of constituting normality and normal choice-making in such a way that they optimize harm minimization practices (Hawthorne 1996; Hawthorne *et al.* 1994; PDAC 1996).

It is important to recognize that, in this process, there is nevertheless a general governmental assumption that fully skilled and informed drug-users will opt for risk avoidance. The process requires no *political* intervention other than the enabling steps of governance to provide information and skills for the subject to deploy as they see fit. As indicated above, government through harm minimization presents itself as neither condemning nor condoning drug use, and while individuals are 'responsibilized' this appears to have none of the punitive connotations that apply to fields of criminal activity with which illicit drug use overlaps. At face value this is founded in the fact that the information about drug risks, appearing as objective and accurate, will present itself as no more than mapping out a *quasi-natural order of risks* rather than imposing an order formed and policed by political governance. The risks appear as probabilistic events triggered by the failure of the user to take necessary avoiding steps. The governmental presentation of risk information is presented as no more than a service provided to enable individuals to chart their own chosen course through the probabilistic course of health, pleasure and social risks presented by drug use. A fundamentally similar model of rational choice is deployed in relation to the category of the 'dependent drug-user', except that here, the greater risks presented by the dependent user are used to justify voluntary subjection to a more intrusive regime.

Dependent Use, Choice and Responsibility

At first blush, the category of 'dependent drug use' appears to be merely a synonym for that of 'addiction'. However, it differs in that the primary technologies deployed to govern addictions (for example, psychiatric and other therapeutic interventions) govern the problem of addiction as a 'disease of the will' and seek directly to restore to the addict a healthy free will. The government of dependent users through methadone maintenance programmes, on the other hand, does not take the dependence as the target for governance. While methadone is regarded as ultimately delivering a way out of dependency, this is neither regarded as a necessary outcome, nor as the primary benefit to the user delivered by the programme. Indeed, it is emphasized that methadone maintenance involves not only continued dependence on opiates, with the associated biochemical risks, but a dependency that often proves significantly more difficult to break (in terms of the severity of symptoms and the period of withdrawal) (HCS 1995). Methadone maintenance programmes under harm minimization regimes have as their primary target the governance of *risk generated by drug dependency*. These risks, and the ways in which methadone programmes manage them, are identified quite clearly in literature made available to dependent users, and include the following:

>*methadone is administered orally (usually in solution with a fruit juice) thereby reducing the health risks associated with injection
>*standard quality control by the administering agency prevents harms associated with drug adulteration

*because methadone does not give the user a 'high', it may be used to stabilise the dosage required by users, thus breaking the spiral of demand for larger dosages at greater cost

*because its effects are longer lasting than are those of other opiates (between 24 and 36 hours) methadone allows increased calculability of lifestyle, and normal patterns of work and life become possible – which in turn produces economic harm reduction and associated risk reduction with respect to the need to commit crime to finance drug use

*because it is legally available at low cost, participation in a methadone pro-gramme reduces risks associated with the violation of criminal law.

(HCS 1995)

Such 'benefits of the methadone scheme' are presented to the user along-side a series of other issues to be considered by a potential participant. These include not only the fact that the user remains opiate-dependent, but also that there are requirements of the programme demanding a regularizing of the user's lifestyle. For example, '(y)ou are committed to attending daily for your dose (and) travel or holidays can be difficult and must be organised well in advance' (HCS 1995). There is not in this sense, as is sometimes implied by critics, a secret agenda of surveillance. As with the transmission of 'accurate' information to responsible users, the effects of the programme, and their associations with the governance of risk, are presented openly to the dependent user as matters for rational choice-making, rather than as matters to be concealed: 'Your treatment team can support, advise and listen to you but basically you have to decide whether methadone is right for you' (HCS 1995).

Again, this voluntarization emerges out of the recognition that compul-sory programmes 'failed' to deliver results because of the fear, stigmatiz-ation and hostility that compulsory treatment created among users. Voluntary programmes, working through the rational choice users' preferences, and based therefore on their recognition of the risk reductions associated with enlistment in such programmes, are held to deliver better results. Governing through choice thus displaces government through coercion not on the basis of 'humanity' (although such ideas are certainly present) but primarily on the basis of optimizing effective rule. Through their participation in the programme, methadone consumers are normalized, and as rational, calculat-ing risk-takers, they enter the sphere of responsible drug use.

Harms to Others: Strategic Moralization

The exclusion of overtly moralizing interventions has been seen as central to the normalization strategy of harm minimization. Certainly in the light of the material discussed thus far, it would be easy to regard the process involved as a strategic demoralization. In other words, while analytically it is not difficult to detect a broadly utilitarian morality at work in harm reduction (Mugford 1993), the tone of texts excludes a judgemental morality which overtly decries drug consumption. This stance is more or less consciously adopted to maximize the effectiveness of technocratic rule (cf. Simon 1987). However, while receiving far less attention, overtly moral and coercive strategies do have a definite place in harm minimization literatures and are deployed with respect to two further categories of subject in the governance of drug problems. These relate to the categories of 'inappropriate use' and the 'drug trafficker'.

'Inappropriate Use'

'Inappropriate use' is a category of drug use that *directly* exposes others to risks. Although this conceivably could include users who, for example, share needles, the category's key reference is to users who drive or who use machinery under the influence of drugs. Here, the liberal concern with the moral culpability of those who harm others becomes more salient. Responsible users, by implication, are those who take into account the implications of their actions for the welfare of others. Accordingly, the primary strategy to be deployed to deflect subjects from 'inappropriate use' is to provide drug-users with the information they need to avoid inflicting harms. This information includes both data concerning the impact of alcohol and other drugs on drivers' reactions and suitable techniques for 'avoiding risk situations' – including the promulgation of the 'designated drive' model, the use of public transport where alcohol consumption is likely and so on.

At this point, the mobilization of morality becomes salient, for the responsibility created – for example in drink-drive advertisements – is clearly an overtly moralized responsibility. Advertisements aimed at responsibilizing users depict the injuries suffered by innocent third parties in drink-drive accidents, the anguish and misery inflicted on their families, and almost invariably include the driver suffering extreme guilt and remorse. Drivers are thus morally manoeuvred to avoid drink or drug-driving but, equally, friends and kin are made morally responsible for ensuring that guests and loved ones do not drive if they are drink-or drug-impaired. While a key strategy of governing responsible use has been seen to be a stance of moral neutrality where risks are linked to the user, this shifts to a morally valorized responsibility for governing risks to others.

Linked with this moral shift comes the deployment of increasingly coercive interventions. The intrusive probabilistic technologies of random breath testing are now a routine part of everyday life for drivers, the vast majority of whom, in a legal sense, have not offended (Walsh and Trumble 1991). Such interventions are justified primarily on the basis of their preventive or deterrent effect, primarily with respect to the risks created for third parties. These technologies and justifications are clearly becoming more generalized. Thus, in the *Victorian Strategic Plan* (HCS 1993) and reforms suggested more recently (PDAC 1996), priority is given to developing effective random drug-testing devices to scan the risk assessment 'gap' between the current capabilities of alcohol testing and those available for policing other drugs – which at present are effectively limited to more subjective means. The Victorian plan proposes to:

> Amend legislation to allow law enforcement to test impaired drivers for drugs other than alcohol for the purpose of legal action, deterrent [*sic*] and investigation into drug driving impairment ... (including) changes to the Road Safety Act to allow Victoria Police powers to take blood and/or urine samples from drivers whose BAC does not correlate with the degree of impairment displayed by the driver. (HCS 1993)

In addition, pre-emptive random drug testing is encouraged for a wider array of settings that are linked with driving. Major parties such as Vicroads (the state road transport authority),

> ... employer groups, transport unions, and the Road Transport Forum will develop new policies on drug use, guidelines for pre-employment medical examination and primary prevention and early intervention programs in the workplace. (HCS 1993)

The effect of such interventions is to reintroduce prohibition, justified not on the basis of particularistic prohibitory moralities of the 'private self' and its pleasures, but out of a moral concern with exposing others to significant risk. The effect, however, is to generate *zones of prohibition*, such as motor vehicles, certain occupations, workplaces or public spaces, entry to which is regarded as a matter of *choice* (cf. Simon 1987; O'Malley and Mugford 1991). People are free to consume drugs, and their freedom of choice in this respect is not problematic *per se*, but their entry to certain zones defined by the risk created for others is prohibited. Even here, however, the primary response within harm minimization discourses is not primarily punitive. Much greater emphasis is placed on the effectiveness of exclusion, whether by entry level detection or by responses to transgression which remove the risk – for example, licence cancellation coupled with driver education for drunk drivers.

'Drug Trafficking'

> Firm and effective law enforcement measures to contain supply must focus on the trafficker, particularly on those who control, direct and profit from such activities. While the trafficker/user dichotomy is not hard and fast, the user, insofar as he or she does not harm others, is primarily a challenge to the health system, the trafficker a challenge to the police system. (Blewitt 1987)

It is crucial to recognize that while, elsewhere in the discourse of harm minimization, new governmental categories have been created for drug use, organized around the problematic of risk, this is not the case with respect to 'drug traffickers', a term imported without change from law-and-order discourses. By and large, it is also the case that the modes for governing traffickers are also fully imported. Thus among the 75 far-reaching proposals for recent reform of Victoria's drug policy along harm minimization lines, there were no recommendations regarding changes in penalty for drug trafficking – apart from suggestions that the sentencing practices of the magistracy and judiciary be assessed with respect to utilizing the full range of penalties available (PDAC 1996) (current legislation allows a sentence of up to $25 000 fine and/or up to 25 years imprisonment for trafficking – including sale of marijuana to a minor). New and more punitive sanctions are being recommended and put in place with respect to confiscation of the assets of persons convicted of trafficking, usually with reverse onus conditions attached (PDAC 1996; Task Force 1992). Indeed, the unusual harshness of such sanctions has been noted by many commentators (for example, Freiberg 1992; Fox and Matthews 1992) in the Australian context. Equally, it is clear that all relevant policy documents adopt a morally condemnatory tone toward drug trafficking. Retention of the language of 'trafficking' – in the face of the explicit abandonment of associated discourses of addiction and abuse – suggests that the demonization and moralization being deliberately abandoned in the latter is being retained and mobilized against this category.

'Strategic moralization' is thus a better description of harm minimization's responses to drug governance than ostensible 'demoralization', which is sometimes regarded as the identifying feature of risk management technologies (Simon 1987), for the programmes selectively focus moral outrage and punitiveness according to the likelihood of creating risks for others. In the case of 'inappropriate use', the primary techniques are self-control through moral responsibility, linked with zonal prohibition and incapacitation. For traffickers, however, the response is sovereign punishment. Yet this distribution of morality and punitiveness is not at all unproblematic. It occurs despite the fact that the view in the harm minimization literature is clearly that blanket prohibition is not necessarily an effective strategy, and may – as in the creation of a black market – be counterproductive (Blewitt 1987; PDAC 1996). This suggests that the deployment of moral responsibility is not so much pragmatic as symbolic (cf. Garland 1991). It is the traffickers who are held ultimately *responsible* for the creation of most drug-related risks, especially conditions leading to drug adulteration, black market price escalation, needle use, and violence and corruption. Moral responsibility has been sheeted away from drug-users – who are governed most effectively by choice, and proportionately refocused on those defined as the creators of harm, the risk producers.[4]

Governing the Future

The probabilism of harm minimization has been linked in this chapter to the general avoidance in such discourses both of 'drug addiction' and 'drug abuse'. Harm minimization could escape these two discourses precisely because it partially avoided determinism/free-will polarity that Eve Sedgwick (1993) regards as their intellectual foundations:

> So long as an entity known as free will has been hypostatised and charged with ethical value, for just so long has an equally hypostatised 'compulsion' had to be available as a counter structure always internal to it, always being required to be ejected from it. The scouring descriptive work of addiction attribution is propelled by the same imperative: its exacerbated perceptual acuteness in detecting the compulsion behind everyday voluntarity is driven, ever more blindly, by its own compulsion to isolate some new, receding but absolutised space of *pure* voluntarity.

In some respects, 'free will' and 'compulsion' are displaced in harm minimization by two parallel but distinct terms – 'choice' and 'risk'. If free will and compulsion exist at opposite ends of a spectrum, this is not the case for choice and risk which are compatible and complementary terms. Choice emerges as a very particular formulation of 'freedom' for it always implies a partial closing down of liberty, its restriction to a number of given possibilities rather than the open selection from an unmarked terrain of possibilities. 'Freedom of choice' allows us to think in terms of variable degrees of freedom without necessarily raising the spectre of a constraint on action produced by an impaired or coerced will. In harm minimization discourses, the dependent user, for example, is not imagined as having the same array of choices that is available to the non-dependent user, for her array has been narrowed by the reliance on gaining access to a drug supply. But she is still imagined as a choice-maker. New choices become necessary or open for the dependent user – such as between enlisting in a methadone programme or not – which do not confront other users. Enlistment in such programmes is understood to increase the array of certain choices open to dependent users – for example, with respect to types of lifestyle that are opened up – but is seen to close down others – for example, those which depend upon a 'freedom' of movement unfettered by the need to arrange methadone supplies.

The imagery of the choice-making drug-user is thus of a 'normal' subject who seeks pleasure through the consumption of drugs, but whose choices are conditioned by an *environment* of risk rather than a restrictive polity. The drug-user is neither totally free nor compelled, but must make choices among risk-bearing options. The prudent individual takes on the role of governing drugs and, on the balance of probabilities, enjoys their pleasures in safety. The feckless individual bears costs to health and lifestyle that, on the balance of probabilities, are delivered by their own lack of responsibility. Prudence based on the advice of expertise is the virtue that emerges from responsible drug use. In the process, however, as Ian Hacking observes,

> The erosion of determinism and the taming of chance by statistics does not introduce a new liberty. The argument that indeterminism creates a place for free will is a hollow mockery. The bureaucracy of statistics imposes order not just by creating administrative rulings but by determining classifications within which people must think of themselves and the actions that are open to them. The hallmark of indeterminism is that cliche, information and control. The less the determinism, the more the possibilities for constraint. (Hacking 1991: 194)

There is, then, a dark side to the expansion of choice that harm minimization seems to deliver to a drug-using society. Now, it is not simply the addict who will be treated, nor the minority of users who are punished. *All* users are exposed to a regime of self-governance, constantly responsible for monitoring their behaviour, governing themselves without pause. Moreover, the probabilism of harm minimization weakens the power of this ability to contest this regime. If tales of the inevitable slide into addiction could be refuted by counterexamples from friendship networks, if the evil vision of the free-will drug abuser could be challenged by reference to harmless recreational users, what can challenge the depiction of a risk based on probability tables drawn from whole populations? The power to define risks and thus to shape self-governing drug use is moved to a more autonomous plane, difficult to challenge from the resources of personal experience.

For all that harm minimization establishes a regime of expanded choice for users, the new relations of expertise that are established deliver the shaping of governance (albeit 'at a distance') into the hands of technocrats. It is technocrats, in the shape of health statisticians, who identify and map the terrain of risks through which the choice-making drug-taker charts their course. It is educational programmes, psychologists and evaluators who develop the techniques of choice making that are held to maximize autonomy: the skills for resisting peer pressure, the development of self-esteem and so on. It is medical programmers and their evaluators who develop the techniques of health risk avoidance and reduction that are available to the choice-maker in formulating a personal programme of pleasure.

The 'taming of chance' thus appears in this domain as the *shaping of choice* and the *identification of risk*. More generally, I would suggest that these two interlinked processes are key features of government in advanced liberalism, for as the domain of our security is increasingly passed over to the responsibility of the 'prudent' individual, then more and more of our lives and resources need be given over to the government of our futures. Only the irresponsible or feckless will leave the future to chance when new probabilistic and risk managerial technologies allow for its taming. At the end of the twentieth-century almost every area of the person has become subject to risk managing technologies that 'allow' us to spread, reduce or refigure risk (Simon 1987). Insurance and other financial technologies now give us the opportunity to manage almost every conceivable form of risk (see, for example, Waine 1992). Technologies of health and fitness alert us to the future consequences of our present actions and provide us with risk minimizing interventions (Greco 1993; Ewick 1993). Programmes of domestic and personal security advise and equip us with the (often commodified) means to defend our bodies against the predations of others (O'Malley 1991, 1992; Douglas 1992). Thereby we are enlisted into programmes of self-rule by being *alerted* to risks in the same moment that we are provided with the technologies for governing them.

Confronted by so many advanced technologies for governing the future, the individual's range of choices apparently expands. But the ambiguity of this choice should now be clear, for while each choice represents the creation of an option, each option represents a further shaping of 'freedom'. Harms that exist only in the *possible* future increasingly must be governed as if they are actually occurring problems, 'objective risks', in the here and now. Increasing commitment of time and effort must be given over to governing the future security of our physical health and fitness, employment, property, retirement and mental faculties. Furthermore, they must be given over to governing the futures of all those others, the members of our 'families' and 'communities', whose futures are increasingly rendered the responsibilities of self-governing individuals under advanced liberalism. Awareness of risks may extend our future and render it more secure. Yet the more that risks are identified and linked to current life practices, lifestyle choices and the acquisition of new commodities of security, so the present is consumed and governed by the future.

Notes

1   This is translated from the general aims of the strategy as outlined here, to specific objectives in particular programmes. Thus, for example, the *Victorian Drug Education Strategic Plan 1994–1999* views a harm minimization approach to drug education as developing 'an awareness of risk situations' and as imparting 'skills to avoid situations of risk and to manage them when they arise' (DSEV 1995).
2   The Directorate of School Education (1995) argues that '(t)he use of drugs, including alcohol, tobacco and pharmaceutical drugs, is common in our society' and that 'many young people will use drugs at some stage of their life', while the Victorian Premier's Drug Advisory Council (PDAC 1996) notes that '(h)arm minimization as a policy accepts that people use drugs on occasions. The challenge for services which come into contact with drug-users is to minimise the harms associated with misuse'. The suggestion seems to be that drug use *per se* is not problematic, and that harms must be the consequence of excessive or inappropriate use.
3   Nor is this fanciful. Major efforts have been made to develop such indicators, and they certainly have been influential in policy formation (for example, Collins and Lapsley 1991; PDAC 1996).
4   Evidently trafficking could be minimized by legalization and regulated drug production. Many harm minimization exponents support this move, but shy away from it as having unpredictable effects. Other factors may also apply. For example in the Commission on which the author served in 1995–96, such proposals were shelved because of the risk of mobilizing opposition which would frustrate other reforms being proposed.

References

Blewitt, D. (1987), *National Campaign Against Drug Abuse: Assumptions, Arguments and Aspirations*, Canberra: Australian Government Publishing Service.
Castel, R. (1991), 'From Dangerousness to Risk', in G. Burchell, C. Gordon and P. Miller (eds), *The Foucault Effect: Studies in Governmentality*, Chicago: University of Chicago Press.
Cohen, S. (1985), *Visions of Social Control*, London: Polity Press.
Collins, D. and H. Lapsley (1991), *Estimating the Economic Costs of Drug Abuse in Australia*, Canberra: Australian Government Publishing Service.
Commonwealth Department of Health (1987), *Drug Education Programs in Australia*, Canberra: Australian Government Publishing Service.
Commonwealth Department of Human Services and Health (1995), 'Briefing Notes on Harm Minimization and Drug Use', unpublished material prepared for the Department of Human Services and Health.

DSEV (Directorate of School Education, Victoria) (1995), *Get Real. A Harm Minimization Approach to Drug Education*, Melbourne: Directorate of School Education.

Douglas, M. (1992), *Risk and Blame: Essays in Cultural Theory*, London: Routledge.

Ewald, F. (1994), 'Two Infinities of Risk', in B. Massumi (ed.), *The Politics of Everyday Fear*, London: University of Minnesota Press.

Ewick, Patricia (1993), 'Corporate Cures: The Commodification of Social Control', in A. Sarat and S. Sibley (eds), *Studies in Law, Politics and Society*, Vol. 13, New York: JAI Press, 137–57.

Feeley, M. and J. Simon (1992), 'The New Penology: Notes on the Emerging Strategy of Corrections and its Implications', *Criminology*, **30** (4), 449–74.

Feeley, M. and J. Simon (1994), 'Actuarial Justice. The Emerging New Criminal Law', in David Nelken (ed.), *The Futures of Criminology*, New York: Sage.

Fischer, B. (1995), 'Drugs, Communities, and Harm Reduction in Germany: The New Relevance of Public Health Principles in Local Responses', *Journal of Public Health Policy*, **16** (4), 389–411.

Fischer, B., P. Erickson and R. Smart (1997), 'The New Canadian Drug Law: One Step Forward, Two Steps Backward', *International Journal of Drug Policy*, **7** (3), 172–9.

Foucault, M. (1991), 'Governmentality', in G. Burchell, C. Gordon and P. Miller (eds), *The Foucault Effect: Studies in Governmentality*, Chicago: University of Chicago Press.

Fox, R. and I. Mathews (1992), *Drugs Policy. Facts, Fiction and the Future*, Sydney: The Federation Press.

Freiberg, A. (1992), 'Criminal Confiscation, Profit and Liberty', *Australian and New Zealand Journal of Criminology*, **25** (1), 44–81.

Garland, David (1991), *Punishment and Modern Society*, Chicago: Chicago University Press.

Greco, M. (1993), 'Psychosomatic Subjects and the Duty to be Well', *Economy and Society*, **22** (3), 357–72.

Hacking, Ian (1991), 'How Should we Do the History of Statistics?', in G. Burchell, C. Gordon and P. Miller (eds), *The Foucault Effect: Studies in Governmentality*, Chicago: University of Chicago Press.

Hawthorne, G. (1996), 'The Social Impact of Life Education', *Addiction*, **91** (12), 9–19.

Hawthorne, G., G. Garrard, D. Dunt, K. Brass, A. Loftus-Hill and L. Bradsley (1994), *Drug Education in Victorian Schools: Policies and Practices in Curriculum and Welfare*, Melbourne: Directorate of School Education.

HCS (Victorian Government Department of Health and Community Services) (1993), *Victorian Drug Strategy: 1993–1998*, Melbourne: Health and Community Service, Promotions and Media Unit.

HCS (Victorian Government Department of Health and Community Services) (1995), Methadone Treatment in Victoria: User Information Booklet, Melbourne: Health and Community Service, Public Health Branch.

Matza, D. and P. Morgan (1995), 'Controlling Drug Use: The Great Prohibition', in

Blomberg, T. and S. Cohen (eds), *Punishment and Social Control*, Chicago: Aldine de Gruyter.

Miller, Peter and Nikolas Rose (1990), 'Governing Economic Life', *Economy and Society*, **19** (1), 1–30.

Mugford, Stephen (1993), 'Social Change and the Control of Psychotropic Drugs. Risk Management, Harm Reduction and "Postmodernity"', *Drug and Alcohol Review*, **12** (3), 369–75.

National Campaign Against Drug Abuse (NCADA) (1987), *National Campaign Against Drug Abuse: Assumptions, Arguments and Aspirations*, Canberra: Australian Government Publishing Service.

O'Malley, Pat (1991), 'Legal Networks and Domestic Security', *Studies in Law Politics and Society*, **11**, 171–90.

O'Malley, Pat (1992), 'Risk, Power and Crime Prevention', *Economy and Society*, **21** (2), 252–75.

O'Malley, Pat (1996), 'Indigenous Governance', *Economy and Society*, **25** (3), 310–26.

O'Malley, P. and S. Mugford (1991), 'Moral Technology: The Political Agenda of Random Drug Testing', *Social Justice*, **18** (4), 122–46.

PDAC (Premier's Drug Advisory Council) (1996), *Drugs and Our Community: Report of the Premier's Drug Advisory Council Melbourne*, Victorian Government.

Reichman, Nancy (1986), 'Managing Crime Risks: Toward an Insurance Based Model of Social Control', *Research in Law and Social Control*, **8**, 151–72.

Sedgwick, Eve (1993), *Tendencies*, North Carolina: Duke University Press.

Simon, J. (1987), 'The Emergence of a Risk Society: Insurance, Law, and the State', *Socialist Review*, **95** (2), 93–108.

Task Force on Evaluation (1992), *No Quick Fix. An Evaluation of the National Campaign Against Drug Abuse*, commissioned by the Ministerial Council on Drug Strategy.

Valverde, M. (1998), *Diseases of the Will*, Cambridge: Cambridge University Press.

Waine, Barbara (1992), 'Workers as Owners: The Ideology and Practice of Personal Pensions', *Economy and Society*, **21** 27–44.

Walsh, J. and J. Trumble (1991), 'The Politics of Drug Testing', in Coombs, R., and L. West (eds), *Drug Testing: Issues and Options*, New York: Oxford University Press.

9 Policing, Postmodernism and Transnationalization

J.W.E. Sheptycki

Omina mutantur nos et muamur in illis

(All things change and we change with them)

Throughout the incandescence of the York Deviancy Symposium, between the late 1960s and the late 1970s, criminology was in a period of more or less permanent scientific revolution (Downes 1988). There is one strand of thinking that suggests that, subsequent to this period of epistemological flux, criminology has become committed to routine research competence in the service of policy-oriented empiricism (POE) because of changes in the funding mechanisms for such research (Rock 1988). Even where the fragmentary nature of criminology is highlighted, POE has been identified as the predominant strain (Ericson and Carriere 1994). 'Crime', Paul Rock tells us, 'now looks more sober, abundant and distressing than before' and thus, faced with the brutal facts of riot, urban disorder and high rates of criminal victimization, criminology is 'no longer a discipline besotted with the idea of big ideas' (Rock 1994: 145–7). It is thus rather pleasingly ironic that a term such as 'postmodernism', with its attendant attitude of theoretical cannibalism – where the intellectual is exhorted to appropriate ideas as the postmodern artist appropriates styles, throwing them together at will, jumbling the different theoretical idioms without combining them into a single coherent language, splashing them on to the page in a celebration of intertheoretical and international elasticity – enters criminological vocabulary at this point.

Just as concepts have ebbs and flows in usage – one might use the term 'fashion' (Thorne 1993; Garland 1995) – they also have etymologies or histories of usage. In the case of the concept of a 'postmodern age' that history goes back much further than most suppose. Indeed, it seems that Toynbee coined the term in the crucial year of 1939 when he wrote that 'our own Post-Modern age has been inaugurated by the General War of 1914–18' (Toynbee, 1939: 43).[1] C. Wright Mills' use of the term in *The Sociological Imagination* (1959), is better known to criminologists (Reiner 1992; Sheptycki 1995).[2] In applying this term these thinkers intended to illuminate a basic transformation in the political economy and the cultural and social order of contemporary societies, imbuing their idea of history with a sense of deep fissure. More recently, and perhaps notoriously, thinkers who have adopted the term have also sought to identify, exemplify and amplify an epistemological break with Enlightenment Rationalism. This break plays on the inevitable irony of historical contingency, seeking only solidarity and thereby eschewing universal truth claims (Rorty 1989). This notion of fissure in both the social structure of society and its philosophical (ideological) framework is, in contemporary usage of the term, accompanied by the stylistic, *née* McLuhanesque, attitude mentioned above as exemplified by Baudrillard, Lyotard and Derrida.

History is not, as Winston Churchill is purported to have said, one damn thing after another. It is a social process of becoming. In trying to write the present as history, the category of the postmodern allows us to approach the present without reference to an overarching and totalizing 'truth' as, for example, Whiggish or Marxist history did. Rather, by writing about the present in contradistinction to what has gone before, and by focusing on processes of disintegration, fragmentation and change, the historian of the present is trying to capture that sense of becoming and, further, to identify where we might be going. It is a dangerous exercise – 'futurology' is the scornful label for such efforts – and yet, even while the study of history cannot help but inspire a scepticism about a recurrent belief in decline, a recognition of deep change is necessary in order to gauge if the degree of fruitful novelty is keeping pace with the obvious destruction. If there were not such striking, and all too often violent, shifts in modes of governance visible in the world around us there would be no point in discussing the nature of the so-called 'Crisis of Our Time' and the character of the turning point which we are said to have reached, or passed, or sighted ahead. Examining the present state of governance permits us to form at least a tentative conclusion about the magnitude of the present epoch. Criminology can, and should, contribute to this intellectual project. This chapter tackles only one aspect of the historical changes in which contemporary people feel themselves to be embroiled – namely, the feeling that crime stalks our cities and the idea that its suppression is neither feasible nor in keeping with enlightened thought. Coupled with this increased sense of insecurity are significant changes in our primary institutions of social control. My analytical focus here is on police rather than, say, the institution of punishment, for it is with this concept, and the practices embodied by it, that the phenomena of crime and social control are most broadly related. However, in order to engage with contemporary manifestations of 'police' we must first discuss its genealogy; we must know where we have come from in order to guess where we are going. *Historia vitae magista* (history is the teacher of life).

A Genealogy of 'Police'

The 'science of police' is much neglected in conventional histories of criminological thought (Reiner 1988), the primary exception being Radzinowicz's encyclopedic *History of English Criminal Law* (1956), the third volume of which is largely devoted to an account of it. Standard histories of criminology make reference to Beccaria and Bentham, Quetelet and Lombroso, but very often fail to mention Colquhoun, or do so only in passing. More obscure figures, such as Georg Obrecht, do not feature in the criminological pantheon at all (Pasquino 1991). The reason for this seems to be the current state of criminology, rather than that the science of police used to be marginal. Indeed, when Adam Smith referred to it as 'the second general division of jurisprudence' he merely confirmed policing as a much broader enterprise than what is referred to by criminologists as 'classical criminology'. The term encompassed the whole art of government in the sense of regulation, management and maintenance of population – that is, 'governmentality' (Foucault 1991). This sense of police is still with us today, as the literature on community policing and its variants testifies (Bayley 1994; Goldstein 1990; Skolnick and Bayley 1986); and yet much of contemporary criminology views the study of police as a mere topic under the more general heading of 'criminal justice systems'. Examining changes in the way social order has been achieved is essential for understanding the scope of the concept.

The concept of police was introduced into the English language during the first half of the eighteenth-century and, as Radzinowicz has noted, it was originally a suspect term derived from contemporary French usage. As previously mentioned, its meaning was cast widely, to indicate something like the government of great cities or the regulation of the inhabitants of a country or city. Pasquino (1991) links his own definition of the term to Foucault's notion of governmentality. Initially, he tells us, police were spoken of positively as *cura promovendi salutem* (concerned with the promotion of safety or the public good). Gradually, a negative definition came to the fore whereby police were conceived of in terms of *cura advertendi mala futura* (concerned to avert future ills). Both Radzinowicz and Pasquino agree, although they use very different theoretical vocabularies, that the notion of policing was gradually refined throughout the eighteenth-century until *circa* 1780, when the task of policing was conceived as being firmly rooted in the role of a uniformed body of men concerned with the maintenance of public order, riot control and crime prevention. Police became, in Robert Reiner's words, 'stout men in blue coats' (Reiner 1988). The first body of such police in the English-speaking world came into being in 1786 with the passing of the Dublin Police Act under the stewardship of Robert Peel, then Secretary of State for Ireland (Palmer 1988).[3] It was not until 1829 that London was given a similar force, and the extension of this strategy for social control over the entirety of the British Isles took practically the rest of the century (Devlin 1966).

Social historians have noted that it was the threat posed by the disenfranchised and economically marginalized 'dangerous classes' at the beginning of the Industrial Age that galvanized the political classes into creating the police institution and giving it a mandate to secure public space through various legal instruments aimed at public disorder, theft and violence (Chesney 1970; Gurr *et al.* 1977; Linebaugh 1991; Jones 1984; Vogler 1991). What this social history makes apparent is that policing gradually evolved as the threat of capital punishment was pared back and the role of the military was gradually confined to the frontiers of the evolving nation-state system. We could say, in terms inspired by Foucault, that the specific form of governmentality practised by the police institution was a manifestly modern one, intended to secure the good order and, hence, prosperity of nationally bounded states. There are, of course, competing (or complementary) definitions, most notably Bittner's (1970) notion that 'police' is best defined by reference to the capacity for the legitimate use of coercion, but this essentialist definition, while undoubtedly indicative of an important feature of the policing function, is too narrow to delineate all of its practices. Indeed, when we consider that British police officers were still inspecting weights and measures in the immediate post-war period (Young 1991) and that the current fashion of community policing may even extend the police role to facilitating the repair of broken windows, Bittner's essentialism needs some qualification. The genealogy of police reveals it to be a form of governmentality based on the rule of law, with a mandate to use force in the maintenance of social order, broadly conceived.

Central to this form of governmentality was the imposition of the nation-state system in Europe and, as this system settled into a more or less stable set of institutional arrangements, so too did the new agencies of social control. Following Weber, sociologists define the state as an institutional form that successfully upholds a claim to bind rule-making over a territory by virtue of commanding a monopoly of the legitimate use of force (Mann 1986). Following Gramsci, sociologists also note that a successful and stable state will not resort to coercion routinely but will obtain a consensual predominance over its citizens, summarized in the concept of hegemony (Jessop 1982). The notion of police which arose in Europe was, in its very essence, an expression of both these ideas. The power of the sovereign state was based on is ability to ensure stability and plenty. The police agencies that emerged during the nineteenth century were the concrete expression of the state's monopoly of coercive force *within* its territory, just as the various branches of the military were the expression of that power at the borders. It should not escape our attention, however, that police had, from the end of the eighteenth-century onwards something of a global reach inasmuch as the 'colonial model' of policing was exported from Europe (Cain 1995; Anderson and Killingray 1991, 1992).

Actually, as the history of our own era testifies, the state system is less stable than this picture suggests. Significantly, however, the system achieved a high degree of stasis in Europe during this period.[4] It was during the relatively peaceful mid-nineteenth-century, when states' coercive forces were exercised by the problems of maintaining *internal* order, that police agencies in the modern sense were established. The revolutions of 1848 that so captured the imagination of Karl Marx loom large here. In general, we may say that nation-states which were established early, such as France, also established a police tradition early and those that came later, such as Italy, lagged behind. In the case of Italy, the *carabinieri* were not established until shortly after the peninsula became a unified state in 1870; in France, the police tradition dates from 1667 (Bayley 1975). The specific form of police institution differed slightly between European countries, but, once police institutions were established within a relatively stable nation-state system, they could go on to develop an internal historical trajectory – that is, one determined partly by their own internal logic.[5] Thus, the process of scienticization advocated by August Vollmer, Edward Henry, Dr Johann Schober and others could unfold, later yielding such innovations as fingerprint classification, radio-dispatched car patrols, intelligence-led policing, and forensic evidence techniques to name but a few (Douthit 1975; Hannant 1995). Of course, this internal history forms only part of the story and, as the tendencies of the nation-state system played themselves out (for example, during both the world wars or by the great multiplication of states in the aftermath of the Second World War), so too was the history of the police affected. Yet as long as that 'inter'-national state system remained, it served as the central reference point for our understanding of policing institutions (Walker 1994). That system is currently undergoing profound change which is visible through changes in police organization.

Four Postulates of Postmodern Police

It has been suggested that the 'belief in the postmodern is almost the touchstone of a new universal truth', and, further, that the use the term evokes the rise of an overarching shift to a new totalized order (O'Malley 1997). In what follows I hope to avoid this pitfall. Rather than trying to grasp the totality of the New World Order – a Herculean task – I propose to use four 'postulates of postmodern police' as a thread to lead us through the labyrinth of conflicting signs, images and data (hyperreality in Baudrillard's terms) about crime and social control. Those postulates should be seen as two dual processes or dyads. The first duality is the marketization of insecurity and of state-provided social control; the second is the transnationalization of clandestine markets and of policing. Together these two twin processes appear as part of the larger global process of the restructuring of the nation-state system – one acting, as it were, 'from below' and the other 'from above'.[6]

The marketization of insecurity

In 1972 the discipline of criminology was stirred by a new idea propounded by a Canadian-born urban planner, Oscar Newman. In his book *Defensible Space; People and Design in the Violent City* (1972), Newman introduced the idea of controlling criminal victimization in public spaces through various tactical innovations, particularly, the creation of 'zones of territorial influence', the fostering of 'natural surveillance' within such zones and, finally, the marking-off of these locales through symbolic boundaries (that is, gates and other barriers). Newman's ideas percolated into thinking about crime control and urban design and, although there were methodological flaws in Newman's original study (Bottoms 1974), the marketing potential of such low-risk, secure environments was seized upon by real estate developers in the USA, where it is estimated that there are now more than 30 000 'gated communities'. It is expected that a further 30 000 will come into being within the next decade (Clark 1995).

The marketization of insecurity is beginning to change the shape of some major cities as they are carved up into zones of 'risk suppression'. Nowadays, 20 or so years after Newman, the marketing of security appears to be a driving force in the reformation of the 'Big City'. Nowhere is this more clear than in accounts of contemporary São Paulo. In her urban ethnography of a Brazilian megalopolis, Teresa Caldeira (1992: 159) has shown how the marketization of insecurity, the fear of crime and concomitant strategies of risk suppression promote a type of policing that bypasses the legal institutions of social ordering in the resolution of social conflict. Private security operates alongside the public police, to erect walls that separate the risky from the at-risk – that is, the poor from the wealthy.[7] In contemporary São Paulo, the security of the enclave has become the *sine qua non* of élite status. Nor is the cultural shift brought about through the strategy of risk suppression peculiar to São Paulo; indeed, the cultural processes underway there invite direct comparison with 'Fortress LA':

> Welcome to post-liberal Los Angeles, where the defence of luxury life styles is translated into a proliferation of new repressions in space and movement, undergirded by the ubiquitous 'armed response'. This obsession with physical security systems and, collaterally, with the architectural policing of social boundaries, has become the zeitgeist of urban restructuring, a master narrative in the emerging built environment of the 1990s ... We live in 'fortress cities' brutally divided between 'fortified cells' of affluent society and 'places of terror' where police battle the criminalized poor ... In cities like Los Angeles, on the bad edge of postmodernity, one observes an unprecedented tendency to merge urban design, architecture and the police apparatus into a single, comprehensive security structure. (Davis 1992: 223–4)

While the merging of urban design and policing into a comprehensive security structure is not without historical precedent, those precedents are decidedly, and despite the pretensions of architectural discourse, *pre*-modern. The reality described by Davis is the 'New Feudal City'.[8] Further, it is also important to stress that these strategies of risk suppression are not confined to a few places. On the contrary, the marketing of secure zones is evident in a multiplicity of American cities as well as in South Africa, Israel, India, Egypt, Indonesia and elsewhere (*Law Enforcement News*, 1992; Brogden and Shearing 1993; Findlay and Zvekic 1993). The process has even found its advocates in the UK (Wheeler *et al.* 1989) and, although Europeans are noticeably less enthusiastic consumers of this form of risk suppression, there are even a few gated communities beginning to emerge in Germany and France (Nogala 1996; South 1994).[9]

The marketization of public policing

Within the literature on governmentality that has emerged since Foucault's death, there has been a concerted effort to analyse neo-liberal strategies of governance. Neo-liberalism is accurately summarized in this literature as a radical programme of government, concerned with correcting the so-called pathologies of the welfare state – in particular, those intrusions into society and the economy wrought by socialized health care, compulsory state insurance, tax-funded social security, unemployment benefits and the like. These mechanisms of the welfare state have, neo-liberals argue, interfered with the efficiencies of the market, sapped the entrepreneurial spirit and introduced a culture of dependence, all of which undermine the 'true' welfare of individuals (Garland 1997a). By the mid-1970s, the rationalities represented by these mechanisms were commencing a retreat which, with the election of Thatcher and Reagan, became a rout. The successful marketization of insecurity discussed in the previous section is symptomatic of this process as is the commodification of services offered to the public by the police, and both are linked to the triumph of cultures of consumption over those of production (cf. Riesman 1950). Robert Reiner (1992) has remarked on how police elites have turned to the languages and style of consumerism. Under the influence of the Audit Commission, police in the UK have undertaken consumer audits, quality-of-service assessments, mission statements, charters as well as adopting the vocabulary of private sector management gurus. Moreover, these affectations are not unique to British police; evidence of this trend can be found elsewhere in the Commonwealth (O'Malley 1996), Europe (Robert and van Outrive 1993) and North America (Bayley 1994).[10]

One of the central strategies of public police agencies has thus become what David Garland (1997b), among others, has referred to as 'responsibilization'. This is currently manifest in the promulgation of 'the partnership approach' in crime prevention and community policing (Home Office 1993), which was perhaps best summed up by Herman Goldstein, doyen of community policing, when he said that 'we must restore a balance between citizen and police responsibilities that reflects a more accurate assessment of actual capacities and acknowledges that effective social control cannot possibly be achieved by hired hands alone' (quoted in Koller 1990). Clearly, the partnership envisaged has a particular balance. Police and community organizations are not thrown together haphazardly; rather, 'partnership policing [is] where police take a *proactive leadership role* in bringing disparate community groups such as the police, elected officials, government and other agencies together to focus on crime and community disorder problems' (Hunt, quoted in O'Malley 1996). The model is of police officers as professional community organizers, and the community policing literature is full of anecdotes and 'heroic stories of police constables being catalysts of change in social housing projects by empowering residents to expel the crack dealers in the tradition of St Patrick and the snakes' (Offer 1996). Criminologists have noted 'the reconceptualisation of policing as a service and the redesignation of the community as customers' (McLaughlin 1992).

Much of what has gone on under the rubric of community policing has remained un-evaluated by professional social scientists and much of what passes for evaluation is merely self-interested reportage produced by individuals who have a direct stake in the success of the projects. It is evident that the motivation of the Audit Commission in the UK, and like-minded bodies elsewhere, is to promote fiscal responsibility and even to cut back the cost of state-provided social control, at least relative to the sum-total of such provision.[11] 'Customerization', as this strategy has also been christened (O'Malley 1997), might be seen as a grab-bag of techniques by which a rump public–police infrastructure is connected with other control providers (not least private security firms patrolling gated communities, or insurance firms). In this bigger picture, public police are dwarfed by the private providers of security. Taken together, the two processes of the marketization of insecurity and of public policing are indicative of a shift in the provision of social control away from the state sector and towards private forms. Some criminologists refer to a 'hybrid model' (Johnston 1992; Jones 1996) wherein private and public forms of security provision work in uneasy alliance, but this picture is too static. If we examine this process over a period of time – since say, the 1970s – it is possible to see that it is not so much a new hybrid but an evolution away from a position where the state was the virtual monopoly-provider of security and social control, towards a situation where state provision is less and less predominant (see Walker 1978; Stenning and Shearing 1980).

The Transnationalization of Clandestine Markets[12]

When US President Bill Clinton announced in his 1996 State of the Union Address that, after years of neglect, 'this administration has taken a strong stand to stiffen our borders ... we are increasing our border patrols by 50 percent', he was not directing anxiety towards a communist invasion or Kidd's band of wild Indians.[13] The issue at hand was brought into close focus by the Deputy Assistant Secretary of State for law enforcement and crime, Jonathan Winer, who later said '[e]very country must develop tough new policies aimed at restoring its borders so that they are again meaningful protection against criminals, drugs, weapons and illegal immigration' (quoted in Andreas 1996). The integration of clandestine markets has become one of the key foreign policy issues, not only for the USA but also for Europe (see Andreas 1995; Hopkinson 1994; Seward 1993). In January 1995, a subcommittee of the Association of Chief Police Officers (ACPO) in England and Wales began a 12-month review of cross-border crime. The (unpublished) report that subsequently emerged became known as the Phillips Report, after Colin Phillips (then Assistant Chief Constable of Greater Manchester), the chairman of the committee who produced it. While it is clear in the report that international crime is not the looming monster feared by some (Martin and Romano 1992) – less than 10 per cent of in-force Central Squad operations were targeted at international crime *per se* – the report did focus considerable attention on what was termed 'market crimes' (Phillips 1996). Phillips was later quoted in *Policing Today* (Howe 1996) as stating that 'market offences are distinguished by the fact that they are committed with the aim to supply an illegal service or product to willing buyers' and, further, that 'these types of offences are often not reported to the police and there is no accurate means of measuring the extent [of them] … all the indications suggest, however, that it is rising'.[14] Although the report did mention other types of offences (for example, specific mention was made of the investigative difficulties posed by serial sexual assault and murders by travelling offenders) most of the energy of police operations in the transnational arena was clearly absorbed by market-type offences: in particular, drugs trafficking (40 per cent); fraud, traffic in counterfeit credit cards, and other monetary instruments (36 per cent); traffic in stolen vehicles (9 per cent); and 14 per cent undefined.[15]

Geographers have long talked about the phenomenon of time–space convergence (Carlstein *et al.* 1978). At its most basic, the point made is that at the turn of the twentieth-century it took four days to travel across North America but, nowadays, the journey has shrunk to five hours. This time–space convergence has had important implications for the reach of markets. In our own era it is possible to have fresh produce from every corner of the globe.[16] Time–space convergence, coupled with the opening-up of borders to trade, advocated by transnational financial regulators (for example, the World Bank, the World Trade Organization, the Organization for Economic Cooperation and Development), has unintentionally magnified the potential for clandestine trade. Opening economies through the liberalization of markets reduces governments' ability to withstand market pressures; after all, countries that follow the tenets of neo-classical economic theory should specialize in those exports in which they have a competitive advantage. This may mean that the only market niche open to some entrepreneurs in some regions is unseemly, to say the least: immigrant labour, white slavery, weapons, plutonium, toxic waste, drugs, stolen cars – all can be brought to the transnational black market to be realized at their truest value. Thus, as free-market reform reshapes the state system, shrinking the regulatory system of the nation-state proper (even while creating or expanding transnational regulatory régimes such as the EU or NAFTA),[17] market prohibitions push to expand the policing dimensions of the state proper. Public policing, as a manifestation of the nation-state's renewed commitment to controlling market prohibitions, is consequently pulled further into the transnational realm.[18] This process was clearly revealed by FBI director, Louis Freeh, in his statement to the Senate Appropriations Committee Subcommittee on Foreign Operations in March 1996, in which he revealed that the number of legal attachés working at the US embassy in Moscow had risen from 20 to

200 during the previous 20 months. The reason given for such a large FBI presence in Eastern Europe was determined to be the presence of organized crime in the marketplace. As Freeh (1996) put it:

> Organized crime activity in Russia includes monetary speculation, manipulation of the banking system, and embezzlement of state property, as well as contract murder, extortion, drug trafficking, prostitution, protection rackets and infiltration of legitimate business activity.[19]

While the spectre of Russian-organized crime is a particularly potent folk-devil, the problems of market-based crime are more commonplace in European discussions. The debate in the House of Lords on the remit of Europol is interesting in this regard. The opinion of the committee was that 'the crimes within the initial remit of Europol ... appear on the list ... because they are particularly transnational in character and therefore require a transnational response' (House of Lords 1995, para 86: 26). Those crimes were revealed to be 'drug trafficking, crime connected with [trafficking in] nuclear and radioactive substances, illegal immigrant smuggling, motor vehicle crimes (in particular trafficking to other States and theft of goods in transit) and illegal money-laundering activities in connection with these forms of crime'. Indeed, the only type of crime mentioned in connection with Europol's remit that did not have some link with clandestine markets was terrorism; and the Lords voted to delay this addition to the list (ibid.: paras 24–9: 12).

What seems clear from discussions within law enforcement circles and from policy-makers is that transnational clandestine markets have become a particular cause for concern. This is not to say that this is a new phenomenon – when Interpol was in its initial operating stage in the 1920s, black market crimes were of some, even considerable, concern (Bresler 1992): however, there is a clear perception that this type of activity has greatly increased since the end of the Cold War. Hence, public police agencies are increasingly drawn into the transnational realm, but this only confirms an already well known tendency.

The Transnationalization of Policing

Transnational policing is not, in itself, a new phenomenon, as Hannah Arendt has pointed out.[20] The transnationalization of policing seems to be part and parcel of the internal history of the police organization in the twentieth-century; certainly as mentioned earlier in discussing 'A Genealogy of "Police"', the exportation of the 'colonial model' in the nineteenth-century reveals policing to be, in a sense, transnational from the outset. In the twentieth-century we may cite the early formation of the International Association of Chiefs of Police (IACP), noting how it fostered the dissemination of European developments in police science, notably fingerprinting (Hannant 1995). Then too, there is the conception of Interpol during the same period (Anderson 1989), even if its realization did not occur until after the First World War. The necessity of transnational policing has always depended on a variety of folk-devils, its efficacy always resting on certain technical means for capturing them. For example, there is the story of Detective-Sergeant Faurot, an NYPD officer who had been sent to London to learn about the Henry fingerprint classification system. As Ethan Nadelmann explains:

> Back on footpatrol in New York he happened to arrest an Englishman who was lurking suspiciously at the Waldorf Astoria Hotel. Uncertain of his true identity, Faurot sent the suspect's fingerprints to Scotland Yard. The reply, some two weeks later, confirmed that the suspect was a professional hotel thief and a fugitive from British justice. (Nadelmann 1993: 85)

The above scenario is striking, not only for the pettiness of the folk-devil in question, but for the length of time that the transatlantic communication took. These days the suspect in question is more likely to be a paedophile and certainly the communication time-lapse is expected to be far shorter.[21] The 'information revolution' has had a profound impact on policing, making the possibility of police communication over long distances a matter of relative ease. In the recent past, cross-border links between police forces have been greatly enhanced by this process, and police managers have been quick to grasp the invitation to transnationalize even further (Sheptycki 1995, 1996, 1997). When politicians and policy-makers highlighted the problems posed by the integration of clandestine markets, they found a transnational police infrastructure already in place. This infrastructure, albeit only skeletal, needed no reorganization of its principal features in order to take on his enhanced mission. Indeed, the major problem for senior police managers is that they have had to share the turf with agencies rendered largely redundant by the ending of the Cold War. In the USA the CIA has been given a role to play in the new transnational police enterprise, while in Britain both MI5 and MI6 have been similarly accommodated. In both the USA and the UK instances, the military and its vast array of technical hardware have also been brought into the frame. What is clearly evident is that the transnationalization of policing is taking place at the convergence of several major global restructurings – the opening-up of global markets, the information revolution and the end of the Cold War. All lend to the enterprise a considerable import, and one which is much beyond a mere continuance of the police fraternity's seemingly natural inclination to transnational networking.[22]

One way to illustrate the exponential growth of transnational police in recent years is to look at the acquisition of information technology intended to foster such efforts. Elsewhere I have shown the growth in macro-structures of information exchange for transnational policing (Sheptycki 1995), including the advent of Interpol's Automated Search Facility (ASF), the Schengen Information System (SIRENE), and Europol's' phone/fax network. My fieldwork in north-western Europe has also uncovered two micro-structures, the Lingua Net Project and the PALMA project, both transnational regional networks for information storage, retrieval and exchange.[23] So-called soft information, or 'criminal intelligence', is exchanged through informal networks which are well-documented (Bigo 1994). This process is also evident within the North American Free Trade Area (NAFTA) – information sharing between Canadian and American law enforcement has been routinized by way of an interface between the Canadian Police Information Exchange Centre (CPIC) and the National Crime Information Centre (NCIC), facilitated by the Automated Canada USA Information Exchange System (ACUPIES) (see Interpol Ottawa 1995). This system allows patrol officers on either side of the border to access their respective national criminal databases on a 24-hour basis. Enquiry response times are estimated to be between three and five minutes. Information types range from expired driver's permits to criminal records to records of convicted persons on supervised release and much else. There is even some indication in the scholarly literature that the RCMP and FBI even have online access to criminal intelligence files *per se* (Anderson 1993: 50) and, certainly in the stratosphere of 'high policing', these linkages have been documented (Brodeur 1995: 96). The research to date on the growth of information technology in police organization reveals a quantum leap in communications capabilities in the transnational arena. This development amounts to an institutionalization of transnational police cooperation (cf. Fijnaut 1995).

Another way to illustrate this is to refer to the growth of legal instruments to facilitate transnational law enforcement (Commonwealth Secretariat 1991, 1992, 1993). The variety of newly available legal instruments, from the highly formalized Mutual Legal Assistance Treaty (MLAT) to the less formal Memoranda of Understanding (MoU) and many others, provide a central pillar in the growth of the transnational police enterprise (Sheptycki 1998). The multiplication of these legal instruments beyond the historical baseline of the Extradition Treaty again shows that the variety of police work and its volume have reached unprecedented proportions.

Discussion

The thesis is that police organizations worldwide have had nation-states as their nesting sites and, further, that the character of the nation-state system is currently undergoing a significant transformation that is both visible in changing forms of policing and constitutive of those new forms. Policing is being transformed 'from below' by the twin processes of the marketization of insecurity and of state-provided social control. The first is a process by which citizens become consumers of security services and the example of the growth of enclave communities was taken to be the *sine qua non* of this process. On the other hand, we can see that the state is being internally transformed. In the social control industry, one sure indicator of this is the adoption of private sector 'management speak' by senior police officers, another is the so-called 'strategy of responsiblization' articulated by senior policy-makers in governments throughout the Commonwealth and elsewhere. Together, these strategies make communities, citizens and other organizations actively responsible for their own risk management and thereby reduce the responsibility of the state, through the public police organization, in this area of social provision. All this must be seen against the background of the ongoing fiscal crisis of the modern state – wherein national governments are suffering from an extreme form of indebtedness. A discussion of these economic facts is beyond the confines of this chapter; nevertheless it seems safe to say that the provision of security and crime control – a virtual state monopoly since the mid-nineteenth century – is poised on the precipice of this fiscal crisis. Already new forms for the management of insecurity are taking shape in the interstices of the old police system. In my estimation they are, if anything, *pre*-modern; but, regardless of the label, they are the harbinger of a significant transformation of the state-system which gains its impetus 'from below'.

In the transnational arena there is also clear evidence of the magnitude of transformation in the nation-state system. Nations are being reconstituted downwards into regions, even as the transnational realm becomes a significant domain for the negotiation of governance. This chapter identified a second set of dual processes occurring at this level and clearly visible to criminologists – namely, the transnationalization of clandestine markets and of policing. These processes are linked, but there is also a sense in which they are independent. On the one hand, the growth of transnational black markets is symptomatic of the freeing-up of global trade generally – that is, this growth is another indicator of the sweeping changes in the state system. On the other, the transnationalization of policing has a long history which has perceptibly accelerated within the last decade. These dual processes are symptomatic of the larger global processes of transnationalization. Following Toynbee, and shifting our vision to the broader historical vista, we might say that these are signs of an epochal shift which, if not on a par with the great withering away of the western Roman Empire and the rise of Christendom, are indicative of a shift at least as momentous as the rise of the Atlantic economies and the colonial hegemony of Europe at the dawn of the Modern Age. Small wonder there are so few certainties, epistemological or otherwise.

For a generation of criminologists locked in the *Realpolitik* of policy-oriented empiricism (POE), this wider horizon may be only dimly visible or, worse, visible only through the kaleidoscopic lens of television news where history is compressed into a 30-second sound-bite. Discourses on the postmodern coloured, as they are, by visions of the 'hyperreal', are one way to force an ironic *dénouement*: the utopia visualized by neo-liberals is falling apart before its completion, the postmodern implodes into the detritus of its own panic scenes. And yet many criminologists are irritated by the confessed intentions of criminologists working in the postmodern vein, who forsake crisis management on behalf of 'the crimino-legal tradition' in favour of a 'strategy of exacerbation' (Young 1996: 3). Whatever else, the progeny of the postmodern era, whose lives are ultimately, if precariously, built on the shifting sands of a transnational state system that is emergent, fragile and insecure, will have to make choices. But those choices will be made on the basis of the unknown, and the barely knowable. A POE-fixated criminology provides too narrow a vision to illuminate the broad sweep of history; its collective product merely contributes more information to the hyperreality industry which endlessly refracts understanding nightly on the television news. The poetic abandon of much self-avowedly 'postmodernist' criminology is meant to be corrosive of this process and yet purveys only a sense of desperation and powerlessness. Caught between forms of governance that, by virtue of their remoteness, continually escape our control and understanding and the overproduction of myopic simulacra of 'valid knowledge' that clouds our vision we merely cope. *De minimis non curat vires* (power does not take account of trifles). No more the Enlightenment's sense of rationality and the historical march of human progress; instead, mere damage control.

Notes

1   Toynbee's use of the term was directed at the eclipse of European civilization on the world stage. Put simply, since the modern period was synonymous with the rise of Europe, the transfer of global political, social and economic power away from that tiny peninsula and its clutch of small islands on the western edge of the Asian landmass

presaged the dawn of a new civilization. Hence the historical cleavage bespoke by the term 'postmodern'.

2   Mills' use of the term, while also pointing to the importance of historical cleavage in social theorizing, points to the importance of an earlier transformation. For him, too many sociological terms were forged in an attempt to understand the import of the industrial revolution and the transition from the medieval to the modern age but, 'generalised for use today they become unwieldy, irrelevant, not convincing' (Mills 1959: 166).

3   The first legislation to establish a police organization in the New World came three years later when the Federal Marshals Service was set up in the new republic of the United States. It had a complement of 12 officers.

4   It should be pointed out that the hegemony of state forms of policing was not so pronounced in the USA where the radical democracy of the 'vigilante tradition' looms large even today (Franz 1969; Brown 1969). We might agree with Tocqueville when he spoke of the 'tyranny of the majority', and said that 'what I find most repulsive in America is not the extreme freedom reigning there but the shortage of guarantees against tyranny'. In this regard he characterized the police as 'nothing but the majority under arms' (Tocqueville 1969: 252). He notes, with a European distaste, the 'anarchy' and 'apparent disorder' that arises from the lack of general regulations for police, a lack which is 'acutely felt' (ibid.: 90). Thus, 'in Europe the criminal is a luckless man fighting to save his head from the authorities; in this sense the population are mere spectators of the struggle'. In the USA, where the 'tyranny of the majority' reigns, the criminal becomes 'an enemy of the human race and every human being is against him' (ibid.: 96). The vigilante tradition in the USA might explain why it is that the marketization of insecurity is so much more advanced there.

5   This broad-brush approach to police history obscures much that is important about the evolution of the various national police traditions and, as Bayley warns, 'by fitting diverse situations into a Procrustean mould, loss of empirical richness is assured' (Bayley 1975: 329). However, the more general point, that police institutions in their modern form were contingent on the development of the nation-state system, is, for the purposes of this discussion, important to establish.

6   Here the reader can see that the notion of the postmodern, especially as it is operationalized in these four postulates, is functioning as what Herbert Blumer (1969) referred to as a 'sensitizing concept'. Thus, in keeping with the spirit of sociological enquiry exemplified by Blumer and other members of the Chicago School, the main emphasis is on the social world, not the abstract concepts. In this view, the social world should be allowed to 'speak for itself', rather than being subjected to the distorting lens of an overly abstracted theorization (Blumer 1969; see also Mills 1959).

7   In São Paulo this partnership is manifest in an extreme form. There the state police (detailed in groups of four heavily armed officers), react to the crime problem with the routine use of violence. Indeed, statistics relating to the number of people killed by the police are announced monthly in press releases as a grim performance indicator of police success in the fight against criminality (Caldeira 1992: 162). Extreme violence by the public police is considered an effective and necessary means to fight criminality. Caldeira, citing a report by America's Watch, notes that 'the military police [which is] a uniformed patrol force, is responsible for summary executions and the civil police [which is] charged with [the responsibility for crime] investigation is responsible for torture' (ibid.: 170). Symbols of class membership are a key factor in police decisions to use force (Huggins 1991; see also Birkbeck and Gabaldón 1996, for a discussion of these processes in Caracas).

8   Los Angeles City Council approved the installation of seven metal gates on public

thoroughfares, effectively sealing off the suburb of Whitley Heights to non-residents. This was later overturned in the California Supreme Court, whose decision referred to these enclaves as a 'return to feudal times' (Lind 1995: 213).

9 Some readers may object that Europe has not seen the emergence of the enclave community. It is too early in the history of the processes of transnationalization that are described here to commit to a European exception in this regard. It should be noted, however, that some research has documented enclavization in the UK (Loader and Sparks 1997), although in a muted form: notably, the absence of 'armed response' and the use of much more subtle symbolic boundaries (traffic-quietening, for example) to achieve the same ends – the separation of the risky from the at-risk. According to these researchers there is a very real worry held by middle-class English people about 'travelling crime' – that is, crime that enters their communities from 'outside'. They talk about a 'violation of the cocoon', giving the sense that people feel a need to retreat from a hostile and dangerous world. The residents of such developments as the Barbican Centre in east London depend on (unarmed) private security to secure the space around the buildings. It remains an open question, but perhaps this is the seed of an armed fortress in London's midst?

10 The beginning of this process in the UK is usually taken to be the Home Office Circular 114 (issued in 1983), entitled 'Manpower, Effectiveness and Efficiency in the Police Service', which, although couched in general and at times vague terms, presented an unambiguous message which sounded more like a recipe for corporate downsizing in the automobile industry than anything previously heard in policing circles. Police managers were given a number of basic options: (1) substitute capital for labour – that is, reduce labour costs through investment; (2) find cheaper forms of manpower (that is, make more use of civilian workers in administration and volunteer police 'special constables'); (3) substitute external sources of supply for internal contracting-out; and (4) improve the management of available manpower (see Morgan 1986; White and Brown 1986). The subsequent history of this initiative reveals that, although the British police were slow to take up this neo-liberal philosophy, they nevertheless came to embrace it with notable enthusiasm.

11 Adam Crawford (1995) argues, further, that the 'appeal to community' found in this literature also serves to shift the blame for programme failure on to the community and away from the police institution. He extends the notion of 'victim blaming' to that of 'community blaming' and notes that many geographical locations have been pathologized as 'no-go areas'. He goes on to argue that this strategy serves to further undermine the legitimacy of state-centred policing since 'the redistribution of the cost of personal and communal safety, from government and state institutions to individuals and groups, raises political questions about the state's competence ... [since it calls] into question the ability and legitimacy of the state to effectively "do the job" of crime control' (Crawford 1995: 112). What then emerges are spaces which are subject to 'forms of extra-state policing and growing vigilantism' and Crawford reiterates a point made by Dahrendorf, warning of the Hobbesian implications if policing becomes merely the exercise of private power (ibid.: 113).

12 I am grateful to Peter Andreas for discussions on this point, whose insights clearly shaped my thinking on this issue.

13 I refer here both to former President Ronald Reagan's worries about communist contagation from Latin America, specifically from Sandanista sources, in the early 1980s and to much earlier worries about cross-border brigandage; specifically 'Kidd's Band of Wild Indians', who operated across the Mexican border in the very late nineteenth century.

14   A report drawn up jointly (but unpublished) by the Ministry of Justice and the Ministry of Home Affairs in the Netherlands in 1992 estimated the total cash turnover of 10 million guilders per annum. The report went on to say that 'Organised Crime thus belongs to one of the biggest sectors of the Dutch economy' and, further, 'predicts a further rise due to the internationalisation of economic traffic' (*Organised Crime in the Netherlands; An Outline of the Threat and the Plan to Tackle it*, 5).

15   A significant, although unquantified, proportion of this was linked to illegal immigration (personal communication to author).

16   An example of time–space convergence in the global market place is the reaction of McDonalds to the BSE crisis in the summer of 1996. Within a week of the panic-induced burger boycott, McDonalds was able to announce that no British beef was contained in their products, and some of it was said to come from as far afield as Argentina.

17   The best recent example of new transnational regulatory/policing bodies is the creation of the Financial Action Task Force in 1989 which, although it is currently housed in the OECD Headquarters in Paris, is not part of that organization. The basic brief of the FATF is the facilitation of the internal or self-policing of the transnational offshore banking system, with specific reference to 'money laundering' and the banking of the proceeds of crime (for a detailed discussion see Sherman 1993).

18   It is important to note that there are older examples of global prohibition regimes. An especially apt one is the case of the anti-slave trade régime imposed by the British navy. This effort at suppressing a global market in human beings was embarked upon in 1807 when the government of the day banned the institution in mainland Britain. This step was extended to the colonies in 1833. Throughout the nineteenth-century Great Britain devoted between a sixth and a quarter of its warships to suppressing the slave traffic. The way in which a global prohibition regime is policed and upheld sheds a great deal of light on the nature of the extant state system. For example, today the pursuance of such a policy would be made, at least in part, through transnational institutions that simply did not exist in the early nineteenth-century; Interpol and the United Nations are only the most evident of these. The crucial point for the analysis pursued here is that, because of the phenomenon of time–space convergence, there has been such a quantitative shift in the vibrancy of transnational markets generally that it amounts to a qualitative shift. For an excellent overview of the history of global prohibition regimes see Nadelmann (1993).

19   The incorporation of contract murder into this list is reflective of the particularity of illegal markets – namely, the absence of a formal apparatus devoted to guarantee the security of contracts. For a discussion of the organizational sociology of organized crime and clandestine marketing, see Arlacchi (1996).

20   Arendt noted that in Europe during the interwar period there were significant dislocations of population and a consequent huge rise in the numbers of 'stateless persons'. She talks in terms of millions of Spaniards, Poles, Italians, Balkans – waves of refugees or economic migrants in the parlance of the day – moving across the newly imposed and reimposed national boundaries. In the resulting tumult 'the nation-state [became] incapable of providing a law for those who had lost the protection of a national government [and] transferred the whole matter to the police ... under the pretext of "national security", the police of a number of democratic countries had embarked on so close and organised a co-operation with the Gestapo and the GPU that one could well speak of an independent police initiative in matters of foreign politics. The co-operation, for instance, between the French police and the Gestapo was never closer and never functioned better than under the anti-Nazi government of the Popular

Front' (Arendt 1951: 284–6). It is evident that Arendt is here talking about police conducting their own foreign policy independently of their respective foreign ministries, which is but an extreme form of what I mean when I refer to the transnational practices of police agencies.

21 I refer to the tragic Dutroux case in Belgium during 1996 which involved a ring of paedophiles operating transnationally within Europe. This case has served to intensify not only the consolidation of Europe's internal security field, but also to offer a rationale for a wholesale reorganization of Belgian policing more in keeping with her neighbours. See the *International Herald Tribune*, 27 August 1996.

22 This natural inclination is also evident in the police custom of referring to their cross-border counterparts as colleagues. It is also evident at the CRI Headquarters (Criminal Intelligence) in The Hague, where all the meeting rooms are not numbered but named after law enforcement agencies. Meeting rooms are officially designated as the RCMP room, the BKA room, the DEA room, the Police Nationale room and so on.

23 Linguanet is the second generation of the Police Speak Project (*Police Speak* 1993) and is thus already well documented. Currently, this system links up police stations at 12 locations in four countries (Belgium, the Netherlands, France and Great Britain) and is expected to continue growing. The project recently attracted some 1.5 million ECUS from the European Union for its further development. The PALMA project (Police, Aachen, Leige, Maastricht) was initiated by police in the Netherlands in conjunction with computer scientists at the Maastricht Technological Research Institute (MTRI). At present there is nothing available in English on this project; however, interviews I have conducted with police officials at the International Contact Centre (ICC) in Maastricht, the Ministry of Interior in the Hague and with computer scientists at the MTRI indicate that the long-term plan for this system is to provide a means of transnational information exchange with regional partners for all Dutch police stations within proximity of the border.

References

Anderson, D.M. and D. Killingray (eds) (1991), *Policing and the Empire*, Manchester: University of Manchester Press.

Anderson, D.M. and D. Killingray (eds) (1992), *Policing and Decolonisation*, Manchester: University of Manchester Press.

Anderson, M. (1989), *Policing the World*, Oxford: Clarendon Press.

Anderson, M. (1993), 'The French Police and Cooperation in Europe', in C. Fijnaut (ed.), *The Internationalization of Police Cooperation in Western Europe*, Deventer: Kluwer.

Andreas, P. (1995), 'Free Market Reform and Drug Market Prohibition', *Third World Quarterly*, 16 (1), 75–87.,

Andreas, P. (1996), 'US–Mexico: Open Markets, Closed Boarder', *Foreign Policy*, (103), 51–69.

Arendt, H. (1951), *The Burden of Our Time*, (1st edn), London: Secker & Warburg.

Arlacchi, P. (1996), 'Some Observations on Illegal Markets', an unpublished presentation for the Economic and Social Research Council Conference on Crime and Social Order in Europe, Manchester, October 1996.

Bayley, D.H. (1975), 'The Police and Political Development in Europe', in C.

Tilley (ed.), *The Formation of National States in Europe*, Princeton, NJ: Princeton University Press.

Bayley, D.H. (1994), *Police for the Future*, New York: Oxford University Press.

Bigo, D. (1994), 'The European Internal Security Field', in M. Anderson and M. den Boer (eds), *Policing Across National Boundaries*, London: Pinter.

Birkbeck, C. and A.G. Gabaldón (1996), 'Avoiding Complaints: Venezuelan Police Officers' Situational Criteria for Use of Force Against Citizens', *Policing and Society*, **6** (2), 113–29.

Bittner, E. (1970), *The Functions of Police in Modern Society*, Chevy Chase, Maryland: National Institute of Mental Health.

Blumer, H. (1969), 'What is Wrong With Social Theory', in H. Blumer (ed.), *Symbolic Interaction: Perspective and Method*, Englewood Cliffs, NJ: Prentice-Hall.

Bottoms, A.E. (1974), 'Review of *Defensible Space*', *British Journal of Criminology*, **14** (2), 203–6.

Bresler, F. (1992), *Interpol*, London: Mandarine.

Brodeur, J.P. (1995), 'Undercover Policing in Canada: A Study of Its Consequences', in C. Fijnaut and G. Marx (eds), *Undercover; Police Surveillance in Comparative Perspective*, Deventer: Kluwer.

Brogden, M. and C. Shearing (1993), *Policing for a New South Africa*, London: Routledge.

Brown, R.M. (1969), 'The American Vigilante Tradition', in H.D. Graham and T. Gurr (eds), *Violence in America: Historical and Contemporary Perspectives*, Washington: USGPO.

Cain, M. (1995), 'Policing Here and There; Reflections on an International Comparison', *International Journal of the Sociology of Law*, **24** (4), 399–426.

Caldiera, T. (1992), *City of Walls*, unpublished PhD dissertation, University of California, Berkeley.

Carlstein, T., D. Parkes and N. Thrift (eds) (1978), *Timing Space and Spacing Time: Vol. 1 Making Sense of Time*, London: Edward Arnold.

Chesney, K. (1970), *The Victorian Underworld*, London: Maurice Temple Smith.

Clark, J.R. (1995), '1995 Law Enforcement Man of the Year, Oscar Newman', *Law Enforcement News*, **XXI**, 436–7, December 1995–January 1996.

Commonwealth Secretariat (1991), *Action Against Transnational Criminality*, Vol. 1, papers from the 1991 Oxford Conference on International and White Collar Crime.

Commonwealth Secretariat (1992), *Action Against Transnational Criminality*, Vol. 2, papers from the 1992 Oxford Conference on International and White Collar Crime.

Commonwealth Secretariat (1993), *Action Against Transnational Criminality*, Vol. 3, papers from the 1993 Oxford Conference on International and White Collar Crime.

Crawford, A. (1995), 'Appeals to Community and Crime Prevention', *Crime, Law and Social Change*, **22** (1), 97–126.

Davis, M. (1992), *City of Quartz*, London: Vintage.

Devlin, D. (1966), *Police Procedure, Administration and Organisation*, London: Butterworths.

Douthit, N. (1975), 'August Vollmer, Berkeley's First Chief of Police and the Emergence of Police Professionalism', *California Historical Quarterly*, **LIV**, 101–24.

Downes, D. (1988), 'The Sociology of Crime and Social Control in Britain, 1960–1987', in P. Rock (ed.), *A History of British Criminology*, Oxford: Oxford University Press.

Ericson, R.V. and K.D. Carriere (1994), 'The Fragmentation of Criminology', in Nelken, David (ed.), *The Futures of Criminology*, London: Sage.

Findlay, M. and U. Zvedkic (1993), *Alternative Policing Styles*, Deventer: Kluwer.

Fijnaut, C. (ed.) (1995), *The Internationalization of Police Cooperation in Western Europe*, Deventer: Kluwer Law and Taxation Publishers.

Foucault, M. (1991), 'Governmentality', in G. Burchell, C. Gordon and P. Miller (eds), *The Foucault Effect: Studies in Governmentality*, Chicago: University of Chicago Press.

Franz, J.B. (1969), 'The Frontier Tradition: An Invitation to Violence', in H.D. Graham and T. Gurr (eds), *Violence in America: Historical and Contemporary Perspectives*, Washington: USGPO.

Freeh, L. (1996), FBI Web Page, March, http://www.fbi.gov/intrcrim.htm.

Garland, D. (1995), 'Penal Modernism and Postmodernism', in T. Blomberg and S. Cohen (eds), *Punishment and Social Control*, New York: Aldine de Gruyter.

Garland, D. (1997a), '"Governmentality" and the Problem of Crime: Foucault, Criminology, Sociology', *Theoretical Criminology*, **1** (2), 173–214.

Garland, D. (1997b), 'The Punitive Society: Penology, Criminology, and the History of the Present', *Edinburgh Law Review*, **1** (2), 180–200.

Goldstein, H. (1990), *Problem-Oriented Policing*, Philadelphia, PA: Temple University Press.

Gurr, T.R., P.N. Grabosky and R.C. Hula (1977), *The Politics of Crime and Conflict*, Beverly Hills: Sage.

Hannant, L. (1995), *The Infernal Machine: Investigating the Loyalty of Canada's Citizens*, Toronto: University of Toronto Press.

Home Office (1993), *A Practical Guide to Crime Prevention for Local Partnerships*, London: HMSO.

Hopkinson, N. (1994), 'Responses to Western Europe's Immigration Crisis', *Wilton Park Paper No. 84*, London: HMSO.

House of Lords (1995), 'Select Committee on the European Communities, EUROPOL', *HL Paper 51*, London: HMSO.

Howe, S. (1996), 'Mind the Gap', *Policing Today*, **2** (1), 20–4.

Huggins, M. (ed.) (1991), *Vigilantism and the State in Modern Latin America*, New York: Praeger.

Interpol Ottawa, RCMP (1995), *The International Criminal Police Organisation: Canada's Law Enforcement Link with the World*, Ottawa: Minister of Supply and Services.

Jessop, B. (1982), *The Capitalist State*, Oxford: Martin Robertson.

Johnston, L. (1992), *The Rebirth of Private Policing*, London: Routledge.

Jones, G.S. (1984), *Outcast London*, London: Penguin.

Jones. T. (1996), 'The Boundaries Between Public and Private Policing', unpublished seminar presentation for the Centre for Law and Society, University of Glasgow.

Koller, K. (1990), *Working the Beat; The Edmonton Neighbourhood Foot Patrol*, Edmonton, Alberta: The Edmonton Police Service.

Law Enforcement News (1992), XVIII (37), December.

Lind, M. (1995), *The Next American Nation*, New York: The Free Press.

Linebaugh, P. (1991), *The London Hanged*, London: Penguin.

Loader, I. and R. Sparks (1997), 'Social Talk and Fear of Crime in Prestbury', unpublished paper presented to the British Society of Criminology, London.

McLaughlin, E. (1992), 'The Democratic Deficit: European Union and the Accountability of the British Police', *British Journal of Criminology*, **34** (4), 473–88.

Mann, M. (1986), *The Sources of Social Power*, Cambridge: Cambridge University Press.

Martin, J.M. and A.T. Romano (1992), *Multinational Crime: Terrorism, Espionage, Drug and Arms Trafficking*, London: Sage.

Mills, C.W. (1959), *The Sociological Imagination*, New York: Oxford University Press.

Morgan, J. (1986), 'Getting Better Use of Police Resources', in *Crime UK 1986; An Economic, Social and Policy Audit*, Harrison, A., and J. Gretton (eds), Policy Journals, pp. 41–9.

Nadelmann, E. (1993), *Cops Across Borders*, Pennsylvania: Pennsylvania State Press.

Newman, O. (1972), *Defensible Space; People and Design in the Violent City*, New York: Macmillan.

Nogala, D. (1996), 'How Policing Gets "Privatised"', unpublished paper presented to the ESRC European Research Conference, Manchester, September.

Offer, C. (1996), 'C-OP Fads and Emperors without Clothes', *Law Enforcement News*, 15 March.

O'Malley, P. (1996), 'Policing, Postmodernity and Political Rationality', unpublished paper presented to the Law and Society Annual Meeting, Glasgow.

O'Malley, P. (1997), 'Policing, Politics and Postmodernity', *Social and Legal Studies*, **6** (3), 363–81.

Palmer, S.H. (1988), *Police and Protest in England and Ireland 1780–1850*, Cambridge: Cambridge University Press.

Pasquino, P. (1991), 'Theatrum Politicum; The Genealogy of Capital – Police and the State of Prosperity', in G. Burchell, C. Gordon and P. Miller (eds), *The Foucault Effect: Studies in Governmentality*, Chicago: University of Chicago Press.

Phillips, C. (1996), 'International, National and Interforce Crime. A Study Commissioned by the Association of Chief Police Officers: Final Report February 1996', unpublished document.

Police Speak: Police Communications and Language and the Channel Tunnel – Report (1993), Cambridge: Police Speak Publications.

Radzinowicz, L. (1956), *A History of English Criminal Law and its Administration from 1750*, vol. 3, London: Sweet & Maxwell.

Reiner, R. (1988), 'British Criminology and the State', in P. Rock (ed.), *A History of British Criminology*, Oxford: Oxford University Press.

Reiner, R. (1992), 'Policing a Postmodern Society', *Modern Law Review*, **55** (6), 761–81.

Riesman, D. (1950), *The Lonely Crowd*, New Haven: Yale University Press.

Robert, P. and L. van Outrive (1993), *Crime et Justice en Europe*, Paris: L'Hamattan.

Rock, P. (1988), 'The Present State of Criminology in Britain', in P. Rock (ed.), *A History of British Criminology*, Oxford: Oxford University Press.

Rock, P. (1994), 'The Social Organisation of British Criminology', in *The Oxford Handbook of Criminology*, Oxford: Oxford University Press.

Rorty, R. (1989), *Contingency, Irony and Solidarity*, Cambridge: Cambridge University Press.

Seward, V. (1993), 'Combatting Drugs Trafficking and Abuse: the Challenge to Europe', *Wilton Park Paper No. 64*, London: HMSO.

Sheptycki, J.W.E. (1995), 'Transnational Policing and the Makings of a Postmodern State', *British Journal of Criminology*, **35** (4), 613–35.

Sheptycki, J.W.E. (1996), 'Law Enforcement, Justice and Democracy in the Transnational Arena; Reflections on the War on Drugs', *International Journal of the Sociology of Law*, **24** (1), 61–75.

Sheptycki, J.W.E. (1997), 'Transnationalism, Crime Control and the European State System', *International Criminal Justice Review*, **7**, 130–40.

Sheptycki, J.W.E. (1998), 'The Global Cops Cometh: Reflections on Transnationalisation, Knowledge Work and Policing Subculture', *British Journal of Sociology*, **49** (1): 57–74.

Sherman, T. (1993), 'International Efforts to Combat Money Laundering: The Role of the Financial Action Task Force', in H.L. MacQueen (ed.), *Money Laundering*, Edinburgh: Edinburgh University Press.

Skolnick, J. and D. Bayley (1986), *The New Blue Line*, New York: Free Press.

South, N. (1994), 'Privatizing Policing in the European Market', *European Sociological Review*, **10** (3), 219–33.

Stenning, P.C. and C.D. Shearing (1980), 'The Quiet Revolution: The Nature, Development and General Legal Implications of Private Policing in Canada', *Criminal Law Quarterly*, **22** (2), 220–48.

Tocqueville, A. de (1969), *Democracy in America*, New York: Doubleday.

Toynbee, A.J. (1939), *A Study in History. Vol. 5: The Disintegrations of Civilizations*, London: Humphrey Milford/Oxford University Press.

Thorne, T. (1993), *Fads, Fashions and Cults*, London: Bloomsbury.

Vogler, R. (1991), *Reading the Riot Act*, Milton Keynes: Open University Press.

Walker, N. (1994), 'European Integration and European Policing: A Complex Relationship', in M. Anderson and M. den Boer (eds), *Policing Across Transnational Boundaries*, London: Pinter.

Walker, S. (1978), *A Critical History of Police Reform*, Lexington, Mass.: Lexington Books.

Wheeler, J., M. Tuck, B. Poyner and M. Pirie (1989), *Curbing Crime*, London: Adam Smith Institute.

White, G. and E. Brown (1986), 'Police Forces', in A. Harrison and J. Gretton (eds), *Crime UK 1986! An Economic, Social and Policy Audit, Policy Journals*, 30–9.

Young, A. (1996), *Imagining Crime*, London: Sage.

Young, M. (1991), *An Inside Job*, Oxford: Oxford University Press.

10 Beyond the Law: The Virtual Reality of Post-Communist Privatization

Maria Loś

One of the key dimensions of post-communist power regimes in Central Europe is the development of new norms and practices surrounding property. The communist party-state's near monopoly over property rights was institutionalized through a complex system of the *nomenklatura* rule,[1] legal prohibitions and central distribution of goods. The large sphere of the second (shadow) economy notwithstanding, state ownership of the means of production (including the, so-called, cooperative property) was the centrepiece of the communist normative order.

To grasp the dramatic nature of changes in that region one has only to imagine the impact which a sudden denial of validity of private property would have on the modern Western liberal state. While, however, such a mental exercise helps to appreciate the normative turmoil that a change in the concept of property may cause in a contemporary society, this analogy should not been taken too literally. Certainly, the communist state's property claims, which extended to both the economy and individual citizens, were not treated as natural or normal to the same extent as private property in Western societies.

Nonetheless, many people in communist countries took for granted the state ownership of heavy industry and utilities, even if they criticized the waste, irrationality and corruption with which they associated it. Their world was structured by the state-cum-party – the two were really interchangeable – which paid meagre wages, supplemented them arbitrarily with various perks and handouts (now mistakenly presented by many Western commentators and former communist elites as 'welfare') and often pretended not to notice the petty appropriation of state property by employees and the much grander criminal schemes by state functionaries. The normative boundaries of the state's ownership prerogative and those relating to the rights and duties of employees were, to put it mildly, murky.

The delegitimation of state monopoly over property rights was expected to shake these rather hypocritical normative arrangements and replace 'nobody's' property – as state property was generally viewed – with a new, more inspiring image of the property owner. Indeed, many competing versions of the latter were to be found in the dominant discourses of the time. They ranged from the timeless 'cornershop-keeper', to the wealthy expatriate to the pre-communist title-holder to the enterprising street vendor (the equivalent of the American shoeshine boy) to the romantic 'robber baron' (trusted to grow, in time, into a respectable capitalist, just as the American ones had done) and, finally, the simultaneously dreaded and wooed multinational company. This colourful discourse, with its broad range of fanciful possibilities, appears now to have played the role of a smokescreen to divert attention from the real-life robber barons who were busy dividing the state economy among themselves – the old communist *nomenklatura* class.

In this chapter I analyse specific forms of property that appear to serve best that class's interests. The main thesis is that the emerging pattern of property holdings in the fledgling post-communist capitalism is a type of *network-based property that is intangible, ephemeral, diffuse, flexible, web-like, neither state nor private and neither domestic nor foreign*. The new type of property holdings can best be described in terms of *'virtual' property* that promises pleasure and profit without pain and liability.[2]

Just as 'virtual reality' allows for the training of pilots while sheltering them from the physical effects of a navigational error, or for the experience of a risk-free sexual adventure, virtual property opens the door to re-creating the gain involved in laying claim to something while avoiding the corresponding hazards and responsibilities. The latter are somehow left behind, since the space in which the virtual property thrives (new-technology-based, information-driven, long-distance, network-based) is characterized by speed, extraterritoriality and frailty of regulation.

The 'something' to which the claim is made may be used, for example, as a security against a new or preferential credit or as a proof of business credibility. While it may not in fact exist, it may be 'virtually' there in terms of its desired effects. Alternatively, it may exist but only ephemerally (destined for immediate bankruptcy or dissolution) as a means of legitimating, transmitting or laundering something else which, in turn, may be but a stage in the virtual property chain. Virtual property-holders use elements of the positive law in a way that both places this property ahead of the law and decentres the state law as a viable tool of regulation.

In my argument, I draw on David Stark's perceptive conception of 'recombinant property' which, however, seems too circumscribed to account for the global economic and normative context of the post-communist transformations, the transnationalization of post-community property rights and the specificity of the class of actors involved. I focus on these aspects in my attempt to explore the nature of normative changes in former communist countries in conjunction with a broader worldwide transition that is likely to have both influenced and been affected by the post-communist transformations. In other words, I presume that the specific shape of the post-communist normative/economic culture has been conditioned by both the particular legacy of the late communism and the specific historical moment in the development of the Western world at the time of communism's collapse.

The 'Recombinant' Property?

Based on his research in Hungary, David Stark describes in an *American Journal of Sociology* article the new type of property relations in which 'the qualities of public and private are dissolved, interwoven, and recombined' (Stark 1996: 1016; see also Loś 1992: 125–8 on symbiotic companies and Staniszkis 1994–5: 33–4 and 1995 on 'hybrid property').[3] He gives an apt characterization of one, commonly encountered, form of this type of property rights arrangement:

> ... a limited liability company owned by private persons, by private ventures, and by other limited liability companies owned by joint stock companies, banks, and large public enterprises owned by the state. (Stark 1996: 1007)

Stark calls it a 'corporate satellite'. Various corporate satellites are likely to be linked to each other within 'metamorphic networks' that restructure existing assets and liabilities. Stark postulates that these complex processes of diversification are a response to a combined market and organizational uncertainty which calls for flexible hedging strategies, 'based in some cases on *profitability* but in others on [bureaucratic] *eligibility*' (Stark 1996: 1014). A result of this manoeuvring between the market and the state, and between their incompatible legitimating principles, is what he calls the recombinant property.

In economic terms, the recombinant property is produced by two simultaneous processes: the decentralized reorganization of assets, resulting in mixed inter-enterprise ownership networks; and the centralized management of liabilities resulting in debt consolidation and transformation of private debt into public liability (ibid.: 997). The main thrust of Stark's theory is that social change, no matter how radical, 'is not the passage from one order to another but rearrangements in the patterns of how multiple orders are interwoven' (ibid.: 995). In other words, the new reality is constructed 'not *on the ruins* but *with the ruins* of communism', whereby credible commitments and coordinated actions are possible because of the persistence of old 'routines and practices, organizational forms and social ties, that can become assets [and] resources' (ibid.) in shaping the new organizational arrangements.

In my view, Stark's 'recombinant property' represents only one version of a broader phenomenon which I have labelled 'virtual property'. Stark based his generalization on his field research in six Hungarian enterprises, a series of interviews and the ownership data about Hungary's 200 largest corporations and top 25 banks. He thus described the uncertainty faced by those involved in business that is registered and fairly traditional (apart from banks, mostly in the industrial, manufacturing sector) and, being formerly state-owned, is now subject to complicated schemes of share and chain ownership.

David Stark's conceptualization seems to refer to a special type of fluid recombination of traditional types of property that produces a highly ambiguous multifarious property rights status, typical of what he calls East European capitalism. It may be useful, however, to explore the concept of virtual property as a genuinely new type of ownership form, inspired by both post-communist and postmodern/industrial transformations.

While Stark offers an original and well documented analysis of the 'recombinant' property, the picture he paints may be lacking some important dimensions, both on global and local planes. For the purposes of this chapter, the following aspects of Stark's theory are of particular relevance:

1   Although Stark notes that 'top- and mid-level managers, professionals and other staff can be found on the lists of founding partners and current owners [of corporate satellites]' (ibid.: 1006) and mentions 'the activation of preexisting networks of affiliation' (ibid.: 995), he does not dwell on the biographical and political specificity of the actors involved in the post-communist economy. His actors appear abstract and anonymous, approximating the universal *homo oeconomicus*.

2   According to Stark, the uncertainty that the actors face results from a combination of the past and new state policies and the inherent uncertainties of the market. He does not search for any other relevant sources of uncertainty.

3   The emergence and prominence of the new, 'recombinant' form of property is treated by Stark as a *response* to the type of uncertainty described in point 2 above 'Recombinant property is a form of organizational

hedging, or portfolio management, in which actors respond to uncertainty in the organizational environment by diversifying their assets, redefining and recombining resources' (ibid.: 997).

4 The recombinant property's main feature is that it blurs the line between public and private property rights to enable those involved to provide ready and favourable *accounts*[4] in both, state-organizational and market languages, depending on shifting demands and pressures. By the same token, recombinant property blurs enterprise boundaries and the boundedness of legitimating principles. Stark's grounding of this phenomenon is purely systemic–organizational, divorced from further global developments.

My specific challenges to this theoretical conceptualization are as follows:

1 Is the identity of the historically specific actors really irrelevant? Are these actors' particular interests, experience, skills and associations immaterial to the choices made at this particular historical (and historic) juncture, when there are no equivocal domestic structural imperatives, and society undergoes an unprecedented transformation?

2 Are there any other important sources of uncertainty, either related to the actors' particular political roots, plans and possible legitimacy problems or to more global, transnational processes?

3 Is it conceivable that the actors involved, rather than merely responding to, deliberately *cultivate* the environment of uncertainty to promote their interests? Could the new type of property be their vehicle of choice for navigation in the muddy waters of their own making?

4 Since 'blurring the lines' is also a part of a larger, postmodern transition, should not the latter be somehow included into the explanation of the ease with which the new property proliferates, crosses borders, and bears plenty of fruit for the post-communist actors? Consequently, is this new form of property just a 'recombination' of traditional types of property rights or a genuinely new type of boundless ownership holding?

Below, I address these problems in three separate sections (combining issues (1) and (2) in one section), which are preceded, however, by a brief sketch of a global environment that may help contextualize these seemingly regional processes.

The Global Transition

Before exploring further the peculiar nature of the post-communist property arrangements, I would like to place them in a broader context of normative changes. I believe that a conjunction of four interrelated forms (or layers) of contemporary capitalism can provide a useful framework for such an explanation.

1   *Globalized post-industrial capitalism.* This refers to the stage of capitalism which involves economic transnationalization and the weakening of the state's capacity to regulate the market; high capital mobility due to the liberalization of international financial rules and new banking technologies; deregulation; the 'global free-market' rhetoric; the blurring of the line between 'legitimate' and 'criminal' economies; a rapid shift to new post-industrial digital technologies; multiplication of forms of capital (for example, access to information as capital); and the emergence of new forms of property (for example, intellectual, suprajurisdictional). It also involves the process of transnationalization of capital accumulation that can be witnessed in the increasingly dominant role of both multinational corporations and their illicit counterparts which, however, are moving rapidly into the world of 'legitimate' business.

   Globalization should not be equated with the modernist pattern of homogenization, uniformization or unification (Santos 1995: 253, 270). Linked as it is with a simultaneous process of regionalization, it is far more complex, ambiguous, and contradictory.

2   *Supranational regional capitalism.* This refers to the tendency to create and consolidate regional markets and to limit the autonomy and relevance of the nation-state. It also implies a pressure on lesser countries to adopt regional rules even before a guarantee of entry has been issued. Furthermore, it leads to the creation of a new hierarchy of states within new regional blocs. For the East/Central European states it may mean that they become a new periphery within the new regional power, the European Union. It also means entering another super-bureaucracy with all its drawbacks and familiar opportunities for corruption, fraud and skilful appropriation of public funds and subsidies. 'Europe' has already become a convenient reference, evoked to justify all kinds of changes or policies or to score points in internal power struggles. General ignorance about the specific requirements of potential European membership allows them to be used as a shield for powerful local and foreign interests.

3   *Globalized mafia capitalism.*[5] This refers to a growing tendency of hierarchical criminal organizations that are specialized in certain illicit markets (drugs, arms, sex trade, gambling and so on) to diversify and form

international business links both among themselves and with more conventional business partners. This in turn enhances their efficiency at raising and laundering huge amounts of capital for strategic investments in foreign or transnational markets. The size of this readily deployable capital may easily exceed the GDP of at least some of the post-communist states.

4 *Post-communist capitalism (or 'red-web capitalism')*. This refers to the formation that emerged from the gradual transformation of the communist ruling (or *nomenklatura*) class[6] into the new capitalist class without leaving behind its heritage. It is a formation founded, on the one hand, on the removal of ideological and political obstacles to the full economic endowment of that class and, on the other hand, on a platform of integration with world/regional capitalism.

The East/Central European states' withdrawal from the Soviet bloc and the subsequent disintegration and anarchization of the Soviet Union have led to a rapid privatization of economic and security relations within that region. Particularly well positioned to steer and exploit this process has been the web of secret services, including the military special services, that formerly linked these states into a single police edifice (Loś and Zybertowicz forthcoming). Moreover, these countries' military–industrial complex – the symbol and legacy of the Cold War – has become the driving force in the post-communist economies' integration into worldwide arms smuggling and illicit trading.

As a result of the Soviet bloc's collapse, the East/Central European countries underwent rapid redefinition of their national and territorial identity, but their long-awaited sovereignty came at a time when the modern concept of the independent nation-state is no longer perceived as a viable or even justifiable entity. Thus, the weakness and vulnerability of the new states cannot even be meaningfully addressed within the new framework of an open-ended and ambivalent process of globalization/regionalization.

This twin process of simultaneous *globalization* and *regionalization* appears to be mediated by a third trend that could be called *'networkization'* or internationalization of social capital. One of the consequences of globalization is a normative vacuum. International legal space is a contested area in which many interests, cultures and pressures – some more dominant than others – converge. It is an immense field where the urgent need for regulation coexists with a profound scepticism about such regulation's totalitarian or imperialistic potential and its practical viability. The sense of global, paradigmatic change and a disillusion with modern concepts underlying the idea of law (rationality, formality, objectivity, closure, specialization, hierarchy, instrumentalism and possibility of planning; see, for example, Cotterrell

1984: 22–4) open this vast space to multiple competing quasi-normative orders used instrumentally by various international networks. They are of paramount importance for doing business in the international arena. Informal network rules replace and substitute for legal regulation, while digital technology and fast transport facilitate rapid internationalization of networking. It may be claimed that this international social capital becomes one of the key features of the global post-industrial economy.

All these processes take place in a time of profound cultural change, whereby turbulent interactions between modernity, postmodernity, and their as yet unnamed successor, result in *paradigmatic chaos* and multiple unsynchronized shifts in our mental landscape.

The Invisible Actors Behind the New Property Concept: Sources of Uncertainty

According to Stark (1996), the convoluted legacy of the communist past and inherent insecurities and inconsistencies of the economic transition produce unprecedented levels of ambiguity and uncertainty within the economic sphere. There may be, however, other types of uncertainty related to, on the one hand, the already mentioned specificity of group biographies and interests and, on the other hand, regional and global processes of change.

A credible explanation of the uncertainty in the economic life of post-communist societies should perhaps include an insight into the ways by which the actors involved acquired their assets, whether they have (or had) any reason to fear reprisals for the past roles/actions and whether they harbour(ed) any long-term political aspirations. Despite the formal legality of some of the state economy takeovers by the *nomenklatura* under the foresightedly revised communist laws, all members of the former communist *nomenklatura* had to feel, at least in the initial stages of transition, some anxiety about possible attempts to hold them accountable for the communist regime's sins. The uncertainty they faced was not simply that of state–market transformation. And the 'accounts' they were carrying with themselves were not simply related to the economy-related uncertainty.

While readying themselves for new opportunities offered by marketization and privatization of the economy, *nomenklatura* networks were also preparing themselves for anticipated retaliatory policies by the winning opposition forces. Although their fears proved by and large unfounded, they were real in their consequences. First, the economic strategies of the *nomenklatura* were bound to be affected by their sense of individual and group insecurity; second, when the anticipated retaliation did not materialize,[7] their mutual protection networks, consolidated during the transition period and fortified by the resources and intelligence of the former secret services, could safely engage in new, even more daring, ventures.

There is sufficient empirical evidence to conclude that transformations in East/Central Europe brought relatively little change in the composition of these countries' elites. The process of the 'endowment of the *nomenklatura*' – launched well before the official collapse of the communist order – has been continued under the new, quasi-capitalist conditions (see, for example, Gabryel and Zieleniewski 1996; Handelman 1994; Łoś 1992, 1994; Staniszkis 1994–95; Tarkowski 1990; Tittenbrun 1992). A large-scale, comparative study of elite recruitment, conducted in 1993–94 in Russia and five East/Central European countries, demonstrates convincingly that, cross-national variations notwithstanding, most members of the new economic elites originate from the old *nomenklatura* (Szelenyi and Szelenyi 1995; Wasilewski 1995; Wasilewski and Wnuk-Lipiński 1995).

This and other research have pointed primarily to the process of reproduction of the former communist managerial elite (or the economic *nomenklatura*) as the new owner–shareholder–manager stratum. This has been described as an almost unavoidable process, given not only their hands-on managerial experience – inaccessible to non-party members, who had been barred from these positions – but above all their 'inherited political assets, which granted them easy access to information, decisionmaking, powerful networks, low-interest loans, etc.' (Wasilewski and Wnuk-Lipiński 1995: 689). They were also best positioned to restructure the assets and liabilities of the state economy so that they could freely exploit the former while leaving the latter to the state (Łoś 1992: 125–8; Staniszkis 1994–5 and 1995; Stark 1996). To achieve this result they have been prepared to go to great lengths to complicate and muddle the new property rights arrangements.

While thorough surveys can reconstruct the economic careers of many members of the former economic *nomenklatura*, it is much more difficult to trace the career paths of the former political *nomenklatura* (members of the party and security service apparatus). It is my contention, however, that by appreciating the 'virtual' nature of property rights in post-communist countries it is possible to get at least some insight into the complicated webs of profit-making schemes by these seemingly propertyless individuals and networks.

Full ownership or even 'recombined' forms of property rights or managerial authority may not offer the same flexibility and profit opportunities as do more inventive strategies based on a subtle understanding of the new logic of business. This new logic is related to the following factors: emergence of new, inexperienced financial markets; inherent weakness of the reforming states; foreign trade liberalization (both domestically and globally); a multifaceted process of transnationalization of markets; and, finally, the opening of the borders between East and West as well as within the two new regional entities, the European Union and the multistate territory formerly occupied by the Soviet Union.

Considerable published evidence – available to anyone interested in piecing together the scattered investigative reports on large-scale economic scandals, dazzling fortunes and internationally connected financial operations – points invariably to the involvement by former party and secret service officials (Grajewski 1996: 14; Handelman 1994; Knight 1996; Loś and Zybertowicz, forthcoming; Raport 1992; Shelley 1994: 347; Sterling 1994; Zybertowicz 1993). They may have few visible domestic property entitlements, but their fleeting property arrangements allow them to draw enormous untaxed profits. These are made possible by: their old networks of connections; insider information; preferential credits and subsidies; possession of sensitive/compromising material useful for blackmail/extortion/political pressure schemes; control over many domestic financial institutions; openness to cooperation with foreign partners, including intelligence services and organized crime syndicates; as well as receptiveness to unconventional lines of international business, including money-laundering, drugs and arms trade facilitation, smuggling, forging of import–export licences, and so on.

Countless examples of spectacular cross-national networking include a gigantic scheme, launched at the beginning of the 1990s, to buy up, at artificially low prices, a large proportion of the Soviet currency in exchange for unencumbered access to, and export of, that country's immense natural resources on the eve of its imminent demise (for the best description of this, see Sterling 1994, Part IV; also Sinuraja 1995: 38–41). The losses incurred by the Soviet (and, later, Russian) treasury ran into many billions of dollars.

In another scheme, a special fund for external debt management (the notorious FOZZ) was established in Poland in the last months of communist rule. While it was designed to surreptitiously buy up the Polish debt on the secondary market, the fund, run by people connected to the Communist Party and the intelligence and security services, became involved in complicated national and international banking and business operations, using several international intermediaries (Bikont 1991; Dakowski and Przystawa 1992; Raport 1992; Zybertowicz 1993). The scam, which continued after the collapse of communism, involved the deliberate misuse of state funds in the range of 1 billion dollars.

The frantic patterns of constant reconstitution of their property rights by these former communist officials may be at least partly explained by their efforts to detach themselves from their communist past, forestall possible expropriation or prosecution and build sound financial foundations for their refurbished political party and their own political careers.

While a flexible and fuzzy merger of state and private property might have been a sufficient strategy for the economic *nomenklatura*, the fears and aspirations of the political *nomenklatura* (party and security apparatus) seem to have led them to search for an even more open-ended concept of property. They have been looking for profit-producing entitlements unencumbered by registration, taxation, materiality or durability – in short, virtual property. This kind of property is a perfect enrichment mechanism for those who need to hide their economic pursuits, who are afraid that their past may catch up with them, who need to generate secret funds to sponsor political activities and who are used to operating surreptitiously.

A good illustration is provided by the efforts of some representatives of the Polish Social Democratic Party to secure a financial base for their organization and provide for its elite. This party – since 1993, the senior partner in the ruling coalition – is the direct successor of the Communist Party and has taken over its numerous assets. Those assets included Western bank accounts in which the Communist Party had stashed considerable amounts of money.[8] Additionally, the nascent Social Democratic Party received a special loan from the KGB to invest in profitable ventures as well as to finance its founding congress and the publication of a newspaper.[9] Private businesses were to be set up in such a way as to attract foreign capital and to distance the ownership from the party itself, while making sure that the profits could be used to finance its agenda (Hugo-Bader 1996; Janecki 1996a, b; Janecki and Szoszkiewicz 1996). A whole host of joint ventures, foundations, joint-stock companies, partnerships and financial organizations were then launched, dissolved, converted and multiplied, with amazing speed. The pattern adopted was meant to make it practically impossible to track down any abuses of trust, appropriation of public money, the use of 'paper' companies or assets as securities, or the actual involvement of the Social Democratic Party or the KGB.

Driven by their unique combination of insecurity, greed and power designs, many former communist officials and agents have skilfully meshed into the broader process of simultaneous transnationalization of organized crime and the world economy.[10] They seem to have both capitalized on, and precipitated, the growing fusion of the two. Sinuraja thus explains the chain-like transactions linking a multitude of economic actors – legal and illegal, domestic and foreign, stable and meteoric:

On the one side of this chain can be a criminal organization (which controls the aluminium factory and Russian traders), and on the other, a quite legitimate Western company (a factory which uses Russian aluminium). In between, a complicated and integrated structure of subsidiaries, joint ventures, various operating linkages, and licensing can exist ...

... if a foreign criminal organization has invested money in the economic sector of Russia, as it is now a good place for money-laundering from abroad, they will have to make sure that their operations and investments are secure ... Networking through cooperation ... will develop further, strengthening the positions of organized crime in both Russia and the West. (Sinuraja 1995: 49)

It can be argued that the global tendency towards blurring the line between the criminal and legitimate economies has a peculiar appeal for people whose earlier experience within the secretive political structures of a monopolistic party/police state has equipped them with unique operational skills and intelligence, a network mentality and organization, as well as with profound axiological nihilism.

It also appears that the post-communist economies have a special appeal for international organized crime and 'mafia capitalism'. The many reasons for this may include: normative chaos; a well established culture of corruption and clientelism; poorly defined property rights;[11] currency and foreign exchange fluctuations; preferential tax treatment offered to foreign investors; abundant opportunities for safe money laundering;[12] the absence of extradition treaties; easy access to cheap military equipment (including nuclear material); and cheap natural resources (at least in some of these countries).[13]

In sum, while the uncertainty of the domestic economic scene has probably played a role in the preference of former communist power networks for locating their capital abroad, their background and the personal/group uncertainty related to their political past and future are vital to understanding their style of operation and preferred forms of property rights arrangements. Furthermore, by internationalizing their ventures, the post-communist networks have linked up with the rapidly globalizing organized criminal economy and, therefore, have also become exposed to its unique pressures and uncertainties.

Reactive or Proactive Actors?

In David Stark's model, anonymous actors react to the structural uncertainty they encounter (domestically) by employing various hedging strategies resulting in a complex and ongoing recombination of property rights. In the preceding section, I pointed to other powerful sources of uncertainty, unaccounted for in Stark's model. Another possible weakness of his model is the construction of the actors' actions purely in reactive terms. Although he hints that they may deliberately contribute to the climate of uncertainty, he does it only in passing and with no broader context. He notes that 'to gain room for manoeuvre, actors court and even create ambiguity. They measure in multiple units, they speak in many tongues. They will be less controlled by others if they can be accountable (able to make credible accounts) to many' (Stark 1996: 1015).

There may, however, be more tangible forces of destabilization at work here – related both to the interests of the domestic post-communist power networks and various international interests. In the immediate aftermath of the communist regime's collapse, the former *nomenklatura* needed to develop effective strategies to influence the overall, legal and political conditions and make sure that new democratic policies did not impede their drive to become the new capitalist class.

Jadwiga Staniszkis argues that while the old informal power networks could not officially institutionalize their power position and property rights, they used various techniques to *anarchize* the state as a method of quasi-institutionalizing their control over crucial economic and political processes. She describes this period as a phase of managerial corporatism that is marked by coordinated efforts geared towards:

- establishing an infrastructure of market institutions that conveniently corresponds to the needs of the group exerting pressure
- ensuring selectively restricted access to the institutions that reduce market risk exposure and operating costs (underwriting facilities, export guarantees, government loan guarantees)
- ensuring the maximum externalization of operating costs along with the maximum internalization of benefits
- influencing the parameters of economic activity. This particularly applies to exchange and interest rate policies (Staniszkis 1995: 36).

In so doing, these corporate networks did not rely on direct pressure on the central authorities, but instead attempted to depoliticize decisions concerning these vital areas, define them as technical matters and relocate them to the bureaucratic level, relatively unaffected by the democratic process. Staniszkis argues that, although this kind of politics remains outside the realm of traditional political institutions (such as parliaments and political parties), the politicians themselves (parliamentarians, cabinet ministers) play an active part in it. Yet their role is not to exercise public control over the political process, but rather 'to oil the wheels of a process which they hope will bring personal gain or party political advantage' (Staniszkis 1995: 47). This leads to the *depoliticization and technocratization* of fundamentally important decisions that are 'being hijacked from the political structures of the state' and to the *privatization of certain components of the state* that are 'being diverted to the promotion of group interests rather than the public interests' (ibid.).

A virtual paralysis of the criminal justice system, especially when it comes to prosecuting economic organized crimes, also appears to be closely related to economic strategies of the new capitalist class and be, at least in part, deliberately engineered. Moreover, a generally shared perception of lawlessness and economic anarchy may be in the interest of various groups striving to make fast profits, control capital-creation-and-accumulation processes, dominate certain markets, and/or impose their own regime of control over new democracies. These organized groups may range from domestic *nomenklatura/* organized crime networks[14] to various foreign mafias to transnational corporations to international agencies to foreign governments or their proxies.

Internationally connected private detective and security-guard companies, employing mostly former members of the communist militia and secret police (Czapska 1994; Hugo-Bader and Wiernikowska 1994; Shelley 1994: 350), are a good example of a lucrative non-governmental regulation of the fledgling markets. Some of these companies are also used as fronts for well developed criminal schemes and are strategically placed to exploit and protect major illegal economic ventures as well as foreign intelligence operations (Hugo-Bader and Wiernikowska 1994: 7–9). Likewise, protection rackets are both a way of ensuring steady income and a mechanism for establishing control over a particular territory or commodity market. By increasing the risks of capital investments, those who profit economically from unstable conditions and exploit them in their political power struggles, turf wars or economic/criminal ventures effectively drive away those potential competitors who prefer a more stable and predictable business environment (see, for example, Shelley 1994: 349–50).

A perception of anarchy legitimizes coercion. In post-communist states, 'organized crime groups attempt to replicate the controls of the authoritarian state' (Shelley 1996: 19). The weaker the state's ability to create and enforce equivocal rules the more justified appears the occurrence of private systems of quasi-regulation that provide mechanisms for adjudication of disputes and enforcement of contracts, while exercising simultaneously exclusive gatekeeping, corruption and deterrence functions.[15] As Fiorentini and Peltzman observe:

> Once a monopoly over coercion has been acquired by a criminal organisation, the latter can perform inside its territory those activities which typically characterize collective decision-maker's intervention in the economy: levying taxes, coercive provision of public goods, and regulation of private agents through non-fiscal tools. (Fiorentini and Peltzman 1995: 14)

The occurrence of a new type of property cannot, therefore, be analysed simply as a reaction to uncertainty, but also as a vehicle of creating it. A climate of uncertainty facilitates and justifies private replication of quasi-state functions and endows the actors with certain credibility under the new, anarchic conditions.

Conclusion: Virtual Property and the Global Environment

The multiple processes that I have sketched in the 'Global Transition' section constitute the context in which the former communist state property is being transformed into quasi-private transnational property. I have argued that the virtual property which became the favoured vehicle for enrichment of the new Central European capitalists,[16] both within their countries and transnationally, is a type of *property that is fluid, easily disposable, convertible, invisible or hidden behind false names or short-lived fronts.* Whereas conventional property is well entrenched in space and time, virtual property is freed from both these dimensions. It is here, there and nowhere; one moment it exists, in another it is no more, or it has become something else. It knows no borders, respects no laws and is easily transferable by wire or other means of speedy communication. It escapes the law by virtue of the speed with which it transforms itself, its cross-jurisdictional reach, its web-like, network-based nature and its fundamental disconnectedness that renders modern, rational law powerless. It is, moreover, a property that comes with an inbuilt mechanism for externalization of costs and losses.

Many features of this type of property have been made possible by the global economic, legal and technological developments and can be recognized in already familiar patterns of mobility of international financial capital. Offshore banking provides an excellent example of an institution that has played an enormous role in the 'virtualization' of financial markets and divorcing them from material economic realities. As described by Chossudovsky:

> ... almost all roads in this tangled financial [both 'legal' and 'illegal'] network lead offshore to the banking havens. Without the cumbersome smuggling of banknotes across international borders, they move and conceal the proceeds of illicit trade through a web of offshore hideaways and a maze of anonymous shell companies. It is here that the criminal syndicates and the representatives of the world's largest commercial banks interact ... The same privacy, technology and lack of regulation that attract the criminals help legal money flow between a parent company and its subsidiary shell corporation. (Chossudovsky 1996: 28)[17]

Yet, despite some obvious commonalities and the shared environment, the post-communist 'virtual property' networks seem to add a new twist to those broader patterns. There are several quite distinct traits of their situation and experience that may help explain their special approach to property issues. They include:

- the lack of exposure to modern/rational economic and legal institutions
- their formative experience within an essentially non-money economy (state, planned, and so on) that never developed a financial sector, means of financial accountability or meaningful currency
- the unencumbered access to the rapidly commercialized, marketized and denationalized state economy
- unprecedented structural opportunities for passing business costs and debts to the state
- the protective security net and intelligence provided by the Soviet bloc's former secret services, themselves active players in post-communist power/property networks
- the continuity of personnel within the justice system, which renders successful prosecution of members of the former ruling class most unlikely
- the communist elites' special behavioural conditioning and mental patterns formed under previous regimes, such as: obligatory 'double talk', duplicity, vigilance and secrecy; duty to support fictitious facades and routine doctoring of official records; heavy involvement in the 'second' (shadow) economy (usually *within* or in a close symbiosis with state enterprises), double reporting, graft and so forth.

A wide range of versatile virtual property transactions has been facilitated by the unclear and shifting ownership status of much of the national wealth of post-communist countries and the inherently problematic conceptualization of cross-national ownership and property rights transfers (see Santos 1995: 291).

The growing transnationalization of markets has not been accompanied by parallel legal developments. Indeed, the concept of legal regulation itself is being challenged on several grounds:

1   its authoritarianism;
2   its inflexibility and impotence in dealing with the complex (post)modern world that cannot be reduced to the juridic (autopoetic) logic;
3   its inherently modern, and therefore obsolete, nature.

The weakness of international property rules makes it relatively easy for the post-communist networks to invest their dubious funds abroad and maintain their anonymity. The rules of operation that they employ are not so different from those used by organized crime syndicates.[18] But the line between the 'legitimate' and 'illegitimate' is blurring anyway and, from their vantage point, the new post-communist capitalists, accustomed to the same phenomenon under communism, do not find it problematic. Not surprisingly, the postmodern questioning of the validity of conventional (or any other) standards of legitimacy or legality becomes embodied and enthusiastically exploited in the practices of these new arrivals on the international scene.

Indeed, the new property rights that are typical of post-communist transformations can best be described by reference to the postmodern vocabulary. Is this simply a coincidence? It is important to realize that the actors who are shaping the post-communist economy from within (mostly the ruling elite/economic underworld of the past regime) have had no direct experience of the democratic nation-state, industrial capitalism or the ethos of modernity. These are empty concepts, of little value in the pursuit of their goals. What they have witnessed through their frequent travels and international contacts, especially in the final, decadent years of their former political lives, was a world of international business seemingly unconstrained by any fixed rules, dominated by transnational corporations and organizations skilled in passing costs to taxpayers or less developed countries, hospitable to international criminal consortia because of their huge financial power, discreet in its provision of banking services, rapidly embracing new technologies and open to new markets, opportunities and new 'friends' from the East. They saw the world at the brink of the twenty-first century and they decided to join it.

The current attack on modernity is above all – and logically – an attack on what have been considered the finest achievements of the Western civilization. This introduces ambivalence – so welcomed by former communist elites – in evaluation of Soviet-sponsored East/Central European regimes, which used to be perceived by their subjects as monocentric (lacking separation of powers), irrational, disorganized, non-representational, anti-civil society, anti-national sovereignty, anti-human rights, anti-liberal and anti-positivistic in their overtly ideocratic conception of truth, in short, *anti-modern*. While these were instinctive, commonsensical human reactions, they were also dependent on and prestructured by the vocabulary and ideals of modern European civilization. Engaging theoretical debates among intellectuals on the relationship of the Soviet communism to modernity notwithstanding, it appears that systemic features which exasperated those countries' populations most can also be characterized as antitheses of the unmistakably modern standards relative to the state, economy and citizenship.

The current anti-modern backlash has inadvertently provided needed discursive tools to ex-communist elites and their public relations experts. This appropriation has been especially conspicuous in countries such as Poland and Hungary in which former communists have re-established themselves, both politically and economically, as the new ruling bloc. Needless to say, the discourse from which they have been borrowing was not the elusive, hesitant, searching discourse of philosophical postmodernism at its best, but a selection of slick clichés that can be deployed for mass consumption and vested with an aura of Western political correctness. While exploiting and subverting the essentially anti-totalitarian post-modern climate, these new/old elites draw on it to legitimize their past and current roles and to fashion for themselves new forms of governance. Governance-through-virtual-property and the make-believe reality that it generates may be among their most effective strategies of bonding with global governance bureaucracies and global financial markets.

Notes

1   The *nomenklatura* principle involved the Communist Party's exclusive right to nominate managers and officials at all levels of the economy, public administration, education, culture, the mass media, the military, the justice system and so forth.

2   In a sense, this continues, albeit in a radically revised version, the earlier situation when the Communist Party elites became accustomed to treating the state economy as their own, enjoying virtually all the privileges of private ownership without having the obligations and responsibilities which normally come with it (Loś 1990: 8).

3   Staniszkis points out that 'hybrid ownership causes state enterprises and foreign trade companies that have been denationalized (although not fully privatized) to become *de facto* a form of organizational-cum-group property. The profits earned are used to set up purely private companies (including ones abroad), to establish interlocking financial interests (with the companies holding each others stock), and also set up – acting in concert – commercial banks and trust funds that subsequently service the original companies while wringing out the last drops of capital from the state sector' (Staniszkis 1995: 33).

4   Stark's 'accounts' connote both book-keeping and narration. They incorporate justifications that draw on 'established and recognized ordering principles, standards, and measures of evaluation' (Stark 1996: 1013). They are both reasons we give to those who evaluate us and reasons we actually take into consideration when we act.

5   I borrow the term 'mafia capitalism' from Arlacchi (1983) who used it in the Italian context.

6   Or, rather, its more dynamic elements. The final period of communism was marked by intense competition within the ruling party class, resulting in the advancement of those individuals and networks that were the most viable candidates for class conversion. They were generally younger, better educated, with military or security connections and managerial skills.

7   While there have been significant differences in the ways of dealing with the past, adopted, for instance, by Hungary, the Czech Republic and Poland, none of them introduced any legal measures aiming at retribution or confiscation of communist officials' wealth. Only in the Czech Republic have they been barred from occupying

important state offices. In Poland and Hungary, well endowed former communist parties were returned to power by general elections in 1993 and 1994 respectively, virtually assuring impunity and security of the former *nomenklatura*.

8   For similar efforts of the Soviet Communist party, see Handelman (1994: 88–91).

9   Handelman's investigation led him to believe that 'the KGB was ... perhaps the most important [player] in bridging the criminality of the old regime with the criminality of the postcommunist era' (Handelman 1994: 92; see also Waller 1994).

10 This process has been facilitated by deregulation of financial markets, liberalization of international commerce, increased mobility of capital, information and people, and regional supra-state bureaucratization (for the latter, see Passas and Nelken 1993; Fiorentini and Peltzman 1995; on internationalization of criminal activities see also Chossudovsky 1996; Mathews 1997: 57–8; Sinuraja 1995; Sterling 1994; Taylor 1992).

11 According to Fiorentini and Peltzman, existing studies indicate that criminal organizations prefer allocating their resources in 'regions where there are problems in the definition of the property rights' (Fiorentini and Peltzman 1995: 25).

12 According to a Russian estimate, about $16 billion have been brought to Russia for money-laundering over a two-year period in the early 1990s (Sinuraja 1995: 46; see also Kapuściński (1994) on the issue of money-laundering in East/Central Europe.

13 For elaboration of some of these aspects, see Shelley (1996) and Sterling (1994).

14 It is difficult to distinguish the two due to a long communist tradition of corruption, clientelism and organized economic crime within the state economy.

15 This happens, for example, on a selective basis, when the state prohibits the production and distribution of certain commodities (for example, drugs) and, therefore, 'effectively abrogates the enforcement of its other laws in the affected illegal markets' (Skaperdas and Syrapoulus 1995: 64).

16 Of course, they also invest in very solid and traditional property – for example, expensive real estate in Western capitals.

17 Among many examples of suspected connections of post-communist networks to off-shore havens is a case of Sergiej Gavrilov, a Russian currently carrying a Belize passport, who has gained control over important chunks of banking in Poland and is involved in the import of Russian oil to that country. The legality of his and his associates' financial dealings has been questioned both by the Polish media and the Main Board for Banking Control in Poland (see, for example, Szemplińska 1997: 18).

18 Margaret S. Beare explains how the latter use a strategy of 'layering' whereby 'a series of otherwise legitimate transactions are carried out which due to the frequency, volume or complexity of the transactions create a paper-trail that is hard or impossible to follow' (Beare 1995: 172).

References

Arlacchi, Pino (1983), *Mafia Business. The Mafia Ethic and the Spirit of Capitalism*, London: Verso.

Beare, Margaret E. (1995), 'Money Laundering: A Preferred Law Enforcement Target for the 1990s', in J. Albanese (ed.), *Contemporary Issues in Organized Crime*, Monsey, NY: Criminal Justice Press.

Bikont, Anna (1991), 'W poszukiwaniu zaginionych milionów', *Gazeta Wyborcza*, 9–11 November, 16.

Chossudovsky, Michel (1996), 'Globalization and the Criminalization of Economic Activity: the Business of Crime and the Crimes of Business', *Covert Action Quarterly*, (58), Fall, 24–30 and 54.

Cotterrell, Roger (1984), *The Sociology of Law. An Introduction*, London: Butterworths.

Czapska, Janina (1994), 'Growing Privatization of Penal Justice and the Personal Security Feelings in Poland', paper presented at the World Congress of Sociology, Bielefeld.

Dakowski, Mirosław, and Jerzy Przystawa (1992), *Via Bank i FOZZ*, Komorów: Wyd. Antyk.

Fiorentini, Gianluca and Sam Peltzman (1995), 'Introduction', in G. Fiorentini and S. Peltzman (eds), *The Economics of Organised Crime*, Cambridge: Cambridge University Press.

Gabryel, Piotr and Marek Zieleniewski (1996), 'Stu najbogatszych Polaków', *Wprost*, 23 June, 3–28.

Grajewski, Andrzej (1996), 'Lustracja po polsku', *Przegląd Polityczny*, (31), 8–14.

Handelman, Stephen (1994), *Comrade Criminal. The Theft of the Second Russian Revolution*, London: Michael Joseph.

Hugo-Bader, Jacek (1996), 'Realista, iluzjonista, lisok figowy', *Gazeta Wyborcza*, 1–2 June, 8, 10.

Hugo-Bader, Jacek and Maria Wiernikowska (1994), 'Ochraniarze', *Gazeta Wyborcza. Magazyn*, 24 June, 6–9.

Janecki, Stanisław (in collaboration with A. Witoszek) (1996a), 'Wielka gra', *Wprost*, 21 January, 19–22.

Janecki, Stanisław (in collaboration with J.S. Mac and A. Witoszek) (1996b), 'Ekonomia polityczna SdRP. Związki towarzyskie', *Wprost*, 28 January, 22–3.

Janecki, Stanisław and Andrzej Szoszkiewicz (1996), 'Kto kontroluje polską gospodarkę? Kolor pieniędzy', *Wprost*, 29 September, 26–9.

Kapuściński, Paweł (1994), 'Pranie na sucho', *Zycie Gospodarcze*, (24), 12 June, 18–19.

Knight, Amy (1996), *Spies Without Cloaks*, Princeton, NJ: Princeton University Press.

Loś, Maria (190), 'Introduction', in M. Loś (ed.), *The Second Economy in Marxist States*, London: Macmillan; New York: St Martin's Press.

Loś, Maria (1992), 'From Underground to Legitimacy: The Normative Dilemmas of Post-Communist Marketization', in Bruno Dallago *et al.* (eds), *Privatization and Entrepreneurship in Post-Socialist Countries*, London: Macmillan; New York: St Martin's Press.

Loś, Maria (1994), 'Property Rights, Market and Historical Justice: Legislative Discourses in Poland', *International Journal of the Sociology of Law*, **22** (1), 39–58.

Loś, Maria and Andrzej Zybertowicz (forthcoming), 'Is Revolution a Solution? State Crime in Communist and Post-Communist Poland', in Martin Krygier and Adam Czarnota (eds), *The Rule of Law after Communism*, Aldershot: Dartmouth Press.

Loś, Maria and Andrzej Zybertowicz (forthcoming), *Privatizing the Police-State: The Case of Poland*, London: Macmillan; New York: St Martin's Press.

Mathews, Jessica T. (1997), 'Power Shift', *Foreign Affairs*, **76** (1), 50–66.

Parchimowicz, Iwona (1991), 'Gra w dokumenty', *Polityka*, 23 November.

Passas, Nicos and David Nelken (1993), 'The Thin Line Between Legitimate and Criminal Enterprises: Subsidy Frauds in the European Community', *Crime, Law and Social Change*, **19** (3), 223–44.

'Raport Wydziału Studiów gabinetu ministra SW' (1992), *Tygodnik Solidarność*, 3 July, 4–5.

Shelley, Louise I. (1994), 'Post-Soviet Organized Crime. Implications for Economic, Social and Political Development', *Demokratizatsiya. The Journal of Post-Soviet Democratization*, **2** (3), 341–58.

Shelley, Louise I. (1996), 'Transnational Organized Crime: The New Authoritarianism', paper presented at the International Law and Society Conference, Glasgow.

Sinuraja, Timur (1995), 'Internationalization of Organized Economic Crime', *European Journal on Criminal Policy and Research*, **3–4**, 34–53.

Skaperdas, Stergios and Constantinos Syropoulos (1995), 'Gangs as Primitive States', in G. Fiorentini and S. Peltzman (eds), *The Economics of Organised Crime*, Cambridge: Cambridge University Press.

Santos, Boaventura de Sousa (1995), *Toward a New Common Sense. Law, Science and Politics in the Paradigmatic Transition*, London: Routledge.

Staniszkis, Jadwiga (1994–95), 'The Politics of Post-Communist Institutionalization in Historical Perspective', Working Paper Series, no. 1, University of Michigan, International Institute.

Staniszkis, Jadwiga (1995), 'In Search of a Paradigm of Transformation', in Edmund Wnuk-Lipiński, (ed.), *After Communism. A Multidisciplinary Approach to Radical Social Change*, Warsaw: PAN ISP.

Stark, David (1996), 'Recombinant Property in East European Capitalism', *American Journal of Sociology*, **101** (4), 993–1027.

Sterling, Claire (1994), *Thieves' World. The Threat of the New Global Network of Organized Crime*, New York: Simon & Schuster.

Szelenyi, Ivan and Szonja Szelenyi (1995), 'Circulation or Reproduction of Elites During the Postcommunist Transformation of Eastern Europe: Introduction', *Theory and Society*, **24** (5), 615–38.

Szemplińska, Ewa (1997), 'Niejasne interesy Sergieja Gawriłowa', *Polityka*, 22 February, 18.

Tarkowski, Jacek (1990), 'Endowment of Nomenklatura, or Apparatchiks Turned into Entrepreneurchiks, or from Communist Ranks to Capitalist Riches', *Innovation*, **4** (1), 89–105.

Taylor, Ian (1992), 'The International Drug Trade and Money-Laundering: Border Controls and Other Issues', *European Sociological Review*, **8** (2), 181–93.

Tittenbrun, Jacek (1992), *Upadek Socjalizmu Realnego w Polsce*, Poznań: Dom Wydawniczy Rebis.

Waller, J. Michael (1994), 'Organized Crime and the Russian State', *Demokratizatsiya. The Journal of the Post-Soviet Democratization*, **2** (3), 364–84.

Wasilewski, Jacek (1995), 'The Forming of the New Elite: How Much Nomenklatura is Left?', *Polish Sociological Review*, **2**, 113–23.
Wasilewski, Jacek and Edmund Wnuk-Lipiński (1995), 'Poland: Winding Road from the Communist to the Post-Solidarity Elite', *Theory and Society*, **24** (5), 669–96.
Zybertowicz, Andrzej (1993), *W uścisku tajnych służb*, Komorów: Wydawnictwo Antyk.

11 Mapping Urban Space: Governmentality and Cartographic Struggles in Inner City Vancouver

Nick Blomley and Jeff Sommers

Here stood Hamilton, First Land Commissioner Canadian Pacific Railway. In the silent solitude of the primeval forest he drove a wooden stake in the earth and commenced to measure an empty land into the streets of Vancouver. (Plaque commemorating the original survey of downtown Vancouver in 1885)

In May 1996, senior Vancouver civic staff met with a group of activists in a small community centre in the city's poorest neighbourhood. At issue were a series of maps prepared by the City as part of a planning and data collection exercise. For the activists, however, the maps were more than a disinterested planning tool. The manner in which inner city space was both named and bounded on these maps was objectionable, particularly as the community with which the activists identified, the 'Downtown Eastside', had apparently been mapped out of existence. This prompted fears that their neighbourhood was being transformed into a mere administrative zone, facilitating the eventual material erasure of their community.

Community activists vowed not to participate in a number of planning exercises targeted at the area, thus invalidating the entire process, until the maps were redrawn. City staff were surprised by the vehemence of the opposition to a mere map, particularly in view of the range of problems that the neighbourhood faces, ranging from gentrification-led displacement, epidemic levels of HIV/AIDS, injection drug use, fears centred around crime and violence, conflicts between gentrifiers and residents and so on. For civic officials, it was precisely these concerns which the maps sought to address

261

by defining a space which could be monitored and acted upon. The process of naming and bounding was seen as largely neutral and they urged residents to tackle the 'real issues', and not be diverted by symbolic politics.

For area activists, however, the two issues were inseparable. Maps were perceived as powerful statements of entitlement and political identity. They spoke not only to a history of past and present entitlements, but also served to constitute a future space. A community newsletter made the linkage explicit:

> There's an old saying that the best way to make people powerless is to make them invisible. Maps are a good way of doing this. When Europeans first came to North America, they made Indians invisible by leaving large blank spaces on maps ... That way they were able to rationalize stealing other people's land ... [T]he City insists that the Downtown Eastside must be gentrified ... One way they can do it is by eliminating the Downtown Eastside from city maps. By leaving a community off a map, they erase the people who live there and make them invisible. That way, the neighbourhood is left open for whatever changes they have ... in store. (Anonymous 1995a)

This clash between community activists and civic officials over the bounding and naming of urban space was one event in a larger and longer conflict over the governance of Vancouver's inner city. During the 1990s social service agencies, property developers, business organizations and residential property-owners joined the dispute between the planners and politicians and the opposing activists. Their confrontation highlights some complex questions concerning the relations between community, mapping and governmentality that we wish to explore here.

We take as our point of departure Nikolas Rose's (1996) discussion of 'reterritorialization' of government. He maintains that the rise of 'community' has become a key vector of government in recent decades. Bonds of solidarity and obligation which have long been situated within the webs of relations that were constructed as 'social' are being increasingly reworked, he argues, through networks of identity and lifestyle that centre on 'community'. The language of political rationality has become suffused with the concept of community, as evidenced by community health initiatives, 'neighbourhood'-based urban planning, security (community policing), economic planning ('community economic development') and so on. These new political languages frame issues and make them amenable to authoritative action, he suggests, by seeking to *act upon* the dynamics of community; configuring the *imagined territory* upon which such strategies should act, and specifying the *subjects* of government as individuals who are seen as allied to a set of community-based beliefs and attachments. Community is not simply the surface on which government operates, he claims, 'but a *means* of government: its ties, bonds, forces, and affiliations are to be celebrated, encouraged, nurtured, shaped, and instrumentalized in the hope of producing consequences that are desirable for all and for each' (Rose 1996: 335).

Certainly, civic officials in Vancouver, along with other Canadian cities, have embraced the language of community. The formation of the community centre in which the May meeting was held, as well as the community spaces which the maps sought to represent, evidenced a respatialization of government that has been unfolding throughout North America since at least the late 1960s. However, the politically charged nature of the meeting, and the apparent significance of maps to that contest, raise some particular issues that we hope to explore in this case study.

The reference made to gentrification and dispossession is our first point of entry. Rose (1996: 334) notes that government through community can entail the mobilization of diverse 'dimensions of allegiance' that configure the individual as identified with the 'community'. Thus community policing relies on a conception of the subject as an 'active and responsible agent in the securing of security for themselves and those to whom they are or should be affiliated' (ibid.: 335). New forms of neighbourhood participation into policing and security, it is felt, will 'reactivate self-motivation, self-responsibility and self-reliance in the form of active citizenship within a self-governing community' (ibid.). Programmes of urban renewal, at issue in inner-city Vancouver, similarly imagine the subject as active and responsible, but the organizing political rationality is now one centred more directly on property.

Real property has long had a special significance in governmental discourse, given its supposed importance in the formation of social and political subjectivities. Its stationary condition supposedly ensures that the owner has a special interest in 'his' immediate community and a stake in a property-owning democracy. Also, within the stream of 'self-developmental' property discourse, ownership of property is seen as a means by which the self becomes constituted as a 'free actor'. 'To attain freedom', for Hegel, 'it is necessary that I have property, for in my property I become an "object to myself". Not to have a sphere of property that is one's own is to fail to attain self-conscious knowledge of oneself as free' (cited in Berry 1980: 79). More generally, Hume argues for the special significance of property in the management of social relations, ensuring social order and the maintenance of society.

The manner in which property and community are linked in the case of urban areas undergoing 'renewal' of 'gentrification', then, could be said to be significant. Programmes of renewal often seek to encourage home ownership, given its effects on economic self-reliance, entrepreneurship and community pride. Gentrification, on this account, is to be encouraged, because it will mean the replacement of a marginal anti-community (non-property-owning, transitory and problematized) by an active, responsible and improving population of home-owners who will 'improve' a community, both physically and morally, 'stabilize' it through their fixity and presence and serve to represent it given their supposed interest in responsible community activism.

But property and the political and social entitlements that flow from it can be configured in different ways. As we shall see below, the activists of the Downtown Eastside seek to advance a locally-based claim to community, based not on individualized entitlements but, rather on a collective form of ownership, rooted in history and shared struggle. Issues of ownership, entitlement and property rights are points of intense controversy in this part of Vancouver as different groups and individuals stake out contradictory entitlements to local space. Opposing claims concerning political identities and citizenship rights – particularly the right to speak 'for' a community – are predicated on some sort of 'propertied claim' (individual or collective) to that community space. Tensions between gentrifiers and those resisting them frequently turn on this axis.

Under such conditions, the definitions of community and the allegiances it invokes can be points of contention. While government programmes increasingly operate on the presupposition that '[w]e can ... , be governed through our allegiance to particular communities of morality and identity', Rose reminds us that there is a 'contradiction' to community.

> Complementarily, imagined communities, created by the activity of local activists or emerging as the reciprocal, as it were, of such governmental projects, can form the locus of the articulation of demands upon political authorities and resistance to such authorities: the language of community and the identity which is its referent becomes the site of new contestations ... The contradictions of community establish a new and agonistic territory for the organization of political and ethical conflicts. (Rose 1996: 336–7)

However, the 'agonistic territory' of community mentioned here is more than metaphorical. This will be our second point, noting the significance of mapping to the construction and contestation of both community and property as a dimension of localized allegiance.

Maps are among those media which Rose and Miller have called 'inscription devices', that serve to render reality 'stable, mobile, comparable, combineable. It is rendered in a form in which it can be debated and diagnosed' (Rose and Miller 1992: 185). As representations of space, maps facilitate the operation of what, they suggest, is a key principle in the exercise of liberal government – its ability to operate through 'action at a distance'. They are created through the labour of a variety of experts and compiled in those 'centres of calculation' that serve as nodal points in the exercise of governmental power. While mapping has long been critical to the organization of governmental power, the rise of community, perhaps, makes it even more significant. If the space of the social is more or less homogenous and transparent, the space of government by community begins to lose these qualities. As social solidarity dissolves into micro-locales and networks of identity and meaning, the government of space becomes more complex and tenuous. These kinds of spatial displacements create uncertainties and instabilities that cry out for the regular, transparent spaces of the map.

But maps are more than 'mere' representations of reality or ways of 'acting upon the real' that enable the government of social life and human conduct. They are, in fact, constitutive of that reality, inscribing power on space, codifying, and thus privileging the meanings that make it recognizable and actionable. The ability to constitute space in this way is a crucial factor in the exercise of governmental power, for it makes possible the regularity which is necessary for the motivation of self-rule. The extent to which governmental (and, indeed, other) authorities are able to mobilize 'the self-regulating capacities of subjects ... [as] key resources' is contingent largely on their ability to render space as transparent, fixed and predictable.

The inscription on the Hamilton monument, with which this chapter opens, speaks of the measurement of 'an empty land into the streets of Vancouver'. The turn of phrase is revealing. The ordering device is uncoupled from that which is ordered, forcing a separation between a space (the 'empty' land) and a practice (measurement and mapping) which itself serves to constitute an order (Vancouver). Its presumption of space as a category which is external to social life makes possible the very idea of space as an object of specialized knowledge and expert representations of which maps are a crucial component. In the representation of this *a priori* space, the map constitutes an 'order'. That order, for Hamilton, is not only one that guarantees quietness of possession and provides for ordered economic transactions through the precision of the survey and the formalization of land transfer. Rather, it is itself order, defined against that which is, by definition, lacking in order. With the cadastral grid – even while still forested – the mapped frontier is rendered transparent and 'opened up' to speculation, in both senses of the word.

Arguably then, the power of the map thus lies in the ways in which its very abstraction and decorporealization serve to depoliticize and naturalize the social and political relations that it inscribes. In much the way that Hamilton is described as measuring an empty land into the streets of Vancouver, so the map seems to exist as what Mitchell (1991) would call an 'enframing' device, seemingly above and beyond the material world of objects. Although power relations are being internalized, they appear to take the form of an external structure. Abstract space helps make a world that exists not as a set of concrete social practices, but as a binary order – individuals and their practices set against an inert *a priori* structure. The map conceals the processes through which it works as an ordering device. Space is marked and divided into places where people are put. The effect is to create a framework which appears prior to and within which objects are distributed. Power becomes submerged, apparently dissolved into the very order which it makes possible.

This is an especially vital operation in the production of community spaces in the city, where the tangled webs of everyday life present ongoing challenges to the orderliness required for effective government. Maps have long been used '… to tame the urban labyrinth, and to represent its spaces as "legible" and "knowable"' (Pinder 1996: 407). With no 'hidden spaces', all is opened to inspection and subsumed within the map. The specification of the geographic territory of the communities that are to serve as the vectors of governmental programming (when those communities are spatial, rather than interest-based) becomes a pressing concern. Under those conditions, the map becomes critical. However, state mapping is more than a neutral 'inscription' of space, but can constitute space in significant and apparently neutral ways. It is these concerns, in large part, that lie behind the opposition voiced by Downtown Eastside activists. The act of 'leaving a community off a map', as they put it, entailed a silent recomposition of the spaces of community. But this did not just entail a redrawing of an 'administrative map', but also a redrawing of the geographies of local propertied entitlements.

As Lefebvre (1991) reminds us, the 'spatial economy' policed by the map is not disinterested, but must be situated in terms of certain social relations. The intersecting interests of liberal governance and those of mapped property are of special relevance to the present example, given the significance of land to both. Property opens space to governmentalizing intervention, making it countable and accountable. Generally, the fixity, visibility and security of land (guaranteed, in part, by the map) is the reason that real property (as opposed to personal property) is given special status by the state (Reeve, 1986). Real property as commodity transforms space not only into equivalent, interchangeable and exchangeable pieces (Lefebvre, 1991). Together with the survey and the map, which are bound up with it, property imposes a grid, enabling the division, classification, quantification and administration of space. As Barthes notes, 'ownership depends on a certain dividing of things: to appropriate is to fragment the world, to divide it into finite objects subject to man in proportion to their very discontinuity; for we cannot separate without finally naming and classifying, and at that very moment, property is born' (quoted in Wood 1992: 70). It is not surprising, then, that mapping has long been seen by liberal regimes as fundamental to the production of political and economic subjects. Harvey, for example, reminds us that:

> 'Rational' mathematical conceptions of space and time, were ... a necessary condition for Enlightenment doctrines of political equality and social progress. One of the first actions of the French revolutionary assembly was to ordain the systematic mapping of France as a means to ensure equality of political representation. (Harvey 1996: 239–40)

Property relations, however, can be configured in very different ways. The way in which propertied entitlements and rights are understood by marginalized populations, such as indigenous peoples, peasants or poor city-dwellers in either the Third or First World, can be very different. If ownership does depend on 'a certain dividing of things', we should not be surprised that the mapping of dominant interests, which frequently challenge such entitlements, are contested, while alternative maps are constructed. The process of cartographic boundary construction and naming, in this light, becomes a critical question. Spatial naming as a means of ordering is of immense political significance. The 'power to individuate within a given spatio-temporal frame is associated with the power to name; and naming is a form of power over people and things' (Harvey 1996: 264).

Under these conditions, the denial or effacement of names constitutes an erasure of alternative forms of political ordering. As Ann Armbrecht Forbes notes, the naming of our immediate environment provides a way of 'entering into relationships with those places, of making them our own, of creating a home'. Conversely, 'when we are forced to live in places according to boundaries, maps and names that are created elsewhere, we in turn become alienated from those places' (Forbes 1995: 70). As one indigenous inhabitant of Nicaragua's coast expressed it, when faced with 'official' maps of the reefs central to traditional culture and economy, 'This is not a map of our reef. This map is like a birth certificate with the wrong names on it' (Nietschmann 1995: 36).

There is extensive evidence of the significance of cartographic naming in the constitution of space and power relations, much of which speaks to the deployment of mapping as a means of resisting domination. Garth Myers, for example, describes the manner in which colonial and post-colonial toponymies in Zanzibar are expressive of the desire to make urban space legible and disciplined, regulating 'who could be where' (Myers 1996: 240). However, he goes on to describe the manifold ways in which such maps are implicitly challenged and redrawn by local residents. Similarly, in their study of black Richmond, Brown and Kimball note the way which African American residents, through both their multiple daily practices and understandings and their opposition to dominant interests, depart from the official maps of the city: '[B]lack Richmonders created a "counter memory", rerembering the creation of the ward as an act undertaken by black people, a distinction that has turned into a place of congregation as well as segregation' (Brown and Kimball 1995: 316–17).

Such remappings, undertaken increasingly by indigenous groups, for example, can rely on 'Western' technologies and modes of representation (such as geographic information systems), or can invoke very different cartographies that better reflect local nuance and complexity. For example, in their reading of the complex overlapping property relations associated particularly with women's traditional uses of the environment, Rocheleau *et al.* call for a 'multipurpose representation that can account for the complexity of the kinds of multiple, overlapping rights and obligations likely to be associated with any one spot on a conventional map' (Rocheleau *et al.* 1995: 64).

At the same time, we must be cautious about imputing some 'authenticity' to such oppositional mappings. Not only can processes of naming and bounding serve to exclude just as often as they include, given the zero-sum nature of mapped space, but the provenance of the map itself can serve to compromise opposition. However, we do need to be attentive to the implication of community maps both in terms of 'action at a distance' and the constitution of hegemonic political subjectivities, and also as a basis for the contestation of such forms of ordering. As we shall see from the Vancouver example, struggles over the mapping of community, and the political and social identities that such maps bound and order, has been a leitmotif of local politics from the very inception of 'community'-based forms of government to the present day.

From Liminality to Community: The Emergence of Gastown and the Downtown Eastside in Vancouver's Inner City

Hamilton's commemorative plaque, quoted at the beginning of this chapter, marks not only a temporal boundary (the arrival of the Western cadastral grid and the effacement of First Nations geographies) but an important spatial boundary between the prosperous central business district to the west and the devalorized east side of the downtown core. Residential gentrification has become the central issue in the eastern part of the downtown, an area which has the dubious reputation of being one of Canada's poorest urban neighbourhoods. It currently contains a large, low-income population that manages to obtain often sub-standard accommodation in the many residential hotels in the area. Years of underinvestment and capital flight have depressed land values in the area to around $70 per square foot, compared to values of around $600–900 square foot for central downtown property. However, this cheap land, zoned for high population densities, in combination with the central city location, an overheated property market, a planning policy that encourages the 'densification' of downtown space and the changing function of the central city within the international division of labour, has begun to attract development capital. In the past few years, a number of developments on the periphery of the area have occurred – most notably, on the former Expo site to the south and west – in addition to more rent incursions by loft developers into the neighbourhood. While realtors begin to salivate over one of their 'hotter markets', area activists call for a policy of 'zero displacement' (Bula 1997: a10).

As land development pressures increase in the eastern section of the downtown, the politics of space and turf – especially questions of mapping, naming and bounding – have also intensified. The resulting conflicts neatly exemplify the ways in which mapping invests the urban spaces of community with morality and economy. Two conflicting communities, each with associated propertied and citizenship claims, are particularly salient – namely, the Downtown Eastside and Gastown. The passion which the representatives and activists in this confrontation bring to problems associated with boundaries and names is explicable partly by the claims to community staked out by each. In order to understand those claims, however, it is necessary to briefly review the historical and social milieu from which they have emerged.

At the time of Hamilton's survey, the locus of Vancouver's financial, retail and commercial sectors was to be found in and around the eastern part of the downtown, in the several blocks of the old Granville town site. His survey, and the associated arrival of the Canadian Pacific Railway, saw investment shift westwards, away from the original town site, in a real estate boom shortly before the First World War. Nevertheless, the east side remained the vital centre of warehousing and transportation, as well as shopping, for the city's predominantly working-class east side population. This area, adjacent to the city's East End slum district, was also known as a district of dubious morality, with dozens of 'dollar-a-day' hotels and cheap rooming houses where loggers, miners, railroad and other seasonal workers congregated between jobs and people new to the city could find inexpensive accommodation. In many ways, it was a frontier version of Chauncey's (1994) New York 'bachelor subculture'. Brothels, bars, nightclubs (legal

and otherwise), restaurants, and religious missions abounded. However, the era of migrant workers drew to a close after the Second World War as corporate interests were consolidated in western Canada and unionization in resource, transportation and construction industries stabilized the demand for mobile labour.

In the post-war decades, these kinds of districts were termed 'skid rows' – the homes of supposedly rootless single men, classified as chronic alcoholics, drug addicts, perverts, drifters and outcasts of various hues. In Vancouver, the area was called 'skid road', after the corduroy logging roads where fallen trees were 'skidded' to the mill. Although the loggers were now fewer in number, the timber industry connotations remained. With growing anxieties about downtown 'decline', skid rows – including Vancouver's – were mapped as pathological spaces of blight and decay, both moral and physical. By the mid-1960s the area was targeted as part of a proposed downtown urban renewal scheme, leading to an intensification of mapping and surveillance which has yet to cease.

But even as they ordered this space, the 'codes and conventions' of official mappings opened up expert discourses and representations to challenge and appropriation as well as the articulation of alternative orders. The planning department's solution to the perception of a blighted slum area was a proposal to extend the planned downtown freeway system through the city's Chinatown and skid road – known officially as the Old Granville Townsite – to service a massive high-rise office project that private developers intended to construct on the waterfront. These two interlinked schemes became strategic flashpoints in a larger struggle over the future of the city. Their proponents represented a corporate–bureaucratic development regime which had dominated civic planning since at least the early 1950s, based on large-scale downtown property and commercial interests. The hegemony which this regime had enjoyed for almost two decades was seriously eroded as it was confronted by emerging social and political forces that crystallized around the issues of the Chinatown freeway and redevelopment versus renovation in 'the old city'. An alliance of ethnic-based neighbourhood groups and radical organizations with small groups of young professionals, especially academics and architects, countercultural entrepreneurs and establishment arts organizations, promoted a version of small-scale development and slow-growth politics that would be formulated in terms of its vision of 'the livable city'. In the course of this contestation, the official mappings were appropriated and 'skid road' was recomposed through two quite different and, ultimately contradictory, visions of the inner city whose remappings continue to resonate today.

The campaign to promote 'the livable city' was carried out through a range of tactics and schemes, including the implementation, by the City, of a regime of Local Area Planning that bounded Vancouver into 22 discrete neighbourhoods. Civic staff, including those from the new department of social planning and community development, sought to engage citizens in the formulation of zoning regulations and social policy. Both officials and citizens deployed a rhetoric of community that permeated this process. Despite the fact that many had not existed until the planners drew the lines on their maps, Vancouver's 22 neighbourhoods were seen simultaneously as communities, constituted through shared histories and memories that underpinned some level of local collective identity and therefore local interest. The representation of urban space was thus inextricably linked with the formation of political identities. Not only did civic departments, aided in their quest by various historical projects, begin an exhaustive cataloguing of the characteristics of each neighbourhood, they sought out, and sometimes solicited, organizations, groups and individuals to speak for, and act on behalf of, their 'community'.

Gastown

The remapping of 'skid road' was both a tool and an event in the conflicts through which communitized forms of urban government crystallized in Vancouver. Notions of community were deployed in a whole range of different forms, transforming the discursive, the institutional and the built landscapes through which this space was materialized. It is in this way that we can understand the emergence of 'Gastown', occupying the original locus of European settlement (known as the Old Granville Townsite). This area's official designation as a heritage site in 1972 was the outcome of a campaign not only of opposition to urban renewal but for the promotion of revitalization. Local networks of entrepreneurial elements, together with arts groups and some local property-owners, had quickly taken advantage of the area's marginal real-estate market and its rapid rise as a key Vancouver countercultural site at the end of the 1960s, transforming the heart of 'skid road' into a fashionable district of boutiques, restaurants and nightclubs. Revitalization, however, was not advocated as an entirely commercial proposition but, rather, as a benefit to the citizens of the city. Gastown, the old city, was constituted as a community resource, a repository of historical memory, social meaning and identity.

In this sense, all of Gastown was a public trust for which civic authorities, as representatives of the community, had the responsibility of nurturing and guiding. Propelled by the alliance of forces that contested its freeway plans, the City began to finance and coordinate the infrastructural changes, such as sidewalks, street lighting and trees, necessary to support increased entrepreneurial investment in the district's buildings. City's 1974 creation of special-

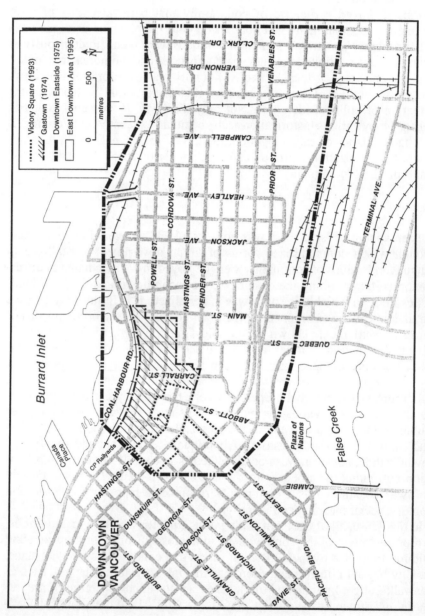

Figure 11.1   Competing mappings on Vancouver's Eastside

purpose 'historical area' zoning was accompanied by the Gastown Historical Area Planning Committee, an advisory body with appointed representatives of tenants, property-owners, businesses and architectural experts to
advise Vancouver City Council on the issues and decisions regarding the
district. Then, in the 1980s, the City recognized Gastown as a Business
Improvement Area in which all businesses were assessed a special annual
levy to fund the Gastown Business Improvement Society (GBIS). While the
earlier Gastown Merchants Association had been a strictly voluntary affair,
GBIS membership was legally mandated under civic by-laws for businesses
operating within the specified boundaries. It provided a way for businesses
to determine priorities and exercise discretion over the spending of nomi-
nally public funds. It also acted as a lobby for the interests of Gastown
businesses.

But if it was a community resource, Gastown itself was not yet a community, although the heritage zoning at least provided a boundary for Gastown
(Figure 11.1). The formalization in Vancouver of a notion of community
framed by the intersection of space and citizenship in the form of residence
made untenable any claims to community by Gastown interests. The predominance of private sector commercial investment combined with a lack of
actual property-owning residents to render the heritage district as a business
precinct, oriented increasingly to tourism. This would change by the 1990s,
as we shall see.

The Downtown Eastside

During the last half of the 1960s, groups of young, politically radical organizers began working in the 'skid road' area, fundamentally shifting the
networks which existed between the mostly church-operated social service
agencies and those of the city and the province. Their arrival signalled the
rise of a new agenda that challenged the dominant rendition of 'skid road' as
the haven of derelicts and transients, seeking instead to articulate a vision of
inner-city residents and citizens whose most pressing problems were poverty, deteriorating housing, unemployment and a lack of access to services.
Increasingly explicit was a claim of occupation and residence. Contrary to
characterizations of the population as shiftless and mobile, activists re-
minded outsiders, 'of the district's stability, of the loyalty of many elderly
men to it, of the small minority who were transients and alcoholics' (Hassan
and Ley 1994: 190). The Downtown Eastside, in other words, was a neighbourhood and a community to which residents could claim some collective
attachment and entitlement. Although the population was (and is) largely
made up of renters, the sense of a collective property claim to not only the
housing but also the communal spaces of the Downtown Eastside is an

important one (Blomley forthcoming). It also provided the conditions for the development of an indigenous organizational base capable of mobilizing local 'citizens' in alliance with other groups, including the City, to address these problems.

Central to that mobilization was a self-conscious mapping strategy. Organizations such as the Downtown Eastside Residents Association (DERA) played a formative role here, struggling to remap 'skid road' as the 'Downtown Eastside'. The term itself derives from these remappings, originally delineated in a 1975 newspaper article by a prominent activist and future member of parliament. At the same time, the boundaries of this space were drawn deliberately widely and inclusively, encompassing a broad swathe of the low-income area to the east of the downtown. This included, we should note, Gastown (Figure 11.1). Note the reference to shared poverty and permanent residence:

> The area designated as the 'downtown eastside' stretches along the harbour from Clark Drive to Burrard Street (except for the Strathcona neighbourhood, which maintains its separate identity). It contains downtown businesses, waterfront industries and a newly developed Gastown commercial-entertainment area which has pushed Vancouver's Skid Road eastward. The residents of the area include many single people who live in run-down hotels and rooming houses, the most visible of whom are the transients, alcoholics and social outcasts on the streets. However, the majority are permanent residents who have lived downtown for many years and include a number of Japanese and Chinese families in the eastern section. (City of Vancouver Archives, Planning Department, Series 69)

The force of this definition, and the effectiveness with which neighbourhood groups had managed to reconstitute space, is revealed by its longevity. For nearly 20 years, this notion of a sprawling Downtown Eastside went unchallenged, even by business operators and property-owners with obvious interests in upscaling the area. From being purely a 'skid road', the 'Downtown Eastside' now constituted a viable 'community' and 'neighbourhood' that had both particular strengths and specific needs. Consequently, local government, planners and the new City of Vancouver Department of Social Planning and Community Development made increased efforts to discover, investigate and provide services for the amelioration of the problems faced by people living in the area. DERA, and eventually other local groups in the Downtown Eastside, were themselves constituted as authorities on the neighbourhood, its residents and the issues taking place there.

DERA, together with other groups in the Downtown Eastside thus attempted to fabricate a spatial order that was initially quite different from that of civic authorities. The space of the 'skid road' slum was reconfigured into that of a community by appeals to history and memory – an effort in which mapping was a central tactic. But it was also a double-edged sword, because it required Downtown Eastsiders to operate on the same terrain of government as those authorities which had so recently dubbed the area a pathological slum. In recasting 'skid road' as the Downtown Eastside, a new spatial order was produced, the ultimate effect of which was to constitute local groups as authorities on the 'problems' of their community, thus localizing those problems. In so doing, the Downtown Eastside was co-opted into emergent community-based forms of governance.

In both the case of Gastown and the Downtown Eastside, then, 'community' emerged as the key vector of governmental power. Both entailed mappings, and both entailed the construction of localized political subjectivities relating to citizenship and propertied entitlements. However, such spatializations were not unproblematic. Two future antagonisms were established, as we shall see below. The first centred on the relationship between the local state and the communities of Gastown and the Downtown Eastside. While both community spaces provided powerful points for state intervention, the specific boundings and namings of these spaces either had, or later attained, considerable relevance to the communities themselves. When the maps began to change with the changing land market, the boundings and namings became points of considerable contention. This was largely so due to the second agonism. As noted, the broad cartographic definition of the Downtown Eastside subsumed Gastown. As we shall see, when Gastown began to advance more formalized claims to community standing, based largely on a gentrifying propertied claim, this subsumption was directly challenged. Along with related remappings, the effect, so far as Downtown Eastside activists were concerned, was to dismember their community and thus efface its governmental claims. To both Gastown and Downtown Eastside activists, maps were seen as constitutive of community spaces and political relations, signalling either a healthy revitalization or a cynical exercise in class politics and social exclusion.

Redrawing the Maps: Gastown Redux and the Birth of Victory Square

The very name of the Downtown Eastside has been a central feature in local politics for over a quarter of a century. A politics of symbolism has been a vital strategic element as local groups struggled for recognition of this district and its population as a neighbourhood and community (Hassan and Ley 1994). But such recognition has always been tenuous and groups making claims to represent the community are ever-wary about shifts in its representation. Nevertheless, for at least two decades, the boundaries and namings of Downtown Eastside had been relatively stable, entering into governmental discourse as a problem in search of a solution.

However, by the mid-1990s, those cartographic and governmental certainties began to give way. Anticipating problems over the direction of downtown development, the City's planning staff initiated a process that attempted, in their eyes, to balance the needs of residents of residential hotels, developers and local property-owners, businesses, and heritage proponents for whom the district was the symbolic heart of the city. The balance which they sought to achieve was to be reflected in a district where students, trendy young people and artists would rub shoulders with the urban poor in a display of tolerance, mutual acceptability and minimum displacement. The plan's goal was to stimulate the kind of low-level reinvestment that would both attract the new population – as residents, consumers or employees – and upgrade the building stock in a manner that was sensitive to the restoration process.

However, the planners chose to act upon a section of the downtown (close to the city's core and thus primed for redevelopment) that Downtown Eastside activists had traditionally claimed as part of their community. Bringing together representatives from the business and property-owning sectors with those from social service agencies and community groups, civic staff conducted a whole series of working groups, committees, workshops, consultations, meetings and tours at which participants were induced to engage in repeated exercises of mapping and representation that not only redrew the boundaries but also renamed the space. In so doing, they tried to produce a new neighbourhood in the city's core, rendering an area which they designated 'Victory Square' visible as a discrete space (Figure 11.1).

Paradoxically, the very process by which Victory Square was actually produced as a cartographic space has been rendered invisible. The complexities of competition and negotiation between and among the various participants, including civic staff, were virtually erased by the apparent objectivity of the mapping process. Instead, this literally invented space appeared, almost independently of its representations, as a fully formed 'neighbourhood', complete with particularized and objective histories and communities. A newspaper article presents the area in precisely these terms, as appearing to exist prior to the ordering that constituted it: '*Perfectly framed* by turn-of-the-century architecture, it is a place of resonance and memories that progress has passed by' (Ward 1997: 15, emphasis added). There is no recognition of the active, and very recent, political construction of this space.

While the creation of this space may have been rendered invisible to 'outsiders', this was not the case for Downtown Eastsiders. Community activists who were drawn into the planning process placed themselves in direct opposition to the construction of Victory Square as a *de novo* neighbourhood. For them, this was the Downtown Eastside. The Victory Square planning programme was treated as a challenge to the spatial integrity of their community, signalling a conscious effort to facilitate gentrification by pushing the edge of the Downtown Eastside eastwards. For one critic, the Victory Square renaming was an instrument of gentrification and dispossession that

> ... betrayed their vision of the future of the area ... And that was downtown, the downtown core, would gradually swallow up the western end of the Downtown Eastside right up to Main Street. It would be cleaned up, gentrified. (Interview with Marg Green, area resident and activist, 18 June 1996)

More sinister still, argued many activists, was the effective balkanization of the Downtown Eastside as it became fragmented into a cluster of smaller, autonomous neighbourhoods. It was seen as:

> ... a systematic attempt to define the Downtown Eastside out of existence, to chop it up into disconnected sections and crowd it out by other 'neighbourhoods' that are dominated by business interests and developers and upscale new settlers. If that were to happen, the people of the Downtown Eastside would lose their unified voice and their power to resist the changes that are so harmful to them. (Doinel 1995)

The plan was thus perceived by activists as a direct challenge to claims of property and citizenship rights which had been promoted over the past quarter-century on the basis of a community identity that inserted the urban poor and residents of single-room occupancy (SRO) hotels as legitimate participants in Vancouver's social and political life. The creation of Victory Square was understood as a recomposition of those rights, nullifying any recognized moral claims to property that might accrue to the community as a consequence of its long-term occupation of this place. Property, the planners and their maps seemed to be saying, was after all, only pieces of property. Activists saw this process as, once again, mapping their constituency out of existence and hence out of power.

That contestation was often cartographic in form, with attempts at renaming, rebounding and reprojecting space. One very direct disruption of the Cartesian map occurred at a planning department 'open house', held in the Downtown Eastside, where activists physically relabelled the 'Victory Square' and 'Gastown' maps with 'Downtown Eastside', causing great consternation amongst city staff (partly at the cost of replacing the maps): 'We won't be rendered invisible by being ignored' (Anonymous 1995b: 26).

But if Victory Square represented a threat to the integrity of local concepts of neighbourhood and community, a gentrifying Gastown district claiming rights to the name of 'community' loomed as a spectre of destruction. Early in the 1990s the ongoing tension that existed between Gastown interests and Downtown Eastside organizations erupted into an open and increasingly bitter confrontation over land use, zoning and development policy in the area. During this period of intense conflict, incoming residential property-owners, occupying condominium developments that have been constructed over the past decade, have organized and allied themselves with business groups to advance residential development in the area and to claim neighbourhood and community status.

State mappings initially called Gastown into being and, in so doing, institutionalized certain forms of localized identity as congruent with the production of 'heritage'-designated properties. Subsequently, legitimized Gastown representatives have engaged in their own mappings, designed to distinguish Gastown from its more dubiously reputable neighbour and to solidify zoning boundaries that are highly fluid with respect to the movement of people. The relations of power which are realized and exercised through the development and transformation of property are thus expunged, as it were, from the map, replaced with renderings of mundane concerns dealing with vectors of criminality, the siting of social service agencies and special needs residential facilities (SNRFs, pronounced SNeRFs in the argot) or the necessity of public funding for property-owners to renovate their heritage buildings.

Thus, the presence of the poor in Gastown, who actually constitute the great majority of the residential population, is explained in terms of the siting of social service facilities and subsidized housing rather than their pre-existent residency. 'There is', one analyst claims, 'a fiercely competitive economic struggle between market and non-market interests ... for finite and shrinking numbers of development sites' (UD&D 1992: 2, 6). As a consequence of the 'subsidies' which they receive from state and charitable sources, such facilities threaten to crowd out the market interests because the latter are not subsidized and, hence, uncompetitive *vis-à-vis* development costs. They also, apparently, attract the poor to Gastown, creating problems for everyone else. 'Advisory' groups established by the local state in the 1970s, notably the Gastown Historical Area Planning Committee (GHAPC) have emerged a key proponents of these claims:

> Gastown has experienced an influx of facilities targeted to clientele at the lower end of the socio-economic scale, which cater to the *socially disabled* and consequently have been known to attract an undesirable element. Ironically, there is a dearth of facilities for *Gastown residents* (GHAPC minutes, 25 September 1996, emphasis added).

Poor people are thus represented as interlopers who are present only to utilize services that are not required by authentic locals. A heritage area, it seems, is not a place for the poor. They must, then, belong elsewhere.

Gastown interests have thus asserted their right to map, name and regulate the space within the boundaries of the Gastown Historical Area – for example, by refusing any subsumption within the boundaries of the Downtown Eastside or even association with the designation 'Eastside'. Opponents are labelled 'outside professional interest groups' or 'negative, self-interested people who have their own reasons to keep the status quo here. Whether they be drug dealers or self-appointed spokes-persons for the poor' (Shason 1995; Anonymous 1995a). Hence, references to the existence and looming threat of a 'ghetto' abound in documents produced by Gastown-based organizations. The contemporary state of deterioration and visible street drug-dealing in the area around Gastown are contrasted with a past golden age of shopping and street life and a potential future of the same. Gentrification, called 'revitalization', is promoted as the key to counteracting the looming ghetto and reviving the prosperous days gone by.

In comparing itself to the image of a deteriorating, burnt-out 'ghetto', Gastown has been successfully able to claim the status of a neighbourhood and community and, in so doing, inscribe on to the landscape a space where the poor are outsiders and property-owners as those with rights of representation and voice.

As in the related case of Victory Square, Downtown Eastside activists have attempted to resist Gastown's claims to a distinctive space and advance their own claims to a wider geographical base for the community which they seek to represent. Refuting the portrayal of their constituency as an 'anti-community' of 'undesirables', criminals and drug addicts and of their space as a slum in need of redevelopment, activist groups have countered these images with their own projections of encroaching 'yuppies' concerned only with their own property values and heritage buildings, rather than the needs of the 'real' community into which they had located. The presence of condominium owners, activists have claimed, is exacerbating already existing problems by promoting the dispossession and displacement that inevitably result from gentrification.

Not surprisingly, Downtown Eastside activists have attempted to affirm their spatial boundings to include Gastown. A stencilled graffito that reads 'I live in the Downtown Eastside' appeared throughout the area, often on boardings around new loft and condominium projects, consciously challenging the aggressive mappings of Gastown interests and the consequent erasure of the poor. At the same time, activists sought to assert the physical presence of the Downtown Eastside, leafleting a developers' sales office in Gastown and demonstrating regularly at the premises of a large, abandoned department store that was earmarked for condominium development. These demonstrations often took a festive atmosphere, with participants sweeping and drawing on the sidewalks, painting the building's windows and listening to music.

The spatial politics of bounding and naming was also explored by a local poet who noted the perils of 'community' in the context of contemporary modes of governance. In an article headed 'Community makes me crazy', Tora argues for the need to redefine a Downtown Eastside community in order to resist the attempts by Gastown interests who 'want to wipe us out'. The problem, however, is that Gastown can define itself as a community and attain official recognition of that assertion. Indeed, the fluid geographies of contemporary capitalism make community even more slippery and potentially oppressive. In the face of the Downtown Eastside, Gastown can say:

> Oh, we're a community too – a business community, a Gastown commercial venture community. They may even reveal themselves as the international offshore holding community, or the community of New World initiatives … with the language they have today, they can make up any number of official sounding titles … At other times in history, in other situations, this 'living here' & knowing one another gave us the right to decide who would move into the area and who wouldn't – but we're civilized & have progressed beyond common sense now, but let's shout into those deaf ears some more. Let's rip the headset off society & make them face the truth' (Tora 1995: 19).

It was in response to the concerns raised about both potential displacement and the escalating intensity of the conflict, that the City initiated its monitoring project to assess the changing land market and social consequences of property development. However, it faced a problem (in part of its own making) of what to name the space it sought to monitor. The question of naming and bounding in this hotly contested zone was a sensitive one. Their initial plans to use the term 'Downtown Eastside' were vociferously rejected by Gastown merchants and loft-owners and a newly enervescent (at the behest of City staff) merchants group from Victory Square. Given these local geopolitics, the term 'East Downtown' was selected by planners as a deliberately neutral umbrella term. However, the zero-sum quality of Cartesian space meant that, inevitably, 'Downtown Eastside' activists were offended, particularly in the context of other remappings, such as Victory Square, as well as a re-emergent 'skid row' discourse in the media.

The space of the East Downtown, renamed and bounded into sub-areas that were labelled as neighbourhoods, only confirmed activists' suspicions that the City was colluding with developers and 'yuppies' in dismembering their community. Activist groups contested this relabelling and appropriation of what they took as their space. Along with the struggles around

Gastown and Victory Square, it was felt that the time was ripe to draw the cartographic line in the sand. Downtown Eastside activists forced the May 1996 meeting with civic staff noted at the start of this discussion. Confronted with the threat of non-participation in their planning programme by some key Downtown Eastside groups, staff acquiesced, and the term 'Downtown Eastside' was reinstated for some of those efforts. Nevertheless, the designated space remains divided into 'sub-areas'. It has also not gone unchallenged by propertied interests, who have objected that the association of 'the words "East" or "Eastside" with Gastown and businesses in Gastown associates [it with] negative images, especially drugs, crime and alcoholism' (GHAPC Minutes, 15 October 1997; GHAPC Minutes, 16 July 1997). In response to these complaints, one planner reassured Gastown representatives that the Downtown Eastside was, in fact, merely a 'zoning district' (GHAPC Minutes, 15 January 1997).

Governing Urban Space

As noted, city planners were surprised at the resolution of Downtown Eastside activists in insisting that the 'appropriate' boundaries and names be reinstated on official maps. In our capacity as both academics and 'Downtown Eastside activists', we were questioned by planners at this stand. In part, this chapter is an attempt to clarify why maps have been so important to community politics in inner-city Vancouver. Clearly, other questions are at stake in the complex struggles over the future (and the past) of this space. However, maps do seem undeniably important as a means by which spaces and associated claims to space can be concretized, and through which conflicting claims to 'community' can be fought over. We have highlighted property as one such terrain of conflict.

In making sense of these questions, certain issues seem particularly salient. Most immediately, this case study appears as an examplar of what has been termed the 'congenitally failing' nature of government: 'the "will to govern"', as Rose and Miller argue, 'needs to be understood less in terms of its success than in terms of the difficulties in operationalizing it' (Rose and Miller 1992: 11). To think of maps simply as political technologies that can render space transparent, or of the related construction of 'community' as a key governmental space can make both appear as relatively unproblematic and uncontested. As we have seen here, mappings of community and related mobilizations of citizenship and propertied entitlements certainly have served as instruments for state intervention in inner-city Vancouver. However, in line with Foucault's injunction to think of power in relational, spatialized and ascending terms, we also need to be sensitive to the workings of complex local networks where community has been mapped, but with reference to a very different spatial and political order.

In moving to these local networks, it is tempting to position them as 'external to rule', as a form of self-sufficient resistance that can conflict with governmental programmes. Miller and Rose, in exploring the contradictions of government, note the collisions between such programmes and a reality 'too unruly to be captured by any perfect knowledge ... [T]he real always insists on the form of resistance to programming' (Miller and Rose 1990: 14). However, as O'Malley suggests, the effect of such claims is to posit resistance as both external to, and an obstacle in, such programmes. His alternative suggestion that we think about the manner in which 'government and resistance articulate, mingle and hybridize' (O'Malley 1996: 310) is useful here. For, despite the oppositional positioning of Downtown Eastside activists and civic planners, the very space of the Downtown Eastside has served as a 'community' site for government programming for the past three decades (indeed, one of the calls made by local activists is for a reinstatement of many of such interventions, such as cooperative housing subsidies). However, despite this 'co-option', the localized provenance of the Downtown Eastside as a space, produced as it was by 'grassroots' mobilization, generates internal instability when city planners start rebounding and renaming this space. To activists, the Downtown Eastside is seen as an organic space, directly produced by local practices. To deny this space is to efface the community.

> City Hall doesn't include the Downtown Eastside on maps of the area. If it isn't here, then where is it? ... There is a very active community in the Downtown Eastside ... Loggers tell tales of their exploits, fishers relate experiences from their lives ... Writers congregate to hear all the stories they can and turn them into articles, novels, plays ... City Hall, the Downtown Eastside may not be on maps of your making, but it is here. (Sanders 1996)

Gastown is different to the extent that it was produced 'from above' by state fiat. However, Gastown activists have deployed a language of community occupation and entitlement, albeit in a more market-oriented form, to reconfigure a zoning area into a 'neighbourhood'. In the case of Gastown, the apparently disinterested language of zoning and heritage has been used to define a social and political landscape. The poor can be 'zoned out' as they conflict with the 'heritage landscape' of Gastown. In this process, the mappings of city staff have similarly been challenged. A social group that one might consider as potential beneficiaries of planning has also emerged as a sticking point in government programmes.

Mapping, then, seems to be a technology deployed both by 'programmers' and by 'community groups'. Again, however, we should be cautious about imputing a divide between either dominant or resistant maps. Recent debates around cartography have sometimes made this distinction, with the mappings of oppositional groups compared to those of state elites. In making this distinction, the implication is that the former are somehow more authentic to the extent that they are not only localized, but also given their apparent resistance to the decorporealization and abstraction of dominant maps. Precisely this distinction was made in the Downtown Eastside, where the mappings of grounded and embodied residents are clearly elevated against the 'expert' spatial representations of the authorities. As one critic notes: 'The residents are the people who actually live here, long term. And our neighbourhood is not just a bunch of lines drawn on a map by planners or developers' (Doinel 1995). More emotively, at a city meeting to discuss a proposal to build 'micro-suites' for low-income residents, one activist demanded 'one [additional] square foot for every man and woman murdered in the Downtown Eastside, for every disabled person, for every child gone hungry, for every addict and alcoholic'. The detached 'square foot' of the developer is here clearly set against a morally superior claim of local residents, who have lived, and died, in the abstract spaces of the development proposal.

This is not to say, however, that 'dominant' maps are, by definition, abstracted or false, nor that local maps are somehow authentic to the extent that they are grounded. Not only does the production of Cartesian maps entail some profoundly embodied processes (not least of which is Hamilton's driving of the survey stake and the clearing of the brush), but the maps of the Downtown Eastside can equally play with the protocols of abstraction. For example, attempts to establish a Geographic Information System – one of the most detached and abstract of mapping technologies – are underway, involving Downtown Eastside activists, academics and planners. However, the desire is not just to obtain an objective rendering of the reality of changing land markets, but also to be able to turn 'expert systems' on their head and to use the authoritative language of the Cartesian map to advance community concerns about the pace of gentrification to outsiders who might otherwise be unpersuaded. In that sense, if the abstraction of dominant maps is at issue, it is as a point of political intervention rather than as a self-evident truth. In other words, the very fact that state maps are powerful definers of local space, to the extent that they speak with the language of detachment and authority, is the reason that Downtown Eastside and Gastown activists wish to contest official maps that they find objectionable, and insist that such maps better reflect their sense of local entitlements. There is an apparent paradox here: state maps are seen by local groups as sufficiently powerful to produce certain spaces (such as Victory Square), but not so persuasive as to be incontestable when those spaces are deemed the wrong ones. Perhaps the only way out of this paradox is through an exploration of the hybridized nature both of resistance and government, and of dominant and 'community' maps.

But if 'community' can be mobilized by dominant interests, this does not, as Rose (1996: 336) reminds us, make it false. Indeed, it is the tangible associations which people have with the local spaces in which they live and the populations and places that make up those spaces that makes 'community' such a powerful vector of governance, for good or evil. For precisely these reasons, we need to be very sensitive to the manner in which such communities are constituted, mobilized, mapped, named and bounded, and alert to the exclusions and democratizations that accompany this process. If the social is indeed dead, as Rose (1996) suggests, such questions have never been more pressing.

Acknowledgements

Versions of this chapter were presented at a colloquium in the Department of Geography at the University of British Columbia (November 1997), and at the Annual Meeting of the Institute of British Geographers, at the University of Surrey, January 1998). We would also like to thank David Demeritt for his perceptive comments. Research was made possible by a grant from the Social Science and Humanities Research Council (401-94-1734).

References

Anonymous (1995a), 'Can you Find the Downtown Eastside on these Maps???', *Newsletter of the Carnegie Community Action Project*, November, 1, 2.
Anonymous (1995b), 'Community News', *Carnegie Newsletter*, 15 December.
Barry, Andrew (1997), 'Line of Communication and Spaces of Rule', in A. Barry, T. Osborne and N. Rose (eds), *Foucault and Political Reason: Liberalism, Neoliberalism and Rationalities of Government*, London: UCL Press.
Berry, Christopher (1980), 'Property and Possession. Two Replies to Locke – Hume and Hegel', in J. Roland Pennock and John W. Chapman (eds), *Nomus XXII*, New York: New York University Press, 89–100.
Blomley, Nicholas (forthcoming), 'Landscapes of Property', *Law and Society Review*.
Brown, Barkley and Gregg Kimball (1995), 'Mapping the Terrain of Black Richmond', *Journal of Urban History*, **21** (3), 296–346.
Bula, Francis (1997), 'Real estate boom looms for Hastings Street', *Vancouver Sun*, 5 March, A10.
Chauncey, George (1994), *Gay New York: Gender, Urban Culture, and the Making of the Male Gay World, 1890–1940*, New York: Basic Books.

City Clerk (1993), City Clerk, Memorandum re: Victory Square Community Planning Program Initiatives.
City of Vancouver Planning Department (1993), Victory Square Community Planning Process, information sheet [ND].
City of Vancouver Planning Department (1995), Victory Square Concept Plan, 5.
CVA (City of Vancouver Archives), Planning Dept, Series 69, 94-D-6, File 1a, DERA Newspapers, 1975–1979, Downtown Eastside Residents Association by Margaret Mitchell, Downtown East newspaper, no. 4, April 1975.
Dansereau, Francine, Annick Germain and Catherine Évillard (1997), 'Social Mix: Old Utopia, Contemporary Experience and Challenges', *Canadian Journal of Urban Research*, **6** (1), 1–23.
Doinel, A. (1995), 'The Incredible Shrinking Neighbourhood', *Carnegie Newsletter*, 1 March, 2–3.
Forbes, Ann A. (1995), 'Heirs to the Land: Mapping the Future of the Makalu-Barun', *Cultural Survival Quarterly*, Winter, 69–71.
Foucault, Michel (1980), *Power/Knowledge*, New York: Pantheon.
Foucault, Michel (1988), 'Technologies of the Self', in H.L. Martin, H. Gutman and P.H. Hutton (eds), *Technologies of the Self: A Seminar with Michel Foucault*, London: Tavistock.
Foucault, Michel (1982), 'Afterword: The Subject and Power', in Hubert Dreyfus and Paul Rabinow, *Michel Foucault: Beyond Structuralism and Hermeneutics*, Brighton: Harvester.
GBIS (Gastown Business Improvement Society) (1995), *Gastown Business Improvement Area Newsletter*, Vancouver.
GHAPC (Gastown Historical Area Planning Committee) (1997), Minutes of 15 January 1997 meeting.
GHAPC minutes, 25 September 1996.
Gregory, Derek (1994), *Geographical Imaginations*, Cambridge: Blackwell.
Harvey, David (1996), *Justice, Nature and the Geography of Difference*, Cambridge: Blackwell.
Hassan, Shlomo and David Ley (1994), *Neighbourhood Organization and the Welfare State*, Toronto: University of Toronto Press.
Helgerson, R. (1986), 'The Land Speaks: Cartography, Choreography and Subversion in Renaissance England', *Representations*, **16**, 51–85.
Kain, R.J.P. and E. Baigent (1992), *The Cadastral Man in the Service of the State: A History of Property Mapping*, Chicago: University of Chicago Press.
Latour, Bruno (1986), 'The Powers of Association', in John Law (ed.), *Power, Action and Belief: A New Sociology of Knowledge?*, London: Routledge & Kegan Paul.
Lefebvre, Henri (1991), *The Production of Space*, Blackwell: Oxford.
Mann, Michael (1993), *The Sources of Social Power. Volume II: The Rise of Classes and Nation States. 1760–1914*, New York: Cambridge University Press.
Miller, Peter, and Nikolas Rose (1990), 'Governing Economic Life', *Economy and Society*, **19** (1), 1–31.
Mitchell, Timothy (1991), *Colonizing Egypt*, Berkeley: University of California Press.

Myers, G. (1996), 'Naming and Placing the Other: Power and the Urban Landscape in Zanzibar', *Tijdschrift voor economische en sociale geografie*, **87** (3), 237–46.

Nast, Heidi and Audrey Kobayashi (1996), 'Re-corporealizing Vision', in Nancy Duncan (ed.), *Bodyspace: Destabilising Geographies of Gender and Sexuality*, London and New York: Routledge.

Nietschmann, B. (1995), 'Defending the Miskito Reefs with Maps and GIS', *Cultural Survival Quarterly*, Winter, 34–7.

O'Malley, P. (1996), 'Indigenous governance', *Economy and Society*, **25** (3), 310–26.

Osborne, Thomas (1997), 'Security and Vitality: Drains, Liberalism and Power in the Nineteenth Century', in A. Barry, T. Osborne and N. Rose (eds), *Foucault and Political Reason: Liberalism. Neo-liberalism and Rationalities of Government*, London: UCL Press.

Pinder, David (1996), 'Subverting Cartography: The Situationists and Maps of the City', *Environment and Planning*, **28**, 405–27.

Reeve, Andrew (1986), *Property*, Basingstoke: Macmillan.

Rocheleau, D., Thomas-Stayter, B. and Edmunds, D. (1995), 'Gendered Resource Mapping: Focusing on Women's Spaces in the Landscape', *Cultural Survival Quarterly*, Winter, 62–8.

Rose, Nikolas (1993), 'Government, Authority and Expertise in Advanced Liberalism', *Economy and Society*, **22** (3), 283–99.

Rose, Nikolas (1996), 'The Death of the Social? Re-figuring the Territory of Government', *Economy and Society*, **25** (3), 327–56.

Rose, Nikolas, and Peter Miller (1992), 'Political Power Beyond the State: Problematics of Government', *British Journal of Sociology*, **43** (2), 173–205.

Sanders, Dora (1996), 'A Real Community: Mapping the Downtown Eastside', *Carnegie Newsletter*, 1 April.

Shamir, R. (1996), 'Suspended in Space: Bedouins under the Law of Israel', *Law and Society Review*, **30** (2), 231–57.

Shason, J.P. (1995), Letter to Gastown BIA Members, Vancouver.

Tora (1995), 'Community Makes me Crazy', *Carnegie Newsletter*, 15 April, 1 and 19.

UD&D (Urban Design and Development Consultants) (1992), *A Discussion Paper of Issues and Topics Affecting the Viability and Growth of Gastown: Suggestions Leading to a Community Plan for Gastown*, mimeograph.

Ward, David (1976), 'The Victorian Slum: An Enduring Myth?', *Annals of the Association of American Geographers*, **66** (2), 323–36.

Ward, Robin (1997), 'Victory Square', *The Georgia Straight*, **31**, 26 June–3 July, 15, 17–19.

Wood, Denis (1992), 'How Maps Work', *Cartographica*, **29** (3 & 4), 66–74.

12 An Intrusive and Corrective Government: Political Rationalities and the Governance of Plains Aboriginals 1870–90

Bryan Hogeveen

In recent years, following the seminal work of Franz Fanon (1963) and Edward Said (1979), there has been an outpouring of theoretical work concerning Europe's colonial past. This emergent work, which runs under the rubric of 'post-colonial' theory, has shifted the manner in which the image of the colonized, their forms of customary law and mode of life have been thought about and theorized. Central to the post-colonial mode of inquiry is the assumption that indigenous writers have been excluded from participation in the construction and constitution of their unique cultural development. Until recently, this stream of inquiry was primarily concerned with 'literary studies which discerned how the other was constructed and deconstructed through literature and documents' (Pfeifer 1996: 6). Post-colonial analysis constitutes an essential undertaking for researchers hoping to understand colonialism, the governance of the indigenous other and the cultural inscription inherent to the colonial project. Recently however, elements of post-colonial thought have been taken into account in governmentality studies (Scott 1995; Smandych and Linden 1996; O'Malley 1996; Ronsbo 1997; Ibrahim 1997). In this chapter I seek to apply post-colonial analysis and Foucault's ideas on government to the study of colonial governmentality in the context of the aboriginals in the prairie region of Canada from 1870–90.

Governmentality, Liberalism, and the Canadian State

In Foucault's (1991, 1988a, 1988b, 1988c, 1983, 1981a, 1981b) analysis of governmentality, scattered over a few lectures and essays, he adopts a unique approach to the analysis of liberalism. While liberalism has most often been referred to as a political ideology that accentuates the optimization of individual liberty and its protection from intrusion by the state, those who have followed Foucault's work (Dean 1996a, 1996b, 1994; Pavlich 1996; Rose 1993; Rose and Miller 1992) have rejected the normative discourse of liberalism and opted for a more critical interpretation of its activity of rule. Liberalism as an activity of rule, as often cited by classical and contemporary thinkers, reflects the natural order of things. But, we may ask, who participates in the privileges of this natural order? In order to discern the nature of aboriginal participation in this order, I will rely on two methodological principles derived from the governmentality literature. First, I will endeavour to refrain from articulating this study with the normative discourse of liberalism. And, second, I will try to understand the activity of nineteenth-century liberal rule in Canada and its rationality by considering not its ideology but, rather, the practices which it intrinsically constructed to shape the domain of government whose parameters were the aboriginal mode of life. Before we came to understand the practical activity of government in nineteenth-century Canada and its work on the mode of life of the aboriginal people of the prairies, we should first situate the Canadian version of liberalism in terms of its development, extension and proliferation.

One of the most evident circumstances to confront the student in search of a distinctly Canadian scholarship of liberalism is the comparative lack of literature. Anyone searching to come to terms with the ideological foundation of his intrinsic governmental rationality must be content with, and satisfy their interrogation with, a collection of extracts from speeches and newspaper articles (cf. Forbes 1985). Canadian thinkers have taken little part in the debate which has taken place around the Western world concerning the fundamental values of freedom, of justice, and of what is essential concerning the human spirit (Underhill 1960). Over the last 100 years Canadians have made great strides towards economic maturity and political autonomy, yet have made little contribution to the discussion of the ideological issues which underlie this development. 'Where are the classics in our political literature which embody our Canadian version of liberalism?' asks a leading Canadian critic (Underhill 1960). But, if there is a lack of Canadian scholarship concerning the underlying principles of liberal government, how did Canada arrive at the present foundation of governmentality? The answer lies in the unique developmental history of Canadian politics and society. The underlying principle for unfolding the ideological foundation of nineteenth-century Canadian liberalism is that it is derivative. It is imported. It is colonial.

The stream of ideas which contributed to the formation of nineteenth-century Canadian liberalism were derived from the teachings and discourse of the English philosophers. Canadian liberals were always happiest and most effective when 'applying to Canadian conditions the traditions of English constitutional development' (Underhill 1960: 132). These ideas provided the foundation on which the Canadian version of liberalism emerged. However, it would not be sufficient to state that Canadian liberalism was merely an extension of its British heritage. Rather, it was shaped by two influences – one social and the other economic. On the one hand, since the 1830s, nativist liberal ideas have produced a unique twist to the British version through the distinctive agrarian mode of frontier life. This economic condition gave Canadian liberalism its conservative appearance. On the other hand, there was a social condition of influence. The first settlers in Upper Canada were United Empire loyalists who had been driven out of the 13 colonies following the American revolution. To the early Canadians, America and its version of democracy brought to mind house burnings, confiscation of belongings and suffering. In 1812 the Americans launched a war of conquest against Upper Canada, thus making certain that those who looked to America for political inspiration had little influence on Canadian sentiment (Kelley 1969). While Canada inherited the British liberal system of state and ideology, it was shaped by social and economic conditions of life intrinsic to the Canadian context (Smandych 1995; Wise 1974; Wise 1965).

The founders of Canada were content to have a constitution similar in principle to that of England. They, nor any other Canadian liberal thinkers, thought it desirable to spell out – to set in stone – the ideology of this foundation of government. Rather, the founders were more concerned with practical philosophy than their ideological antecedents. John A. MacDonald, the first prime minister of Canada, proclaimed the spirit of the nation when he stated that he found it unjustified to 'waste the time of the legislature and money of the people in fruitless discussions on abstract and theoretical questions of government' (cited in Cambell, 1996). MacDonald and the initial members who made up the Canadian House of Commons were more concerned with the intrinsic exigencies of the country, such as its expansion and internal communications. They had other ends to meet and correct.

The Canadian liberal rationality of government was influenced by the ideology of the English stream, but it was also shaped by unique economic and social conditions. However, while this constituted the foundation of the practical activity of government, we are left with the following question: how did the Canadian state respond, take action against and correct the problems that it faced? Will ideology explain and illuminate this? Hardly. In order to evaluate and understand the unique version of Canadian liberalism we must understand, and come to terms with, the intrinsic problems and exigencies which it sought to correct and govern. Instead of viewing Canadian liberalism as an ideology, I argue that liberalism must be seen as the power and capacity of the state to act on and govern actions. In this way liberalism refers not to ideology, nor to a normative framework, but rather to a political rationality of government which functions within a realm of exigencies and intrinsic problems encountered by the state which claims to embody its principles. What is left over from the interaction between political rationality and the intrinsic problems encountered by the state is often quite different from the premises it is based on. While liberal ideological principles are the foundation on which government is erected, it is only the backdrop against which the state governs its conditions.

In light of the above discussion we are able to envision the possibility of a Foucaultian governmentality approach concerning the governance of the plains aboriginals. The first step in this process is to understand that the normative framework of liberalism is insufficient when discerning the practices of government which affected the lives of the aboriginal people. Instead we must look to its rationality – that is, the means through which it sought to realize the ends intrinsic to it. Furthermore, the liberal rationality of government cannot be deduced *a priori*, but must be viewed from, and understood in, the context of the domain that it sets out to govern. To illuminate the liberal governmentality of the domain constructed around the parameters of the aboriginal mode of life, we must first address and understand the intrinsic exigencies with which the Dominion of Canada was confronted on the secession of land from the Hudson's Bay Company (HBC). In order to do so, we must examine, on the one hand, the rationality of government by the HBC and, on the other, the aboriginal culture and the HBC's effects on it.

The Rationality of the HBC and the Aboriginal Mode of Life

In 1670 a Royal Charter was granted to the Hudson's Bay Company which gave it the exclusive right to govern the territory of Rupert's Land, or what is now most of western Canada (Smandych and Sacca 1996; Smandych and Linden 1995). In the years that would follow, the HBC would initiate an intrinsic rationality of government which responded to the unique exigencies of the fur trade. It sought to articulate a political rationality through which it would govern not only the space of Rupert's Land, but a domain constructed around the parameters of the fur trade. The domain of the fur trade was the end governed by the company. This end is circular. It resides in the security of the HBC itself.

The rationality of government which embodied the HBC was that which sought, above all else, the security of its existence in relation to competition, settlement and the harsh conditions of life in the Canadian north-west. These intrinsic concerns mediated against the accumulation of furs and, ultimately, profits. It is these problems which were governed by the Company. However, to secure its interests, the HBC relied on the aboriginal mode of life as a means to this end. In order to be productive, the aboriginal mode of life (aboriginal people being the proletariat of the fur trade) had to be protected from alien intrusions in the form of missionaries and other philanthropists whose intent was to shape their existence in ways which were contradictory to the ends of the company. Alternatively, to produce more efficient hunters, this mode of life had to be modified by the introduction of European commodities such as guns and ammunition. In relation to the aboriginal mode of life, the rationality of government initiated by the HBC had to strike a careful balance between intrusion and non-intrusion.

In this, we are able to envision the beginnings of the intrinsic HBC rationality of government, which sought to both shape and secure the knowledge of the indigenous people, not for reasons residing in the population but, rather, as a product and function of its rationality. The aboriginal people were a means to a desired end. The ends of the company were not so much concerned with the aboriginal population – its current functioning, its troubles and conditions of life – only that it existed and functioned in a 'right' manner. What results from a mentality which seeks only the existence and preservation of itself is a domain of government whose parameters encompass only the amelioration of its own intrinsic problems.

Intrinsic Principles of Government and the Shift in the Rationality of the Fur Trade

Throughout the early period of government, the HBC perpetually sought means to maximize its profits. In addition to using a series of other practices to encourage trade, the company attempted to encourage aboriginals from the interior to trade at Hudson Bay but, despite the practices put in place, profits remained relatively stable. The company's monopoly was brought to issue in 1749 before a select committee of the House of Commons that heard testimony from 20 witnesses who had knowledge of the manner in which the company operated in Rupert's Land (Great Britain, House of Commons 1749). Many intermingling concerns were addressed by the committee, including: criticisms of the company's monopoly; whether an agricultural colony could be established in the territory; and whether the trade in furs could be expanded. In relation to this last concern, two possible schemes were proposed. The first was in accordance with the principles laid down by the classical economists. The second took into account the intrinsic concerns and problems of a fur trade domain of government in Rupert's Land.

According to classical economists, if the company was to give a 'better price' to the aboriginal peoples for furs they would be able to accumulate more furs and thus increase their profits. 'Tis a greater price would encourage the Indians to kill more' (Great Britain, House of Commons 1749; 239). Robson, a stonemason, provided the committee with a similar opinion that if 'the Standard of Trade was more advantageous to the Indians, a greater quantity of furs and pelts would be brought' (Great Britain, House of Commons 1749: 220). This scheme, while consistent with the 'natural' trade in England, was in opposition to both the cultural complex of the aboriginal peoples and the dynamics of trade in the hinterland of the north. In 1769 Andrew Graham (1969) found that the aboriginal peoples would only trade for what they required to sustain their existence. Without effort, they could procure between 70 and 100 beavers, thereby satisfying all their wants, before coming to trade again. This meant that, if the aboriginal people were given a 'better price' for trading furs, they would need to trade less, not more. The dynamics of trade in the northern areas of the country also mediated against the 'rules of economy' set out by the classical economists. It was found that the French traders would intercept the Cree on their way to the Bay and trade with them before they reached the HBC trading posts. In this way, the French would secure the lightest and best furs before the HBC had a chance to trade (Rich 1991). Those in England failed to take into account the intrinsic problems and concerns of trading with a population which did not share the same sense of property, and failed to recognize the intense competition which existed within the fur trade. Although giving a better price for goods sold is a sound tactic to induce a population to trade, it ignores the intrinsic conditions of the fur trade and the mode of aboriginal life.

How, then, could the HBC increase profits, given the fact that the French were intercepting furs coming to the Bay and the aboriginal people 'would kill no more Beasts than what is sufficient to purchase Commodities for the year' (Great Britain, House of Commons 1749: Thompson, 223). The only way to govern this domain was to develop a rationality to manage the fur trade which responded to its exigencies. In order to procure more furs, and thereby achieve a greater profit margin, the HBC decided to eliminate the middle trader by situating inland trading posts along the Saskatchewan River. This solution responded directly to the problems encountered in trading with the aboriginal peoples: on the one hand, it enabled more nations to come to trade directly with the company; on the other, it curbed the number of furs which were lost to the competition.

Starvation/Alcohol/Disease – Implications of the Intrinsic Rationality of the Fur Trade

In addition to introducing an economic rationality and the commodities which accompanied it, the fur trade introduced European vices, disease and excess which shaped the aboriginal culture in other ways. One of the most destructive of these intrusions was the use of alcohol as a trading commodity. While these intrusions of alcohol and disease had critical consequences for the shape of aboriginal culture and social organization, it was perhaps the increased strain on the traditional resources of the prairies which had the greatest impact on the shape of their lives. The rationality of governing the fur trade domain, where profits were the ultimate end, served to undermine the subsistence economy of the aboriginal peoples. Isbister, a former resident of Red River once stated that:

> Owing to the numerous hunting excursions which the demands of the fur trade render necessary, and to the great slaughter of animals consequent thereon, the only present resources of the country have been gradually diminishing to such an extent, that the larger part of the native population can no longer find the means of supporting life from the produce of the chase, or the natural productions of the soil. (Isbister 1857: 6)

Before the intrusion of the European mentality of accumulation, the aboriginal people subsisted in harmony with the natural order of things (Binnema 1996). However, when a mentality of government exists which seeks only the security of itself through the means of aboriginal people, a certain shift in culture emerges. The intrusion of a fur trade mentality into the aboriginal mode of life, the expansion of that mentality, and the commodities used to create and sustain it, as well as the resulting disease, had important cultural, economic, political and social implications for the aboriginals. Their ability to carry on a traditional mode of life was undermined by the intrusions of vice, disease, commodities and a fur trade mentality. When the fur traders of the HBC receded after the secession of land to the Dominion of Canada the scarcity which was the product of their intrinsic rationality of government and the intrusions into their lives did not cease to have implications for these aboriginal peoples. Rather, the scarcity of game and introduction of alcohol and disease were part of the conditions which the Dominion problematized and the aboriginal people sought to ameliorate.

The Discursive Constitution of Space and Intrusion by the Antecedents of Liberal Government

The geographical space of Rupert's Land comprised 'a territory which is one third larger than all of Europe, covering a space sufficient for the establishment of kingdoms and empires' (Gladstone 1857: 7). Yet the vast amount of space controlled and governed by the HBC was not opened to settlement but 'treated as if intended by God and nature for no better purpose than the breeding of wild beasts and vermin, in order that a set of private adventurers might make the greatest possible profit out of their skins' (Gladstone 1857: 8). The space of Rupert's Land was one of the primary means to the desired end and was to be safeguarded from the intrusion of settlement. The only exception to this determination was for those whose sole purpose was the facilitation of the company's ends. Nevertheless, no cement walls were constructed around this space and nor were armed guards positioned on the border to control entry and settlement. How, then, was this space governed? If the territorial space into which the HBC introduced an intrinsic economic rationality was concerned with extracting profits from the territory which it governed, how was it possible to organize, defend and manipulate this space to the company's advantage?

To this end, the company discursively constituted the geographical space which they governed as unfit for colonization. One prime example of this is Sir George Simpson's testimony before the select committee inquiring into the affairs of the HBC, in which he maintained that Rupert's Land was unsuitable for cultivation. However, in his 1847 book, *Journey Around the World* he painted quite a different picture, frequently comparing the countryside of Rupert's Land to that of England (Simpson 1847, vol. 1: 46). At one point he marvels, 'nor are the banks less favourable to agriculture than the waters themselves to navigation, resembling, in some measure those of the Thames near Richmond' (ibid.: 53). However, 16 years later, when governor of the HBC, he seems to have changed his mind. In reference to the question posed to him concerning the cultivation and colonization of the territory governed by the company, he had no hesitation in expressing his opinion that no area of this territory was fit for settlers (Great Britain, House of Commons 1858).

As a traveller, Simpson marvelled at the splendour of the territorial space over which the company governed, but as commissioner, he could only find disdain. By constituting and perpetuating this discourse the HBC was able to secure the space against settlement. For example, in 1858 the government of the united province of Canada sent an expedition to Red River to see if it was possible to, first, reach it and, second, establish a 'chain' of communication. The expedition finally expelled the discourse perpetuated by the company, as evidenced in the following:

> Before Mr Dawson's exploration, the rocky, broken structure of the country was thought to present an insuperable barrier to further extension except at an immense expenditure: but his examination led to the discovery of a good line. (CSP, vol. 7, no. 31, Return to an Address from the House of Commons, dated 18 November 1867 for Correspondence, Report of Proceedings and other documents, in Possession of the Government relative to the Hudson's Bay Territory: Mr Folley).

To guard the space in which they conducted the fur trade, the HBC discursively designated it as unfit to sustain life. A second way in which they managed and preserved a beneficial status quo was to charge excessively high prices for land, further discouraging settlement. By discouraging settlement through these two means the HBC was able to guard and preserve the fur trade. However, in the opening years of the nineteenth-century this state of affairs was to be intruded upon by a small group of Scottish settlers under the auspices of Lord Selkirk.

In 1811 the Scottish colonizer, Lord Selkirk, sent a group of settlers to establish the Red River colony at the junction of the Red and Assiniboine Rivers. The great majority of these settlers were of Roman Catholic denomination, and this was reinforced by the presence of French Canadian fur traders and the Metis in the area (Huel 1996). Since there was no Catholic priest among them, much to the outrage of the settlers, Selkirk invited Bishop Plessis to Red River in order that he might make provision for sending a priest to the settlement. In 1818 this request was fulfilled. Two Catholic priests were sent to the colony with detailed instructions to 'rescue the Indian population from barbarism' (Plessis, cited in Huel 1996).

A unique feature of the missionary activity in Rupert's Land was that it did not begin until 150 years after contact (Smandych and McGillivray 1999). What happened in the 1820s to condition the intrusion of missionaries into the fur trade domain? First, the emergence of a settlement in the territory brought with it a concern for religious instruction. Another influence was the Protestant evangelist movement in England, which, in other parts of the world, made efforts to convert indigenous people to Christianity (Smandych and McGillivray 1999), making it perhaps inevitable that they would turn their attention to the aboriginals of Rupert's Land. In addition, John West, a Protestant missionary, was sent to Rupert's Land to serve as the chaplain of the HBC. Much to the dismay of the company, however, West commenced a programme of instructing the aboriginals in the ways of Christianity. The company was opposed to such an endeavour, as it posed a threat to the security of the fur trade. For 150 years the HBC had been able to conduct business in the region free from intrusions that had the potential to significantly alter the shape of the fur trade. The missionaries' conversion activities initiated a divergent form of government in the space of Rupert's Land and introduced an important shift in the governance of the aboriginal peoples. While the HBC endeavoured to secure the aboriginal mode of life in the interests of profits, the missionaries sought to shape it in relation to the conversion of their souls. In this shift there is a pivotal unsettling of the ends–means relationship which foreshadows the rationality of liberal government.

The Emergence of the Liberal Rationality of Government

> It is the business of the speculative philosopher to mark the proper ends of government. It is the business of the politician, who is the philosopher in action, to find out proper means towards these ends, and to employ them with effect. (Edmund Burke 1770: 29)

The date 1 December 1869 marked the beginning of a fundamental shift in the government of the aboriginal peoples of the prairie region of Canada. This is the date the Dominion of Canada paid the HBC £300 000 for the land occupied by the company. With this change, a new rationality of government would emerge – one which would attempt to shape the mode of existence of the aboriginal people not with a view towards divine salvation, nor one with circular intents but, rather, one which was constituted by numerous ends and multiform tactics which were employed to achieve these ends.

With the emergence of this rationality it is possible to witness a series of shifts in government from its former configuration. With the HBC we saw a rationality which sought to reflect back, and secure itself. That is, the practices disposed were aimed at nothing other than the accumulation of profits. While it may seem as if the HBC has a multitude of concerns – space, profits, inland forts, a fragile resource base – these concerns must not be seen as independent of the end pursued but, rather, as implicit within the ultimate end. When the administrative apparatus of the Canadian state emerges in the West we envision a subtle but significant shift in the ends–means relationship. What were once means to an end now become ends in themselves. What once was the ultimate end passes into the background.

What emerges is a new rationality of government concerned with a new manner of thinking about, and acting upon, both the population and the territory. In the remainder of this chapter I will endeavour to decipher the implications of this shift for the aboriginal peoples of the prairies.

With confederation in 1867, the Dominion of Canada became a group of European colonists who enjoyed the benefit of 'free institutions' – to be members of a 'free people', to engage in free trade and market competition and to be citizens of a state subject (for all intents and purposes) to no other state. This is the liberty that they valued. The early Canadian liberal, Sir Wilfred Laurier, in a lecture given in Montreal, stated that Canadian liberalism, when stripped to its bare essentials,

> ... and seen in its true colours, is the love of lawful and necessary liberty, of progressive freedom, which results from the natural conditions of progress and not from *sudden shocks* which dangerous spirits would wish to impart to it. Such are the characteristics of Canadian Liberalism. (Laurier 1887)

Freedom of progress and liberty from unnecessary intrusion into everyday life are essential both to the human condition and to the spirit of Canadian liberalism. At the same time, however, all too often Canada, and similar self-declared liberal countries, refuse to concede the privileges of liberty in the same sense to 'other' individuals and groups who carry on their mode of life in the same geographical and social space. Individuals and groups are excluded from partaking in the liberal spirit; they are denied access to that which is, according to Laurier (1887), essential to the 'progress of the human spirit'. If liberalism is exclusive, it is also intrusive – striving to constitute and shape others in its own likeness. Liberalism, wherever it has reared its righteous head, is exclusionary. Here it shows itself to be narrow and one-sided and contains a contradiction which cannot be rectified by its principles. In such places – South Africa, Australia, Canada, Ireland – the antithesis of the liberal spirit emerges.

The Euro-Canadian members of the early Canadian community were smug idealists who cherished the British ideals of individual and national liberty even, at times, overextending its colonial heritage and principles (Underhill 1960). When Alexander Mackenzie visited Britain in 1875 as Liberal premier, he found, quite to his disappointment, that few there shared the Dominion's devotion to the spirit of liberalism and the Empire. 'I have listened a lot', he once wrote home, 'and I conclude that Canada is more British than Britain' (Thompson 1960). This self-righteous adherence to the cherished principles of liberalism was accomplished at the expense of, and jealously withheld from, certain segments of the population deemed unworthy of such entitlement.

It would seem plausible that if the Canadian state followed the principles of liberalism, the aboriginal mode of life, with its dispute settlement techniques, religion and other cultural institutions, should continue to realize, enjoy and be protected from intrusion upon their liberty. However, when the liberal rationality of government emerged in the Canadian prairies the aboriginal peoples and their mode of life was intruded upon by practices which sought to establish a normalized order of things. The rhetoric of liberalism can lead us to overlook the ways in which Dominion of Canada endeavoured to harmonize, constitute and intrude upon the mode of life of the aboriginal peoples in relation to the incumbent order. However, in nineteenth-century Canada an emergent liberal order, based on principles shared and enjoyed by the Euro-Canadian population, came to intrude significantly on the lives of aboriginal peoples.

Problematizing the West: Treaties, Reserves and the Domain of Government

To say that the aboriginal people were simply the victims of settlement and extension of a normalized and prescribed order would be to deny their role in shaping the policy constituted to govern their lives. While the ends of the emergent rationality of government sought to intrude upon a geographical space previously discursively and overtly closed and introduce a new mode of existence, the aboriginal peoples also had ends which they wished to establish in relation to these. In 1871 Sweetgrass, a prominent leader of the Cree nation, forwarded a message to Lieutenant-Governor Archibald stating the following concerns:

> We heard our lands were sold and we did not like it; we don't want to sell our lands; it is our property and no one has a right to sell them. Our country is getting ruined of fur-bearing animals, hitherto our sole support, and now we are poor and want help – we want you to pity us. We want cattle, tools, agricultural implements, and assistance ... our country is no longer able to support us. Make provisions for us against years of starvation. We had great starvation the past winter, and the smallpox took away many of our people ... We want you to stop the Americans from coming to trade on our lands, and giving firewater [alcohol] and ammunition and arms to our enemies the Blackfoot. (Morris 1880: 170–71)

The aboriginal concern was not to open a space for settlement, not to introduce a new rationality of government, but rather to secure the space which they inhabited and to improve their living standards which were conditioned by the rationality of the fur trade.

The emergence of a new rationality of government denotes a new concern for space – a concern to open up the territory which had for so long been governed and gated by the HBC. Aboriginal people recognized that the takeover by the Canadian government would bring about many other negative changes. In response to the concerns and actions of the aboriginal peoples, the Dominion of Canada negotiated a series of seven treaties between 1873 and 1876 which surrendered aboriginal title to the land. While the Canadian state intended only to concede spaces of land and cash annuities, the aboriginal peoples sought that which would help to solidify their future. The Ojibway and Saulteaux of Treaty 3 rejected this initial offer from the state in 1871 and again in 1872. It was not until 1873 that the state ceded to their demand for livestock, horses, wagons and farming implements which then became standard articles of the treaties (Public Archives of Canada, Record Group 10, vol. 3571, file 124–2; vol. 3603, file 2036).[1]

An important provision of the treaties was the setting aside of land as reserves for the bands of aboriginals at the increased proportion of one square mile, or 640 acres per family of five (Canada. Sessional Papers, Department of the Interior, vol. 35, number 22, 1872, p. 14).[2] Governor Archibald explained that the Dominion would 'lay aside for you lots of land, to be used by you and your children for ever. She will not allow the white man to intrude upon these lots. She will make rules to keep them for you' (Begg 1894).

While the treaties ultimately functioned to cede the aboriginal title to the land, perhaps the capacity of the treaties and the creation of reserved lots of land was more than opening a closed space, more than the cession of a territory. Perhaps it was for the closing of space, for the constitution of a domain of government – one designed to divide and constitute the aboriginal mode of life in relation to the intrusive prescribed mode of European life. The aboriginal mode of life and their concern for space ultimately rationalized their exclusion from the privileges of liberalism and the intrusion of practices of government to harmonize their actions. Once the Dominion of Canada obtained title to the western portion of the country it was able to open this portion of the country for settlement. However, the extension of citizenship and participation in the emergent order of things excluded the aboriginal peoples. If they were to participate in this order their values and mode of life would have to be harmonized in relation to it.

The relationship of difference is here ordered and *othered* once and for all. On the one hand, the aboriginal mode of life is othered – in other words, boundaries are set between the aboriginal mode of life and that of the emergent and prescribed Euro-Canadian one that is valued and placed in opposition to the 'other' (Salvatore 1996). On the other hand, and implicit in it, is the ordering of aboriginal culture – that is, the process of normalizing and harmonizing the aboriginal mode of life with the newly emergent order of things. This process – of othering/ordering – does not emerge with the immersion of the Canadian state in the west. Rather, it emerged with the early settlement of the territorial space, with the introduction and intrusion of missionary practices and the drawing of the aboriginal peoples into a foreign 'justice system'. However, where a rationality of government is extended and inscribed to perpetuate its own ends, these practices and ends will not flourish, but are seen as secondary to the interests of sovereignty. When attached to a rationality of government which seeks to establish and intrude a mode of life, the process of othering/ordering becomes not only pertinent, but fundamental to the ends of the emergent Dominion.

The aboriginal mode of life was not valued in relation to the emergent Euro-Canadian one and thus was to be shaped, moulded, and 'imbued with the white man's spirit' (CSP, vol. 53, no. 12, 1980, p. 165, Reed). The emergent liberal order is in marked opposition to the aboriginal mode of life. It is a difference which is to be divided out and excluded from privileges enjoyed by the included. It becomes a status of exclusion which marks those who share its values and mode of life as a domain – a domain of intrusions to govern and shape their mode of life. This status is othered, and the new mode of life made functional, through the demarcation of the aboriginal mode of life as a domain of government to be shaped, harmonized and ordered in relation to the prescribed mode of Euro-Canadian life. To render the othered status of the aboriginal mode of life functional, government disposed two practices to designate it as such and divide it as a domain of government. This process of marking and dividing was initiated by the signing of the treaties: however, in addition, government sought to both physically divide the aboriginal mode of life through reserves and, legally, through status.

While settlement on reserves was in no way compulsory these areas designated a space of government where the demarcation of aboriginal peoples as other could be immediately ordered. However, this is not to say that the aboriginal peoples refused to settle on, or determine, the site of their reserves, but rather that, within a few months of the signing of the treaties, they had already begun the process (RG 10, vol. 3625, file 5489, Christie to Laird, 7 October 1875). Some bands formally requested the Dominion surveyors to mark out their space (RG 10, vol. 3626, file 5894; vol. 3635, file 6647). Clearly some of the aboriginal bands were ready to commence a new life on their reserves. While the reserve provided the aboriginal peoples with a space to enter a new mode of existence, it also served another important function of tangibly setting out the boundaries between the aboriginal mode of life and the emergent one. By allocating plots of land for the exclusive use of the aboriginal peoples, the Dominion of Canada effectively divided their mode of life from the emergent order and constituted it as a domain of government.

An essential element in the process of othering a people is the issue of membership. That is, in order to govern a population, and constitute it as a domain of government, it becomes qualitatively necessary to define the material on which to work. However, the definition of this material, and the inclusion or exclusion from that population, is what Derek Smith (1993) terms an 'inauthentic ethnic category' – that is, one whose definition was not derived from the cultural members, but rather from criteria generated entirely from an administrative source. The definition of the aboriginal person, and the material which was to be worked on and harmonized, is embedded in Canada's constitutional documents (British North America Act 1867) as well as, in later Acts directly aimed at consolidating the administration of Indian Affairs (Indian Act 1876). If the reserve was to be the space where the programme of government was to be realized, the legally defined mode of life of the aboriginal peoples was to be the domain into which this was to be intruded.

Inducing Change: Practices of Government

The status of othered demarcates a governmental domain of intrusion. The ultimate end is the creation of an individual who is not 'othered', but embodies the prescribed mode of life. Here then, the status of the aboriginal peoples is to be known and governed not as a category in and of itself, but in relation to a normalized mode of life. It is referred to, and is defined, in relation to an outside which is both legally and spatially constituted as a normalized mode of life which is embodied in the Euro-Canadian order of things. This becomes a category of inclusion and exclusion where the othered is at once differentiated and ultimately marked as a domain of intrusion.

The reserves and treaties served to mark and divide out a legally constituted category of individuals and groups as a special community of probationary citizens and a domain of government intrusion. The definition and division induced its effects so long as the individual aboriginal person continued to follow and engage in the constituted mode of life. The process of marking the aboriginal mode of life as 'other' has a dual function: on the one hand, it privileges and constitutes one mode of life over another; and on the other it marks the deviant material as a domain of government. Its main function, however, is to make visible the gap between the two. In marking this division as a domain of intrusion and making it functional through spatial division, government was confronted with a problem of how to induce the prescribed change.

The answer to this problematic of government was not a simple one. In the space between the mode of existence of the Euro-Canadians and that of the traditional aboriginal one, many factors intermingled, one being the conditions of existence in the prairie region. The rationality of the fur trade had introduced a mentality which sought the accumulation of furs; however, this had certain important effects on the fragile resource base on which the aboriginal peoples depended. Given this factor, government was left to consider 'what measures can be taken to prepare the Indians for the time not far distant when the buffalo will be a thing of the past' (CSP, vol. 40, no. 11, 1877, Laird: xii).[3] The solution to the problem, for individuals such as J.A. MacDonald, came down to

> ... a choice between two evils. We cannot allow them to starve, and we cannot make them into white men [*sic*]. All we can do is endeavour to induce them to abandon their nomadic habits, and settle down and cultivate the soil. (Canada, Debates, House of Commons, 23 April 1880: 1693)

Governing the Choice of Actions

The means of bringing these objectives into being was through a complex set of practices disposed by those who governed to induce, train and shape the mode of life of the aboriginal peoples. Note here that I am not concerned with the 'coercive tutelage' (Dyck 1991) of government, nor the 'destruction of the tribal organization' (Carter 1990) but with the practices of government which sought to structure the possible field of actions of the aboriginal peoples.

How did those who governed the domain of the aboriginal mode of life endeavour to attach them to agriculture and settle them on reserves? According to Agent Markle of the Department of Indian Affairs:

> It must however be remembered that our great desire is to educate and to persuade the Indians to do what is right because every step made by such method is valuable, where as apparent restrainment, to which in reality is the result of coercion, can only be of value so long as the restraining force is in operation. (Markle to Birtle, 12 May 1887, RG 10, vol. 3598, file 1361)

It was no use coercing the aboriginal people to stay on the reserve and farm, for as soon as the coercive apparatus was removed any perceptible gains would be lost. Instead, it was necessary to structure their actions through practices of government which were to intrude and shape it. That is, 'no one can at once force an Indian to take hold of the plough and keep stead at work' (Dewdney, CSP, vol. 43, no. 11, 1880: 100). To govern the actions of the aboriginal peoples, to settle them on reserves, to induce them to commence an agriculture mode of life required that government devise certain practices to govern the *choice* of actions of those who constituted the domain of government. It may be better to think of this in terms of conducting as opposed to coercive domination or destruction. To conduct signifies the action of leading, and guiding the possibility of actions and putting in order the possible outcomes of government (Foucault 1983). To govern a domain, to shape its mode of life, is to govern the choice of actions. It is to 'lead' or 'induce' the aboriginal peoples to shape their mode of life in relation to the Euro-Canadian one.

Implied in this conception of government is an element of freedom which cannot be included when the defining discourse is coercion and domination. In this way, resistance is not merely something to be added in at the end of a chapter, but is a fundamental part of the government project. It is implied. It is a requisite for the practices of government. Considered in this way, government is action upon the actions of the aboriginal peoples. But does this mean that those who chose to engage in agriculture were consenting while those bands who refused to take up this mode of life were resisting and had to be coerced? In my opinion, the nature of the project to govern aboriginal peoples cannot be captured using this dichotomy. What is pertinent in this consideration is an understanding of the conditions of life which confronted the aboriginal mode of life, the ends of government and agency of the indigenous peoples.

If given the unrestrained choice among modes of life, one could assume that the aboriginal peoples would choose to continue in their traditional one. In the treaties there was a stipulation that

> ... you will still be free to hunt over much of the land included in the Treaty ... you will be free to hunt over them, and make all the use of them which you have in the past ... the Queen, though she may think it good for you to adopt civilized habits, has no idea of compelling you to do so. This she leaves up to your *choice* and you need not live like white men [*sic*] unless you can be persuaded to do so with your own free will. (CSP, vol. 35, no. 22, 1872: 16, emphasis added)

The fact that this mode of life existed and was offered as an alternative was not a precondition for its acceptance; rather, the choice to engage in agriculture or to 'live like white men [*sic*]' must be seen as tied to the practices of power which governed the choices of the aboriginal people. However, practices of government, on their own, would not be sufficient to induce the aboriginal peoples to take on the prescribed mode of life. Rather, these practices were mediated by and through the conditions of existence on the prairies. Consider the following comments made by the Commissioner of Indian Affairs, Dewdney, when on an inspection of Crowfoots band at Blackfoot Crossing:

On arriving there, I found about 1300 Indians in a very destitute condition, and many on the verge of starvation. Young men who were known to be stout and hearty fellows some months ago were quite emaciated and so weak they could hardly work. (Dewdney to Dennis, RG 10, vol. 3696, file 15266)

Given the conditions of existence of Crowfoot's band, it is not difficult to imagine how government sought to intrude a new mode of life and how (some) aboriginals welcomed it. The conditions of life on the prairies were such that the traditional means of subsistence would no longer support them in the way in which they had in the past (Hagarty to Laird, RG 10, vol. 3695, file 14924). Furthermore, alcohol abuse perpetuated by American whisky traders and disease added to these conditions. For many bands, these conditions in and of themselves, gave sufficient motivation to settle on their reserves and commence agriculture. However, on the other hand, the practices of government were also mediated by these conditions of life. In order to achieve the ends of governing this domain – settlement on reserves, the undertaking of agriculture and, ultimately, the amalgamation with Euro-Canadian society – certain practices of government, which linked up with the conditions of life on the prairies, were disposed to structure the actions and govern the choices of the aboriginal peoples.

Governing Through Consumption

The shift from a rationality of government based on the intrinsic ends of a fur trade company, to one with liberal tendencies, introduces a shift in the ends of government and the means to govern. No longer is the aboriginal mode of life to be encouraged in the interests of government. No longer is the space of the west to be closed to settlement. In its place is intruded a rationality of government which seeks to establish a prescribed order. In liberal political discourse, order is often used rhetorically, in that it is paired with legality. However, what is order? Is it law? Can it be obtained through the disposing of a single practice of government? Hardly. Order can be seen as corresponding with a mode of life consistent with Euro-Canadian values and institutions. It can be conceived as an 'order of things' – a manner of living and carrying out an existence which implies structure, values, and a prescribed mode of life. To have order then, implies not only law, but an arrangement of 'things' consistent with the Euro-Canadian mode of life. While law, and a force to govern it, may have been sufficient to maintain and establish an order of things with the prior rationality of government, it is not a sufficient condition for the realization of it in the emergent one. This is not to say that law is an unimportant practice for the governance and convergence of order, but that it is merely one of a cluster of practices disposed by those who govern to ensure a right arrangement of 'things'. A liberal order does not find its end in itself, nor does it find its end in law, but implies a plurality of ends and a cluster of practices to realize these ends. What becomes of interest then, is not law, *per se*, but the manner in which government works on, arranges and structures the mode of aboriginal life.

The conditions of existence on the prairies following the signing of the treaties had important implications for both the aboriginal mode of life and the practices of government disposed to shape it. While the ideology of liberalism goes against the granting of charity, the control of food consumption for the prairie aboriginal peoples was deemed necessary to both keep the aboriginal peoples from starving and, perhaps more importantly, maintain them on reserves. Denying food to the aboriginal peoples meant they would look for it elsewhere which in turn meant that the practical availability of settlers' cattle would become an attractive alternative (Satzewich 1996). It was also thought that, if the Dominion did not provide some form of subsistence for the aboriginal peoples, they would 'commit depredations amongst the settlers' (Macloed to Vankoughnet, RG 10, vol. 3721, file 23666).

The Dominion's initial system of providing food for the aboriginal peoples was to administer rations[4] to a selected chief for distribution among the members of the band. However, this plan was deemed unsuccessful due to 'complaints of unfair allotments' (Morris to Laird, RG 10, vol. 3625, file 5495). In response to this, Agent Mackay endeavoured to introduce a system by which a government agent, in 'ascertaining the number of families would divide the provisions themselves among the heads of families' (Mackay to Laird, RG 10, vol. 3625, file 5495). While this system mediated against unfair allotments of rations, it functioned to 'help those who refuse to help themselves' (Markle to Birtle, RG 10, vol. 3598, file 1361). Through this system the government agents encouraged the aboriginal peoples to continue with their mode of life. In 1879 the system of the 'distribution of rations without rhyme or reason' was terminated (Wadsworth to Denny, RG 10, vol. 3609, file 3380) and replaced by a policy whereby agents were directly responsible for the amount of rations distributed (Dewdney to Vankoughnet, RG 10, vol. 3576, file 309a). T.P. Wadsworth, an Indian agent, acquaints us with the system he referred to as 'rationing Indians':

I do not confine myself to give each Indian 1 pound of beef and ½ pound of flour per day precisely, but look upon the regulation ration as an average, or rather the maximum that may be given. Families that do little or no work, I give less than the amount, and so am able to give parties that work for themselves, or do work on errands for me a little more. In that way I am able to get a great deal more value for the amount of rations. (RG 10, vol. 3605, file 2950)

Wadsworth's words show us how government agents rewarded those actions which were deemed normal or positive while simultaneously 'correcting' actions deemed undesirable. Value is attached to the classification of actions. In this way the idle, or those individuals who embody the negative pole of actions, are encouraged to work in the 'right' manner through the desire to be rewarded, to receive relief and gratification in the same way as the diligent. Government agents were not merely prohibiting traditional actions, but encouraging the adoption of a more convergent way of life.

The limits of a chapter such as this do not allow for a complete description of the practices invented, constructed and disposed by government to shape the domain which was the aboriginal mode of life. However, the previous example serves to highlight the mechanics of government practices. First, as has been evident throughout, practices of government are tied to, and link up with, the conditions of existence which faced the aboriginal people. Where else, except in reference to this domain of government, could the practice of withholding provisions of food be disposed to govern actions? In this way, practices are not viewed or interpreted as being universal, nor functional in any other domain. Practices specifically, and government generally, are linked intrinsically to the exigencies of the population which is to be acted on. Practices to govern actions are invented and given prominence among only the population which is their end. Second, there is an attachment of value to actions. That is, if an aboriginal person is busy farming and settled on the reserve, his or her actions are deemed desirable and normal, and thus deserving of gratification in the form of rations. However, if there is a positive pole of actions, there must be an inverse. If an individual is engaged in 'other' occupations – ones that are consistent with their traditional mode of life and thus in opposition to the prescribed one – their actions would be governed negatively. Third, practices of government presuppose an element of freedom and agency of the governed. Implied in the practices of government is a free and active subject, who requires actions to shape their actions. Freedom is the material which is being worked on. It is the mode of life of the aboriginal people. It is the deviant material. To engage in traditional actions is resistance. If the aboriginal peoples were not resisting the intrusions of a prescribed mode of life, there would be no need for practices of government. Freedom, then, is an implied and requisite part of practices of government. Lastly, there exists a government agent who sees and classifies actions. This implies a form of surveillance and a knowledge which is indispensable to the government of aboriginals. The mechanics of conducting the mode of aboriginal life are tied to a system of training based on the logic of classification and gratification which is linked to the conditions of existence, the freedom of the governed and the objectives of government. To induce their effects, a form of surveillance needed to be exacted which would render actions visible and subject them to the correcting and classifying gaze of a government agent.[5]

Colonial Governmentality: An Intrusive and Corrective Government

In this chapter I have tried to offer a framework for understanding colonial governmentality by focusing on questions which relate to the political rationality and the pragmatic government of the aboriginal mode of life. The aboriginals and their mode of life were subjected to a series of intrusions by successive rationalities of government, each with conflicting ends. If I were to rely solely on the ideology of liberalism and the discourse of colonialism, the intricacies, shifts and practices would escape notice. In fact, the differences in the processes of transformation and the continuity between the two rationalities would remain embedded within the discourse that surrounds them. However, to explore and unravel how the domain of government converged around the parameters of the aboriginal mode of life was constituted I have relied on, and developed, a series of themes to come to terms with this complex historical reality.

The first theme pertains to understanding political rationality as opposed to ideology or discourse. Above I set out two rationalities of government, each with their unique concerns, problems and the intrinsic manner in which they governed them. In coming to terms with these diverse rationalities of government, the first matter to discern is the end to which government was exercised. The first rationality discussed above concerned the manner in which the HBC managed their interests in the fur trade by articulating a rationality of government that designated a space for the intrusion of a series of practices which were disposed to arrange and constitute a domain of government. However, this statement cannot be differentiated from the rationality of liberal Canadian government and must, instead be linked to a series of observations made concerning the ends realized by the company. If we consider what distinguished the HBC from the liberal rationality which followed, we can see that the destination of government was contained within itself. In this way, for the HBC, the destination, or the point of application of power, was twofold: space and the aboriginal mode of life. Both were essential to its ends. A series of complex practices were therefore invented and disposed to secure the ends of the company and would have certain fundamental effects on the shape of the aboriginal mode of life. The rationality of the HBC constituted a field of intervention fundamental to the aboriginal conditions of existence and to understanding the rationality of government which followed. When the HBC ceded the territory over which they governed to the Dominion of Canada a fundamental shift in the rationality of government emerged. No longer was the end of government embedded within itself; instead, the aboriginal mode of life itself now became the domain of government.

The discourse of liberalism stresses freedom and non-intrusion into individuals' lives where differences, among individuals (religion, social position) are declared irrelevant to their qualifications for inclusion among those who enjoy liberties offered of the 'natural human spirit' (Hoernle 1969). The principles of liberalism were not born of the cultural contingencies and contact of the emergent frontier, but rather on blank pages of philosophers such as Rousseau, Mill, Bentham and Montesquieu. In their theories attention was centred on the consideration that all class-based inequalities between humans were unnatural. All differences among humans, when considering the totality of humanity, became irrelevant. The formula of liberalism asks the state to consider human units as though each were as like any other, 'as one atom of a given element is like any other atom of that element' (Hoernle 1969: 124). In the theoretical ramblings of the 'great classical thinkers' this ideology was to apply to all individuals everywhere, whatever their culture and structural position in the societal regime.

Ideology, as Deleuze and Guttari (1977) have stated, 'explains nothing'. However, this is only partly true. Liberalism is an ideology which is scattered throughout the notebooks of history. Rather than relying on ideology, the best 'approach to a theory of liberalism' and its practices 'is by way of the concept of man's [*sic*] power to do' (Hoernle 1969: 109). In this, liberalism refers to a political rationality of government which functions within a realm of exigencies and intrinsic problems encountered by the state claiming to embody its principles. The wake of the interaction between political rationality and the intrinsic problems encountered by the state is often quite different from the premises upon which it is based.

The Canadian frontier, with all its exigencies, was a context of which the classical thinkers on liberty were apparently aware and with which the Dominion of Canada was not concerned. The 'rights of humans' are the rights of those who embodied the prescribed mode of life, while the divergent are divided out and excluded until such time as their mode of life is in harmony with the prescribed one. In short, when confronted by difference the Canadian state was quick to abandon the fundamental principles of liberalism. Instead, difference legitimized, and continues to legitimize, intrusions into the mode of life of the aboriginal peoples.

To unfold a contextualized account of the government project – whether it be by the HBC, the liberal Canadian state or another form of colonial government – at any historical moment in time the researcher must be cognizant of the constituted domain of government, the conditions of existence experienced by those governed, the intrinsic problems encountered, and the nature and effects of the political rationality which preceded it. By observing these convergent constituents of the history of government–governed relations we are able to observe the complex linkages inherent to the colonial context.

Notes

1   From here on, this will be referenced as RG 10 followed by the volume and file number.
2   From here on, the Canada Sessional Papers will be referenced as CSP followed by the volume and number. It should be noted that in 1880 the Department of Indian Affairs annual reports were no longer included in the reports of the Department of the Interior.
3   The buffalo was a staple of the aboriginal subsistence base.
4   Generally rations consisted of 1lb of beef (later bacon) and ½lb of flour per aboriginal per day (Wadsworth to Agent Denny RG 10, vol 3609, file 3380, July 1882).
5   For a more detailed discussion of mechanisms of physical surveillance by Indian agents, see Hogeveen (1998).

References

Begg, A. (1894), *History of the North-West*, Toronto: Hunter, Rose & Co.

Binnema, T. (1996), 'Old Swan, Big Man, and the Siksika Bands, 1794–1815', *The Canadian Historical Review*, **77** (1), 1–32.

Burke, E. (1770), *Thoughts on the Present Cause of Discontents*, Dublin: Oxford Press.

Cambell, C. (1996), *Parties, Leaders and Ideology in Canada*, Toronto: McGraw-Hill, Ryerson.

Canada (1867), *British North America Act*, Ottawa: King's Printer.

Canada, Debates (1880), *House of Commons*, Ottawa: King's Printer.

Canada, Sessional Papers (1870–9), *Annual Report of the Department of the Interior*, Ottawa: King's Printer.

Canada, Sessional Papers (1880–90), *Annual Report of the Department of Indian Affairs*, Ottawa: King's Printer.

Carter, S. (1990), *Lost Harvests: Prairie Indian Reserve Farmers and Government Policy*, McGill-Queens University Press: Montreal and Kingston.

Dean, M. (1994), 'A Social Structure of Many Souls: Moral Regulation, Government, and Self-Formation', *Canadian Journal of Sociology*, **19** (2), 145–68.

Dean, M. (1996a), 'Putting the Technological into Government', *History of the Human Sciences*, **9** (3), 47–68.

Dean, M. (1996b), 'Foucault, Government and the Enfolding of Authority', in E. Barry, T. Osborne and N. Rose (eds), *Foucault and Political Reason: Liberalism, Neo-Liberalism and Rationalities of Government*, Chicago: University of Chicago Press.

Deleuze, G. and F. Guttari (1977), *Anti-Oedipus: Capitalism and Schizophrenia*, New York: Viking Press.

Dyck, N. (1991), *What is the Indian Problem? Tutelage and Resistance in Canadian Indian Administration*, St John's: The Institute of Social and Economic Research.

Fanon, F. (1963), *The Wretched of the Earth*, New York: Grove Press.

Forbes, H. (ed.). (1985), *Canadian Political Thought*, Toronto: Oxford University Press.

Foucault, M. (1981a), 'Michel Foucault, "History of Systems of Thought, 1978"', *Philosophy and Social Criticism*, **8** (1), 238–41.

Foucault, M. (1981b), 'Michel Foucault, "History of Systems of Thought, 1979"', *Philosophy and Social Criticism*, **8** (2), 353–69.

Foucault, M. (1983), 'The Subject and Power', in L. Dreyfus and P. Rainbow, *Michel Foucault: Beyond Structuralism and Hermeneutics*, Chicago: University of Chicago Press.

Foucault, M. (1988a), 'Technologies of the Self', in L. Martin, H. Gutman and P. Hutton (eds), *Technologies of the Self: A Seminar with Michel Foucault*, Amherst: University of Massachusetts Press.

Foucault, M. (1988b), 'The Political Technology of Individuals', in L. Martin, H. Gutman and P. Hutton (eds), *Technologies of the Self: A Seminar with Michel Foucault*, Amherst: University of Massachusetts Press.

Foucault, M. (1988c), 'Politics and Reason', in L. Kritzman (ed.), *Foucault: Politics, Culture and Philosophy, interviews and Other Writings*, New York: Routledge.

Foucault, M. (1991), 'Governmentality', in G. Burchell, C. Gordon and P. Miller (eds), *The Foucault Effect: Studies in Governmentality*, Chicago: University of Chicago Press.

Gladstone, A. (1857), *The Hudson's Bay Company versus the Magna Charta, and the British People*, New Haven: Research Publications.

Graham, A. (1969), *Andrew Graham's Observations on Hudson's Bay, 1767–91*, London: Hudson's Bay Record Society.

Great Britain, House of Commons (1749), *Report from the Committee on the State of the Hudson's Bay Company*, London: Irish University Press Series.

Great Britain, House of Commons (1858), *Report from the Select Committee on the State of the British Possessions in North America which are under the Administration of the Hudson's Bay Company, with Minutes of Evidence*, London: Irish University Press Series.

Hoernle, R. (1969), *South African Native Policy and the Liberal Spirit*, New York: Negro University Press.

Hogeveen, B. (1998), 'An Intrusive and Corrective Government: Political Rationalities and the Governance of the Plains Aboriginals, 1870–1890', unpublished master's thesis: University of Manitoba.

Huel, R. (1996), *Proclaiming the Gospel to the Indians and the Metis*, Edmonton: University of Alberta Press.

Ilbrahim, A. (1997), 'Tale of Two Sudanese Courts: Colonial Governmentality Revisited', *African Studies Review*, **40** (1), 13–33.

Isbister, A.K. (1857), *A Few Words on the Hudson's Bay Company: With a State-*

ment of the Grievances of the Native and Half-caste Indians, Addressed to the British Government through their Delegates now in London*, London: C. Gilpin Publishers.

Kelley, R. (1969), *The Transatlantic Persuasion: The Liberal Democratic Mind in the Age of Gladstone*, New York: Knopf Publishers.

Laurier, W. (1887), *Lecture on Political Liberalism Delivered by Wilfred Laurier Esq., MP, on the 26 June in the Music Hall Under the Auspices of the 'Canadian Club'*, Quebec: Morning Chronicle.

Morris, A. (1880), *The Treaties of Canada with the Indians of Manitoba and the North-West Territories Including the Negotiations on which they were based*, Toronto: Belfords, Clarke, and Company Publishers.

O'Malley, P. (1996), 'Indigenous Governance', *Economy and Society*, **25** (3), 310–26.

Pavlich, G. (1996), *Justice Fragmented: Mediating Community Disputes Under Postmodern Conditions*, London: Routledge.

Pfeifer, K. (1996), 'Modernization and Indigenous Knowledge', *Peace and Social Change*, **6** (1), 41–59.

Public Archives of Canada, Record Group 10, Department of Indian Affairs Records.

Rich, E. (1991), 'Trade Habits and Economic Motivation among the Indians of North America', in J. Miller (ed.), *Sweet Promises: A Reader on Indian-White Relations in Canada*, Toronto: University of Toronto Press.

Ronsbo, H. (1997), 'State Formation and Property: Reflections on the Political Technologies of Space in Central America', *Journal of Historical Sociology*, **10** (1), 56–73.

Rose, N. (1993), 'Government, Authority and Expertise in Advanced Liberalism', *Economy and Society*, **22** (3), 283–300.

Rose, N. and P. Miller (1992), 'Political Power Beyond the State: Problematics of Government', *British Journal of Sociology*, **43** (2), 172–205.

Ross, A. (1856), *The Red River Settlement: Its Rise, Progress and Present State, with some account of the Native Races and its General History to the Present Day*, London: Smith, Elder and Company.

Said, E. (1979), *Orientalism*, New York: Vintage Books.

Salvatore, R. (1996), 'North American Travel Narratives and the Ordering/Othering of South America', *Journal of Historical Sociology*, **9** (1), 85–110.

Satzewich, V. (1996), '"Where's the Beef?": Cattle Killing, Rations Policy and First Nations "Criminality" in Southern Alberta, 1892–1895', *Journal of Historical Sociology*, **9** (2), 188–212.

Scott, D. (1995), 'Colonial Governmentality', *Social Text*, **5** (3), 191–220.

Simpson, G. (1847), *Narrative of a Journey Round the World, during the Years 1841–42*, London: Colburn Publishers.

Smandych, R. (1995), 'Willian Osgoode, John Graves Simcoe, and the Exclusion of the English Poor Law from Upper Canada', in L. Knafla and S. Binnie (eds), *Law, Society and the State: Essays in Modern Legal History*, Toronto: University of Toronto Press.

Smandych, R. (1999), 'The Exclusionary Effect of Colonial Law: Indigenous Peoples and English Law in The Canadian West to 1860', in L. Knafla and J. Swainger (eds), *Essays in the History of Canadian Law, Vol. 8: The Middle Kingdom: The Northwest Territories and Prairie Provinces, 1670–1945*, Toronto: The Osgoode Society.

Smandych, R. and R. Linden (1995), 'Co-existing Forms of Aboriginal and Private Justice: A Historical Study of the Canadian West', in K. Hazlehurst (ed.), *Legal Pluralism and the Colonial Legacy: Indigenous Experiences with Justice in Canada, Australia and New Zealand*, Aldershot: Avebury Press.

Smandych, R. and R. Linden (1996), 'Administering Justice Without the State', *Canadian Journal of Law and Society*, **11** (1), 21–61.

Smandych, R. and A. McGillivray (1999), 'Images of Aboriginal Childhood: Contested Governance in The Canadian West to 1850', in R. Halpern and M. Daunton (eds), *Empire and Others: British Encounters with Indigenous People, 1600–1850*, London: University College London Press.

Smandych, R. and K. Sacca (1996), 'The Development of Criminal Law Courts in Pre-1870 Manitoba', *Manitoba Law Journal*, **24**, 201–57.

Smith, D. (1993), 'The Emergence of Eskimo Status: An Examination of the Eskimo Disk List System and its Social Consequences, 1925–1970', in N. Dyck and J. Waldram (eds), *Anthropology, Public Policy and Native Peoples in Canada*, Kingston and Montreal: McGill-Queen's Press.

Thompson, D. (1960), *Alexander Mackenzie: Clear Grit*, Toronto: MacMillan Company of Canada.

Underhill, F. (1960), *In Search of Canadian Liberalism*, Toronto: MacMillan Company of Canada.

Wise, S. (1965), 'Tory Factionalism: Kingston Elections and Upper Canadian Politics, 1820–1836', *Ontario History*, **47** (2), 205–25.

Wise, S. (1974), 'Liberal Consensus or Ideological Battleground: Some Reflections on the Hartz's Thesis', *Canadian Historical Association, Historical Papers*, 1–14.

Index